The NATURE And PURSUIT Of LOVE

The NATURE And PURSUIT Of LOVE

The Philosophy of Irving Singer

Edited By David Goicoechea

Ⓟ Prometheus Books

59 John Glenn Drive
Amherst, NewYork 14228-2197

Published 1995 by Prometheus Books

99 98 97 96 95   5 4 3 2 1

Library of Congress Cataloging-in-Publication Data

The nature and pursuit of love : the philosophy of Irving Singer / edited by
   David Goicoechea.
        p.   cm.
   Includes bibliographical references.
   ISBN 978-0-87975-912-4
   1. Singer, Irving. 2. Love.
B945.S657N37   1995
128'.4—dc20
                                                                    94-40405
                                                                    CIP

Contents

6   Contents

PART TWO. THE HISTORY OF THE QUESTION

PART THREE. CONTEMPORARY FORMULATIONS

PART FOUR. SPECIAL PROBLEMS

Preface

As the year 2000 approaches, the Brock Philosophical Society of St. Catharines, Ontario, is celebrating two thousand years of philosophizing about the nature of love. This celebration takes the form of a conference each year for three days on the weekend closest to St. Valentine's day. To date, four conferences have already taken place and the fifth in a series of ten is being planned. This decade-long meditation on love began in 1991 with a three-day colloquium on the trilogy of Irving Singer, *The Nature of Love*. Besides this monumental three-volume work, Singer's books on love in the operas of Beethoven and Mozart and on love and sex were also discussed. The present volume is a compilation of papers delivered at that conference, together with others that have been contributed more recently. However, the conference was even more comprehensive than this volume indicates: there were also papers on love in the great tradition of the English novel, on St. Augustine, on Indian love as Bhakti, and on love and the person. Irving Singer was indefatigable and stimulating in opening the response to each of the twenty-four papers and in giving his keynote address.

Professor Singer's lifelong study of love has both theoretical and practical dimensions. Practically, he has been very concerned about exploring the nuances of romantic love and married love in order to find what the conditions must be if the two are to be compatible and mutually supportive. This problem arises with courtly love in the Middle Ages, and it becomes a crucial issue for the Romantics in subsequent centuries. As Singer theorized about love in the history of literature and the history of ideas, he came to focus on this issue through his reading of Anders Nygren and Denis de Rougemont. In puzzling over the relation between *eros* and *agape,* Nygren seemed to be relating eros to romantic love and agape to married love at its best. De Rougemont argued, in his influential book *Love in the Western World,* that all of Western literature, from *Tristan and Iseult* to *Anna Karenina* and beyond, has shown that passion, and romantic love in general, between man and woman cannot survive marriage. According to him, romantic love is to be found only outside of marriage. De Rougemont is critical of romantic love in a way that Kierkegaard also is.

By developing a concept of "bestowal" that is similar to Nygren's notion

9

of agape in some respects, Singer rebuts de Rougemont's approach to the nature of romantic love. What de Rougemont says about romantic love and marriage may possibly apply to the French tradition, but it is not true of the English tradition or many others. From Shakespeare to Milton to George Eliot and Dickens down to D. H. Lawrence, the English have tried to find a way to let romantic eros bring forth married love and to let marriage contribute to romantic aspirations. During the conference it was argued by Professor Brian Crick that Singer was right about the difference between the English and the French. But then he went on to claim that the English tradition had more concern about fathers and daughters than about husbands and wives.

Another aspect of Singer's approach to this classical problem is his interpretation of courtly love as a humanistic, life-enhancing enterprise. This difference between him and Nygren, on the one hand, and de Rougemont on the other, has great importance for Singer's explorations into the meaning, origin, and development of humanism as a whole. Did the humanistic attitude originate with Ovid, or was it already prominent in the Song of Solomon? After all, the Shulamite might have been a sovereign humanist before the ladies whom Ovid depicted, and long before Eloise in the Middle Ages.

Singer's philosophical and phenomenological approach is evident throughout the present volume. It begins with two television interviews with Robert Fulford, in which Professor Singer discusses his work on the nature and pursuit of love in the Western world from antiquity to the twentieth century. These interviews with Singer serve as a preparation for the main portion of this book, that is, those papers on Singer's philosophy delivered at the 1991 Brock conference, several of which have since been revised, together with the new ones written for this volume. The book ends with Singer's extensive response to the contributors. His "Reply to My Critics and Friendly Commentators" serves to articulate his most recent thinking as well as to reformulate many of his earlier ideas.

By emphasizing the nature and history of love as bestowal, Singer provides a provocative introduction to a meditation on the agapeic tradition as well as various others. His attempt to give equal importance to the element of appraisal can be seen as a healthy criticism of certain formulations of the agapeic perspective. That he is an American pluralist, naturalist, pragmatist, and humanist through and through makes his philosophy very intriguing in relation to contemporary continental thinking about love. In working out his somewhat Postromantic approach, Singer takes a position in current thought not far from that of French postmodernism.

David Goicoechea
Brock University
September 1994

Two Interviews with Irving Singer on the Nature and Pursuit of Love[*]

[*]Partly revised versions of television interviews originally broadcast on TVOntario. Copyright © TVOntario. Reprinted with permission.

Irving Singer on the History of Love

Interviewed by Robert Fulford

FULFORD: One of the fascinating ideas that emerges from your work is the difference between love as feeling and, on the other hand, ideas about love. And I think you've made the point that the feeling of love is universal among human beings, whereas ideas of love are extremely particular to a culture or historic period.

SINGER: Well, I modify that in emphasizing attitudes of love rather than feelings, since people are often capable of love and experience love without having any one feeling such that they can say "Ah, that is the feeling of love." And something comparable must be true of other species as well. Love is related to biological forces—what used to be called instincts—running throughout the mammalian species and possibly other creatures, too. The way they respond to their instincts, the way they use them, the way they interpret them (which human beings do constantly), the way people in different eras build systems of thought and religion—that varies tremendously.

FULFORD: Today, a major issue when you hear people talking about love, as opposed to writing about it, when they speak about it among themselves, a major issue seems to be a conflict between commitment on the one hand and passion, immediate passion on the other hand. I think that's something really that is there in the literature going a long way back.

SINGER: Yes, I think it does, and the conflict you mention is especially important in the twentieth century. There's a book by Bertrand Russell called

Marriage and Morals, in which Russell addresses himself to this question in a very interesting way. He advocates romantic passion, and even says that anyone who's never experienced it has missed out on a great deal that's important in life. But once one gets married, he insists, one has to devote oneself to the children and to the family situation, and romantic passion no longer has any place. This represents a split between passion and commitment that I consider unfortunate and generally unwholesome. The big problem for philosophy and for behavior in our age consists in trying to find some way of overcoming that split in such a way that romantic passion is amenable to commitment, which by and large means marriage, and marriage or comparable long-term affiliations can incorporate something like the romantic passion with which a relationship may have begun.

FULFORD: Whenever someone like Russell becomes articulate about love and his or her experience of it, the idea of transcendence comes in here. The idea that when you are in love, when you have felt this thing that we've been feeling for thousands of years, and we all think about differently, when you feel this thing you become something greater than you were. There's a wonderful passage in Pasternak's *Dr. Zhivago,* where he says when we were expressing our love, Lara and I, physically but also far beyond physically, I felt that we were with all history and, indeed, with the gods and so on. It's a beautifully phrased expression of what many people feel. But where does that idea come from? Where do we start noting it in the history of our civilization?

SINGER: It's a great idea and it begins with Plato, who is possibly the greatest philosopher in the Western world. In Plato you get the idea that love is an instinctual means by which human beings transcend their limitations in time and space. Christianity picked that up and interpreted the transcendence in terms of religious concepts of a divinity who was himself outside of time and space. But in later traditions, as in medieval courtly love and in Romantic love of the nineteenth century, you get a kind of naturalization or even humanization of love inasmuch as it need not be elicited by an ultimate Platonic form, or the Christian God, but rather issues from the mere experience of oneness between human beings on earth. Love as transcendence beyond this world is a magnificent idea. Unfortunately, it's wrong.

FULFORD: It's wrong even though Plato held it and many others repeated it?

SINGER: Yes.

FULFORD: Now, when you say wrong, why do you believe it's wrong? Transcendence, I mean, many people think they've had this experience.

SINGER: I'm a critic of that tradition, though I recognize its great importance and derive many of my own ideas from it, because it falsifies the way in which love is related to normal responses that belong to us as parts of nature rather than as entities that escape or rise above nature. Love has to be understood in terms of what happens to ordinary men and women in their ordinary relationships throughout their lives and in terms of the world that they live in. There's something in the *achievement,* something in the grandeur of having attained a relationship of love, which may be called "transcendent" in the sense of being wonderfully desirable and a consummation, but love does not take us into some transcendental realm beyond our natural state. Once you think that way, it becomes very hard to see how mere mortals like us are able to experience it.

FULFORD: So it's part of your philosophic project to really destroy the idea that we transcend ourselves mainly in love. You want to bring love down to being part of our worldly concern.

SINGER: Yes. That's exactly what I wish to do. I believe that the old tradition that thinks of love as transcending ordinary life neglects the way in which we belong to what George Santayana called the realm of matter. We arise from and live in a material order, and we are governed to a large extent by our physiological as well as our psychological makeup. If we're going to make sense of how ordinary people love each other, then we can't define love as being transcendent of the ordinary world they live in. When love succeeds, it is a transcendent good but there is no transcendental object that necessarily defines its being. The relationship of love is something that people, men and women, establish in their day-by-day experience with each other— assuming they have learned how to do so.

FULFORD: You mentioned that the idea of transcendence goes back to Plato. And, of course, the Greeks began many of our concepts of love, our ways of thinking about love. For them it was really an elite preoccupation, wasn't it? Almost a preoccupation of philosophers or people who defined themselves as philosophers.

SINGER: Elitist in various ways. The most interesting ideas about love in the Greek world are homosexual ideas that presuppose that love involves a kind of intellectual friendship only men can have with one another. Certainly that is an attitude we have long since outgrown. We foresee now the possibility of friendship between men and women that will enable them to attain the kind of heightened love relationships the Greeks were seeking. Their attitude was also elitist insofar as the philosophers were thought to have a special faculty that enabled them to make that transcendental leap we were just talking about. If one no longer defines love in this way, there is no reason why ordinary people can't love as well as the Platonic philosophers. In the history of ideas, courtly and Romantic concepts have, in effect, been a kind of democratization of Greek thinking about love. They encouraged the belief that everybody can possibly attain a love worth living.

FULFORD: Democratization, first of all, in bringing in half of the human race. Because in the Greek concept, as you say, it was basically a male-to-male concept.

SINGER: Right.

FULFORD: That's where the real love of that kind could exist. And women were sort of a side issue, weren't they?

SINGER: They were not treated seriously. Certainly they were not treated as people who were capable of love. Aristotle even wonders whether women are persons—whether they are metaphysically the equal of men—that is, in their souls—and whether they have a humanity equal to what men have. We believe that he was obviously wrong. Our great challenge nowadays, when women are achieving equality in so many areas of life, is to see what kind of love is available to them as well as to men in the present world.

FULFORD: Among the Greeks, as they thought about it they must've noticed that they—many of the men—felt passion for women—enough passion to have children. But that man-woman passion was not, in their way of thinking, to be elevated into anything really exceptional or magical or anything like that.

SINGER: Right. It was not to be dignified.

FULFORD: Not to be dignified.

SINGER: Or given ideal status. Love is, and always has been, a great ideal in the Western world, and the idea that the passions of ordinary men and women could be dignified as love was very threatening to the Greeks. In a sense, Christianity introduces that possibility since every person, every child of God, could hope to aspire toward the love of God. But in Christianity there wasn't a full realization that in their natural condition men and women could attain an authentic love independent of the love of God. The church's ideas about marriage, for instance, were very wholesome inasmuch as they saw it as a sacramental bonding of male and female. But that was only because marriage was considered a partnership within the community of people seeking God. The church failed to see that men and women, in or out of marriage, can achieve a kind of natural love that may be equal to the love of God.

FULFORD: The courtly, really medieval, tradition was partly based on Christianity, partly looked back to the Greeks, but developed something of its own.

SINGER: Right. There you find the process of democratization beginning. The ideas in courtly love are sometimes Christian, sometimes neo-Platonic, except that it is the relationship between men and women that now becomes the focal point. Very special men and women. The man would be a great hero, particularly a military hero; the woman would be the most beautiful female around. They would both be . . .

FULFORD: Of noble birth.

SINGER: Often of the highest birth. Queens and princesses. They would be exceptional examples of what men and women can become. But they were men and women in nature, and that made a very big difference. That was the beginning of this process of extending the ideal of love to ordinary people.

FULFORD: But it was a very special and exceptional kind of love that the courtly troubadors sang of, in Provence and such places. They sang of a very special kind of love, self-sacrificial, of course, and something very, very much beyond what we think of as ordinary, everyday love.

SINGER: In a sense, yes. Still it wasn't special in the way that some scholars have thought. There's a tradition, I'm sure you know, that thinks of courtly love as being based on frustration, self-abnegation, denial of one's talents and capacities; and there was a segment within courtly love that took that attitude. But there are other varieties of courtly love in which the satisfaction of one's instinctual needs is very much recognized and accepted. It's just that since the men and women were so outstanding they were expected to show their love in noble and extraordinary ways. Courtly and Romantic love was generally very ethical, highly idealistic, concerned about great achievements of the spirit that men and women could experience in their relationship with one another. Only that could prove they really had a bond of love. The warrior would have to go out and do heroic deeds, and the woman would have to be the faithful beloved who waits for her lover to return from his glorious enterprises.

FULFORD: And she would be the inspiration of the warrior, too. He would fight for her, fight to glorify her.

SINGER: Right. But he was also fighting for the right to attain her. He was fighting for the ability to have a reciprocal relationship. He wasn't fighting merely to be frustrated by her.

FULFORD: Right. But to deserve her also.

SINGER: To deserve her love. Precisely.

FULFORD: But in that context, I think, the tragedy of love was born. Is that fair to say? That is, the idea that you could have a doomed love and it would still be extremely beautiful.

SINGER: It's doomed and it's tragic because the world doesn't understand it. I think that's the message of courtly love. The medieval world understood the importance of marriage. But that was not the same as love. Marriages were primarily economic or political arrangements. They could include sexual love between the spouses but often didn't.

FULFORD: Certainly in the class we're speaking of, which is the nobles and the royals and so on.

SINGER: So if there were a love relationship of the sort that courtly love advocated, that might have to occur outside marriage, and therefore, to some extent, outside the social order. The tragedy arises when love and marriage come into conflict. The legend of Tristan and Iseult in the Middle Ages portrays what happens when the two are separated and do come into conflict with each other. The woman and the man suffer terribly despite their heroic attempt to accept and harmonize the values of both marriage and love.

FULFORD: The possibility that is in the medieval and the Renaissance period of dying for love—Romeo and Juliet in Shakespeare most famously—and it being somehow admirable and beautiful—that was a product of that age, wasn't it?

SINGER: Right. But remember, it's not very much different from the idea of dying for any ideal. Many people have died for love of country. Many people have died for reasons of religion. Human beings are programmed, I think, to construct ideals which then become so important that they are prepared to die for them. Love is a supreme example of something that people have either died for, or felt they'd be willing to die for, because it is such a magnificent ideal. And that's part of the meaning, I think, of courtly ideas about love: that the men and women are so greatly dedicated to love that their life no longer matters to them once they realize they cannot attain its ideality here on earth.

FULFORD: The love is greater than everything else, including their life.

SINGER: Not that they want to die, but they are ready to do so if they have to choose between life and love.

FULFORD: The ideal, the central idea on which mass communications, mass fiction are based today, is Romantic love. A couple of hundred years ago this ideal grew up and filled literature and so on. Where did that Romantic idea of love come from?

SINGER: Well, to some extent it comes from what we've been talking about—the Platonic origin, the Christian context, the desire to humanize and democratize Platonic and Christian ideas through courtly love. And then there was the reaction against courtly love, which took place in the sixteenth and seventeenth and beginning of the eighteenth centuries, when people felt that courtly love was just too elevated and unrealistic. It was in fact too far from what ordinary human beings actually experienced. As a result, a split occurred during the period represented by rationalist philosophy on the Continent—mainly in the seventeenth and early eighteenth centuries—a split between the conditions needed for people to live together well, in an orderly marriage for instance, and the conditions demanded by courtly love, or in general, idealized sexual love of any sort. There was a great skepticism on the part of Montaigne, Descartes, and many others about the ability to harmonize married love with sexual love. Romantic love arose as a reaction against that.

FULFORD: A reaction against that separation of the two things.

SINGER: Yes, it was a reaction against the skeptical attitude on the part of the previous century.

FULFORD: Right.

SINGER: History often runs in terms of action and reaction and, in this case, the concept of Romantic love was an attempt on the part of people in the nineteenth century to respond to the cynicism of their predecessors in the seventeenth and early eighteenth centuries. In doing so, they went back to courtly love, Platonic love, Christian love . . .

FULFORD: And combined them all. And they were really saying to their grandfathers or their great-grandfathers of the enlightenment of the seventeenth and early eighteenth centuries: we want to put aside your coolness, your rationality, your skepticism. We want to commit ourselves in our poetry, our thinking, our feeling, to this whole full-bodied love of man and woman.

SINGER: Right. And such love was more accessible to large numbers of people in the nineteenth century because of industrialization that had brought a relative degree of wealth to Europe. Social customs had changed—families and parents didn't have the power to choose who would marry whom to the extent that they had previously. Individuals could carve out their own destiny. And when individuals do that, they generally want to marry somebody they can love. Romantic love provided an intellectual framework in which one could justify and explain individual choices that young men and women were now making, partly on the basis of sexual preferences but also on the basis of idealizations that transmute such preferences into a special and authentic kind of love.

FULFORD: So the new economy of the industrial age was providing opportunities for people to leave home and set up their own lives.

SINGER: Right.

FULFORD: And Romantic love, through the poetry and fiction of the day, was there to say you should direct your feelings this way: fasten them on this one man, this one woman, and that will be your deepest, fullest commitment.

SINGER: Moreover, with some hope of success. At the beginning of the tradition of Romantic love there was a great deal of optimism. This was related to the French Revolution and to the feeling millions of people had in Europe that now we'd create a new world: we have erased the old order; the old regimes are crumbling throughout each of the countries in Europe; we can have all sorts of democratic possibilities, one of which involves the freedom to choose somebody in accordance with our own taste, and to do so with the justification of living up to this great ideal that has evolved in Western thought over a period of centuries. It was a time of great hope, great optimism, great buoyancy. Romantic poetry and philosophy lent themselves to all this very readily.

FULFORD: And that was really a flowering of an idea that had been there all along. Now there was a chance to play it out.

SINGER: It had been there but submerged, not fully democratized, not extended to the large numbers in the population that may previously have felt inclinations to love.

FULFORD: I realize it was expressed in a thousand or ten thousand ways, but how would you sum up that ideal of Romantic love?

SINGER: Well, one way of doing that is to think of it in relation to Christian ideas about love. In Christianity there is a transcendental entity—God—who is outside of time and space, and love consists either in his bestowing love upon the world, for no reason other than this belongs to his nature—in Christianity, God *is* love—or else love is creation searching to respond to God's love, to return it reciprocally to him. As a result of all sorts of things that were happening in theology and in philosophy, Romantic love reverses the slogan "God is love" and says that love is God, that wherever you find love you are experiencing God. Once you make that shift, it's no longer necessary to think in terms of a transcendental entity, to think of a goal of love outside of time and space. Love exists in the world and God is present at the moment in which you are actually achieving love. The whole theological emphasis beyond this world is reversed, inasmuch as the highest ideal is now to be found in a certain kind of fulfillment or self-realization within this world. That is the democratization in Romantic love: it is not limited to philosophers or theologians, or saints. It is not a part of traditional religion. It is a consummation, a completeness in terms of what people feel for each other as fellow creatures in nature and because they are carrying out their individual search for goodness as human beings.

FULFORD: There's something really beautiful in that concept of love that comes down from the nineteenth century and the late eighteenth century. We've spent a long time, I guess, since the late nineteenth century, chipping away at it.

SINGER: Right.

FULFORD: And there's a kind of split that's developed between what you would call realism, on the one hand, and Romantic idealism on the other. Where does the realist critique of that beautiful ideal come from?

SINGER: Partly it comes from within Romantic love, and partly it comes from without. In the nineteenth century, ideas about Romantic love divided into two traditions—one of which I call benign romanticism, and that's what we've been talking about—and the other of which is Romantic pessimism. By the 1850s, many of the hopeful, positive, affirmative Romantic ideas about the ability to achieve love in this world were being questioned by many thinkers on purely Romantic grounds. Among the philosophers, Schopenhauer is the greatest example of a pessimist who simply says this is not the way the world is. There is a phenomenon that can be called romantic love and it is extremely important in human life, but it is a trick on the part of nature to get us to reproduce. It should therefore not be thought of as a quasi-religious experience that happens between men and women. Instead, Schopenhauer argued, the amatory state manifests material processes that have very little to do with what people *think* is motivating them when they fall in love. As a result, a division developed within Romantic theory in the nineteenth century. But also there was a growing scientific awareness that possibly we need other categories of analysis in order to explain why it is that people become emotionally involved with one another. A great deal of what we recognize as behavioral science and the science of human relations develops out of this realist tradition that thinks of love in wholly un-Romantic ways. Freud is the foremost example of that in the twentieth century. But in a sense everybody who deals with what's called affective studies nowadays—that is, the study of how people respond to one another through their feelings—is more or less within the realist tradition.

FULFORD: I used to hear people say years ago, you're not in love with her or with him: you're in love with the idea of love. That was really an implied criticism, wasn't it, of what we've been talking about—the idealization of love.

SINGER: It's a criticism to the extent that if you tell a woman that you love her and it turns out that you're only interested in the idea of love, she has a right to be offended. She also has a right to suspect you because if you're only in love with the idea of love then you could just as well make the same protestation to another woman tomorrow when you've got tired of her. There's always the danger that a relationship is going to be inauthentic or fragile if the man or the woman is more in love with love than with the particular person that he or she thinks he or she is in love with. I think that's true. On the other hand, however, you could defend the attitude by saying it shows that one's concern is not merely sexual, that it's not just the interest of a business arrangement in which you hope to benefit from the other person and are prepared to reciprocate by giving him or her various compensations. If you are motivated by devotion to the ideal, your love can't be *totally* wrong or dishonest. But it's still very dangerous.

FULFORD: But one thing it does is to link you with this whole history of the idealization of love going back to courtly love and back to Plato. The idea that the human being should be in love.

SINGER: Right. That's a very interesting and important point, because human beings are so constituted that they feel the need to identify themselves with great idealistic traditions. One of the reasons why people buy works of art, or reproductions, and put them on their walls is not necessarily to look at them. In fact, after a few days they probably become so habituated to these art works they forget they are even there.

FULFORD: Yes.

SINGER: But they are there and they serve as a way of saying to oneself, and to one's friends, and sort of proclaiming to the world: I believe in art; I believe in this magnificent, creative ability that human beings have.

FULFORD: And I'm connected to the tradition this painting represents.

SINGER: Right. And that is supremely true about love. One reason we do love and feel the desire to love is because we realize that this is the embodiment of a superlative ideal that elevates human nature beyond what it might otherwise be.

FULFORD: Thank you very much.

SINGER: Thank you.

Irving Singer on Love in the Twentieth Century

Interviewed by Robert Fulford

FULFORD: In terms of what has been written, thought, and said about sex and love in the twentieth century, surely Sigmund Freud is the embodiment of the most important set of ideas. How does a philosopher who deals with love approach Freud's work? I know you've dealt with him at least twice in your trilogy, *The Nature of Love.*

SINGER: And differently. In the first volume I thought of Freud as defending a tradition that is related to what I call appraisal as opposed to bestowal. By appraisal I mean the way in which people look for benefits in other persons that they can selfishly enjoy in themselves; whereas by bestowal I mean people making one another valuable through the act of love itself. I thought Freud misunderstood bestowal, failing to recognize it as a creative phenomenon in life. Given his predominant interest in what people can get out of each other, Freud's insight was limited to appraisal. By the time I wrote the third volume I began to see the great wisdom and profundity in Freud, inasmuch as he realized better than anybody else, I think, how important it is for people to be able to derive benefits from each other, how important it is for people to act in their own self-interest, how important it is for them to get goods out of each other that they cannot find anywhere else. I believe he is absolutely right about that. One can't hope for success in love or marriage or any intimate relationship unless the relationship is so constructed that each of the members will derive important goods, benefits, values from each other. Bestowal is fundamental in love, and I still think Freud is confused about that. The ability to create value *by means of* the relationship itself is crucial for understanding the nature of love. But Freud was right as far as the importance of self-interest is concerned.

FULFORD: That, of course, set him sharply aside from the whole Christian tradition of love, didn't it, because in that tradition—which still exists, of course—the idea of self-sacrifice was very much a part of love.

SINGER: In Christianity there is a tendency to identify love with self-sacrifice. God so loved the world that he gave his own begotten son to save it. This sacrifice on the part of divinity, for no reason that we can fathom, is considered definitive of God's being. God is love and love is self-sacrificing. Freud has no respect and no tolerance for that attitude toward love.

FULFORD: When it's brought down to human life where one loves simply out of one's goodness, that would be presumably the human portrayal or acting out of God's goodness. For me to love someone must involve great sacrifice on my part.

SINGER: Whereas the Freudian tradition thinks of that goodness on which one's love is based as an expression of one's own self-fulfillment. It's good for oneself that one should love others, and that's why we're able to do it. It's not really self-sacrifice but rather self-realization. This healthy-minded attitude is fundamental in all of Freud's thinking.

FULFORD: Freud, of course, is part—though the most important part—he's part of a much larger approach to love which is unique to our time. I mean scientism or the scientific approach to love, where one looks at love through psychology, even physiology and so on. Has that changed the way philosophers deal with love?

SINGER: Very much so. I believe that is the great opportunity of the twentieth and twenty-first centuries. If you start with the fundamental idea of health—healthy-mindedness, which I think is basic to psychoanalytic thinking—then the project for science and philosophy is to analyze what the nature of health is, what are the ways in which we can understand human development, individual development and social development that would maximize this healthy-minded capacity to love; and also what we can do to make the world more receptive to it. That's a very important task for philosophy, but it's based on scientific investigations that give us facts about our material nature. This seems to me to be the hope of the future.

FULFORD: But there is a whole tradition of quantifying sexual expression which goes back to Kinsey and maybe beyond, where you add up the number of this or the number of that, and then twenty-five years later there's a Masters and Johnson tradition which—not limited to them in their clinic but spread over the Western world—which is a physiological approach to sex. Now isn't this narrowing down the whole business of man-woman or man-man or woman-woman relations?

SINGER: Well, it would be if one thought that by solving problems of sexology you're automatically solving problems about the nature of love. These are two different fields.

FULFORD: They're two different fields but one depends very heavily on the other.

SINGER: They can, and in fact I've been trying to do work in both fields. But I think of them as working at different kinds of questions. The sexological enterprise explains human nature in terms of sexual behavior and sexual instincts, to the extent that the instincts actually exist. The questions about love would be questions about how those instincts and how those sexual forms of behavior can be used. Once we understand what the nature of sex is, we can then answer questions about how it should be properly enacted for the sake of achieving relationships of love. The two enterprises can therefore be coordinated and suitably harmonized. But very little of this work has been done as yet. That's why I think of it as the promise of the future.

FULFORD: One element of this which comes up a great deal, both in public and I imagine in private, is the contrast or the conflict of lust versus love. Many, many people find that dealing with one without the other is very, very difficult. How does the philosopher approach such a knotty issue, a thorny issue, I should say, as that?

SINGER: Did you say knotty or naughty?

FULFORD: K-N-O-T-T-Y is what I said.

SINGER: It's both. I myself think that there's nothing in the reality of sex which in any way precludes the possibility of love. It's by means of our body that we're able to express our feelings and our attitudes. Sex is one of the most vivid and most important ways of showing love that we may have for another human being. It isn't automatic that by carrying out sex successfully we're going to achieve love, and it isn't necessary to use sex in order to express our love. Some people, for instance couples who've been married many years, may have little of a sex life any longer but still enjoy a very rich love life. Some people can have very active and gratifying sex lives without a great deal of love. There is, however, the ideal of harmonizing the two which is the ideal of sexual love, and that is a magnificent ideal. In pursuing it, we function fully and completely as sexual creatures while also functioning fully and completely as loving human beings toward one another, toward the children who result from our sexual love, and possibly toward the world that sustains us in the ability to have this kind of sexual love.

FULFORD: There is a very widespread belief—certainly expressed through the media and dramatic fiction—that loveless sex is much more present among us today than it was a few years ago and that somehow the love has been driven out of sexuality. Some of that may be the result of social conditions or whatever, but is it in any way a result of how we've thought about sex in recent years?

SINGER: Well, there's much more sexual experimentation, but there's little reason to think that the human race has flourished as long as it has without a great deal of sex. And much of that surely was loveless in the past. Whether there is more loveless sex now than there was before, I really doubt. Certainly there's more loveless sex among the unmarried than there was in earlier periods since fewer people feel the need to get or remain married nowadays. On the other hand, I think those who have loveless sex are probably the first ones to say how much better it would be to have sex with somebody one does love. The ideal of sexual love—of a love that is sexual; of a full and satisfying sex relationship that also involves love—is still quite strong today. It's just that people are freer to experiment with all possible alternatives or methods of approach to the ideal, and often they don't succeed.

FULFORD: The twentieth century has produced many, many critiques of the ideals of Romantic love that were left to us by the previous century. Perhaps one of the most striking came from all the existentialist writings of the last thirty to fifty years. The idea, really, in existentialism is that we're all so alone on this earth—perhaps I shouldn't be explaining to a philosopher what existentialism means. But it certainly presents a critique which adds up to the impossibility of love, because people are so alone and our isolation one from another is so great that it can't be bridged by this fiction of the nineteenth century called Romantic love. How have you tried to approach that?

SINGER: The most prominent existentialist is Jean-Paul Sartre. But if you examine his life's work you find a very different sort of picture from the one you've described. What you've just referred to is true and accurate for his early period. Books like *Being and Nothingness* argue that, because of the isolation of individuals, love of a quasi-Romantic sort is impossible. In his later writing, however, he changed tremendously. In a posthumous work that came out in 1983—*Notebooks for An Ethics*—Sartre develops an idea of love as an attaining of interdependence with other people. There he argues that people are such that their social nature requires them to form a kind of unity, a kind of oneness that can only occur as a result of love, particularly sexual love. In existentialism as a whole one finds these different elements. In the work of Simone de Beauvoir there exists a similar development. In her book *The Second Sex*—which has had much importance in feminist circles and for people generally—she emphasizes how women in our present male-dominated society don't have access to an authentic, genuine love; that's one of the evils of male chauvinism. But at the same time she holds out the hope that some day women will be able to experience interdependence that will be authentic, that will recognize their autonomous differences from men, and that will be a complete, satisfying, sexual love. So even in existentialism you get these different developments.

FULFORD: You mentioned *The Second Sex*. In some ways it's seen as the beginning of feminist studies in the current period. But out of feminism—that book and the seven thousand that followed—there emerges a serious criticism of Romantic love and of the concepts of love by which our society lives. I know you've thought about the feminist critique. How do you deal with it?

SINGER: There again I don't see any single critique. I see a complex of problems that have elicited different kinds of responses on the part of feminists. Some radical thinkers—T. Grace Atkinson, for instance, in her book *Amazon Odyssey*—say that men and women are incapable of loving each other, that there's something in the difference between the sexes that makes it impossible for a man to love a woman or for a woman to love a man. But other feminists see this as the great challenge for our society; that if equalization occurred and women were truly treated as the equal of men, then there might be possible an authentic love of a very desirable sort. Still other feminists have claimed that men can't love, that there is something in the nature of male sexuality that orients it toward lust or appropriative sex even when it thinks it's acting out of love—that men just can't love: only women can. Still others hold that men and women can both love but women do it better than men.

FULFORD: That's a strong argument.

SINGER: Yes, it is. Nevertheless, it seems to me that what Atkinson says is wrong—there does exist the possibility of authentic love between men and women—and that, in a sense, what the more moderate people say is also wrong. It isn't that love is impossible in our society but only that it is not as likely to succeed, is not as strong and as healthy a phenomenon as it would be in a condition of total equalization between men and women. So there again one finds a great hope for the future: that when women are treated as equals, there may be a richer and finer kind of love that men and women will share beyond anything they can have in a society which is troubled—as ours is—

by these questions about the relative status of the different sexes. As for the idea of women being better able to love, I think that's ultimately mistaken, too. Men and women are equal in this respect as in many others; they're both capable of love. Women experience a different kind of love from men, partly related to their being able to have children and therefore innately possessing certain nurturing capacities that men have to acquire through learning. So there are differences between the kinds of love that men and women may attain. But that's why it's important for them to join in an authentic love for one another: they can benefit from each other's different kind of love.

FULFORD: One feminist critique, however, maintains that romantic love has cheated women. It really doesn't exist. It's a fiction. Women are sucked into it. As in a dream, they walk toward marriage and are then put in a subservient position, and it was love that did them in.

SINGER: I think there is some truth to that. Many women have identified with the aggressor, so to speak—to use Freud's term—for reasons of love. They felt, well if I love the man then it doesn't matter that he sometimes treats me badly, that in general he doesn't treat me as his equal, that I am forced to do things that he's not required to do, that I am expected to remain faithful but he can be free to range through other sexual possibilities; since I love, I should submit to it all. If that's the feminist critique, I believe it's correct. This isn't a criticism of heterosexual love, however—it's a criticism of the way in which it has been misused by women as well as men. In the case of the women, for reasons of their own weakness; strong women are able to overcome this kind of difficulty.

FULFORD: In recent times we often hear in relation to men and women the verb "merge." That's a part of the goal of many people who seek love today.

SINGER: Yes.

FULFORD: How do you react to that fashionable verb?

SINGER: I think the idea of merging is very dangerous. Because it's an idea that in order to love another person, the two of you have to become some new . . .

FULFORD: Third.

SINGER: Yes, a third kind of entity in which each of you loses your individuality. I think this is foreign to human nature. I don't think one can lose one's identity. All one can do is distort it in the attempt to merge. In order to explain love between human beings one needs a wholly different system of concepts. In the third volume of *The Nature of Love* and in my book *The Pursuit of Love,* I develop ideas about a sharing of selves, about interdependence as well as autonomy, about love as a relation that has nothing to do with fusion or merging between two people. I don't think the concept of merging explains the intimacy that men and women are really looking for. They succeed in loving one another, they learn how to share each other's personality, they learn how to join forces in a common enterprise, they learn how to communicate effectively, they learn how to benefit from an interdependence such that each can count on the other to be interested in one's own welfare. They learn to have faith in the sustenance that they can get from each other. This is a very exalted achievement. I'm not saying it happens easily, but when it does happen it provides all of the goods that people have thought they wanted when they used the language of merging. The concept of merging is pernicious because it encourages people to submit and lose themselves, to forget what they actually want, and to spurn responsibility for their actions.

FULFORD: In a sense the most exalted ideals about love in the nineteenth century are really the most popular ideals about love in the twentieth century, aren't they?

SINGER: Yes. There is a filtering down that always takes place in the history of ideas.

FULFORD: In the nineteenth century the poets and the novelists, perhaps (the serious ones) spoke of this exalted, beautiful ideal of love which today we find on the movie screen.

SINGER: Right. And I, too, think the ideal of sexual love is beautiful. It's a beautiful idea and it's a beautiful ideal, and it's one that ordinary people nowadays can feel they have access to in a way that they might not have at any other time in the Western world, and still don't have access to in many other cultures. Potentially, I think, it's an ideal that all human beings can honor and pursue, but in various societies it has not been tolerated or actively cultivated as it has been in the Western world. One of the advances of the twentieth century is the fact that this kind of interest is now available to so many people. But like every other good that becomes accessible, having been popularized, the ideal is liable to misinterpretation and misuse. That's where philosophy comes in—to keep us on our toes. Progress means criticizing the past, particularly the way in which it has been appropriated by the present.

FULFORD: Yes. Just when humanity thinks it has things sorted out, there's someone such as yourself or the other philosophers in the long line who are there to tell us that that's not quite the way it is.

SINGER: The father of philosophy is Socrates and he described himself as a gadfly. And it's the function of the gadfly to keep biting, gnawing away at perceived truths in the hope of getting closer to authentic beliefs.

FULFORD: But that ideal, that nineteenth-century Romantic ideal, is now the everyday content of Harlequin books, popular movies, soaps, and so on. What has replaced it at the sort of higher intellectual level where those poets of the nineteenth century lived when they were creating the Romantic love ideal? What's living there now?

SINGER: Well, I think we're still going through a period of digestion and critique, and surely some of the best poets are critics of Romantic ideas. It's fashionable among intellectuals to distance themselves from Harlequin romances and from soap operas. I don't read Harlequin romances myself and I don't watch soap operas. But I respect the humanity in them and I believe it's a great challenge for philosophers to make sense out of it. In that regard I don't despair of Romantic interests. I want to understand the workings of imagination in them, and I think philosophers should examine this, and every other way of pursuing love, with whatever analytical and scientific tools are now available.

FULFORD: Is it possible to say that we are still actually in the Romantic era? That when we put out books called *The Romantic Reader, The Romantic Period,* and so forth, in a way we're still within that way of thinking? Aren't we?

SINGER: Yes, we're still preoccupied with questions that the Romantics raised. I think that's true. Incidentally, those questions are only about two hundred years old, which is not a very long time, given the number of generations that are involved, for thought to keep working at such problems. But we are tending, I believe, toward a new world in which those questions will be resolved.

FULFORD: Those questions, of course, dealt with many other things besides love. But what's the most important question that they raised regarding love?

SINGER: I suppose the most important question about love is whether human beings can have it in a nontheological setting, in other words without trying to orient their responses in ways that were previously dictated by the church or by religious traditions which claimed to have final, absolute answers predicated upon extranatural truth. The big question is whether human beings can manage on their own in a cosmos that may not be as benign as previous generations thought. I interpret romanticism as part of the humanistic effort that encourages people to work out their destiny for themselves, creatively and with freedom of self-expression. That, I think, is the greatest challenge of romanticism. But that, I also think, indicates the direction in which we're heading. Religious and spiritual ideas will have to be recast in terms of everyday truths that we discover ourselves rather than dogmas that have been handed down by earlier authorities.

FULFORD: What is the future of love as an ideal? You know, you've chartered it as carefully as anyone ever has, through the minds of people who've lived over thousands of years; but you must've thought: where does it now go from here?

SINGER: I believe it will involve the search for greater and greater personal enrichment, greater and greater recognition of the diversity of emotional values that human beings can enjoy. That's why pluralism is, for me, such an important approach in philosophy. In the pluralist attitude one doesn't assume there is a single correct answer to human problems. One doesn't assume that the human condition is unitary, or similar to questions in mathematics, for instance, for which you have to find the one and only right solution. In matters of our humanity there isn't any question of that sort, and, therefore, there isn't any single answer to be found. There is only a series of explorations, and these vary from culture to culture, and from individual to individual. The function of the philosopher is to legitimize and to explain, to make sense out of the ways in which a whole gamut of imaginative possibilities may all be equally authentic. This doesn't mean that every answer is acceptable, since you can have dishonest answers and you can have answers that are based on falsehoods. Consequently there's room for the scientist to say: Oh, but this dogma has no foundation in empirical fact; and there's room for the logician to say: This or that notion is inherently inconsistent. There's room for criticism on the basis of these factual or logical criteria. But still one can tolerate a wide panorama of different kinds of responses, and this can have a great deal of immediate importance in terms of social behavior. When I was young, there was a very limited range of relationships that human beings were allowed to enter into. If you didn't act in accordance with this limited range, you were considered either wrong or deficient or sick, and you were generally made to feel very uncomfortable. What I find as the present tendency, and what I foresee as the future for humankind, is a world in which an indefinite number of alternatives will be made available to men and women, the emphasis being on success within whatever lifestyle is chosen by the individuals themselves, as opposed to expectations arbitrarily imposed. In other words, even greater democratization, and possibly anarchy, in which individuals and groups will be able to determine on their own the way of life they want to cherish and pursue. Eventually the human race may succeed in living up to this pluralistic ideal of love more than it has thus far. That's the reason I wrote my books in the first place—to encourage people (and myself) to find new, enriched, more creative, more imaginative ways of making sense out of our need to love.

FULFORD: Thank you very much.

SINGER: Thank you.

Introduction to the Papers

David Goicoechea

According to Irving Singer, love in its passion and commitment is an attitude of appraisal and bestowal. Appraisal is the exploring quest of the lover's joyous desire. Bestowal is the creative care for the beloved's personal welfare. Singer's appraisal of passion makes of him a romantic. His commitment to bestowal makes of him a personalist, a humanist, and a pluralist. It is the tension between the *eros* of his appraisal and the *agape* of his bestowal that brings the passion to the monumental project of his thinking, as it does to the mystery of love and its history.

At the beginning of his trilogy, *The Nature of Love,* Singer sees bestowal as love's necessary and most important condition. Thus, in criticism of Freud, the twentieth century's most influential theorist of love, who reduces love to self-seeking desire, Singer is more a personalist than a romantic. He argues that there is no true love unless in bestowal it is attentive to the beloved person. Against both Freud and the Greek tradition Singer argues that bestowal's recognition and creation of the alterity of the agapeic tradition is necessary to love and perhaps even sufficient.

But as the years passed by and Singer meditated on such prominent European theorists as Denis de Rougemont and Anders Nygren, and as he considered the criticism of his fellow American pragmatists and naturalists, he moved much more toward Freud and the eros tradition, arguing that bestowal may be necessary but that it, like appraisal, is by no means sufficient. In moving from the passionate young man's praise of commitment to the committed older man's praise of passion, Singer went through the great debate

33

about love and marriage. How can marriage survive the romantic attitude? How can the romantic survive within marriage?

So the questioning remains about appraisal and bestowal. The tension between them has been, is, and will be. Singer's universal vocabulary fits the friction between Plato's black and white horses, between Aristotle's "opposites that attract" and his "birds of a feather that flock together." It fits the friction between Platonic *eros* and Aristotelian *philia*; between the Mosaic Covenant and the more universal bonding of the Davidic Covenant; between the generosity of Jesus and the judgment of the apocalyptic Christ; and between the upward striving eros and the downward bending agape.

And yet, according to Singer, love is not only the interplay of appraisal and bestowal. It is also a way of idealizing. Singer optimistically sees love as growing from primitive naturalistic idealizations of sex to the transcendental idealizations of Christian Platonism to the humanistic idealizations of post-romanticism. For this reason he is critical of Santayana and Freud. For Santayana sees the beloved only as a replica of some chosen perfection, while Freud regards the beloved merely as a substitute for that person who loved us when we were incapable of loving anyone but ourselves. Singer wants to love ideals as a way of loving persons rather than use persons as a way of loving ideals.

The idealizing involved in both appraisal and bestowal raises the question of love and its emotional cognition. Singer is opposed not only to Freud and Santayana for their tendency to treat love as an activity of self-deceiving projection, but, for similar reasons, he opposes Denis de Rougemont and his approach to *Love in the Western World*. As Freud reduces agapeic bestowal to self-deceit, so does de Rougemont reduce erotic appraisal to false idealizing. De Rougemont views Western literature from *Tristan* to *Anna Karenina* as a surrender to the erotic potion that destroys marriage. Singer argues, however, that, especially in the English tradition, there has been the quest to create the true love that allows the romantic to infinitize marriage and marriage to eternalize romance.

As Singer pleads the case for bestowal against Freud, he discovers not only de Rougemont, who writes entirely about erotic appraisal in order to show that it is deceitful and unethical, but he also enters dialogue with Anders Nygren, who writes entirely about agapeic bestowal in order to show its incompatibility with eros. But Singer is far more shocked by the extremity of the anti-appraisal of de Rougemont and Nygren than he is by that of Santayana and Freud. Thus, while defending his synthesis in volume three of *The Nature of Love,* Singer reveals new reasons to appreciate the Freudian economy of self-seeking eros.

All along Singer is clear about the necessity of the bestowal that lets there be love instead of desire. But as he defends bestowal against mere appraisal, he comes also to appreciate the necessity of appraisal. For human beings, as they grow in love, must make demands upon the beloved so that they too might become bestowers who fulfil the needs of the lover. Appraising eros must contribute as necessarily to bestowing agape as bestowal does to appraisal, or there will be a breakdown in the bonding love.

In order to interrogate Singer's conception of love as the bonding that takes place through appraisal and bestowal, Goicoechea compares Singer with Nietzsche and his conception that love is the interplay of the will to power and the eternal return. Is the will to power an appraising activity by which living beings grow toward higher life? Is the love of eternal return a test of bestowal by which the lover examines himself concerning the quality of loving negation and affirmation? The point of the comparison is to question whether growth in love and the love of love are as essential to love as are appraisal and bestowal.

Throughout the trilogy Singer implicitly concerns himself with the question of love and personal growth. He believes that we have grown from a primitive naturalism to a transcendental idealism, to a postromantic humanism. His vast treatment of the details of love's history seeks to verify the hypothesis of a growing progress. Since he himself grew from a positing of appraisal and bestowal to a defense of bestowal, to a defense of appraisal, he believes that the life sciences can perfect love today. Singer hopes that his work is contributing to love's growth. And yet, as Platonists and Cartesians have argued, comparing degrees of perfection is possible only if there is some transcendent standard that lets the mind know that the present is not enough.

The standard is love itself and implies that all love is a loving of love itself or adoration. As Singer reveals at the end of volume three, he has come to focus throughout the course of his thinking upon falling in love, being in love, and staying in love. Falling in love is an appraising by which lovers, in a bestowing, leap from the everyday world to the love world. Being in love is a continued bestowing by which lovers remain in an attitude of positive appraisal. Staying in love is the maturing creativity by which lovers work and play at passionate commitment. But for these three to make sense, a fourth category is implied and that is the category of becoming a loving person. The ideal of being a loving person is revealed as we fall in love, fail in love, and grow in love. The drama of Nietzsche's *Zarathustra* is primarily a postmodern story about becoming a loving person. Once the rewarder-punisher god is dead, it is asked, "What kind of loving person should we try to become?"

The death of the transcendental signified bursts forth into a plurality of perspectives that all should be loved. Nietzsche's is a pluralism of values and of loves, and so is Singer's as he struggles to become the person who can love not only his dog but especially his wife and all whom he meets. Most of all, Irving Singer's is an existential project in which he is always seeking because he loves love to grow into a more loving appraising and bestowing.

Russell Vannoy, in his creative exploration of love, tests what he calls the classical theory of Singer by presenting two cases as a challenge to Singer's view that love is the imaginative, creative bestowal of value. In Vannoy's experience of love at his senior prom and in his mother's relation with her seven husbands, bestowal is either not there or it is demeaning or useless or masquerading as appraisal. Singer's classical view would explain love as the interplay between appraisal and bestowal, but Vannoy is cynical of a worthy bestowal ever really invigorating appraisal. Thus Vannoy is perhaps cynical about love itself, for mere appraisal seems to be a grim and sorry spectacle.

Perhaps Vannoy is not really cynical about love but cynical only about the way many people love and about the way classical views account for love, for in closing his paper he asks a very intriguing question, one that our ten-year love celebration will be exploring in a variety of ways. The question is, "Have we gone wrong somewhere in the way we have conceptualized personal love?" Singer's account points out three great classical moments: the Augustinian, the Lutheran, and the postromantic. Likewise Zarathustra treats of the three metamorphoses of the medieval camel, the modern lion, and the child. What has gone wrong with the medieval and modern models? For what model are we postmoderns searching?

Singer and Vannoy seem to agree that love as mere appraisal will be a grim and sorry spectacle. Singer's search has led him to affirm personal love, then humanistic love, and finally pluralistic love. Perhaps the Middle Ages emphasized the personal, the moderns the humanistic and it is our task to explore pluralistic models of the classical synthesis. Not every pluralism satisfies our quest for the ideal interplay of appraisal and bestowal. Vannoy questions his mother's loves as well as his own. He wonders how appraisals that suit my standards give rise to a qualitatively different attitude of bestowal.

But is this not the great postmodern question of difference? Is there an original identity from which differences arise? Or is there an original difference that permits of pluralism? Perhaps we go wrong in thinking about personal love if we first posit unity and then try to be pluralists. Vannoy seems to think that bestowal and alterity must be derived from appraisal and egoism, and so he becomes cynical of generous love. However, perhaps Singer does not try to derive bestowal from appraisal, for he does recognize the origin of bestowal within Judaeo-Christianity. Perhaps on this key point Singer differs from Nietzsche, who seems to derive the many perspectives from the monism of an original will to power.

The Brock Philosophical Society's ten-year love celebration is based upon the belief that true personal love was born upon earth in human form 2,000 years ago. As Irving Singer has defined it, true personal love is an attitude and activity of bestowal which is open to, and perhaps even dependent upon, appraising desire. Paul Gooch concurs with Irving Singer that even within the magnificent accomplishment of the Greeks, any conception of bestowing personal love was lacking. Aristotle came closest with his benevolence and beneficence. But for Aristotle the friend is another self, and he has not entirely captured what the best friendship is like. He misses the intimacy that is based upon openness. Aristotle's philosophy is not open to alterity and difference. While Gooch agrees with Singer on this, he cannot agree with Singer's notion of bestowal as a pure gift to be offered without value or merit in the beloved.

Gooch likewise concurs with Singer concerning Socrates. As a lover Socrates reached such heroic heights as to be possessed of a semidivine love. Plato thinks of Socrates as he does of eros personified. Socrates loved beauty as a way to goodness and wisdom, and yet the criticisms of Alcibiades are apt. Socrates can be charged with hubris and displacement. He is too proud to joyfully affirm in love the merely human; his love finds any human bond or feeling unfitting. Socratic love has nothing of the personal within it. In fact, Gooch is even more critical of Socrates than Singer, for Gooch does not see Socratic love as human at all. It is perhaps mystical and beyond our world.

Gooch regards Platonic love as belonging to our world in that it does not bypass the first two rungs of Diotima's ladder of love as does the Socratic. Plato's love is more like the best Aristotelian friendship in that it is a mutual sharing between two individuals. It may erotically aim at the form of the good and erotically start with a bodily form of beauty, thus differing from the Aristotelian philia. But it is a relation between humans rather than with the Socratic *daimon* that keeps him morally aloof. However, Gooch agrees with Singer that Platonic love cannot account for the love of persons qua individuals. Singer thinks that personal love requires a spontaneous bestowal of value in spite of imperfections, while Gooch thinks that it requires an openness to vulnerability and a commitment to work for the good of the other.

Gooch raises questions about both appraisal and bestowal. He would agree with Singer in thinking that the Greeks are not concerned with nor aware of a love of persons. But whereas Singer would say that they lack bestowal, Gooch denounces that term and says rather that they lack openness to alterity, and that they shy away from vulnerability and commitment to work for other as other. But in being concerned about the other only insofar as he is the other half of my soul and my own, the Greeks, as Gooch understands them, make you wonder even about the appropriateness of the term appraisal. Does Singer want to say that Aristotelian philia with all its traits is only a matter of appraisal? Does he also mean that both Socratic and Platonic eros in all their traits are likewise all properties of appraisal? Gooch explicitly questions the philosopher's urge to simplify in terms of bestowal, and implicitly he makes you question how much of a role appraisal can play.

However, in approaching love Singer's sense of category is more than matched by his sense of the concrete. Just as Gooch praised him highly for treating all the essential traits of love in the early appraisal tradition, so does Graeme Nicholson admire him for his fine sense of detail in his nuanced understanding of the early bestowal tradition. Out of the vast world of the Bible and concurring with Singer, Nicholson focuses upon love insofar as it is related to submission to the law, knowledge, and truth. Biblical love is a disciplined love that begins with an overcoming of egoism by a loving submission to law. Singer centers his treatment around law or *nomos* or Torah. And Nicholson agrees that essential to love in the Bible is the idea in John's first epistle that we may know Him if we keep His commandments.

Nicholson's main point is to indicate the necessary link between love and knowledge in the Bible. This is very important because love is often thought of as a merely subjective feeling, and Singer is often criticized for having a conception of bestowal that lacks objectivity. Nicholson shows that at the roots of the agapeic tradition love is constitutive of the essence of knowledge. When you love someone or when you are a loving person, you can see many more values than the nonlover. Love need not be blind for it can also open the eyes. After showing that love is of the essence of knowledge, Nicholson then shows that truth is of the essence of love. Submission to the law opens one to the other so that one can see the person and the personal values that are hidden from those who have not been transformed into true love. So false love can be a deceitful projection, as Freud shows, but true love can bestow by cultivating the hidden. Truth can be in us if our whole life is just; it is a matter of integrity and submission to the law. If we love one another, then we will know God, for God is love, the love that first bestows itself so that we might bestow to receive more bestowal. Therefore, if one is disciplined into a sense of justice toward the widow, orphan, and stranger by meditating on the law of the covenant day and night finding therein all one's delight, one's bestowal will be able to cultivate hidden values.

Finally, Nicholson argues that incarnation is the essence of truth. As love lets there be knowledge and truth lets there be love, so incarnation lets there be the truth that is Jesus' body and that becomes the embodied bond of those who love. When the Word became flesh it was able to suffer and die. Thus, as Singer shows in his analysis of nomos love, the love of submission develops so far that it becomes not only the transformation of Job, but even the atonement of the suffering servant. Love as embodied dialogue submits to the truth of law so as to give glory to suffering and death, and so as to innocently atone for the guilt of others and thus to stop the momentum of evil even in such a way as to reveal to lovers that their love is divine.

In his paper, "Ovid and Courtly Love," Kevin McCabe suggests the vast array of love which Singer treats from Rome through courtly times and into the Renaissance. Singer is especially sympathetic to Ovid and his influence, for he sees Ovid as erasing love's transcendental idealizations, thereby becoming the forerunner of medieval humanism. In working out the art of sexual love, Ovid focused upon the earthly ideals that Singer admires in that more northerly strain of the courtly and the Renaissance. But McCabe does not make the celibacy-adultery distinction and thus is not as admiring of the Ovidian strain as is Singer in his ideal of mixing love and marriage. Since McCabe is content to see the Ovidian art of love as a phenomenon of an urbane youth culture, he is not concerned to retain any of it within a mature, ethical, and religious married love.

McCabe raises the question of now the medieval mentality could ever come to appreciate and accept the Ovidian contribution. Was not Ovid an unethical and irreligious materialist? Therefore, would he not be an opponent of the Christian Platonist? In answering this question, McCabe seems to disregard and even give evidence against the majority approach which distinguishes the troubadour celibacy lyrics of Provence from the *trouvère* adultery narratives of the Celtic realm. Was not Guilhem IX, the first courtly poet of Provence, the closest imitator of Ovid and an advocate of philandering? So perhaps it is hard to assume that the later northerly movement was more Epicurean and the southerly more Platonic. Be that as it may, Singer is not a Christian Platonist: he builds upon his ideal of love in accordance with the appraisals and bestowals of his own experience and judgment.

At this point serious questions might be raised about Singer's bestowal in terms of the personal and the humanitarian. Vannoy thinks that a spontaneous and unwarranted bestowal is too inadequate and contradictory a notion ever to lift one out of the sorry spectacle of wanton appraisal. Gooch suggests that true bestowal appraises with demands such as the Lord had when dealing with his people Israel. Nicholson suggests that if bestowal is to be worthy, it has to be cultivated into an attitude of true knowledge through the discipline of submission to the law of justice. Singer criticizes the Greeks because they lack the personal love that is an imaginative and creative bestowal of value upon the beloved who is a person in her own right. But Singer praises Ovid as a humanist because he gets rid of any transcendental idealization, even though Ovid has no sense of ethical commitment.

So is Singer's Ovid a humanist without being a personalist? Ovid treats the beloved not as a person in her own right but as a means to his own idealizing ends. Singer only seems to suggest some bestowal with Ovid and Lucretius. Does he think that there is some bestowal involved in the Epicurean affirmation of love for women and sex? Or is Singer's preference made only in terms of appraisal? Are the Romans better lovers than the Greeks simply because there is a more healthy appraisal in their Epicurean humanism than in Platonic transcendentalism? To clarify these questions concerning bestowal is it necessary to distinguish several senses of bestowal in Singer's usage? Is the phenomenon of bestowal to be found in every falling in love? Is not the Freudian projection a kind of creative bestowal? In this very general sense does not even the Platonic lover have a kind of imaginative and creative bestowal? Can the Aristotelian friendship which has no falling in love have a kind of bestowal in its benevolence and beneficence? Or is bestowal to be connected only with love of persons?

As a Thomist, Walter Principe feels at home with Singer's idealization of love as appraisal and bestowal. In friendship Principe sees the mutual knowledge as appraisal and the mutual benevolence and beneficence as bestowal. This may indicate the kinship of Singer's synthesis with that of Thomas, who always sought to balance nature's true appraisals with grace's true bestowals. But in spite of the kinship of balance which relates him to Thomas, Singer is still critical of the merging and the determinism of the magic and of the suicide which he detects to be the implication even of the Thomistic *caritas* synthesis. Principe seeks to defend Thomas from these criticisms.

Principe points out that a great deal of Thomas' philosophical labor is put into what Principe calls the phenomenology of "being-in." Augustine had already begun this phenomenology, as had Plotinus, when in his *Confessions* he argued that there could not be more of God in an elephant than in a sparrow. Principe argues that a firm distinction must be made between the way bodies can be in one another and the way in which spirits can "merge" or be in one another. Ideas can be in a mind in a very different way than tea is in a cup or traces in a brain. This suggests that lovers and their attitudes, passions, and feelings should not be reduced to merely material things and thought of only as juxtaposed instead of as mutually inhering. Singer is very appreciative of those artistic Renaissance mergings of Ambiguity, Paradox and Irony and these are already semi-mergings that lie between those realms of sparrows and elephants and of persons and ideas, as does the love merging. As Father and Son can merge in the Holy Spirit, so can lovers merge in love without losing their individuality. As the Holy Spirit emerges from the mutual love of Father and Son, so can God through his Spirit be one with a person.

Singer, who is also highly concerned about the problem of human freedom, thinks that Thomas, even in his Aristotelian version of caritas, forfeits human freedom in upholding the divine creativity of all. If God must bestow all man's power upon him, then how can man have free and personal appraisals? Vannoy, Gooch, and Nicholson see this as Singer's problem just as Singer sees it as Aquinas': according to these scholars Singer so conceives of bestowal that he denudes genuine bestowal of any appraisal and thus takes away from free appraisal its realistic opportunities. Principe, who identifies Singer to a great degree with Thomas, tries to help them both out by arguing that again we should not become entrapped within a materialistic metaphor and realize that a nonmaterial causality can operate between God and persons as well as between human lovers. The Holy Spirit's empowering yet freeing presence is like the power of a lover's bestowal that lets flower forth hidden qualities that at first only love could see. Love is a creativity that lets both lover and beloved become creative.

Singer's ultimate criticism of Thomas and the caritas synthesis is that it makes of love a matter of magic and of suicide. Principe seems to agree with this, pointing out that the key distinction between Thomas and Luther is that Thomas believes in love as transformation whereas Luther sees love as a realistic project in which the lovers remain *simul peccatores et justi*.

Using a culinary metaphor, Luther argues that even though lovers can become one cake with God by the pouring down of God's love, they always remain a lower and sinful layer of the cake. Thomas thinks that love's transformation can significantly justify them to the extent that they are no longer sinners. This transformation from sin to justification would be seen as a death or suicide of the old self so that a magical new birth can come to the lovers. In the light of Principe's focus on transformation it can be seen that Singer's criticism of Thomas is frought with an artistic ambiguity and irony, for, like Shakespeare, Singer fashions so finely tuned an ambiguity that magic and the suicide of the old self often appear in Singer to be the glory even of realistic married love. One cannot imagine in Singer's world a love that in its idealizations and bestowals is not magical and powerfully transformational.

With John Mayer's paper, "The Marriage of Love and Reason," Irving Singer's philosophy of love becomes much clearer, for Singer is above all a pluralist. Adducing as examples the words "dog" and "rat," Mayer shows that the word "love" has a vast variety of analogous meanings so that in loving love the thinker has to be open to an even more unlimited world than would be before him if he were thinking about dogs. Irving Singer looks out at the world of love and he sees affection, eros, friendship, and agape. He sees love among the Greeks, Romans, Hebrews, and Christians. Aware of non-Western loves, such as the Hindu and Buddhist, Singer makes it his task to explore the great plurality of loves. He begins by dividing all of love into three parts: appraising, bestowing, and idealizing and perhaps idealizing belongs to bestowing in its widest sense. Singer sets out to appraise all the important loves of the Western world and show how they give meaning to life.

Mayer, who identifies very much with Irving Singer, exemplifies the pluralist at work, thereby showing more simply just what Singer has been doing all along. Mayer is not adverse to being typecast as having a good bit of the rationalist and the puritan within himself. However, modernism from Descartes to Hegel was an exaggerated rationalism which brought about a strongly dualistic antagonism between the rational and the passionate such that its ideal love separated the sane and rational love of marriage from the passionate and romantic love outside marriage. Both Singer and Mayer see such exaggerated rationalism as irrational and closed to their type of pluralism. In their move toward a postmodern perspectivism they see reason not only as representational but also as appraising, bestowing, submissive, and romantic.

As creative pluralists Mayer and Singer see the puritans as seeking to bring forth another important form of ideal love. The puritans from Milton to D. H. Lawrence want to show that within marrage there can be a robust passion and sexuality. It is over this issue that Singer takes issue with de Rougemont, for the latter portrays passion and marriage as incompatible; the puritanical discipline, on the other hand, aims to let sex and passion promote the love and growth of the married couple while at the same time marriage aims at promoting the continued growth of the Ovidian and courtly Art. Puritanism is based upon a rational approach to faith to modernize the Adam and Eve relationship so that in their mutual devotion the married couple might work out their earthly blessedness together. Puritanism itself is a lived pluralism which, with effort, seeks to harmonize into its ideal love the worthy of other ideals.

Do the rational and the puritanical reveal anything about love that will further the exploration of the appraisal-bestowal relation? Puritanism as a serious modern interpretation of Christianity would seemingly have within it a strong element of bestowal. But does not the rational suggest the appraisive so as to raise suspicion about the ability of bestowal to be nonjudgmental? Singer's notion of bestowal might be organized around his treatment of agape according to Nygren, which is: (1) spontaneous and unmotivated in contrast to erotic desire for goodness, (2) indifferent to value in contrast to erotic preference and evaluation, (3) creative of values in contrast to erotic response to value, and (4) initiating of fellowship with God in contrast to nondivine eros. But was not God pleased that his creation was good? Could you conceive of the puritan work ethic as indifferent to value? Though divine bestowal might be creative is that possible for the human? Could even the predestined puritan not work out his salvation? As Singer moves more toward appraisal, is it not toward the appraisal within bestowal and therefore toward a conception of bestowal that is less like that of Nygren?

Irving Singer the pluralist seeks to meet the challenge of defending an ideal love that affirms the truth of each; thus he defines love as an appraisal that includes the eros and the philia of Socrates, Plato, and Aristotle. He defines love as the bestowal of nomos love and agape which he defends against the charges of Freud and Santayana. Against the transcendentalism of Christian Platonisms, Singer himself defends the humanistic love of the *trouvères*. Against the mere aestheticism of Ovid's Epicureanism he argues for the sexuality of the puritanical work ethics. Now in order to supplement his personal humanistic pluralism he argues for the passion of the romantics who are benign. In order to support such an ideal Singer has to defend himself against such charges as Robert Perkins presents from the thought of Scheiermacher, Hegel, and Kierkegaard, for Perkins and Singer collide head-on over the issue of whether or not Schlegel's *Lucinde* can be benign.

Singer sees Schlegel's *Lucinde* as the single most important expression of romantic ideas about love, marriage, and sex. The fundamental thesis with which Scheiermacher agreed is that the activity of sexual appraisal can be the means by which a person can grow into the realm of spiritual bestowal, just as the spiritual can aid the growth of the sensual. When Julius and Lucinde fall in love with each other, they each experience an integration of an under-developed personality. Through Lucinde, Julius is able to develop a more sensuous expression. The meaning of their marriage consists primarily in the psychological events that take place through their sexual consummation. Of course, a truly romantic marriage cannot happen between just any couple, as Milton would agree; therefore, an important part of psychological growth is romantic confession by which Julius realizes his long path of wandering and erring before he finally merges naturally with just the right person.

Singer sees *Lucinde* as an example of benign romanticism because in it marriage and the romantic promote one another. Thus Julius thinks that love and marriage with Lucinde allows him for the first time to be truly and naturally ethical. Hegel criticizes Schlegel for missing the social dimension of ethics, just as Kierkegaard will criticize Hegel for missing the individual. Schlegel is aware that the good intentions of the rational alone are not enough to let everyone be ethical in practice, for good intentions might pave the way to hell unless one is passionately motivated and energized by romantic love. Perkins points out that Schlegel is deceived about his own intentions to let the sensual and the spiritual support one another; he sides with Nygren in arguing that agapeic bestowal can only be in contention with appraising eros and, then, that the romantic can only be an ethical enemy. Singer agrees with the good intentions of Schlegel but would be wary of the antipersonal model of merging.

Schlegel sees romanticism as a religion of love in which Julius and Lucinde are priest and priestess to one another. Their sexual expression can be for them a sacrament that renews and refreshes them as if it were a kind of grace. While Singer appreciates such humanism and naturalism, Perkins sees it all as mockery and gross parody. Kierkegaard, too, though he might appreciate an erotic leap, sees it only as the movement of recollection that precedes any truly religious love of the other person as other. Perkins levels many charges against *Lucinde*'s shortcomings in its aesthetic, ethical, psychological, and religious dimensions—charges Schlegel himself might have accepted as he was making his move toward Catholicism. But in any case, while Singer, too, is a postromantic romantic, he does retain many of Schlegel's ideas, not the least of which is Schlegel's definition of love as the passionate, the sensuous, and the friendly.

Singer's meeting with Kierkegaard has to do with love of persons. Singer writes that by the time Kierkegaard wrote *Works of Love,* his "thinking about the love of persons would seem to have atrophied" (*The Nature of Love,* 3:48). Love of persons has always been very important to Singer; all his criticisms of appraising love derive from its lack of a proper bestowal of personal love. Love without the personal, according to Singer, is not love. It is only desire that would have to be narcissistic. Thus Singer thinks that *Works of Love* goes awry, for it so loves an ideal that it forgets the love of a person. However, Sylvia Walsh argues that *Works of Love* is above all one of the finest books ever written about personal love. The problem seems to be that Kierkegaard and Singer have two very different conceptions: Kierkegaard, like Kant and Jesus, thinks that a loving person should love all persons because of the value of their personhood. Singer, on the other hand, thinks that personal love is a spontaneous bestowal of value upon the beloved so that she alone is loved for her unique and irreplaceable qualities.

The question of personal love also involves the issue of humanism. Walsh points out that Singer criticizes Christian Platonism because it is a transcendentalism that destroys any humanism. She, however, argues that love of God and love of neighbor are so related that love of God does not take away from love of persons but love of love promotes the love of persons. But Singer does not think that love realistically extends to all other persons because we fall in love with only one. Humanism and personalism for Singer mean that we should love a person in his or her own right rather than for an ideal. The early Singer thinks that if we love a person because of the ideal of love, we are antipersonalistic and antihumanistic. However, as Singer grows into the new position which appears toward the end of volume three, is he not moving toward the position of Gooch, Nicholson, McCabe, Perkins, and Walsh?

Perhaps as Singer's philosophy of love is developing, his very pluralism means that he is creating a dialectic that brings him closer to Kierkegaard than he realizes. Singer thinks that Kierkegaard drops the dialectic once he leaves off writing pseudonymously and moves on to the acknowleged works such as *Works of Love*. But is it not the case that the chief dialectic for Kierkegaard is between the appraising aesthetic and the bestowing ethical loves of the early writings and the Christian love of *Works of Love*? In *Point of View* Kierkegaard claims that he was a religious author all along, which would make him a pluralist with as many voices as Singer. Walsh argues that Christian love does not cancel any noble eros or noble philia but redoubles them. That is, the Christian could still romantically love his beloved provided first that he loved her as a person or neighbor. Does not Kierkegaard treat the pluralism of loves and does he not show how to solve the problems which Vannoy, Gooch, and Perkins have raised? If the young man and the other persons at the dance were first of all loving persons with respect for each other, then their appraisals would not be so shocking. There would be a bestowal that would make them fitting.

Singer thinks of Kierkegaard as an antiromantic romantic, which could be a title that applies to Singer himself. Insofar as the young man is a pessimistic romantic and Judge William is a benign romantic, Kierkegaard is antiromantic when he allows these loves to dethrone themselves. But he remains romantic insofar as he only dethrones and still retains these loves in a renewed transformation. But Singer is antiromantic to a much lesser extent, for he dethrones loves of neighbor and gives romantic love the throne even though personal love and bestowal are allowed to remain in attendance at the throne. Singer is antiromantic to the extent that he thinks that bestowal and being a loving person have a place even though it is secondary to appraising romanticism. Total romanticism wants the throne for appraisal alone and gives no recognition to personal bestowal. Even the late Singer does not go that far.

Pat Duffy Hutcheon's meditation upon Singer's prolonged encounter with Freud's theory of love focuses our attention upon the very logic of love. Is the ideal interplay of appraisal and bestowal to be viewed according to the logic of noncontradiction in accordance with the square of opposition and thus arranged according to the Platonic hierarchy? Or are appraisal and bestowal more ideally related according to a dialectical logic of contradiction in which opposites are not opposed but implicational so that they can be synthesized in a meaningful totality? Or are appraisal and bestowal more honestly viewed according to a third logic's mixing of opposites which lets appraisal bestow and bestowal appraise?

While Singer always appreciated some aspects of Freud's complex theory of libidinal love and even moved toward his tough appraisal, Hutcheon organizes Singer's criticisms of Freud around five points, the chief of which is "confusion." Hutcheon thinks that Freud's overall theory is not confused but needs to be understood as an unfolding according to the logic of Hegel's dialectic. She thinks that Singer does not see the dialectic of the Freudian unfolding and thus finds him confusing. Also, making Freud understandable does not make him credible, and in this Hutcheon is perhaps more critical of Freud than is Singer. But what separates the incredible and the confusing? Might not Singer grant Hutcheon's dialectical reading of Freud and then ask her if she would grant that it is incredible because it is confusing?

Are not Hutcheon and Singer both working with a third logic of the mixing opposites which, because it is unthematic and implicit, allows them to move in the same general direction but with some difficulty in understanding each other? Is not Singer's postromanticism concerned with an ideal love that must mix appraisal and bestowal? Is not Hutcheon's post-Hegelianism based on such insights as the Darwinian law of organic causality which has a peculiar mixing of opposites whereby future consequences feed back into the past of a species' history? Perhaps Singer has found the new logic primarily in the ambiguities of love in literature and music, but is very open to the scientific corroborations of a Hutcheon. Perhaps Hutcheon has found in biology, physiology, and experimental psychology the need for the new logic. Even though she castigates the existential, she might find in Singer an analogous evidence for a postpaternalistic logic that is ethically suitable.

If Hutcheon and Singer were to agree on the third logic, could they agree more on the question of Freud and bestowal? Perhaps Freud did discover in history a few elite altruists; but was he not still opposed to the bestowing ideal? Would the third logic not help with the problem of dualism? Maybe Freud needs to be a monist and dualist at once even as a justly merciful lover must judge and a justly judging lover be merciful. Maybe there is a need for an essentialist norm even for those who advocate a pluralism of loves—if not only in the way Hutcheon makes a case for the interaction of the phenotype and the genotype, then at least in the sense in which Singer uses the norm of a proper mix of appraisal and bestowal. Finally, is it not because of their common third logic that Hutcheon and Singer agree that child development should not be reduced to sexual development? Do we not sense the common logic of Singer and Hutcheon as we look together at the looking glass reflections and behold a giant eros astride a world forever doomed to *coitus interruptus*?

As John Nota thinks about love according to Singer from the viewpoint of Thomas Aquinas and Max Scheler, strange things happen. As Nota points out, Singer is critical of the position Nota himself adopts while Nota is critical of Singer's position. One might not expect such an emphasis on criticism, for Singer appears to be more like Aquinas than almost any other philosopher in his openness to the vast variety of different kinds of love. Singer's appraisal-bestowal synthesis is, like Aquinas's, a very open approach to the caritas synthesis; Max Scheler, too, has a vital-spiritual love synthesis that brings him to criticize any reductivism. But as all these philosophers would agree, growth in love takes place not only through the bestowal of mutual admiration but also through bestowal's critical appraisals. Therefore, let us consider their mutual charges about love not being correct in its giving, forgiving, and redeeming.

Few would disagree totally with St. John of the Cross that love is the giving of gifts. But this is a key point of the discussion in *Zarathustra*: Nietzsche thinks that it is even more blessed to know how to receive properly than it is to give. Singer also, in both volumes one and three, borrows D. H. Lawrence's notion of "the greed of giving." Bestowal for both Scheler and Singer is not only a giving but, most of all, bestowal is an open-handed receiving of the values of the beloved with a yes and amen. Scheler's notion of love as an upward movement brings out this receptivity, for love is that guide which imaginatively leads to ever new discoveries. If anything, perhaps Singer is too giving in his understanding of bestowal as primarily creative. Perhaps Scheler's notion of love's giving and taking in creative discovery and discovering creativity would help Singer answer the criticism of Vannoy and Gooch that his concept of bestowal is too fraught with subjectivity.

The notion of love as forgiving is very different in Nota's context of becoming a loving person and Irving Singer's context of creating a romantic marriage. Nota is concerned with loving all persons and thus a universal forgiveness of all, even our enemies. Singer's concern is with the lover's bestowal that overlooks the beloved's faults and forgives her offenses. The later Singer emphasizes the demands of tough love which are necessary if one is to mature into "staying in love." The dispute comes down to the definition of the person. Aquinas sees the person as an individual substance of a rational nature. Perhaps the early Singer would essentially agree with that. But, as Nota points out, Scheler stresses that the person is a dynamic unity of acts, thus emphasizing the father's forgiving love to the prodigal son and the forgiving love of Jesus toward the sinner, Mary Magdalene. Indeed, forgiveness is essential to love because in our finitude there is a necessity of guilt that love alone can heal. Because the person is always in the making, love needs to be a constructive criticism of creative bestowal.

But the notion of the person as a dynamic unity of acts is especially significant in its moral and religious implications concerning the role of redeeming love in repentance and rebirth. Singer clearly emphasizes that God is love according to John the evangelist, Aquinas, Kierkegaard, Scheler, and others. But Singer disagrees with this, for, he asks, how can love be a person or how can a person be love? However, what is a person if not fundamentally one's attitude of love? Against Descartes and the Greek tradition which sees the person as a thinking thing, Scheler argues that the person is one's loving attitude. I am not so much an *ens cogitans* (a thinking being) or an *ens volens* (a willing being) but an *ens amans* (a loving being), love is my crystal form. One's obituary might best show the unity one has become especially through one's various acts of love. If we are always failing one another in our growing love, then we continue to need a love's help that is greater than our own.

Sartre's treatment of the ideal love also raises important questions about the way in which Singer, following *Lucinde,* conceives of that ideal. According to Thomas Flynn, who admires the essentials of Singer's interpretation, Sartre first thought of ideal love in *Being and Nothingness* in terms of consciousness and then in *Cahiers pour une morale* in terms of praxis. Within the context of free consciousness love is a useless passion. When one autonomy falls in love with another autonomy, conflict results. For if my autonomy appropriates your autonomy there is sadism; conversely, if your autonomy appropriates my autonomy there is masochism. When I look at you looking at me I sense your unlimited freedom to think of me in any way you want; therefore, I try to defend myself by getting you to love me so that you will only think well of me. If I do not capture your freedom I feel abused. If I capture your freedom I am frustrated, because to be loved by an automaton rather than an autonomy is not the fascinating affirmation that I desire. So in *Being and Nothingness* the classical ideal of appraisal and bestowal is shown to be impossible if you and I are only autonomous.

However, once Sartre has shown the impossibility of love in the freedom context, he makes his way step by step toward the context of love's practice. Sartre's Hilda, in his play *The Devil and the Good Lord,* shows that we need to let go of our strict autonomy and recognize that we need to care for others in a community. Sartre's *Saint Genet* demonstrates that this conversion involves a generosity so that the lover is like the artist who is offering a gift. The gift is the offering of our own ego or our own autonomy. Authentic love depends upon the ambiguity of the sexual and the benevolent, which could be the tension between Platonic eros and Aristotelian philia. But the conversion from duality to ambiguity is deeper than that. Many attempts at love as giving can still remain inauthentic. Sartre's paradigm for the lover is the artist who is authentic when he offers the gift of his work to the other without defense. Love and art should be generous acts which involve confidence and risk. If I am willing to risk my defenses for an ideal love, I will be able to love persons authentically.

The early Singer conceived of the ideal lover as an appraiser who would desire the beloved with a Sartrean fascination and then give the gifts of bestowal in a spontaneous freedom. That Singer was very benign and saw no great conflict between eros and bestowal (bestowal is agape without God). But as he matured Singer saw the conflict that Augustine, the pessimists, Kierkegaard, Scheler, and Sartre each emphasized. He saw that lovers would come to hate each other. He saw their rejection of each other as authentic appraisal. What is the ideal of love to be at this point of pessimism? How do Sartre and Singer illuminate the question as we bring them together? The mature Sartre thinks that authentic love will "reveal the being-in-the midst-of-the-world of the other and assume this revelation and hence this being in the absolute." For Sartre there is an assumption about the value of love itself that lets the lover have confidence and take the risk of loving. It is the same confidence which the artist or the writer has. Is this absolute the "for itself-in-itself" which *Being and Nothingness* denied? Sartre writes of a demand-appeal, an exigence, that calls forth love. When Singer reaches the pessimistic moment, what is his ideal love? Does he have an absolute that can make demands upon him? Does not Singer's philosophy demand that there be a law of love in order for love to give life meaning when a particular love fails?

With Marvin Kohl's paper, "Love and Liberty," the penny drops, for now it becomes clear what has been going on both in Singer's theory about love as a mix of appraisal and bestowal and in the papers about that theory in the first love celebration. Hardly anyone, including Singer himself, has been content with the theory. Singer changed his own theory and moved away from the primacy of an unconditional and spontaneous bestowal to the primacy of a demanding, conditional and even rejecting appraisal. Bestowal, which is supposed to be agape, can easily become the greed or resentment of giving as Lawrence and Nietzsche see it. In a certain sense, as one reads Kohl, one sees that what he and Singer and Nygren and Fromm are doing is making a devastating criticism of agape by revealing further what might be called the arrogance of agape and thus its failure as love. If agape or bestowal is really only an unconditional giving, then it will never be much of a love, as Kohl points out. Any love worthy of the name has to take into account love and personal growth through demands, hardship, and sacrifice.

David Goicoechea was somewhat aware of this when he thought of love as mere appraisal and bestowal and said to himself: "NO, there has to be more, namely, adoration and personal growth." Russell Vannoy was pretty sure our classical modern model had gone wrong and especially the notion of an unconditional bestowal. Paul Gooch pointed out that in the Bible God's love is creative only by being very judgmental, hard, and demanding. Graeme Nicholson totally agreed with Irving Singer that in the Bible love has to be a nomos love in which the very core of that love is a rigorous submission to the law of love. Robert Perkins expressed a high Nietzschean mockery and indignation against any romanticism that forgets love's law and demands. For Kierkegaard agape has to be a love of strict duty in which we rigorously aim at promoting an appraising love in each other. Scheler argued that there are two loves with two infinities which collide because each makes demands, and even though agape bends down in parental care its law is totally rigorous. Sartre, exactly like Kohl, shows that if there is to be true love it has to go beyond liberty and take hard creative risks. So any bestowal or agape that is only a namby-pamby giving has to be a superficial farce and a self-defeating flop.

If agape is understood as a bestowal of unconditional giving, then it deserves all the criticism it quickly arouses. Perhaps in practice there often is a bestowal that is not love because it does not pay enough attention to make demands, and just leaves the so-called beloved at an unhealthy and wayward liberty. But as an ideal should there be a bestowal without appraisal? In other words, is not appraisal essential to bestowal? As Singer and Nicholson make so clear the Old Testament never advocated mere bestowal, for the very essence of love was submission to the law of love which made great demands. The mosaic covenant as interpreted by the Elohist and Deuteronomist was a totally conditional covenant which stressed that if you submit to the law, you will receive the promise. The Davidic covenant of the Yahwist and priestly traditions was unconditional in the sense of being a *berith olam*, or an everlasting covenant, that would last forever. But that never meant in the least that Torah was put aside or that the people of Yahweh were left as total libertarians. The new covenant first prophesied at Jeremiah 31:31, which Jesus saw himself as fulfilling and not cancelling, was also an everlasting covenant with never-ending forgiveness as well as a nomos, though it was written on the heart.

The point of Singer's later emphasis on appraisal and of Kohl's argumentation about caring love is that if bestowal does not go beyond liberty, it is arrogant. A bestowal that does not really do its best for the beloved's best is a bestowal that is lost in itself and not sufficiently other-oriented. The very point of the whole biblical tradition was to establish an other-oriented moral love with an adequate care. It would seem that a nondemanding bestowal is a misinterpreation of the traditional unconditional bonding. Unconditional never in the least meant nonappraising. Because of the centrality of nomos in agape, bestowal is anything but a nonjudgmental love. An interpretation of agape as a nonappraising bestowal is a leading of the lamb to the slaughter. Nygren, Fromm, and Singer may be doing that; therefore, it is no wonder that Singer had to change his theory. But true agape never was a mere bestowal. Ideally it was always a caring, as Kohl thinks ideal love should be.

Stanley Clarke makes explicit a fourth category besides the "falling in love," "being in love," and "staying in love," namely, "making love," which greatly concerns Singer and which he thematizes. Besides making the category explicit Clarke clearly distinguishes three important senses of the term, namely: the everyday sense in which lovers bond through sexual and other activity; the technological sense in which scientists might help lovers bond through drugs, counseling and any sort of therapeutic technique; and the theoretical sense in which scientists might make their kind of model of love as distinct from other theoretical literary, religious, and philosophic models. As an authentic pluralist Irving Singer is as wonderfully open to the scientific models as he is to the other three types. All the participants of the first love celebration are unanimous that in the trilogy he has made a magnificent description of the great variety of models of love in the Western world. His sense of the concrete is marvelous, although there is much debate about his sense of category even as it mixes with the concrete, as is seen in the case of "bestowal."

Singer is very thorough in his treatment of "making love" in the colloquial sense of that term. Not only is sexuality an important aspect of Singer's theory of Ovidian, courtly, and puritanical love but he has written a whole book on the subject, *The Goals of Human Sexuality*. The Western tradition since perhaps around 200 B.C.E. in Judaism has thought of the sexual act as a goal-oriented activity. The priestly morality thought in terms of the purpose of procreation or pleasure. Singer goes beyond those goals and thinks in terms of making love so that lovers might fall in love, be in love, and stay in love. Clarke suggests that sexuality is not a goal-oriented activity. In sex we need not represent a purpose or goal for ourselves and then try to attain it in some pragmatic manner. Rather sex is more an expressive activity such as smiling or playing. Lurgener's lover would give anything to have those fingers touch him. He would offer procreation, pleasure, or the goal of falling in love. Clarke wants to take "making love" beyond a goal-oriented pragmatics into an expression of meaning through metaphor that indicates a different world. The overall direction of becoming a loving person might best set love-making in a context that will let it make love. Even staying in love is so small an ideal as to be self-defeating in its egoism.

That scientists might make love in their test tubes, as it were, is an idea that is very appealing to Singer, the naturalist and humanist. He has a great hope that natural scientists and social scientists will be able to assist lovers in making love and growing in love. Clarke agrees that parts of love are such that scientists could, in principle, "manufacture" them; he seems to think that these parts are the mechanisms of falling in love, including fixation of attention, wanting to be near the beloved, and imaginative embellishment. Since the scientist qua scientist might study such mechanisms, it is plausible that he could find ways to control and cultivate them. But Clarke argues that love in the main is a historical process of contingency and dynamic intersection, and that since a great deal of it just happens it is radically unpredictable and scientifically intractable. "The historical features of love guarantee that no complete or even general scientific theory of love will be forthcoming." Because scientific theories about love must be so limited, Clarke would seem to imply similar limts on the engineering of love.

So the primary question has to do with the ability of scientists to make scientific models of love. If they do not, then they do not have sex qua scientists nor cultivate love qua scientists. It is noteworthy that Clarke thinks that Singer finds the boundaries between scientific possibility and scientific impossibility to be the distinction between appraisal and bestowal such that bestowal is outside of science. Thus in Clarke's mind the whole question of love and scientific humanism, at least in the way Singer treats it, comes down to the distinction between appraisal and bestowal. Like so many others, Clarke has his doubts about this distinction. While Singer thinks it is the imagination and creativity of bestowal that places love outside the realm of scientific method, Clarke sees scientific possibilities concerning imagination and creativity. Singer can only be so optimistic about science and love because he ignores the contingencies of love's historical processes.

Irving Singer's lifelong work has been a meditation of joyful wisdom in all its sorrow and glory, in all its awe and reverence upon the bond of love between the male and the female. Now in fear and trembling before the mysteries of the feminine, the masculine, and the combination of those two awesome forces, John Mitterer takes up from the psychologist's perspective what has been the focus of fascination for most of literature and so much of religion, for the lateral thinking of philosophers and in our time even for the various kinds of scientists. The question of romanticism and marriage which is also the potion of popular seduction in the soaps and romances is by no means narrow, parochial, or particular. Singer and Mitterer must certainly be convinced that meditation on this one love bonding is also a thinking on any bonding between human and human, human and the universe, the human and the divine, and nation and nation. All the complexity of human relating touches this issue of the battle of the sexes, of the sweet converse of man and woman.

Mitterer radiates with the electric excitement of a young bull moose approaching the heart of the territory of a great old bull in full power and rut. In effect he is indirectly autobiographical when he narrates the story of Iron John and the boy with the golden ball. For Mitterer and Singer meet at that ideal moment which is called *kairos*. Mitterer is alive with the sense that at this postmodern moment, 2,500 years of Greek thinking are exploding into new kaleidoscopic patterns of the male-female relation. Singer has wondrously brought together for him that vast historical mountain range of so many great peaks all touched by that common design of the appraisal-bestowal pattern. Now Mitterer sees bursting before his eyes all the condensation and displacement of that cathected design as he watches Singer in one last grand view represent the West's erotic history in a vast display of variations on that common theme of male domination. This is the moment for Mitterer to be freed from the prison and to leap forth with the golden ball of Zarathustra, Foucault, and Rorty into a new territory beyond Platonism, beyond patristics and scholaststics, beyond modernists and pragmatists.

But as Mitterer explores the moment of transition from a psychology of domination to one of equality, and as in his thinking that lets go of knowing he makes the transition from *philia* to that *philias* that perhaps shows the ideal equality of father and daughter—that daughter who is perhaps the dove of Nietzsche and Derrida—he sees that he is locking horns with Singer not to dominate but rather to explore in dance the realm of the wild. Singer has begun to explore the wild in woman that results in hatred and suspicion and even rejection, and Mitterer is seeing that it is related to the wild between men and men. Can there be a more mature dancing in the realm of the wild that will let violence between men and women be lessened? (And by the way, why is *philias* in the accusative plural?)

But, of course, it is not all true that Mitterer is taking the bull by the horns of that appraisal-bestowal dilemma, for he is an ironist who knows that the point is not to get the right theory of love but rather the right practice of love, or, as the Shinto priest put it, not to have the right ideology or theology but just to dance. Mitterer approaches the domination theory of Singer and the others not in order to dominate them, but in order to dance with them. After all, maybe that is all that bull moose are doing. Maybe they are driven by clusters of associations so charged and intense that it looks to humans as if they are trying to dominate each other, while in reality they are only dancing with one another in order to see who will dance with the cows and in the territory. Mitterer the psychologist is seeking to dance with metaphysicians; but before he can do that, does he have to dehorn them? In our dreams we guess that the dance of the cow and the bull has to do with the dance of the bull and the bull and we postmoderns want to dance without violence. We wonder if there can be an ethics first that then uses metaphysics. If we let the mind rest from such Platonic categories as appraisal and bestowal, will domination diminish?

John McMurtry is concerned that Singer's theory of love fails to recognize and to develop the moral dimensions of love so that good and bad loves cannot be clearly distinguished. McMurtry thinks that Singer's lack of an ethics from and for love has to do with: (1) the subjectivism of Singer's approach to bestowal and his general lack of any clear grounds of value from which to tell good from bad in romantic relationships, and (2) his uncritical pre-supposition of traditional patriarchal and proprietary structures of sexual love. But from his bestowing, "patriarchal," and nonfoundational approach Singer has responded to McMurtry's objections and shown in effect that his is a consistent and sensitive approach to the morality of love. In order to consider how Singer is on the way toward meeting McMurtry's very worthy demands that a philosopher of love should take into account, we might note the morality of Singer's judgments about the lack of bestowal and see how he avoids the pitfalls of patriarchy through sensitivity of expression. We may consider as well how his pragmatic pluralism finds moral directions by avoiding a foundationalism that weakens morality with pretentions to universality.

Many have thought that Singer's bestowal is subjective and incapable of being a love that makes the moral judgments that love should make. For the most part Singer sees bestowal as only one element of love; therefore, when it is coupled with appraisal there is no such problem. When Singer treats the pure bestowals of agape, perhaps he does forget that there is a discernment even in the generous love of the evangel. In any case, it seems that Singer's finest moral sensitivity has to do with his notions of bestowal by which he finds fault with the whole Greek tradition of eros and philia because it fails to arrive at a personal love that bestows upon the beloved the values of personhood, thereby failing to treat the beloved from the beloved's own realistic point of view as an end in her- or himself. Throughout the trilogy, but especially in the first volume, Singer clearly, consistently, and forcefully insists that love is not true love unless it has the bestowal that imaginatively recognizes the beloved as a person to be respected rather than as only a means to be used. Singer is judgmental of Plato, Aristotle, Ovid, and Augustine, among others, because they do not exercise the proper bestowal that allows the beloved to be enjoyed, cherished, and cared for instead of primarily used. Singer does not miss in the least the most important distinction of Kant, namely, that love be attentive to the beloved as a person and not merely a thing. Singer is not subjective because of bestowal but it lets him be objective.

John McMurtry's sensitivity to literature and authors such as Rousseau indicates another great strength of Irving Singer's approach. Singer's project conveys that the way a writer expresses his meaning is as communicative and convincing as what he directly represents. Thus while Singer may not make a great patriarchal assault on patriarchism and heavy handedly uncover its proprietory pathology, his subtle shift away from de Rougemont to show the concern of the English tradition for working out a happily married love becomes on Singer's part a masterful exercise of moral pedagogy. What a humanizing lesson it can be to read his treatment of Donne, Spencer, Shakespeare, Milton, and the English tradition down to Lawrence to see how the great exploration of antipatriarchal pathology has taken place!

Singer, as well as McMurtry and Mitterer, can move the unconscious so that the *anima* in all of her loving welcoming can have a place with those territorial aggrandizements that we so often overemphasize. McMurtry's call for a foundation such as the biological membrance as a value in terms of which judgments can be made is resisted by Singer. As a humanist, Singer resists for ethical reasons any idealized signified of an archeological or teleological type. He makes his evaluations about each particular situation from the background of his personal intelligence that is informed by his lifelong consideration of philosophy, literature, and art.

To bring to a close the first of ten communal reflections on 2,000 years of love, Mark Widner's beautiful presentation of music accompanied by reflection (or of reflection interwoven with music) leads us all to consider the interplay of love and the arts in our world, especially the world of Irving Singer and his philosophical reflection. Widner's presentation reflects Singer's project in such a way as to again bring to the fore such important questions as those posed by McMurtry. Widner's focus on the nature and place of manipulation in *Don Giovanni* and in the person and lifework of Mozart himself leads us all to consider Singer's categories of the sensuous and the passionate with which he approaches the complex phenomena of love in the operas of Mozart and Beethoven. In *Mozart and Beethoven: The Concept of Love in Their Operas,* Singer's approach lets his reflection mirror the thought of Kierkegaard on the question of love in its relation to the aesthetic, the ethical, and the religious. Kierkegaard has been hailed by Wittgenstein as the greatest moral thinker of the nineteenth century; perhaps Singer's approach can be understood as being sensitive to the efficacy of an artistic indirect communication.

We might now take a parting look at the sensuousness of Zerlina, the passion of Leporello, and the judgment of the Commendatore upon the Don, and the music of Mozart's world. In his hall of musical mirrors, as Mark Widner reflected the *Don Giovanni* of 1787 in the Piano Concerto in D Minor of 1785, Mozart recalled for all the sensuous loveliness of the "Andiam" duet, of the merging of the Don and of Zerlina, "in a music cute at first with a gentle mocking laughter that ingratiates itself more fully with a creamy, sliding motion in the left hand and then the upward glide of the left hand that goes off into juicy mellow chords capped by a bit of frothy virtuosity in the right hand." The sensuous can be as playfully lovely as Mozart shows it to be; yet, if it is not ordered in the direction of commitment to the beloved, it has, as Widner shows, the triviality of a mere simulation of feeling.

This Zerlina scene must reflect the thousand and three in Spain and all the other moments of merging ecstasy for which the Don lived. McMurtry would say that due penalty is paid for disregarding the biological membrane that makes all suffer and the Don die. Widner points out that the more we look for it, the more love is remarkably absent as a genuine, lasting concern in this opera. Singer shows how the cat-and-mouse game is one which the

Don controls through the seduction and the conquest of all. Kierkegaard's pseudonyms, the young man and the victorious hermit, seem to indicate how the god plays with the mouse that is man, so that we are each led along from stage to stage unless we rebel and prefer to remain stuck like a miswritten word not wanting to be corrected.

And so the Don is conquered by death in such a way that in hindsight we see that all along it was death and not life in his sensuous game. Both Widner and Singer clearly show that love must be committed passion, and that the Don, by being merely sensuous, failed to be a lover. Of course, the Don could have sought to accommodate women and thus not have been intentionally malicious; therefore, Commendatore would have come to him as "O Statua gentillissima." But because the Don was merely a boyish clown, death was "vecchio buffonissimo."

But in any case the sensuous alone remains mere frivolity even though as the Don surely knew in its essence it is the adorational ecstasy which alone gives meaning to life and of which Singer's trilogy sings. For the sensuous must become passionate, as appraisal must become bestowal, and if that happens, then we are on the way to keeping alive the "Andiam" which the Don and Mozart in their mourning have kept alive for us; for their saddest thought, Kierkegaard has argued, is our sweetest song.

The question of pluralism arises for Ric Brown as he thinks about Irving Singer's treatment of love and sex from a pluralist's viewpoint. Singer thinks, for example, that science can contribute greatly to our love life. John Mitterer has cautioned against any grand views and seeks wisdom about living in myths, poetry, meditation, and certain rites of passage. In "The Goals of Human Sexuality" Singer thinks about sexology and its possible contribution to understanding and promoting good and loving sex. In critically reflecting upon such theories of the orgasm as those of Freud and Masters and Johnson, Singer does think that orgasms can be distinguished physiologically and psychologically into two types, and that there can be mixtures of the two plus unlimited varieties of the three. While Singer's pluralism leads him to affirm any healthy type of sex, Ric Brown is concerned about the apparent hierarchy in which Singer sees the mixed orgasm as better than the passionate and the sensuous. Should a pluralist make such evaluations or should he think that the variety is all to be treated equally? With this we see the difficulty of science and theory.

In practice each kind and nuance can have its place just as Dante's Piccarda could affirm her place in heaven even though others among the blessed might be higher. In the heaven of orgasm where there are many mansions, would one in sensuous orgasm be envious at that moment of possibilities of passionate or of mixed orgasm? The question of pluralism raises the issue of sexual ethics. Singer seems to think that ethically the right approach is to affirm any type of healthy sexual act, and yet still to recognize the traces of hierarchical and dialectical evaluations even though they are erased. Singer seems to sense that merging is the great enemy of pluralists. Throughout his theoretical thinking he is critical of love as merging as it often appears in the literature of romantics and mystics. Singer's model for love is to see two people uniting in love as in a marriage of individuals, but never merging so as to lose personal identity. Yet, Brown shows in "Goals of Human Sexuality," in his pluralistic approach to the sexual act Singer does write of passionate sex as if it were a merging in which there is an apparent erasure of individuals. At the beginning of *The Nature of Sympathy* Max Scheler offers a phenomenology of several kinds of emotional identification and then writes of the metaphysical unity of the sexual act. It is interesting that in practice Singer is enough of a pluralist to affirm what he is opposed to in theory. For this reason I think he is a genuine pluralist.

Can there, then, be an ethics? Is Singer not caught in the relativity of a Nietzschean nihilism? Are not ironists like Mitterer and the Shinto priest caught in the same dilemma? Mitterer has argued that there is an ethic of domination implied in the Platonic approach and probably in the Hegelian as well. So a relativism or pluralism is the denial of an unethical ethics. But must pluralism be a relativism that is nihilistic? Perhaps the irony of Singer speaks to this question, for with one voice he speaks against merging and with another he speaks in favor of it. The orgasm itself has many voices, each of which may contain in turn a number of contradictory voices. But perhaps the irony of these many voices can be a beginning of ethics. When persons face each other in the sorrow of their eyes and voices perhaps they start to respect each other and to avoid what brings sorrow into the eyes and voices of their partners. Perhaps a metaphysics does not found ethics, althought it may attempt to voice the infinity of its voices.

Brown notes that as Singer moves from "The Goals of Human Sexuality" to the third volume of the trilogy, he becomes even more pluralistic. The "I love you" of "falling in love," "being in love," or "staying in love" can have different voices in the sensuality or passion of each. As lovers merge in the dance of lovemaking—and there is only the dance—the creative exploration of their multivocal exploring can become the ecstatic wailing of the wild. It can be a song of imploring that is almost like praying, or the cry of deploring that calls forth the response of responsibility. It is fitting that Singer becomes ever more pluralistic as he expresses the monism of the merging of orgasm. For the many that are radically different but collected are not the many that emerge from the one always to be one.

In Tim Madigan's judgment Singer's latest work, *The Pursuit of Love,* still focuses upon the question of love's ideals which has guided Singer throughout the monumental work of his trilogy. It seems that for both Singer and Madigan the relation between pluralism and norms is the terrain to be mapped; perhaps this is still but a variant on finding the right mixture of appraisal and bestowal. For what is pluralism but the attempt to have the most bestowing attitude possible toward each person and toward each theory of love and ideal of love? And what are norms but ways of appraising in order to be fair in the bestowal of resources so that one does not suffer as the result of bestowals on another?

Singer and Madigan both stress the importance of ideals, seeking to make clear their dangers as well as their benefits. Singer learned especially from Shakespeare that loves that are too idealistic can be vicious and hateful. Madigan's humanism seeks to unmask antihumane ideals that in the name of love are self deceitful and violent. It is this common concern about the dangers of the ideal that brings Madigan to criticize Singer's ideal harmony. Madigan's ideal, which was also the ideal of the early Singer, is to be as bestowing or as pluralistic as possible. Thus he is opposed to Singer's ideal as a harmony of love of persons, love of things, and love of ideals. Madigan thinks that many for understandable reasons will not be able to have such a harmony in their lives, although their way of approaching the other is still valuable and lovable. The later Singer concluded that the best way to love others is to keep putting before them the best norm possible, and that must be what Madigan is doing as he somewhat antipluralistically offers his criticisms to Singer.

So, is there any clarity concerning this question of the relation between love's norms and ideals? According to Madigan, Singer concludes that philosophers are unable to formulate rules of love which all people must follow, although they can assist in the endeavor of determining for each individual what is the most likely path of love to pursue. Perhaps this means that the chief rule of ideal love is to be very other-oriented as a bestowing listener. This pluralistic attitude should then strive to develop the judgments of good appraisal even to share with others. Madigan demonstrates the bestowal of good listening with a reading of Santayana's life, art, and theory that further demonstrates why Singer has always worked so much with the lovemaps of Santayana's charting.

And so it comes down to pursuing love with maps which we explorers in the chaos of love keep making. Following a fifty-year scrutiny of these lovemaps of the Western world, Singer's last word seems to be: "Don't worry too much about ideals, even those of appraisal and bestowal, for in the end it is the love of persons that counts most of all. That is, even these maps are there but for us. And if love for a person can lead us to discard them, that is most surely a sign of just love. For we have but intelligence and each other to trust. As Derrida might have said concerning such maps: "I am founding an entire institution on counterfeit money, by demonstrating that there is no other kind. There is only one good institution, my love, and it is us."

Part One

Erotic Appraisal
and Agapeic Bestowal:
The Origin of the Question

1

Appraising—Bestowing—Growing—Adoring

David Goicoechea

Is not Irving Singer's trilogy, *The Nature of Love,* a philosophy of love, a history of love, a writing of love, and a loving of love? Is not Friedrich Nietzsche's *Zarathustra* a philosophy of love, a history of love, a writing of love, and a loving of love? Might not a reading of Nietzsche in Singer's terms clarify something of Nietzsche's philosophy and history as well as reveal more about Singer's writing and loving? Might not a reading of Singer in Nietzsche's terms magnify even more the nature of love throughout history and intensify even more that writing of philosophy?

When Professor Singer reads Nietzsche's philosophy of love as centered around the concept of *amor fati* in terms of will to power and eternal recurrence might he not be treating what he would call the essence of love as an idealizing evaluation to be understood in terms of appraisal and bestowal? For is not the will to power but a double sort of appraisal made up of negative, reactive, servile preferences and of affirmative, active, noble preferences? Is not the eternal return related to the bestowal that is either one of disgust or of love for the fated smallness of man and the monster chance? Would not a Nietzschean reading of Singer thus help to clarify Singer's two sorts of appraisal which could let a man see either a home or a lady with both an objective and a personal evaluation, and would it not provoke thought about the bestowal which moves from a more critical personalism to a less critical pluralism?

After interlacing the philosophy of Singer and Nietzsche might not the confluence of their two streams of history clarify the focal points of their historical selections even though Singer's paradigm through love's history is

61

the love between the man and the woman and Nietzsche's is the cosmic love of all existence? Does not Singer believe that he can illuminate affection, friendship, humanitarian love, and love of God even while concentrating on erotic personalism? Is not Nietzsche's working out of the *amor fati* just as all inclusive and in *Zarathustra* is it not centered on the male and the female of the two *Dance Songs*?

Can Singer's reading of love's great historical moments: the Platonic, the biblical, the courtly, the romantic, and the Postromantic flow with Zarathustra's stages of love in the camel of Christian Platonism, in the lion of the Enlightenment and the lioness of Romanticism and finally in the child of Postromanticism?

Will not Singer's writing of love, when put in a mixing bowl, as it were, with Nietzsche's love literature, reveal an abundance of love's essence that exceeds the appraising will to power and the bestowing *amor fati,* for does not bestowal develop with a growing just as appraisal comes forth from an adoring? Is not Nietzsche's story of Zarathustra a drama of love's growth from camel's, to lion's, to child's such that Zarathustra grows from disgust at to love of his fate? Does not Singer's trilogy undergo radical growth even as he thinks each love should mature from falling in love, to being in love, to staying in love?

Cannot Nietzsche's writing of love reveal from the adorational depths of its Dionysian joy why Singer might grow in the direction of giving more value to the appraisals of erotic preference, for though love may not be time's fool the lover becomes love's fool already in the appraising?

Might not the cross fertilization of Singer and Zarathustra clarify what could be called their loving of love which has to do with the standard of a perfect love that guides both thinkers in their philosophizing, in their historicizing, and in their writing even as they grow toward some better love? Did not Zarathustra divine a sort of ontological argument for a perfect love when the retired pope suggested that those who believe that God is love do not have enough regard for love? Is not Singer guided all along to perform his works of love, part of which will have been his writing on love in order that he might make explicit the best love possible?

Thus, is not the direction of this meditation guided by a quest for love itself which resides at the germane core of each of us which we think can be cultivated by the deepest love of Zarathustra's heart by the deepest love of Irving Singer's heart?

A PHILOSOPHY OF APPRAISAL

Professor Singer's philosophy of love concerns the interplay of appraisal and bestowal. But for the sake of clarity four theses about the nature of appraisal need to be picked out first of all and understood before it will make sense to do the same with bestowal, and then see the two in their mixing and finally in their essential oneness. Two theses mark out the stance of the early Singer and two explain how his philosophy is growing through a fuller appreciation of appraisal. Thesis one is that appraisal is the cause of love. Thesis two is that appraisal is the basis of the great *eros* tradition from Plato to Postromanticism. Thesis three is that appraisal is not only love's cause but also an element that constantly accompanies bestowal. Thesis four is that appraisal can lead to rejection which can make love even more profound.

As Professor Singer meditates on love throughout the 1,300 pages of his trilogy, he sees appraisal as the primary seed with which all love must necessarily begin. Appraisal is a positive response of feeling which appreciates, cherishes, and desires. It is a preferential feeling that knows value both in the beloved bearer and for the lover. Appraisal as desire for perpetual possession of the good is seen by the early Singer as the necessary but never the sufficient condition for love from Plato throughout the West's Hellenic tradition.

By the end of volume three, Singer is concerned that he has not sufficiently appraised appraisal, for appraisal should not be the only condition that initiates love and lets there be bestowal. This natural and self-seeking preferential desire is not only an egoism that the lover should outgrow as he becomes more and more perfected in bestowal. Rather, appraising desire should itself develop. Singer seeks to solve the problem that haunted romantics from Tristan and Andreas Capellanus to Freud. A woman loses a lover when he becomes her husband. If a lover marries his muse she no longer amuses. Singer seeks to remedy this sad state of the nonaffair. He wants marriage to remain somewhat romantic. He wants the love of personal bestowal to foster at least the friendly appraisals of Aristotle and perhaps even the rapturous replies of Plato.

Is it not at this point of the key problem of romantic love that Singer approaches Nietzsche? Though the terminology of Singer's clear and well-balanced American philosophy is not that of the tortured Dionysian, does he not take much the same heroic direction? The later Singer sees appraisal not only as always accompanying the lover's bestowals, but even as coming forth in rejections. Singer knows that eventually the relationship will lose some of its sexual urgency. He knows that it will come to include periods of anger, boredom, disgust, and hatred.[1] He knows that appraisal can exercise itself in various kinds and nuances of rejections which, however, can make love more profound.[2] This fits well with Nietzsche's axiom that: "Whatever does not kill me strengthens me."

Appraisal for Singer is primarily evaluation. Will to power for Nietzsche is primarily evaluation. According to Nietzsche our emotional cognition of values depends upon our preferential ranking of values. If a lover appraises the beloved positively, then all the beloved's values can be joyously affirmed. If one's value hierarchy should undergo a reversal, if one should fall out of love and, perhaps, into hate, then positive values can become negative values. Nietzsche expects love to undergo such reversals: "Whatever I create and however much I love it—soon I have to oppose it and my love: thus will my will have it."[3] The later Singer has come to this insight that love's appraisals will become rejections. But he also has the Dionysian insight that this might be for the sake of a profounder love.

But this has been at least since the good news of Nietzsche's innocent and generous Jesu whom, by the way, Singer appreciates,[4] a portion of the traditional wisdom at least for those who take love seriously. For it has not only been said that: "You shall love the Lord your God with your whole heart, mind, and soul and your neighbor as yourself." But for the serious likes of Nietzsche and Singer it has also been said: "If any man come to me without hating his father, mother, wife, children, brother, sister, Yes and his own life, too, he cannot be my disciple."[5] Nietzsche asked: "Must we not first of all hate ourselves if we have to love ourselves?" Can this really be the good news that the appraisals of love will become rejections for the sake, however, of making love more profound?

A HISTORY OF BESTOWAL

From the beginning Professor Singer appraises bestowal as the actualization or the very practice of love. Once again to simplify as far as possible, four of his theses on bestowal might be spotlighted. Thesis one sees in the give and take of love bestowal as the giving that is altruistic. Thesis two sees bestowal as the core of the agapeic tradition for the past 2,000 years. Thesis three sees bestowal as loving the person rather than just his or her attributes. Thesis four sees the possibility of excessive bestowal which D. H. Lawrence called "the greed of giving." The first two theses govern the trilogy throughout while the latter two mark out its later thinking.

According to Singer, appraisal is only desire and does not become love until it is coupled with that imaginative and magical metamorphosis which brings the lover to behold his beloved in an artistic and near hypnotic celebration that can even make dear all her faults for him. There is in Singer's bestowal the wonderful ambiguity of a magical creativity plus a personal realism. Thus he appreciates from the popular song the following words that betoken bestowal:

Not that you are fair, dear,
Not that you are true,
Not your golden hair, dear,
Not your eyes of blue.
When we ask the reason,
Words are all too few!
So I know I love you, dear,
Because you're you.[6]

Bestowal lets the lover love the beloved person even beyond her bless-ings so that if she should be possessed of a fault or two even they can become angelic. And if her wondrous beauty nearly brings him to his knees his trust will always proclaim that she is ever so much more.

With this notion of bestowal as the imaginative magic that lets the lover discover even the hidden person, Singer is ready to read the history of love outside and before the agapeic bestowal. In his judgment neither Greek idealists such as Plato, Aristotle, and Plotinus nor Roman realists such as Lucretius and Ovid knew of the fullness of love's bestowing magic. For the object of their love was not a human person. The beloved's beauty might lead to Beauty absolute. Friendship could let friends be mutual means to virtue. Purging oneself of the many could merge one with the one. The lover might use marriage as a cure for love's insanity or the artist of love might use the other for pleasure alone. But in any case the idealizing imagination never focused on the person as an end in herself.

Thus, love that saw itself predominantly as the bestowal of personhood came on the scene 2,000 years ago when out of its Hebrew roots agape as the divine bestowal made possible the magic that never sought primarily to use the beloved as a means to one's ends, but instead to perform the works of love for her.

Professor Singer reads the history of love in the West as the growth of this agapeic bestowal in its mixing with a variety of conceptions of erotic appraisal. The medieval mixings were in their seminal reasons an Augustinian mysticism and a courtly humanism. Augustine's caritas synthesis did appreciate that the word's becoming flesh allowed the trinity of divine persons to reveal the worth of human persons, but that seemed to be of little avail to the Augustinian appraisal which could still reject the mother of his child.

In the twelfth century, Heloise's bestowing love moved beyond Abelard's Augustinian appraisal to a more humanistic love of Abelard himself. And for the *trouvères* of the north even more than for the troubadours of the south, the poet no longer primarily loved a lady that he might sing the better or the knight that he might fight the better or the saint that he might pray the better, but rather she was loved in her own humanity, and sexuality became appreciated as lovemaking.

In the modern era, the Lutheran and Puritanical purifications freed bestowal from its egocentric appraisals, allowing it to be transformed in unexpected romantic directions, for modern love consists of the transition from "The Divine alone is love," to "Any love is divine." For Luther the divine bestowal of God's agape "could descend upon a married couple, sanctify their love, and thereby cleanse their moments of closest contact—sexual as well as nonsexual—of all impurity. Their union would then become a vessel and a manifestation of divine love as it works its goodness through the world. From this point of view, sexual love in marriage was itself a holy communion with the Godhead."[7]

In a wonderful fashion, especially for me, a Catholic who never clearly thought of all this before, Singer shows how, from Donne through Shakespeare to Milton and through the tradition to D. H. Lawrence, the emphasis is not on working out one's perfection, but in cooperating with grace in working out marriage. The whole Platonic-Augustinian tradition through mystical love and courtly love never put its entire literary effort into the problematic intricacies of love and marriage.

Given the receding of Christian Platonic appraisal with the reformational emphasis on bestowal a shift becomes possible away from egoistic ladders or any meritorious ascents up out of the cave. Milton says it all when he has Adam choose identification with Eve rather than rectitude. At this point Singer chooses Milton's bestowal over the Augustinian quest which rejects the woman. The Romantics never reject the woman either, for they take seriously the idea that God is love and thus they would hold that true divine love should bestow upon Adam the grace to opt for Eve. They see love itself in its romantic form as "The world's holy, eternal, creating, primal energy."[8] True romantic love bestows upon lovers the ability to overcome obstacles either in death or in marriage.

Thus, in his reading of the history of love in the ancients, medievals, and moderns, Singer bestows upon bestowal the primacy over appraisal and he sees history as making progress in its growth toward greater bestowal. But in the course of his experience and meditation he has come to diminish the role of bestowal in, I think, a more Nietzschean direction. Toward the end of volume three he writes:

> In the first volume of this trilogy, the idea that love is appraisal was shown to be the basis of the great eros tradition in Western philosophy. I criticized several of its proponents—Plato, Aristotle, St. Augustine, Freud, Santayana—for having ignored the element of bestowal, thereby misunderstanding the role of appraisal as well. I continue to think my criticism was valid. What I now see more clearly, however, is the degree to which these thinkers were right in their insistence upon appraisal as a crucial ingredient of love.

The search for need gratification which motivates so much of human behavior belongs to the core of all intimate relationships. In love one not only accepts the other despite inadequacies, but also one feels free to reject her because of them.[9]

Milton, in the love that God bestowed on him, felt free not only to have Adam reject God, but also to argue for the divorce rejection. As Singer comes to appreciate love's ability even for the positivity of negative appraisals, is he not moving closer to Nietzsche's idea of confrontational friendship and negative appraising that we see between Zarathustra and Lady Life in the two Dance Songs, which, by the way, end with the affirmation of the Yes and Amen Song?

It seems that the give and take of love is such that the greater becomes the bestowal the more realistic can become the appraisal. The person and the attributes are so united that not only the attributes, but even the person is oft in need of negative, rejecting appraisal. A bestowal that is so excessive that appraisal cannot become realistic kills rather than quickens true love. But let us not forget the wisdom of love. A mutual bestowal that is still so fragile that it cannot trust realistic appraisals must bide its time and quicken so that it does not kill true love.

A WRITING OF GROWTH

According to Professor Singer, love is the interplay between an explorative appraising that seeks fulfillment and a creative bestowing which is benevolent to the beloved. Throughout history there has been a vast variety of the mixings of these two elements of love. As we attend to Singer's writing there is, I think, a third element that emerges as essential to love and that has to do with love and personal growth. Love is not only a loving of the beloved and a loving of the self, but it also is a loving of its own growth.

Perhaps the growth of love can be focused upon if we consider the new ideal which Singer finds in Nietzsche's notion of becoming what one is.[10] Caritas glorifies the growth that comes from seeking perfection. Luther claims that man transcends himself only by realizing that he cannot transcend himself. With Nietzsche a new concept of growth comes on the scene. Singer appreciates Nietzsche very much: he sees him as the gateway to the postromantic. Scientific or physiological and psychotherapeutic explorations of love receive a new initiative with Nietzsche. Singer not only gives him the last word at the end of volume one, but volume two ends with much that is Nietzschean. What Singer finds most troublesome with Nietzsche is his philosophy, that is, love as the will to power and *amor fati,* or the love of eternal recurrence. But it is the very conjunction of will to power and love of eternal recurrence which makes clear what growth in love means to Nietzsche. And I think this is much the same conjunction toward which the later Singer is working his way. In order to explain Nietzsche and Singer on love's growth we might speculate as to how they would view the examples of Piccarda from Dante's *Divine Comedy*.

Singer introduces the example of Piccarda in order to show the contradictions of the cosmic circuit in which God loves himself through all things and all things love one another in God. At an early age Piccarda had entered a convent and taken her vows. Later she submitted to her brother's wish to marry her off for political purposes, so she renounced the higher way and lived only the lower life of devout Christian marriage. When Dante meets her in a lower realm of heaven he asks her about the very problem of love's growth. How can she be joyously happy in a lower realm? Must not a lower love be unsatisfactory? Piccarda answers that God's will is her peace. Dante, Santayana, and Singer find her problematic. Singer thinks: "In the medieval heaven there can be no reciprocity between persons. Piccarda and all the celestial hosts are just pawns within the game that God eternally plays in the process of loving himself. They do not love themselves, for they no longer have a separate self. They do not love others for others have no selves either. They do not love God, for it is he who does all the loving. . . . It is not love and certainly not the love of persons."[11]

If Zarathustra met Piccarda he, too, would wonder about her lack of need for any higher love. That is the point of part four of *Zarathustra* in which Zarathustra, like Dante, has pity for the higher type who still could go much higher. For Nietzsche, love is the will to power which always seeks to go beyond to a higher love. In his view all things want a higher life and can never be content with mere survival. The will to power seeks growth in two typical ways: through its noble, affirmative, active forces, and through its servile, negative, reflective forces. Each person and each history is an interplay of these two types of contending forces. Zarathustra is a personification of the will to power through Western history from the original Zoroaster until Nietzsche who has gone beyond good and evil. Zarathustra, as the camel, would be like Dante and Luther, wondering why Piccarda does not have a divine discontent. Zarathustra, as the lion, would be the humanist who, within the limits of reason alone would seek to bestow upon Piccarda a more enlightened worldview. But Zarathustra as a child has come to see that both appraisals of questing eros and the bestowals of the gift-giving love are not of the essence of the will to power's most affirmative, active, and loving possibilities.

The renunciations of a rejecting eros as it denies the lower rungs of the ladder and the depths of the cave are unmasked as a resentful and deceitful failure of love. The bestowing virtue is praised at the end of part one but a new love is promised; for bestowal, too, is unmasked in its pompous, ponderous, proud pretensions. Parts two, three, and four of *Zarathustra* dramatize the discovery of the greed of giving. Enlightenment giving is revealed beginning with "The Night Song" as a cold, callous, cacophonous calculation. Zarathustra grows into the insight that higher than the love that grows with rejection and the love that seeks to give is the love that receives what is with a yes and amen. Love grows most when it does not live in order to grow and when it does not love in order to give, but when it appreciates with joy what is. That is exactly the way in which Piccarda loves. As an expectant mother she loved in accordance with the imperative of pregnancy, which guided her to love all with care for the sake of her child. But then she entered into the kingdom of love which for Nietzsche and his evangel is here and now. She came to love the eternal circuit with a yes and amen. For sorrow may want children and heirs for the morrow. But joy just wants itself again and again for eternity.

As Singer moves toward a pluralism that is ready to affirm each love and reduce none of the differences, is he not approaching the *amor fati* which is Nietzsche's attempt at a most thoroughgoing pluralism? But a tension arises for both Nietzsche and Singer, for how can they affirm at once an all bestowing pluralism and a critical and even rejecting appraisal? Or, in Nietzsche's terminology, how can *amor fati,* which is a totally affirmative yes and amen saying, be consistent with a striving and critical will to power? In short, how can yea-saying bestowal and nay-saying appraisal promote one another? If will to power seeks growth and progress and if the eternal return denies any essential progess how can the will to power affirm the eternal return? How can the quest for progress will the denial of progress?

A LOVING OF ADORATION

To organize our thinking about this enigma of love we might consider, first, Singer's approach to Nietzsche on the enigma; second, Nietzsche on the enigma; third, a Nietzschean approach to Singer on the enigma.

Professor Singer appreciates the critical powers of Nietzsche. He recognizes that Nietzsche is a nay saying genius. And yet Professor Singer also knows that Nietzsche thinks that it is most important to be a loving, yea sayer. This is important to Professor Singer for he, too, judges it best to be an affirmative philosopher and he too thinks that love is primarily an affirmative appraisal and an affirmative bestowal. So while Professor Singer, the pragmatic empiricist, greatly appreciates Nietzsche's empirical criticism, he also wrestles hard with the cosmic *amor fati* which might give sense to our postromantic love.

After writing "The concept of *amor fati* cannot be salvaged by the notion of either will to power or eternal recurrence," Professor Singer[12] goes on to say:

> At times, however, Nietzsche ignores his pseudoscientific hypothesis and unashamedly speaks as a moralist. He tells us to live our lives as if each moment would henceforth recur eternally. The question he asks is: "Do you desire this once more and innumerable times more?" This involves a commitment to the infinite future, but not to the eternal recurrence of the past. And that makes all the difference. Instead of the categorical imperative or a crass concern about rewards and punishments in another world, Nietzschean ethics of this sort bids us to treat decisions as if their outcome would never end, as if their consquences would be with us forever. If we took that attitude, would we not make the greatest effort to render each moment as full and satisfying as possible? Would we not live for the maximum creation of goodness and beauty in this world?[13]

In this short passage does not Professor Singer indicate in a very clear way the primary meaning of the will to power? When he writes that eternal recurrence might ethically have to do with "the greatest effort to render each moment as full and satisfying as possible," is he not expressing what Nietzsche calls the will to power? Is not "living for the maximum creation of goodness and beauty in this world" a definition of will to power?

Likewise, is not Professor Singer making the key distinction when he works with the ethical import of eternal return rather than the scientific speculations on the same? Zarathustra himself is at first nauseated and disgusted by the thought of the eternal return, for he, too, like Professor Singer, saw it as an abomination that would destroy any ethics and lead to nihilism. But, as Professor Singer suggests, Nietzsche discovered an interpretation of eternal recurrence that transforms the depths of nihilism into the greatest affirmation. The interpretation which Nietzsche finds is ethical. It can be acceptable to postromantic man in a way that the Platonic-Augustinian afterlife or the Lutheran Kantian calculation could never be.

Nietzsche knows that the will to power can will ways of loving that look good but are self-deceitful. Will to power's loving of eternal return is the way out of this self-deceit and this great ressentiment. Zarathustra comes to see in part three, thirteen, "On the Convalescent," that if he has the eternal return as his ethical standard, he can be free of ressentiment. If he approaches someone or something, especially the littleness of man, and if he can say, I love it and I want it to return again and again in just this way, he knows he is affirmative and active and not resentful. He could not will the eternal return of that object just as it is and still have a predominant hatred and revenge even at the subconscious level. Nietzsche with the standard of the eternal return is primarily interested in seeing to it that he is loving in a just and noble way. This is the beauty of Professor Singer's interpretation. He sees that the will to power's highest way is made possible by an ethical eternal return.

But Professor Singer still has his doubts. He is still a bit like the convalescing Zarathustra. He interprets the ethics of eternal recurrence as a consequentialism which will logically involve an unending past as well as an unending future. For the further we stretch responsibly into the future the longer will become the past of our responsibility.

Does not Zarathustra at the end of part three disclose an interpretation of loving eternal return that fits right in with Professor Singer's basic thrust? In the "Second Dance Song" he sees life as a woman: She is unfathomable and frightening. She can go mad at any time and plunge him into chance. A woman, like life, can reject you at any moment, for life is wild, exploitative, and unpredictable. She suggests that he often thinks of rejecting her. Man, too, is equally fickle, forgetful, and rejective. They sing that they are a pair of good-for-nothings beyond good and evil. And yet, all the more reason to love one another. For whom else do they have? Their original joy has fated them together. Zarathustra comes to see that if he believes in love then he will have to stay with this woman for life. What else can he do but believe in love? They have had great joy together before and in their joy they said yes to each forever. If there has been such great joy then it should last for all eternity. That is *amor fati*. *Amor fati* is simply the will to power's most creative way of loving. *Amor fati* is simply the joyful love of the eternal return of joyful love.

But what is this joyful love except adoration? When the young Augustine went away to school at Carthage, he was excited most of all because he was in love with love. When the maturing Luther moved away from caritas was it not because he believed in and needed an adoration greater than any the Augustinian way could give him? When Nietzsche and Singer and we postmoderns have to go beyond the appraisals of Augustine and the bestowals of Luther is it not because our love of love is carrying us along into love's beyond?

Is love's deepest essence really appraisal? Is it really bestowal or an ever-growing life? Are not these three the overflow of our love of love? Are they not the practice of and the quest for adoration? Does not Professor Singer's great exploration of love work with that assumption from beginning to end? Why did he choose as a young man to be a philosopher of Love? Was it not that he loved love more than anything? Why did he choose as a writer to focus on bestowal as the very heart and core of responsible love? Was it not because he loved person and fidelity and would even sacrifice a kind of adoration out of responsibility to his faith in love? Why at the end of the trilogy does he return to appraisal and value it even in its rejections if it is not because he has always been a Dionysian lover of adoration? With Nietzsche he knows of a love whose joy is so great that he nearly throws himself—oh, half hurls himself off into love's abyss of chance, off into the unknown. That love beyond reason which, however, has a reason of its own is adoration.

Professor Singer loves the Platonic-Augustinian appraisal. He loves the Lutheran-Kantian bestowal. But of both of these he is leery. However, there is an appraisal-bestowal synthesis or an eros-agape fusion of which he is not the least bit leery or critical. And that is the confluence of eros and agape in St. Francis, who always kept the rhythms of the courtly song pulsing through the singing of his whole loving life. In Franciscan love there is an honest, humorous, humble health which he loves without rejection. Perhaps Nietzsche and Singer, and we postmoderns are daring Franciscan nominalists who know that love will always exceed our theories. Is it not a loving of all existence in joyful love and a loving of joyful love in all existence that moves us to fall in love and to make love to be in love and to remain in love?

Professor Singer's three volumes have three pictures. The Adam and Eve of volume one must portray appraisal. The fig leaves alone show the appraising mentality. The funny little merging blocks of volume three must suggest a dear and faithful bestowal. But I suspect that the picture of volume two is most close to the heart of Singer and Nietzsche and Francis. For it is the picture of adoration that in its growing can affirm the other two. It is the picture of a Singer of love for whose praises of love we are most thankful.

NOTES

1. Irving Singer, *The Nature of Love* (Chicago: University of Chicago Press, 1987), 3:386.
2. Ibid., 3:396.
3. Ibid., 2:12.
4. Ibid., 3:75.
5. Luke 14:26.
6. Singer, *The Nature of Love*, 1:146.
7. Ibid., 1:242.
8. Ibid., 2:387.
9. Ibid., 3:396.
10. Ibid., 3:336.
11. Ibid., 1:357.
12. Ibid., 3:81.
13. Ibid., 3:83.

2

Loving, Appraising, and Bestowing

Russell Vannoy

I

I first became puzzled about the nature of love at a high school dance many years ago. Occasionally there were dances called "men's choice" or "ladies choice" in which the two sexes lined up at opposite ends of the floor. The members of one sex would then quickly cross the gym and select the most desirable dance partner they could. Refusal by those selected was theoretically possible but it was considered most discourteous to do so. Although benevolence was hardly on our minds as we dashed to our partners, many a love relationship was either begun or confirmed in this all-important selection process. Those of us who were not so desirable held back and let the most attractive partners have their pick, since it seemed perfectly natural that the handsome quarterback was destined to love and marry the blonde cheerleader.

It was a small Missouri town in the Bible Belt, and we were all at that time good Christians who had been taught that we should bestow value on the "undesirables." But it didn't work that way at the senior prom. (Nor has it ever worked at the countless faculty parties I've attended, even though physical beauty was now often replaced by hierarchies of spiritual beauty.) We divided others (and ourselves) into the eminently desirable, the moderately and minimally desirable, and the hopelessly unlovable. The least desirable were simply left sitting there; indeed, had some benevolent soul like Erich Fromm picked one of them, he or she would have viewed it as merely an act of charity rather than the sort of love one wanted. A gratuitous, unmerited bestowal of value, to their chagrin, would only have reminded them that they had no appealing qualities that merited love. Interestingly, anonymous sex uses the same hierarchy of degrees of desirability, albeit on much narrower criteria. This should give pause to those who feel that love has some kind of absolute superiority over plain sex. Nor is it the sexual component of romantic love that generates the hierarchy. Prospective friends are assessed in the same way.

A sensitive person surveying this grim prom scene might wish that all of us were irresistibly lovable. This clearly wouldn't work, however: No one would be assured of the exclusivity or constancy of love, and my being selected would mean nothing since one person would be as effective as anyone else in stimulating romantic passion. There is another possibility: What if everyone found one person irresistibly lovable and the feeling were invariably mutual? But once again the self-esteem that comes from being chosen or selected would not be possible. Choice would have to be excluded in such a world since there would be no guarantee that everyone would be chosen. Indeed, when love is this automatic, I am being loved by an automaton. Even the couple on the otherwise deserted island in the film *Blue Lagoon* felt that they were chosen in the sense that either of them might have rejected the other as a lover. Thus if the senior prom symbolizes the loveworld, it is not just a contingent fact that some were either left out or viewed as less than desirable. Indeed, these unfortunates seem, perversely, to be conceptually necessary if the loveworld is to function as one of choice and selectivity.

Some of us did—or thought we did—find love at the prom. If, however, love means cherishing the beloved for his or her sake and being concerned primarily for his or her well-being, how did such idealism manage to arise in the decidedly unidealistic setting I have described? How did appraisals of what suits my standards manage to give rise to a qualitatively different attitude of bestowal of value on the beloved who is now cherished for her sake?

It is not enough, as Theodor Reik claimed, to say that a beautiful rose can arise out of manure. Just try smelling a rose when there is a lot of manure around. And if you clip it (i.e., divorce bestowal from appraisals), the rose dies. Erich Fromm once made the remarkable claim that one cannot love a woman unless one also loves all women. From this it could plausibly follow that if one is a sexist toward women one is not in love with, one does not somehow become a knight in shining armor when one is alone with one's beloved. As the battered spouse problem shows, Fromm is probably right, even though he was quite wrong in ignoring appraisals altogether.

Here is another possibility, and it is one that may reconcile Professor Singer's seemingly contradictory claim that love involves both self-interested appraisals *and* bestowals of value that cherish the beloved for her own sake. Does a favorable appraisal of someone stimulate my imagination so that he or she is ultimately seen to have perfections that others cannot see? Like all pleasures, passion that is aroused by someone's appealing qualities wants to escalate in intensity. Barring unusual circumstances, no one wants to have or to give only a moderate sexual experience; the same is true of romantic passion. This means that both the good and the less than lovable qualities must be seen as progressively more appealing. The closer to perfection they seem, the more passion is aroused; and the more passion is aroused, the more perfect they seem. When sexual or romantic passion is quite intense, fantasy becomes, as it were, reality in the phenomenology of the loveworld.

Since passion can only be aroused by certainty about its object and is confused by ambiguity, these perfections are not seen as the "as if" reality we attribute (say) to someone playing Hamlet in the theater. We identify with the actor, yet we are peripherally aware that it is still a play. Singer holds that the perfections we attribute to a lover are "as if" perfections because he does not wish to defend the old charge that the romantic lover is deluded. Since, however, Singer is a pluralist, he should grant that the loveworld (erotic reality) is just as valid in its own way as the ordinary reality which scornfully labels the realities of the loveworld as delusions.

Indeed, in ordinary reality where we are rational, purposive realists, the language of love can't even get off the ground. If I feel the need to flatter her during breakfast by saying "You're perfect," she would either laugh or feel that she has been given an impossible standard to fulfill. Saying, "I love you" when leaving for work is a perfunctory ritual. If I were to state the truth as defined by ordinary reality and say "I love you because your good qualities outweigh the bad ones," a fight or tears would soon follow when I am commanded to list just what those deficient qualities are. If love is defined by its reasons, then in the real world it becomes the passion that dare not speak its name.

If the one I originally selected on the basis of a favorable self-interested appraisal is now seen as having wondrous perfections in the loveworld, then it would seem that my attitude would change from one of self-interest to worshiping the goddess before me. The phenomenology of cherishing someone is that I think primarily of what I can do to please her. I don't think of myself when I am fixated on someone else. One must use terms like "perfection" and "goddess"—love talk that is ludicrous in ordinary reality—since it requires quite a leap of the imagination to leave self-interest behind and get into the orbit of bestowal of value for the beloved's own sake. The use of the term "perfection" does not mean that one sees a dolt as a genius. Were that true, I really would be cherishing a fantasy rather than the person she is. What is meant is found in the classic example of the ugly mole that is now seen as a beauty mark.

Now, however, a grave problem arises within the loveworld itself in the attempt to transcend self-interest by worshiping the other. The other person, if she loves me in return as I wish, will also imaginatively endow me with perfections as well. The more valued I feel, the more I value the source of my value. She in turn values me even more in response to my valuing her. I in turn then value her even more because of her escalatory bestowal of value on me. The escalation of valuing is either the cause or result of the escalating passion. The climax of this familiar feedback process is that each becomes an absolute value for the other.

One would hope that all this would result in an ultimate experience of mutually enhanced self-esteem and cherishing of each other. Since, however, love commands that I view myself through the eyes of the one who is valuing me, I become an absolute value for myself—something quite different from an innocent sense of heightened self-approbation. The movie star who is an absolute value for her adoring fans must struggle to keep this adulation in perspective lest she begin to think that she can ignore their wishes. In the heated atmosphere of the loveworld, however, keeping things in perspective is quite out of the question. Indeed, if I feel myself to be a being of absolute worth, then when I see myself through the eyes of another, don't I eventually see only myself? It was once said of Anais Nin that when she looked into someone's eyes, she saw only mirrors that reflected her own image.

If I have become a god both for myself and for the other, then, even if I can see the other person, I cannot see her as being equal in value to me. I would egoistically be cherishing myself more than her, and her cherishing me would only be a means to my own fulfillment. If, however, I am still aware that my absolute value depends on her, then it cannot really be absolute since it depends on how someone else feels. Since I know that she sees herself only through my eyes, I must take this a step further and imagine that she has merged with me and has no independent existence. Only then could absolute value, if it is to be absolute, see itself as the source of its own being. When she has ceased to exist for me as an independent person, however, she can no longer be cherished as a beloved.

One might, however, argue that none of this need be true, that there is nothing implausible in holding that we are both absolute values for ourselves and for each other. But consider another problem with this scenario. The phenomenology of cherishing at this intensely romantic level (although not in everyday reality) surely requires that I will be fixated on what is an ultimate value for me. If I can think of myself at all, I will see myself as virtually nothing in comparison with her. (Imagine Woody Allen on a date with Marilyn Monroe.) But then how can I identify with her in the sense of seeing the world, including myself, through her eyes—eyes that say I am an absolute value for her and thence for myself as well? The situation I am describing seems to require that I feel simultaneously like a worm and like a god. Even if I could manage to do so, however, it would throw both romantic passion and cherishing into a state of utter confusion. But perhaps this need not always happen either. Yet passion and selfless adoration, when they begin to escalate in romantic arousal, want a guarantee that they will not self-destruct at the peak that passion and cherishing also desire.

Furthermore, if I am being a kind of artist in imaginatively endowing her with these perfections, then am I not (like all good artists) imposing my own vision on what I see—a vision that pleases me but which may or may not please her? The perfections one lover saw in me included my bald head—something I'd desperately prefer to ignore. Cherishing someone is, therefore, no guarantee that self-interest is not primary even though the phenomenology of cherishing ordinarily excludes any awareness of self-interest.

Allow me to return to my senior prom once again. If love is generous and kind, then Singer's imaginative bestowal of value should have been aimed at those who were the least attractive. To see an ugly person as Cinderella would be the ultimate imaginative leap and it would be the most generous bestowal of value imaginable. But the undesirables for whom love might have meant the most (in the way the food would mean the most for a starving man) never found anyone bestowing value on them. There was no rational reason for avoiding them; after all, they were not moral, intellectual, or physical monstrosities. Like Gertrude Stein's (misquoted) comment about Oakland, there was just no there there. If one believes that romantic love is a dispensable luxury and that being ignored shouldn't have bothered them, I'd note that they were friendless as well. Nor did they much care for each other. Were one to approach the other, she'd probably say: "You're after me only because no one else will have you." They would certainly not have been consoled by the quaint notion that there is a deity who loves only them—a Nietzschian revolt of the nerds.

Nelson Algren once said, "Never fall in love with someone worse off than you are." Perhaps he meant that one could never be sure that one was not merely being used by supposedly lesser mortals in order to elevate their status. Or the desperate may be searching for a savior, and anyone above them will do. One would then not be loved as a unique being. Nor could the savior gratuitously and benevolently bestow self-respect without wondering whether he was in love with the person or merely in love with the ultimate challenge of bestowing value where he could perceive none to exist. If, however, one's amorous imagination is inspired by some appealing quality in the beloved, then this is not a problem. One has a reason for bestowing value that lies outside oneself. Trying to discuss the bestowal of value in agapeic terms when dealing with romantic love—as Professor Singer sometimes does—is a problem in his otherwise fascinating chapter on appraisal and bestowal.

It may seem puzzling that the aesthetic imagination, but not the amorous imagination, can bestow value on things that are not ordinarily seen as having any appealing qualities. The grouchy, hideous baglady takes on a certain bizarre charm when viewed with the aesthetic attitude. Edward Hopper took scenes that were as drab as the undesirables at my prom and endowed them with a certain mystery and vibrancy in his paintings. The erotic imagination, however, requires something appealing to begin with so that passion can escalate to the point where we want not only to look but to touch and interact in other ways as well. Here the *eros* tradition in the philosophy of love is right on the mark.

If the undesirables were ignored, the eminently desirable ones had so much value showered on them that they had to struggle not to become so enchanted with themselves that they couldn't love anyone else. Indeed, bestowing value on our blonde cheerleader seemed redundant. Bestowal is often defined as giving something as a gift. The beautiful cheerleader was, however, already given (or so we thought) all the gifts she needed by nature. Caught up in the phenomenology of perception found in the loveworld, our dazzled eyes saw her value as being inherent. So what was there to bestow on her? We could only passively respond to her overwhelming presence. One thing that all this means is that Singer's conception of love as an imaginative bestowal of value doesn't account for those who are commonly viewed, rightly or wrongly, as being the most desirable partners.

One might argue that such persons are not really viewed this way, that our feelings about conventional or official beauties are highly ambivalent. We felt that Marilyn Monroe was everything anyone could want which, perversely, was the reason why we couldn't love her. Wouldn't one feel inadequate in the presence of a goddess? Or how does one have sex with what one views as a living work of art? And what does a goddess who *seems* to have everything need of a mere mortal like me? These difficulties may be true for some persons, but the cheerleader solved the problem of others being intimidated by her overwhelming desirability. She simply married another official small-town beauty—the quarterback. Although they were deities to us, it can be as lonely at the top as at the bottom of the erotic scale. They needed each other, and they are now grandparents. From what I know of them they appear to fulfill Singer's ideal of "staying in love." I would, therefore, still offer this case as a challenge to Singer's concept of love as an imaginative, creative bestowal of value.

II

My mother, who has been married seven times, once told me that a man is like a library book. One should read it and cherish it and then return it to the library. After all, who wants to read only one book or read the same book for the remainder of one's life? When boredom sets in, find another book—or another man. Did she really love any of her husbands? The neighbors and her rejected husbands didn't think so; they claimed that she was self-centered. Maybe *she* no longer needed them, but they still needed her. And they felt that she was selfish in dropping them merely because she no longer found them interesting. Singer, however, correctly notes that with love individual appraisals are subjective; thus there seems to be no objective criterion for evaluating her decision. Indeed, her husbands were caught up in the dilemma that all lovers face: They want to be cherished for their own sakes, yet their self-esteem requires that they be chosen because they have appealing qualities. To have appealing qualities, however, means that these qualities must suit the needs and interests of the one they love. But this then means that they cannot have a reason to complain about any alleged egoism when their qualities no longer fascinate.

One might argue that there is nothing that is necessarily egoistic, in a vicious sense, in seeking the heightened self-esteem that comes from being selected for my appealing qualities, or from choosing someone who meets my needs and interests and having my love reciprocated. Self-esteem is, after all, a basic good. Romantic passion, whether or not it has a sexual component, is, however, notoriously subjective and whimsical. It cares not a whit about whether its object feels abandoned if it dies for reasons that do not make any rational sense. Benevolent persons often bemoan the fact that they can no longer give their partners the kind of love they want to give. Even if one worked very hard at restoring one's passion, this would be insulting to one's lover since it suggests that it is quite a struggle to find her qualities appealing. In the film *Making Love*, the husband discovered that he was gay and could no longer sexually satisfy his wife. He promised his wife that he would still be her friend, but she screamed: "I don't want just friendship: I want passion." Indeed, she acted as if she believed her rights had been violated, something that is nonsense in ordinary reality but which seems quite reasonable in the loveworld. When passion is strong, it greedily wants a guarantee of permanence that it itself shows it cannot provide when it dies and forgets that its erstwhile object ever existed. If love desires a guarantee of permanence, the fact that staying in love often happens is irrelevant when that guarantee is missing even then. This charge against romantic passion is not new. Surprisingly, however, it can be true of friendship as well. Right now I am tired of my longtime friends in Buffalo and I yearn to move somewhere else to make some new ones. They are as wonderfully kind, witty, and charming as ever, and they don't deserve my neglect.

I should like to return to analyzing my notorious mother in order to see if she ever rose above the level of appraisal into bestowing value.

Mother did cherish her husbands as she cherished her books while she was interested in them. But her cherishing a book was constantly a function of her appraisal of whether or not it was worth continuing to read it. If it began to become boring after the second chapter and no relief was in sight, she returned it to the library. And so it went with her husbands. Her men could, of course, have changed their identities in order to please her. But then she would, if Derek Parfit is right, have been loving a new husband rather than the old one.

Indeed, her cherishing of something for its own sake seemed to be a fragile epiphenomenal reality in relation to her appraisals of her husbands' worth rather than being a robust mode of valuing in its own right. If there were any bestowal of value, her appraisal of another's worth was right there deciding whether or not this bestowal should continue. The ways in which bestowals of value cease—Paul Simon's "Fifty Ways to Leave Your Lover"— perhaps reveals that this is true of all bestowals, even though one may not be aware of the appraisals one is making when one feels one is merely taking delight in the sheer presence of the beloved without any thought of one's own needs.

One might argue that all of this is quite wrong-headed, that there is a confusion here between being interested in someone and serving one's self-interest. Can't an interest in helping someone be a reason for one's love? Surprisingly, it is rather difficult to explain where and how altruism fits into personal love, even though it would be a contradiction to say that one loves someone yet cares not a whit for his or her well-being.

In its purest form, the altruist chooses the one who needs him or her the most. This does not, however, guarantee the security of being loved any more than would an egoistic choice. For once my needs have been satisfied or my most pressing problems have been solved, the altruist—like the nurse in a hospital—will want to move on to someone who needs her help more than I do. Nor could someone motivated primarily by altruism allow her passion to escalate to a point where I am seen as perfect; for then she would feel quite unneeded. Furthermore, although the altruist wants her love to salvage my self-esteem, being chosen because I was a basket-case would destroy what little self-esteem I had to begin with. Finally, two perfectly altruistic persons who gave no importance at all to their own self-interest could not give anything to each other. If I want nothing for myself, no one can give me anything. This parallels the failure of a relationship between two totally egocentric persons who both want either to get without giving anything in return or to get more than they are giving.

These latter points were made in Alan Soble's *The Structure of Love*. Soble concludes that if one uses extreme cases, the ideal relationship would be between a total egoist and a total altruist. But this would not work either. The egoist wants to be seen as perfect and also to have others serve his interests. But if he is seen as perfect, the altruist would feel that he or she would have nothing to give and the relation would collapse. If the altruist did attempt to satisfy the egoist's needs, then the egoist could not see himself as perfect but rather dependent on someone else.

Suppose, however, that one backs away from extreme forms of altruism and egoism and discusses love in terms of a mixture of self-interest and altruism. But how is this mixture to be proportioned? If the other person's needs and my own needs are equally valuable, then my altruism will not know what to do with a bed-ridden lover who can no longer satisfy my equally important self-interested concerns. If love is equal amounts of give and take, this view is commonly rejected by philosophers of love as a tit-for-tat business relationship. It is also alarmingly close to the you-do-me-and-I'll-do-you ethic of non-exploitative anonymous sex, where it works quite nicely.

On the other hand, I may be primarily altruistic and view my own interests as being secondary, although not utterly unimportant. If, however, my altruistic lover tries to imaginatively understand my needs and see them as I see them, then he will see that I see their fulfillment as being of secondary importance. If he fulfills my needs and sees their fulfillment as I see them, he will feel that what he has done is of secondary importance as well. If he avoids this and sees my needs as being of primary importance to him and acts accordingly, the recipient of his kindness will feel annoyed that so much attention is being paid to what to him is of secondary importance. Altruism must consider how the other person feels about the benefits he or she is receiving. Finally, if my interests were primarily benevolent and secondarily self-interested, then I would likely choose someone whose problems I can help resolve outweigh his or her romantically appealing qualities. No one, however, wants to be chosen as a beloved with that sort of criterion. Even worse, the more my failings are resolved, the less appealing I would seem to be to someone who believes that being helpful is a very significant factor in loving someone. Although my attempt to work out the relation between altruism and egoism in personal love has failed, it may be that someone else can do better.

III

While the tone of this paper may seem to be rather cynical, my problem is rather one of conflicting emotions about love. If some sort of personal love is a basic good, one would like to see it fall under the norms of distributive justice and rescue it from the sorry spectacle of my senior prom. Yet that would seem to make it a public rather than a private matter. Even in private matters, however, one often does try to be fair to everyone involved, e.g., giving equal amounts of cake to one's friends. Elizabeth Telfer holds that selectivity and exclusivity actually benefit the unloved since the heightened self-esteem that comes from being loved makes one more benevolent toward the loveworld's rejects. I have not myself seen any evidence that this trickle-down theory of benevolence is true. Romantic lovers seem to be withdrawn from the world, and friends become cliquish. Have we gone wrong somewhere in the way we have conceptualized personal love? There is, alas, no space left to answer that question here.

POSTSCRIPT

I am deeply indebted to Irving Singer's classic opening chapter on appraisal and bestowal in the first volume of his trilogy. Although his remarks about falling in love, being in love, and staying in love in the third volume are interesting and valuable, it was the first chapter of the trilogy and the ways in which appraisal and bestowal were used to analyze philosophers of love in subsequent volumes that fired my imagination.

3

A Mind to Love:
Friends and Lovers in
Ancient Greek Philosophy

Paul Gooch

The vast boundaries of Irving Singer's work are easily admired; but his sureness in dealing with specific thinkers is all the more impressive when one assumes the task oneself of distilling their views on love. In what follows I cannot promise noticeable improvement on Singer's account of Socrates, Plato, or Aristotle; worse, I will have to overlook many of the issues he raises. My aim is not comprehensiveness, but rather to suggest approaches to a sympathetic grasp of what these three grand sources of Western thought contribute to the study of love; to stir up some few doubts; and perhaps to alter some emphases in Singer's account in order to open up further exploration.

The title of my paper, like love itself, has more than one meaning. If I am looking *for* a mind to love, my search is for an individual whose thinking is admirable rather than for a pretty or handsome face. But if I am *of* a mind to love, I am entertaining possibilities, sorting out courses of action, making plans. All that is activity of mind, not a passive experience of invading feelings and emotions. To be of a mind to love is thus distinguishable from being in the mood for love—unless of course one can't tell one's moods from one's mind. My title thus puts up questions about the object of love, and about love as mental and intentional activity. Since our three Greek thinkers lived in the bright Mediterranean light of rationality, it is often thought that love among the philosophers is intellectual, directed by mind toward mind. By the end we should have some idea how this is, and isn't, the case.

My musings fall into two chief parts. Perversely, and in blatant disregard of historical sequence, I'm going to begin with Aristotle. He has a scope and order which may help us get the main themes out for inspection. We will turn back after that to Socrates and Plato for what we'll see is a greater complexity in both form and content.

I. ARISTOTLE

Aristotle's presentation of friendship and love is surprisingly full, in itself and as a proportion of his ethical writing, The eighth and ninth books of his *Nicomachean Ethics,* which explore the notion of *philia,* constitute a fifth of the entire treatise: as Antony Price remarks,

> a modern work on ethics and moral psychology which gave that much space to friendship would seem quaint; that is only in part because modern moral philosophy has become obsessed with one's obligations towards people one does not know.[1]

To characterize the whole of this discussion of philia as having to do with *friendship* as we conceive it would perhaps be misleading, since our term often exclucles family and erotic relationships (we say "friends *and* family," or "not lovers, just friends"). But Aristotle, in working out the nature of philia, has reflected on a range of personal and social relationships: he's thought about what family ties are like, what it is to live in close and more distant companionship, in social and political communities, in passionate feeling and in relation to God. As we'll see, however, he places a premium on one particular kind of relationship, in the belief that only certain kinds of people are capable of being friends in the fullest sense.

Let us start, though, not with that or with formal definitions of friendship, but with the assumptions about friendship which lie scattered across Aristotle's text. For if we plunge too quickly into the prickle of difficulties raised by that text, we may fail to see that Aristotle has indeed planted his ideas in the right soil.

I propose that Aristotle assumes there are three major distinctive marks of friendship, For brevity's sake I'll call them: (1) stability, (2) sharing, and (3) emotional involvement; but each requires some explication.

(1) That friendship should have some significant duration over time is a given for Aristotle; he dismisses short-lived, unstable relationships from the category (viii.6²). And he is right: none of us would disagree that (as the Loeb

translation has it) "the wish to be friends is a quick growth, but friendship is not" (viii.3). Friendship is best when it persists through good times and bad.

(2) But of course length of time is in itself insufficient to turn a relationship into a friendship, as lifelong enemies demonstrate. The second distinctive mark, then, is expressed by Aristotle in many places throughout our text. Several times he points out that there is nothing so characteristic of friends as their "living together" (viii.5; ix.10)—that is the "most choiceworthy thing" for them (ix.12). As he remarks in bk. viii ch. 5, prolonged absence disintegrates friendship. The terms Aristotle uses (such as "to pass one's days together") clearly mean more than spending time together in physical proximity.³ It is the sharing of aims and enjoyments that is important: friends pursue things together such as drinking or sports or philosophy (ix.12). Aristotle cites the proverb "What friends have is common" (viii.9), and finds several occasions to use the term *koinônia* for an essential feature of friendship (*en koinônia gar hê philia*, viii.9; *koinônia gar hê philia*, ix.12). Under the idea of sharing, then, we must understand this commonality of interest and activity.

(3) But one cannot think of sharing without inquiring into the affective lives of friends, their attitudes and emotions. Aristotle's affective vocabulary includes terms and phrases such as these:

- Friendship requires *familiarity* (*sunêtheia*) and trust (*pistis*) (viii.3; viii.6), a *trust* (*to pisteuein*) that they would never wrong each other (viii.4).

- Among the chief marks of friendship is spending time together and *enjoying one another* (*chairein allêlois*) (viii.6), *delighting* in each other or the same things (*chairôsin allêlois ê tois autois*) (viii.6), *sharing joys and sorrows* (*sugchairein, sunalgein*) as their own (ix.10).

- Friendly affection involves *intensity* (*diatasis*), *desire* (*orexis*), and *familiarity* (*sunêtheia*) (ix.5).

We may say then that for Aristotle the emotions and attitudes of friends are summed up in a familiarity that involves mutual trust, delight, and fellow feeling.

Now given these assumptions I should expect Aristotle to think of friendship as a stable life of shared familiarity over time. Although nowhere defining friendship in just these terms, Aristotle does affirm such characteristics in bk. ix ch. 4 when he lists five distinguishing marks of friendship. Friends (1) will and promote the welfare each other for each other's sake; (2) wish each other, for the sake of the other, to continue in life; (3) spend time with each other; (4) choose the same things; and (5) share the same feelings.

It's noteworthy that in this little summary the question of *motivation* has surfaced. Till now the marks of friendship might have been exhibited in relationships where the partners are out to get something for themselves—where, conveniently, they are able to live a life of shared familiarity because it turns out to be good for each of them. Aristotle finds self-interest to be an unsatisfactory motivation for the best sort of personal associations, partly because it too easily erodes the stability of well-developed friendships. In bk. viii ch. 2, he points out that there are three reasons why one might be friendly with another person: for their usefulness in advancing your own interests, for the pleasure you get out of the relationship, or for the sake of goodness. This "goodness" isn't the good they can wish or do for you, because that is simply the first motivation, utility; it seems rather the goodness in them which you admire or which you will for them. Both utility and pleasure are inherently unstable: what's useful changes with our needs; what's pleasurable alters with new interests. And both appeal to self-interest. So good friendship (his term is *teleia philia,* viii.3: commentators call this "perfect" or "complete" friendship), the kind that is trustworthy, depends upon wishing for the good of the friend, not just for your own good. This observation, surely correct, moves Aristotle to ask just what kind of person it is who can sustain reliable friendship. His answer: the virtuous person.

We cannot digress here to explain in detail what a virtuous person looks like for Aristotle. But if you hold in mind a picture of someone who has developed through careful choices a character disposed to act in morally excellent and wise ways, you will have the essential features.

What does friendship between two such people look like? In bk. viii ch. 3, Aristotle sets out four claims. First, these two, since both are good, wish goods for each other (having this attitude of benevolence is part of what "being good" means). Second, not only are these two good persons good in themselves (and therefore pleasant and useful); they are also good for each other (beneficence, the *doing* and not just wishing of good, is part of goodness as well)—and so they are useful and pleasant for each other, too. Third, the two of them are thus highly like each other in goodness, attitudes, and wishes. And fourth, their goodness, being a deliberately developed disposition of character, is durable, meaning that each of them will persist in benevolence and beneficence. They each are of a mind to love the other.

So far, so good. Crucial to friendship is a genuine regard for the welfare of the other, and morally good people are those who take up such attitudes. But what in the moral psychology of good people enables them to act and wish for the sake of the other instead of from their own needs? How do they get into this mind? Aristotle answers, in bk. ix ch. 4, that they have *the proper attitude toward themselves.*

In part this answer reflects the truism that you can't love somebody else very well if you don't much like yourself. Self-doubt, self-hatred, self-denigration:

these illnesses soon curdle relationships; and they lead to impossible devices by which we attempt to reconcile irreconcilable desires. Aristotle assumes, again rightly, that decent friendship is founded upon self-esteem. However, his answer about taking up the proper attitude toward yourself is more complex than that. He thinks that to enjoy any kind of friendship at all, you need to exhibit *toward yourself* the same marks of friendship as you do toward others. You need (if I may phrase his points this way) to have some idea of your own welfare and how to achieve it; to want to keep living your life; not to find it impossible to be alone; and to have relatively stable desires, interests, and life goals which define you as a person, But there's more. Aristotle also believes that, in order to take up this attitude toward yourself, *you* must be a virtuous person. It's not difficult to see the reasons. Only the good are not misguided about what is best for them, and work actively toward that; only the good understand that what needs to be preserved and safeguarded is not just life itself but their moral wisdom. They best enjoy their own company; they, too, enjoy such integrity of personality that their choices and interests are always consistent. Regarding themselves in these ways, they are friends indeed: for (in the famous phrase) a friend is another self. So the virtuous best exhibit fully developed friendship: they set their minds on loving, and they set themselves to love the minds of each other as the best parts of themselves.

We have moved, you will appreciate, from a characterization of friendship which was fairly innocuous (friends enjoy a stable, shared familiarity) to an explanation of motivation containing claims which many readers have thought suspicious. I'll mention only two. The first is that the most developed kind of friendship is possible only between morally good people; the second is that these morally good people are themselves the best object of their own love. These claims are suspect: surely love and friendship are richer than Aristotle allows; and surely it is unsatisfactory that the good, for all their talk about the altruism of friendship, really only love themselves deep down.

The second point deserves more comment than I can offer here, since Aristotle is careful to distinguish between selfish love and self-love. He would be puzzled by the suggestion that one should not want the very best for oneself, and because the real friend is another self he would see no conflict between two friends promoting each other's good at the same time as promoting their own. That brings us back to the first claim, about the nature of perfect friendship, so let us concentrate on this issue. To keep it in perspective, we must reiterate that Aristotle's chapters include much about family love (four or five times he tries to account for the peculiarly strong nature of maternal love[4]); and he is well aware of other sorts of love such as erotic passion (this is mentioned in at least eight places[5]). So it would be ungenerous to accuse Aristotle of ignoring the rich variety of human affections and attachments. Is the issue rather that Aristotle should not assume there to be such a thing as most developed or perfect friendship? Should we prize the uniqueness of each kind of relationship, holding it incommensurable with any other? But anyone who is willing to speak of love generically cannot quite take this line. On Aristotle's own ground he is licenced to speak of most developed philia because of his criteria of stability, equal sharing, familiarity, and mutual concern for the good of the other. We can object to the inappropriate downgrading which familial affection and erotic passion receive in his treatment, a downgrading emphasized by Aristotle's tendency to isolate people in categories of relationships where they experience only one kind of philia at a time. Nevertheless we may, at least for now, grant that people may enjoy a kind of complete friendship, not unlike Aristotle's fully developed philia, within their various relationships. I say "not unlike" deliberately, however, for I do think Aristotle has not entirely captured what the best sort of friendship is like. And that is the question at issue.

Suppose we had two top-notch human beings who spent long years in shared pursuits, each the equal of the other in the moral and intellectual virtues. As Aristotle knows, without an emotional and affective familiarity theirs is more a tiny society for mutual admiration than a strong friendship; but the familiarity requisite to the trustworthy bonds of friendship involves not just delight in goodness but something else Aristotle misses: an *intimacy* and an *openness* to the other. We use terms such as vulnerability and risk when we speak of intimate relationships, for they permit a sharing not only of like interests but of the secrets of the heart. A friend welcomes those fears and fantasies, those aspirations and exasperations, too private to be part of our common trade with the world. I cannot truly wish for your goodness if you allow me only as far as its tidy rooms; you cannot promote my goodness by closing off the cellars of my secrets.

It follows from this that Aristotle has in fact distorted what really good friendship is like. In trying to find the basis for stability and shared equality, he has invoked a view of human excellence which makes us too self-contained and divine, entirely contrary to his view of our relation to the gods, who cannot be our friends because they are too far above us. For Aristotle, the best of friends admire the characters of their partners and will to keep their goodness going. Experience teaches, however, that even the best of us fall short of the glory of God. Without an intimacy, in which we are naked and unashamed before each other, there is no complete friendship.

It also follows that, if openness is the crucial mark of intimacy, then such intimacy is available to those who perceive themselves as less than the best exemplars of humanity. In missing this, Aristotle, aiming for the highest, closes off the deepest kind of friendship from the many who in fact enjoy it, who through acceptance and commitment stick together for each other's good.

We should try to connect my comments about openness to Singer's criticism of Aristotelian friendship. Singer's complaint is that Aristotle's love of the goodness in another person fundamentally misses what it is to love another *as* a person instead of *for* some quality or other. An important part of what it is to love is to care about others, not for their goodness, but *despite their imperfections*. It is to bestow a value on them which they do not have, to treat them in a way incommensurate with their virtues (1:90), because creative and autonomous love is not proportionate to merit (1:96). That generates a picture something like this. By common agreement, person A has so much moral, intellectual, and social value; but since people do not (and indeed cannot) love everybody according to such a scale, then when B loves A, B adds some extra value onto A. This extra is not across the board, but is entirely person-dependent. Singer thinks of this extra value as generated spontaneously, without reference to any other value (that's what 'autonomous' must mean here). That will help explain why only one Jill will find just this Jack attractive while the rest of the world scratches its collectively puzzled head. Aristotle's perfect love misses this essential feature in having excellence in the beloved generate just the right amount of love in the lover.

In exposing the idea of intimacy I have not found its essential feature to be the bestowing of unmerited value on the beloved. In fact, I'd like to suggest that, whatever usefulness there is in the notion of bestowal for the observer of a relationship, the notion does not work well in the psychology of loving. If I thought your love was added from nowhere, and if I seriously believed that my love for you was entirely a matter of my giving you a gift you didn't deserve, decent relationships would be more fragile than they are. What is pure gift, answering to no value in the beloved, can be withdrawn as spontaneously as it was given—without explanation, without justification. Intimacy does not work on such principles. In stressing vulnerability, openness, and nakedness, I propose that we recognize in intimacy a trust into safekeeping of our very selves, we are open where we believe that what we give will not be disdained, mocked, spurned, or destroyed. That includes being accepted in our weaknesses, but it also includes opening up our best parts as well. And it also means, as I said above, a sticking together for each other's good. This "for the good" is not quite an Aristotelian admiration for an excellence already there (though that could be a part); it is a commitment to protect, cultivate, and nurture what's grown to be valuable in the other and in the relationship. If that is what Aristotle may be made to mean by "willing the good" for the other, he does have something which the idea of "bestowal" by itself manages to miss.

In sum, then: Aristotle has identified many of the right ingredients for friendship, but in shutting out everybody but the morally excellent from the place of perfect friendship he has gone wrong. If we accept his reasoning that where people are first-class human beings there they may become first-class friends, we nevertheless cannot accept that it's just their goodness that makes their friendship good. Instead it is an intimacy which characterizes deep friendships between all manner of people. To enjoy intimacy friends do need to be of a mind to love, but what they love is more than a mind.

II. SOCRATES AND PLATO

I turn back now to Aristotle's predecessors, Socrates and Plato, where the Aristotelian advantage of systematic analysis is traded for a many-layered manifestation of love in speech and action. Plato, writing dialogues rather than lecture notes, actually *displays* human relationships in ways that Aristotle's talking *about* them does not. In the conversations of his fictive *personae* Plato exhibits (sometimes directly, more often indirectly) the kinds of attitudes his characters hold toward each other: watching Socrates with Lysis or Agathon or Alcibiades or Phaedrus can be as instructive as listening to the words between them. Further: because we are dealing with a literary construction of speech and characterization, it is important to appreciate the distance between Plato as author and the actions and beliefs of his *dramatis personae,* including— and this is important—his Socrates. And that leads directly to the thesis I'm about to argue: that we may discover in Plato's writings a Socratic love distinct from the Platonic love which everyone believes they know so well.

This distinction is not commonly made, so let me say how I am *not* about to defend it. One can understand the possibility of a difference between the Socratic and the Platonic if we are dealing with different sources for the historical Socrates' beliefs and behavior: the Socrates of Xenophon, for instance, may speak and act in ways not entirely concordant with Plato's views about love and friendship. But I will forswear historical investigation, just as I began by ignoring chronology, in order to learn what Plato's fictive Socrates may teach us about friends and lovers; and only then will I ask how Plato's own understanding of love relates to this Socratic love.

Now if we enjoyed the luxury of a whole conference on the topic, we would canvass the dialogues to ask how our fictive Socrates is portrayed in his relationships, his style, attitudes, interests, motivations, and the like. Who claims friendship with him? What are his overriding commitments? We would also attempt to extract Socrates' own beliefs from what he says about love and friendship—not always an easy task when listening to the master of irony. But we don't have this luxury, so you must be content for now with my portrait of Socrates assembled from observations about his treatment of acquaintances and friends in such dialogues as the *Euthyphro,* the *Apology,* the *Crito,* and the *Gorgias.*

What interests me in these dialogues is the number of times Socrates uses terms like *friend* or *companion*, along with friendly epithets like *good* or *noble fellow*, for his interlocutors. But even more interesting is the variety of emotions and attitudes these terms are made to carry. Take Euthyphro: Socrates praises him on many occasions, but we are not long into the dialogue before suspecting Socrates of playing with this poor victim of epistemological conceit. The purpose of their discussion is highly serious, for if Socrates can learn from Euthyphro the nature of the holy he will be able to defend himself against the charges of impiety at his trial. The dialogue's failure to discover the holy should then be tragic. Instead it is ironic, ending in the intentional diminishment of Euthyphro.

The vocabulary of friendship is peppered throughout Socrates' encounter with Polus in the *Gorgias;* but here the terms are downright sarcastic as Socrates wrings the truth out of Polus by giving him as good as he gets in the tricks of argument.

We might expect better from the *Crito,* as a dear friend and longtime companion visits Socrates to persuade him to save his own life by leaving prison. Yet Socrates quickly brushes aside the evident distress of an old friend, paying no attention to his feelings but focussing only on impersonal moral principles. When Crito's emotional state prevents his continuing the discussion, Socrates turns to the laws of Athens to carry on—only Socrates' own imaginative creations seem worthy partners in this argument.

And as a last bit of evidence, recall Socrates' defense before the jury. What is most striking about the *Apology* is Socrates' refusal to save his own life. His commitments are to truth and goodness; but unlike our commitments (which include self-preservation, as Aristotle well understood), his are absolute and override all interests. Nothing is more important than goodness, nor can any human bond or feeling stand in the way of this singleminded pursuit.

This is, of course, not all to be said about Plato's fictive Socrates. But I suggest that the portrait that emerges is of a man whose consuming passion is the goodness of his soul. He is in love with goodness and truth, obsessed be getting things—his conduct as well as his ideas—right. That matters more than reputation, more than wealth or position, more than life itself. And it certainly matters more than family or friends (especially family, since they don't seem to be of much help in the quest). But for all his self-possession and self-containment, Socrates is not turned utterly inward. Just the opposite: he can't stop talking to people. That might suggest that he needs their contribution to his quest; indeed, he sometimes claims as much. Yet we are not really convinced by his behavior that this is so. Everybody who talks with Socrates turns out to be at a disadvantage; nobody is invited into the conversation on equal terms. It's hard to give Socrates many marks at all on the Aristotelian scale for decent friendship. No one is allowed to share equally in his life.

Nevertheless, these characterizations are not sufficient for constructing a notion of Socratic love, for we have not yet considered what Socrates actually says himself on the matter: surely his words must figure largely in any assessment of the nature of his kind of love.

When we turn to the *Symposium* we find that Socrates says little in his own person: his understanding of love is not his own, but comes from his teacher, the prophetess Diotima. Diotima tells the young Socrates that she is confident he will be initiated into the lesser mysteries of love; so we should recall what these involve, and ask ourselves whether there is enough evidence about Socrates' character and pursuits to assess her prediction.

Socrates' own report to the dinner party makes it clear that he got to understand the basics from spending time with Diotima. He got right, for instance, that one must not characterize the loving in the same way as the beloved. The object of love is goodness and beauty and wisdom. The experience or process of loving, since it is a felt lack of these objects, is intermediate between an utter absence of these qualities and their complete possession. Socrates also learned that the desire, which is love, is a desire to possess its objects—that is, love is not appreciation at a distance, but a desire to turn into something better, to give birth to something, to become a certain kind of being; and to become this forever, in a stable and unchanging way. That state of perfection is the immortality humankind seeks, but in which no human being can fully participate. So we substitute children, poetry, articles, books, pupils, named chairs, laws, institutions—all in an attempt to find enduring happiness. All this Socrates reports himself as having learned; of its truth he is persuaded.

It is nonetheless one thing to agree with the theory, and another to begin to practice it. The theory requires that one locate the good and the beautiful, and bring them to birth in beauty. And it offers, in these lesser mysteries, some steps to take. Has Socrates indeed begun? Has he become skillful in love (*deinos* in *erôtika,* 207c3), as he wanted to be? The path seems to be this. One must discover within a great desire for the birth of wisdom and goodness. Not everyone has this. But if it is there, one must search for the beautiful that will bring goodness to birth. The ugly cannot generate goodness, so beautiful bodies will be attractive. But something else is better: a beautiful soul in a beautiful body, in whose company one may give birth to an enduring goodness.

Now we can believe that Socrates' soul is striving to bring to birth wisdom and beauty: we could not imagine a better candidate for love's work. But (and here is the point crucial to my reading) we know of no close association between Socrates and another person, no intimacy in which beauty has begotten beauty. The *persona* Plato creates seems better placed in the next steps, among the Greater mysteries. Here the attachment that produced the birth of beauty is released. The lover better appreciates the beauty of soul, so that physical beauty is less important; then particular beauties are left behind as he enters upon contemplation of that "great sea of beauty."

That Socrates belongs near the threshold of the final mysteries is confirmed in the similarities between his persona and Diotima's description of the daimon Eros. That daimon is impoverished, spends his time outdoors, goes barefoot, is tough rather than tender, and is neither human nor divine but intermediate between gods and men. In characterizing Socrates as Eros, Plato removes him from normal relationships between lover and beloved, isolating him as Love itself. Think how different Socrates is from the lovers the others have praised: for Phaedrus, for Pausanias, and for Aristophanes, the virtuous and healing benefits of love come only through relationships that are special and even unique. But Socrates has no such relationships. How then has Socrates' goodness come about? Not from any attachment Pausanias would recognize: we hear of no satisfactory teachers for Socrates in, say, the *Phaedo:* and here in the *Symposium* his teacher is a woman—who, though she gives him instruction, is not at all presented as the possible object of his erotic interest. Socrates has managed to make it up the ladder of love; but he has gone beyond the human in ways inaccessible to our understanding. And by some ironic feat he has managed to do it on his own.

All this is confirmed in Alcibiades' drunken speech, which charges Socrates with hubris and displacedness: he doesn't fit. Worse, he refuses not just Alcibiades' erotic advances but also the exercise Diotima recommends—he doesn't allow Alcibiades to acquire virtue through intimacy between lover and beloved. Although Alcibiades' complaint expresses the pique of his particular relationship to Socrates, Socrates' character is nevertheless accurately reflected here. The object of his affection—indeed his passion—is not this or that beauty but the beautiful itself, because goodness and wisdom are there as well. "Socratic love," if the term means the love that the *persona* Socrates exhibits, has nothing of the personal in it. His supposed interest in others is an ironic verbal masking of his inner preoccupation with goodness; he neither appreciates nor delights in other people, nor does he actively help in their seeking salvation or improvement. He loves, but is not loving.

I imagine that Singer will not dissent from my conclusion, for one of his major criticisms is that for Plato persons are not the object of love. We may perhaps push this a little further, however, by comparing Socrates with Aristotle. Aristotle's friends at least love each other's *minds,* but it's hard to say that loving a mind is what Socrates is after. Minds belong to individual souls, are centers of rational consciousness. What Socrates seeks is the final goal and object of all knowing: the forms of the beautiful and the good. I had earlier remarked that Socrates does not get high grades on the Aristotelian scale. Now we can appreciate that this is not because he is uncaring, passionless, or self-absorbed. It is rather because, in removing himself from our world to care about the eternal, Plato's fictive Socrates has passed over to the realm of the divine. I stress again that we have no idea how he has managed this, because he hasn't followed his own prescriptions gotten from Diotima; and this heightens the idealization of Socrates as perfect lover. Since this Socrates is not flesh and blood, but divinized, I must temper Singer's view that Socrates, just by existing as he does, "serves as a living proof that the human condition Plato wishes to advocate is actually possible" (1:48). The love of Socrates, like justice in the ideal state, is capable of only imperfect realization in our world.

And what is Plato's attitude in all this? How does this view of Socratic love fit into the familiar picture of *Platonic* love? (I speak of a picture familiar to those who know Plato, not of the common understanding of Platonic, suspiciously nonerotic, relationships.⁶) My answer is that Plato's view of love must include the whole practice in the *Symposium*, including the non-Socratic step of intimate and productive friendship between two lovers of beauty. In the theory Plato constructed for Diotima to hand on to his fictive Socrates, Plato included this important element of attraction between individuals, an attraction to be channeled into an ascent to the beautiful and the good. In another beautiful person the lover delights, and brings goodness to birth with him. "Such men share an intimacy with one another," says Diotima, "which is far deeper than one coming from children and enjoy a surer affection, because they have taken part in the creation of more beautiful and immortal progeny." (*Sym.* 209bc, trans. Groden). Plato wrote extensively and compellingly about this in the potent imagery and sexuality of the *Phaedrus:* here Plato contemplates the possibility of an inner transformation into goodness through a disciplined and redirected sexual energy, in company with another likeminded friend. More (and here he moves beyond the *Symposium*), Plato does not disapprove lapses from erotic self-control in lovers whose aims are not fully philosophical as long as their fidelity is built upon honor rather than the satisfaction of sexual desire. It is true that the final goal of *eros* in Platonic love remains the eternal forms, so that its object is the divine and unchanging rather than changeable human beings. But personal relationships between suitable lovers leave a crucial role in Platonic love, a role absent from Socratic life and love.

My claim is not quite what Martha Nussbaum is after in her fascinating studies of the *Symposium* and *Phaedrus*.⁷ She believes Plato presents in the passionate attachment of Alcibiades to Socrates a choice between deep personal love for an individual, and the cool rational impersonal love of Socrates. Further, by the time he came to write the *Phaedrus,* Plato had himself fallen in love and so warms the heart of his Socrates toward the young Phaedrus. Against this reading I move to side with Singer, whose fundamental criticism is that Platonic love fails radically because it cannot account for the love of persons qua unique individuals. The object of Platonic love is goodness and beauty; but since no individual fully instantiates this object, we can never finally rest our loving attention on the real people around us. I move in this direction because I cannot find any example in Plato of individuals who *practice* Platonic love in ways that prize unique individuality. Nussbaum is right to ask about how Alcibiades regards Socrates; but there is a host of other friends inhabiting Plato's dialogues, all of whom regard him as special. They are devoted, sometimes fanatically so; they cherish him as irreplaceable; they extol him as divine. That their deep affection is of uncertain reciprocation makes it no less love on their part. But what is it that they love about Socrates? Not the little idiosyncrasies that make people lovable in their particularities; rather, it is Socrates' unwavering commitment to goodness, his exemplification of the virtues in a life that has already begun to pass beyond the human. What Socrates loves is inaccessible to them; but in him they find the images of that reality which he seeks, and love in this one, unique and irreplaceable place that which he himself loves. So Socrates is loved *as* an individual without being loved *for* his individualities or particularities; he is loved rather for his embodiment of those transcendent values to which, Plato believed, we aspire for the sake of enduring happiness.

So I conclude that Platonic love, too, is idealized rather than instantiated in the dialogues. Nevertheless I do not place myself all the way with Singer about the impersonality of Platonic love. In *theory* at least, this love may be experienced by two friends who channel the erotic energy created by their relationship, who cherish in each other throughout their lives what is beautiful and good. In such mutual sharing they may enjoy personal aspects of a love which, if not for everybody, may be no less love for that. It may recall Aristotle's most developed friendship, though with two qualifications. First, where Aristotelian philia appreciates and enjoys the good, willing to perpetuate that good in another good friend, Platonic eros strives toward a good imperfectly grasped, it is a creative and transforming love, not content with the human condition but striving to transcend, to turn us into something else. Second, Aristotelian friends appreciate their minds as the best parts of themselves, but Platonic lovers charge up their eros from a beauty that is represented in bodily forms; they pass to beautiful minds, but end with beauty itself.

CONCLUSION

I have argued that loving persons qua persons requires an openness to vulnerability and a commitment to work for the good of the other, rather than a spontaneous bestowal of value in spite of imperfections. There is just time, though, to say one last word about imperfections. They are so lavishly sprinkled around that none of us misses out. What kind of love will accept us knowing and not ignoring our flaws and blemishes? Not Aristotelian philia, not Socratic eros, not Platonic love. Ancient Greek friends and lovers, when they are of a mind to love, look for the good or strive for the beautiful; and where because of imperfections they set their minds on a transforming love, it is the divine to which they aspire. The gods themselves never love us; how could they?

What then of agape, that divine love of which the Hebrew and Christian scriptures speak?

> When Israel was a child I loved him
> and out of Egypt I called my son.
> The more I called them the more they went from me . . .
> Yet . . . I led them with cords of human kindness
> with bands of love
> I was to them like those
> who lift infants to their cheeks
> I bent down to them and fed them.
>
> Hosea 11.1–4

This sounds, perhaps, like Singer's spontaneous bestowal of value on a cosmic scale, accepting in spite of imperfections, tender in its appreciation. Agape, it would be tempting then to say, is human love writ large and extended past the normal breaking point. God's patience would love longer, God's long-suffering accepts more from us, than our parental love can manage. Even the best of us have limits to the amount of nonsense we can take without walking away, or else devising tricks on ourselves to preserve our unhealthy and needy desires. Is it that God, being blessed with omniscience as well as patience, escapes the cognitive dissonance into which the best of us nonsense-takers fall? Does God just keep on loving for the sake of being loving?

There is something profoundly wrong in this. Though it knows no limits and never finally shuts us out, God's agape is anything but passive acceptance. It has its work to do on us, a work not content to bestow value without creating and cultivating goodness according to the divine purpose. Agape may always leave the door open, but the room in which it operates is full of all manner of equipment for spiritual exercise and even surgery. Plato ought to understand that love may transform, even if neither he nor Aristotle conceived a divine interest which loves us in the sinful present for the sake of a future glory. Or so I maintain: but I have already strayed into the topic of the next paper.

NOTES

1. A. W. Price, *Love and Friendship in Plato and Aristotle* (Oxford: Clarendon Press, 1989), p. 159.

2. References are to the standard chapter divisions of Books viii or ix of the *Nicomachean Ethics,* rather than to lines, for the sake of readers without a Greek text.

3. The Greek terms are verbs such as *sudzên* and *sunêmereuein.* As Terence Irwin notes, "Aristotle is not thinking of people living in the same house (which was not a very important center of a Greek man's life), but of shared activities" (in his translation of the *Nicomachean Ethics* [Indianapolis: Hackett, 1985], p. 360, note on 1157b18).

4. Mothers are mentioned at viii.8, viii.12, ix.4 (twice), and ix.7. They are exemplary of loving in that they can keep up love even when their offspring, adopted by others, don't know the identities of their mothers and so cannot love them back. Their strength of love is related to the amount of time spent with their children, and the pains they went through to have them.

5. In passages in viii.3, viii.4, viii.6, viii.8, ix.1, ix.5, ix.10, and ix.12.

6. On the latter, see P. W. Gooch, "Platonic Love: Some Lexicographical Curiosities," *Notes and Queries* 234, no. 3 (September 1989): 358-60.

7. The most developed versions are in chapters 6 and 7 of *The Fragility of Goodness* (Cambridge: Cambridge University Press, 1986).

4

Love and Knowledge in the Bible

Graeme Nicholson

Like Irving Singer, Northrop Frye has taught that the Bible is no property of synagogue or church, but a work offered to all humanity. Frye and Singer opened the Bible to everyone, first as literature, then as philosophy. Yet both Frye and Singer respect the great rabbis and the great Catholic fathers and painters; as well as the passion and inwardness of Protestant faith. Neither is scornful or mocking toward the long history of the reverent reception of this Scripture. For beyond the literary depth and the cognitive power of the Bible, the professor of philosophy or English has to see something further: *why* the Bible was chosen by synagogue and church, and *why* they sprang from it. Anyone who undertakes to express what the Bible is for us in our time will also have to think in the horizon of history. We see that the covenants of Moses and Jesus were the irreplacable archetypes for all our communities in the West—the great national and ecclesiastical communities, the monasteries and the Mennonite communes, the synagogues and parishes, and also our very families. From the dissemination of this scriptural witness, our culture (or better, our cultures in their variousness) were forced by the practice of listening for evidence of the love of God. Falteringly and inadequately, we accepted that as the norm for the relations of love within our communities; moreover, at least as an expressed ideal even though all too rarely in practice, divine love was the ideal for our relations to the stranger, the outsider: "Love your enemies."

To discuss this ideal leads us into the territory of Irving Singer's chapter on *nomos*. We translate this Greek word at times as "law," at other times as "righteousness" or "justice"; it would be translated into Hebrew as *Torah,* which itself indicates, in English, "law," or perhaps better, "teaching," and hence at times even covenant. That is the cycle of themes my paper will be dealing with. Here at the start I must point out how discerning it was of Singer to include a study of this matter in a major book on love, to present love also as nomos. Obviously, this is only one element in divine love, just as it is only a single element in love altogether: Singer does not challenge the longstanding custom of using the name of *agape* for the highest ideal of love in the New Testament. That custom has likewise seen agape in the scriptures of the Old Testament, and Singer does not challenge that reading either. Yet in the sequence of his chapters, Singer puts nomos directly in front of his discussion of agape; it was a wise instinct that made the one the immediate antecedent of the other. Proposing nomos, righteousness, in this position implies a central role for Law and Torah in the philosophy of love. Singer subtitles his chapter "Submission to God's Will"; indeed, that is also the very meaning of the Arabic word *islam.* This restores nomos to its true place in the vocabulary and architecture of love, and helps to undo one of the unfortunate effects of the Pauline and Lutheran critique of law and its righteousness.

I. LOVE

We are to think of the love-relation between human beings as existing within the family community, the political community, and the religious community. Within the brief compass of this paper, however, I shall focus on the love between God and man. I have tried to suggest in my opening remarks that divine love is the formative substance of Western culture, the divine-human relation being the vital force for reshaping communal relations. The passion and inwardness—we might even say romanticism—of the human reception of God's love, and the outpouring of love for God, are everywhere in both testaments, but I shall take my selection mainly from the book of Psalms. And even confined to the psalter, we have to be selective, so I'll focus particularly on some psalms that are expressions of love, where the love's character and emphasis is especially on the law—psalms of thanksgiving for the Torah. The monumental Ps. 119 is the great exemplar, yet we find the theme distributed throughout, beginning even from the very first psalm.

> Blessed is the man that walketh not in the counsel of the ungodly
> Nor standeth in the way of sinners
> Not sitteth in the seat of the scornful.
> But his delight is in the law of the Lord,

> And in his law doth he meditate day and night.
> And he shall be like a tree planted by the rivers of water. . . .

Such a one does not walk with ungodliness, he does not stand with it, he does not sit with it, and such a one is not free either by day or by night from thinking of the *torah* of the Lord. This is the man of the law, whom Singer links to nomos. This is the man the King James version always calls "righteous," in its translation of the Hebrew *zadik,* the name given this man at the end of Psalm 1. This psalm's praise of the *zadik* involves the very points that will concern me throughout this paper. There is further praise for the "testimonies" and "precepts" of the Lord in many other psalms, as well as praise for the *zadik* who lives by them—e.g., Ps. 19: 7-14, and Ps. 32. I must, however, elucidate the subjective nature of these songs of praise.

Let us grasp, first of all, that the didactic theme cannot be as dry as the modern reader might suppose; we'll say something about the disposition of delight (*hephetz*) that is mentioned here, so improbably for the modern reader. We shall try to follow that didacticism in its inner core. Let us look at Ps. 25 for one treatment of the didactic theme that has clear resonances of emotional depth. We hear the prayer of one who *desires* to receive instruction:

> Shew me thy ways, O Lord, teach me thy paths.
> Lead me in thy truth, and teach me:
> For thou art the God of my salvation;
> On thee do I wait all the day.

Anyone who has the *disposition* thus to be instructed will and must affirm the goodness as well as the wisdom of the teacher.

> Remember, O Lord, thy tender mercies and thy loving kindnesses;
> For they have been ever of old.
> Remember not the sins of my youth or my transgressions.

We have been taught by the power of this Hebrew lyric poetry inside the very soul of the *zadik,* no longer regarding him from a distance, standing like a tree by the river water. And there are many passages in the psalms that embody the song or cry of the *zadik,* not, as in Ps. 25, as the repentant one, or the beginner, who first desires to receive instruction, but as the mature soul who lives out his days and nights in the contemplation of the law that he has learned from the days of his youth. Ps. 119 brings us inside the soul of the mature *zadik* who devotes his life to meditation on the law, and for that reason I would say that we have a psalm here that is no longer didactic but *contemplative*:

> The bands of the wicked have robbed me;
> But I have not forgotten thy law.
> At midnight I will rise to give thanks to thee
> Because of thy righteous judgments.
> I am a companion of all them that fear thee,
> And of them that keep thy precepts.
> The earth, O Lord, is full of thy mercy:
> Teach me thy statutes.

Such poetry as this, which fills the psalter, is the song of the righteous man. In measured rhythm, line after line drops, inscrutable, repetitive, opaque in English. The song of the righteous delights in simple contrasts between the ways of the godless and those of the righteous. But it sings of the godless only in order to illuminate a facet of the righteous. It mentions different times of the day, seemingly to add variety and movement, but in effect it shows that the righteous man is abiding and constant throughout all times. It sings of the ages of man—but the law is the same for all ages. It praises the righteousness, justice, faithfulness, and loving kindness of God, but these are not really different attributes demarcated consistently. It praises testimony, statute, law, ordinance, and precept—but not as if these were in essence different from one another. It refers to the many organs of the body—the heart, the tongue, the limbs, the ear, the eyes, and the lips—but are they not all of one intent, to abide by the testimonies of the Lord? The single profound thought of the song is that the law is the *delight* of the righteous man. The inner disposition of delight is possible because the personality of the Lord, righteous and faithful, shines within his very words, his Torah, given to Israel. It is deeply familiar to the son of the Torah, for Israel has known the Lord for many centuries. And now like delights in like; the righteous delights in the righteous. In the spoken, sung, and written words of the Torah, the righteousness of the Lord has become the righteousness of Israel, and when the Israelite meditates on the statutes of the Lord, the delight rises out of renewed intimate recognition of like.

The law is in a way the transparent cloak of the Lord, for his righteous will shines in it and through it. And the son of the law is likewise a transparent bearer of the righteous will of the Lord. When the Lord, Torah, and Israel are all "righteous," what is meant is that they are all at one. Righteousness, *zedek,* means harmony, a covenant between man and God.

To turn now to Singer, in his chapter on nomos, we see that he does treat the mirroring of man and God through Torah or nomos, especially on p. 245 of vol. 1 of *The Nature of Love,* observing that the core of this relation is constituted by reverence. Singer adds (p. 246) that "reverence often turns into love," speaking, of course, of the love of man for God that will eventuate from human reverence for God. Yet I am sure that he would not dispute that the very covenantal harmony that first brought that reverence about had been initiated at the beginning by the loving kindness of God, or that there was also a human love for God dwelling from the very beginning within the covenantal reverence.

A bit later, Singer addresses the link of love with righteousness or justice, the very theme he took up in a chapter devoted to explaining why nomos is to be seen as one of the variants of love. He is concerned not to offer an overly simple account of the relation. "Nowhere in the Old Testament is love *identified* with justice or righteousness. Unless one lived righteously, one could not love God: this is implied on every page but it does not constitute a definition" (p. 251). And yet I think Singer saw as well that the demarcation was rather too strict, that the relation is indeed closer than that, so he adds on the following page this qualification: "For *nomos* is not obedience itself so much as the *acquiescence* in obedience. It is man adhering so thoroughly to the will of God that breaking the enunciated commandments becomes a moral impossibility" (p. 252). Still that version also gives rise to further reflections that must lead us into deep philosophical and psychological waters. If Singer means to differentiate obedience qua outer acts (behavior) from nomos qua inner disposition, his discussion is bound to recall the tormented critique of St. Paul in Romans and Galatians, in which the perfunctory performance of "the works of the law" will never satisfy God, who also demands an inner joy in obedience, i.e., who demands a spiritual love, a nomos in Singer's sense. What St. Paul wanted was precisely the inability to sin, Singer's "moral impossibility of breaking the enunciated commandments." Realizing, however, that he could never have perfection in that sense, Paul sought salvation through a gospel that surpassed the law.

Yet I think the reader of the psalter can avoid applying this differentiation between obedience (works) and the acquiescence in obedience (a spiritual nomos). The reader can understand, in other words, a unity between love and justice, so long as the loving personality of the divine teacher can be discerned in the code of law. I would say that we should be ready to identify love qua *nomos* with justice and righteousness, where the loving personality of the teacher is recognized with delight. It is not that one must repudiate Paul; rather, one must interpret him. In particular, one has to grasp his situation in the light of his own world, the *change* in religious teaching and practice in the interval between the composition of the psalter and his own day. There was in Paul's time a tendency to woodenness and a decay in spirt in the strict application of the Torah. The history of Protestantism manifested a similar pattern between the sixteenth and the twentieth centuries, with the renewal of spirit through the passion of Paul being, for many Protestants of the twentieth century, a great and inspiring archetype, especially for so-called neo-orthodoxy and existential theology. However, these developments should not prevent us, in our own times, from discovering something in the psalms themselves that for Paul and many of his followers was in a certain way occluded.

II. KNOWLEDGE

It is in connection with the contemplative prayer, the sort we find in Ps. 119, that I can explain the meaning of the title of my paper. The *zadik* (righteous man) has not only loyalty and faithfulness toward the Lord and His statutes. He is also one who has received *instruction* from the Lord, a torah or teaching, and hence he is one who has *knowledge*. And it is my contention that love and knowledge belong profoundly together. Where the Bible speaks most clearly about love, there is a knowledge that lies at its heart. And, likewise, where there is knowledge, there is a love that is at its heart. The Bible reader must seek to understand the belonging-together of the two. The term that is most central to the psalms, and indeed to the Pentateuch and the prophets, for expressing love is *hesed* (normally translated as *misericordia* by St. Jerome and "loving kindness" by the King James version) primarily the love which the Lord manifests toward his people, for instance, in revealing his law to them. Harmony of *zadik* with *zadik* springs from the original love or *hesed* which the Lord showered on his people through his Torah to bring them into accord with himself. That is why the song expresses love, which is also why it expresses knowledge. For the Torah of God is the truth, which all ages and nations yearn to know.

Yet while the contemplative has a knowledge of the Lord and of His testimonies, he also has a yearning for a deeper union—not only a deeper identification of himself with the law and the details of its injunctions, but also more intimate concourse with the *Lord*. Love can never lose its perpetual search for deeper and deeper identification; it is infinite in its aspiration and in its own substance. This shows up in the secular romantic transcriptions of love, so central to English literature. Recall Juliet's words in *Romeo and Juliet*, Act II, Scene II:

> My bounty is as boundless as the sea,
> My love as deep; the more I give to thee,
> The more I have, for both are infinite.

But what this implies in the present context is that we do not understand knowledge either, until we see its character of infinity. So we have to ask as well what the biblical authors tend to understand by the term "knowledge."

After that we can look again at Singer's treatment. We'll mention a case of purely human interaction and knowledge, and then one involving human knowledge of God.

The process of acquiring knowledge seems often in the Old Testament to be as follows: First, there are words spoken, at which point the question is whether the hearers would believe them or not. Then something is presented for the eye, and this confirms the report. At that point, one can speak of knowledge. Yet, as I shall insist, at this point one could equally well speak of belief. In 1 Kings 10, the Queen of Sheba came to see for herself whether the reports she had heard concerning the wisdom and prosperity of Solomon were true. "She came to test him with hard questions . . . ," and Solomon answered them all.

> There was nothing hidden from the king which he did not explain to her. And when the queen of Sheba had seen all the wisdom of Solomon . . . there was no more spirit in her. And she said to the king: The report was true which I heard in my own land of your affairs and of your wisdom, but I did not believe the reports until I came and my own eyes had seen it; and behold the half was not told me; your wisdom and your prosperity surpass the report which I heard.

Hearing in this case had been insufficient to compel belief from the skeptical queen—she had to see with her own eyes. This was not a movement from "mere belief" to knowledge, but from unbelief to a state that is described *either* as belief *or* as knowledge.

Let me pursue my point that the case is no different when it is a matter of the human knowledge of God. There is an example in the fourth chapter of Exodus. God has called Moses to go to the people of Israel to tell them that the Lord, the God of their fathers, had appeared to him and told him to lead them out of their Eygptian bondage. Among the many doubts that troubled the soul of Moses when the Lord gave him this assignment was the fear that the people would not believe him. So God promised that he would perform a sign.

> If they will not believe you . . . they may believe the latter sign. . . . And Aaron spoke all the words which the Lord had spoken to Moses, and did the signs in the sight of the people. And the people believed; and when they heard that the Lord had visited the people of Israel and that he had seen their affliction they bowed their heads and worshipped.

The people who saw believed, and their belief is not something less than actual knowledge. I think there is not a single text in the Bible in which belief is said to be different from knowledge, or that implies that a "mere belief" is in some way inferior to knowledge. Indeed there are texts linking the two emphatically together, such as this declaration that I quote from the prophecy of the second Isaiah:

Ye are my witness, saith the Lord,
And my servant whom I have chosen:
That ye may *know and believe* me,
And understand that I am he:
Before me there was no God formed.
Neither shall there be after me. (Isa. 43:10)

There is another aspect of the biblical writing about knowledge that holds as well for the writing about belief—the link to deeds and action. In both the stories we quoted (1 Kings 10, Exod. 4) the result of the belief, or knowledge, is an action suited to the thing believed. When the doubts and unbelief of the Queen of Sheba were dispelled by the very sight of all Solomon's riches, and the living experience of his wisdom, she was transformed by her new certainty and showered gifts of all kinds upon the king.

She gave the king a hundred and twenty talents of gold and a very great quantity of spices, and precious stones; never again came such an abundance of spices as these which the Queen of Sheba gave to King Solomon.

Indeed this story tells us still more about knowledge—that in its fullest realization (between the king and the queen) there is the generosity and even love that shows up in showering gifts. When she knew him, she loved him. Moreover, this love cum knowledge is reciprocal.

And King Solomon gave to the Queen of Sheba all that she desired, whatever she asked, besides that which Solomon gave of his royal bounty.

Likewise we read at the very end of Exod. 4 that after the people heard the words and saw the signs, "they bowed their heads and worshipped"— and precisely, now at the start of Exod. 5, begins the story of the departure from Egypt. They are prepared to follow Moses and the Lord. When we know *and* believe, that will prompt our movement, not just our thought; after all, we think with the heart, the *central* organ of the body.

Here we could return for a moment to Singer again, for his comments on nomos and obedience are as relevant to the topic of knowledge as they are to love. After all, the possibility of knowing *without* appropriate action is just the huge, mysterious question philosophers know as the problem of *akrasia* or moral weakness. The key positions on this were those of Socrates and Aristotle. Socrates held (see especially *Protagoras* 351b–358d) that one who does wrong cannot really be said to know it is wrong, just as Singer, as we noted, expected the person of nomos to be incapable of sin. The biblical quotations we have made seem to lend support to Socrates' view, and also to Singer's interpretation of the Bible. Yet, as is well known, Aristotle replied to Socrates (see especially *Nichomachean Ethics,* bk. VII, ch. 3) that a person can on occasion fail to apply something that he knows in general. In this way, Aristotle's view was akin to that of Paul in Rom. 7; yes, I know what the Lord requires of me, but I still cannot do it! How shall we respond to this most difficult question? Surely our intuition of the *infinity* of love and knowledge plays a role here. To love and to know God is to be desirous of the ever-continuing way into ever-increasing intimacy and concourse. The Socratic paradox keeps its force only where we think in a geometric style about what is just or what is moderate: as if to know a virtue and to have a virtue were the acquaintance with the stable outline of a finished and perfect Form. Biblical intercourse with God calls our attention instead to the infinity of the *itinerarium mentis in deum.* And I think Singer would be prepared to grant that infinity belongs to the constitution of biblical love as well as biblical justice, hence that perfection even in obedience is in principle beyond reach.

III. TRUTH

There is a further relation between love and knowledge that we must introduce. Let us begin with a look at the Hebrew verb we translate as, "to believe." Its primary root is *aman,* "support," as pillars support a doorway or as parents support a child. Participles formed from this root mean "firm" and "trustworthy," i.e., what is sustained by adequate support or provides adequate support. The noun *emunah,* translated as "faithfulness," has the sense of "trustworthiness," that on which you can depend. One of the verbal forms based on this root *aman, ne'eman,* means "to be trusty, reliable." And a cognate form, *he'emin,* means "to trust," hence, "to believe." But we cannot find in classical Hebrew a noun that would be properly translated as "belief," still less "opinion," i.e., nothing properly like the Greek nouns *pistis* and *doxa.* Although those words are indeed used in the Septuagint, modern Hebraists cannot accept them uncritically. It appears that when ancient Hebrews distinguishes the noun *emunah* from the verbal root, the noun acquires such force or strength that it conveys much more than the notion of belief. It means both faithfulness, and also faith in the sense of "trust." Yet it is clear enough that the verb *he'emin* often does mean "to believe," as in the sense of believing signs or words. Very likely, there was no occasion to differentiate a *belief* from an item of *knowledge*. Although at the level of verbs there is a difference—*yada'* must be translated "to know," not "to believe"—the difference does not hold for nouns.

And here is the most remarkable circumstance of all: another word from this same system, the noun *emeth*, is to be translated at times as "truth," and at other times—as merely another alternate form of *emunah*—as "faithfulness." Thus (a) the idea of truth in the Hebrew language is linked directly to the verb for "believe," not to the verb for "know"; moreover, (b) it is linked directly (to the point of overlap) to terms for "faithfulness" and "trust"; and (c) the whole system revolves around a verbal root that signifies "to support," "hold up."

Now I shall try to show from the psalms that truth, too, stands in an intimate relationship to love.

Not only etymology of these Hebrew words but, more surely and convincingly, the thought patterns of the psalms make it clear that the *truth* is that opinion which we can base ourselves, upon which we can lean, and that which affords us sustenance and support. Nowhere is this more clear than when the psalmist calls upon God as the truth, or the truth of God, or the God of truth, *el-emeth.* Let us quote again the lines from Ps. 25:

> Shew me thy ways, O Lord, teach me thy paths.
> Lead me in thy truth and teach me:
> For thou art the God of my salvation;
> On thee do I wait all the day.

Here, truth is like a way or a path, the way of the Lord. To the way there also belongs the landscape through which the pathway leads. Truth here is preeminently not an abstraction (the common feature of all true statements), but a reality; and this reality lies outside ourselves—it is the path and the country that is open to receive us if we make our entry. Other texts make it clear that truth enters the soul of man because he has entered into the truth, the pathway of God. The point is that we become grounded in the reality we enter—whether that be truth or the opposite. They who lift up their soul unto vanity will then swear deceitfully. The soul acquires truth or falsity depending on the reality in whose midst it walks. We see this thought expressed in Psalms 31, 40, 57, 69, and 89, and most economically in Ps. 43:

> O send out thy light and thy truth:
> Let them lead me;
> Let them bring me unto thy holy hill,
> And to thy tabernacles.

Or, to revert to a scene from the narratives of human interaction, we can grasp how the way of truth differs from that of treachery and lies, both in the stories of Genesis and the Book of Kings. Ancient Hebrew does not distinguish between the man and the word—if the man is true, the word he speaks will be true. Thus Joseph tested his brothers "to see if there is any truth in you" (Gen. 42:16). Man and word are true with one truth: whoever is true and faithful (see, e.g., Jer. 42:5) will give true testimony. True words express the true soul, and are not a momentary configuration, expressing by chance one isolated truth or event. Prophets who prophesy the truth do so because they are true prophets. False prophets prophesy only lies. In 1 Kings 22, Ahab and Jehoshaphat are preparing to make war with Syria, and in accordance with custom they inquire for the word of the Lord. To ask for the word of the Lord was not to determine the course of the future as today we would find out a weather forecast. It was more in the nature of a religious observance, paying one's respects to the Lord. And so when truth was revealed to be bitter they were able to go on ignoring it; indeed they imprisoned the prophet Micaiah to signify their control over what he had said. The most interesting point in the story is that the king of Judah was not satisfied with the word of the four hundred prophets who told him, "Go up, for the Lord will give [Syria] into the hand of the king." He turned from them and said, "Is there not another prophet of the Lord of whom we may inquire?" Ahab knew that Micaiah was a true prophet of the true God, with a true word because his prophecy was always the opposite of what Ahab knew himself to be—a sinful overreacher: "I hate him for he never prophesies good concerning me, but evil." When Micaiah was brought before the kings, he mocked them with an ironic prophecy: "Go up and prosper." But the king of Israel was enraged: "How many times shall I adjure you to speak to me nothing but the truth in the name of the Lord!" Though his life was a lie, he could not bear to hear the lie from the mouth of the true prophet, even though the lie was what he wanted to hear, and even though he acted upon the lie. For even Ahab the false knew that the soul of Micaiah was true, and that it must be spoken out in true words.

The psalmists call upon the God of truth, *el-emeth,* to deliver them from pain and destruction. They seem to imagine the salvation as being brought from chaos to stability and firmness.

> I waited patiently for the Lord,
> And he inclined unto me, and heard my cry.
> He brought me up also out of an horrible pit, out of the miry clay,
> And set my feet upon a rock, and established my goings.

Or again:

> I lie in the midst of lions
> That greedily devour the sons of men.
> Their teeth are spears and arrows,
> Their tongues sharp swords. (Ps. 57:4)

In the following passage from Ps. 69 I emphasize words that translate *emeth* or *emunah*. This psalm is the most extreme in the imagery of chaos:

> But as for me, my prayer is to thee, O Lord.
> At an acceptable time, O God,
> In the abundance of thy loving kindness
> Answer me with thy *faithful* help.
> Rescue me from sinking in the mire,
> Let me be delivered from my enemies
> And from the deep waters,
> Let not the flood sweep over me
> Or the deep swallow me up
> Or the pit close its mouth over me.

Ps. 32 has another description of desolation, moving progressively inward:

> My eye is wasted from grief,
> My soul and body also.
> My bones waste away. (vv. 9-11)

The next group of verses describes the psalmist's status in the midst of the world:

> Those who see me in the street flee from me.

Yet it is from here that the psalm moves to a passage of redemption and joy in God the savior:

> Let thy face shine on thy servant.
> Save me in thy loving kindness.
> Let me not to be put to shame, O Lord,
> For I call on thee.

Here and in many other psalms the *emeth* of God is connected with his hand, his power to rescue us:

> Into thy hand I commit my spirit.
> Thou hast redeemed me, O Lord, *faithful* God.

To be redeemed is to be raised from the pit, to be rescued from chaos:

> I was beset as in a besieged city.

A besieged city is just the opposite of what the Lord is for us: a strong fortress and a rock (vv. 1–4). It is to this *emeth*, faithfulness or truth, that the psalmist appeals when he urges the destruction of his enemies:

> Let me not be put to shame, O Lord, for I call on thee.
> Let the wicked be put to shame, go dumbfounded to Sheol.

We find the motif of God's solidity and trustworthiness and rescue from chaos in a number of other psalms: 86, 138, and 146, but let us look especially at Ps. 85, where the psalmist is giving thanks that the Lord has looked in favor upon the land, and beseeches him to show favor once again. The word *emeth* takes its place here in a messianic vision:

> *Hesed* and *emeth* will meet; *zedek* and *shalom* will kiss;
> *Emeth* will sprout up from the earth; *zedek* will look down from the sky.

The function of *emeth* is to stand upright like a tree, for it stands firmly on the earth. And all these powers are blended with the good increase of the earth in the vision of this psalm, showing us that *emeth* is a state of affairs in which the flesh rejoices as much as the spirit. It is something in which we come to participate, no more an abstraction than joy. *Emeth* not only is a mood or quality of the soul that cleaves to the Lord, but it has a self-subsistence. If it is wrong to think that *emeth* in man is only an opinion or belief, it is also wrong to think it is only the moral attitude of faithfulness. It comes to us from outside as a messenger of God.

The psalms proclaim that God is faithful—that he is true to us. The divine name *emeth* means the whole personality of God insofar as he sustains us, saves us from the pit, and gives us the path in which to walk. Now that above all is what we humans *love*. Where salvation, grace, and rescue come through his truth and his faithfulness, our deepest response of love is awakened. Yet there is a resistance to God that is also a part of this human response. Where *emeth*, truth, and faithfulness lies outside of us, we see that God is more fundamental to us than our own self. The divine quality of being fundamental, the basis, the support, is what we mean when we say that God is truth. This is not to identify God with the truths of the world, however, for in comparison to him, they appear profoundly false. But it is to say that he is faithful.

IV. THE NEW TESTAMENT

The fourth gospel carries us to a vision of incarnate truth in dialogue with men. As Jesus travels about, he divides those he meets into two groups, for his presence brings out either belief or hate. When John speaks of "the Jews," he means those who could not hear the word. "He who is of God hears the word of God." Truth is the bond that attaches those in whom the ground is prepared for the word of truth. It unites the Samaritan woman and Nicodemus to Jesus, yet in the case of the Pharisees it is the truth of God in Jesus which is precisely the divisive force. "Because I tell you the truth you do not believe me." The truth of Jesus (which is of God) is given to the world in his words. The truth that is uttered is, to be sure, something that is dark, surpassing the understanding of the world; yet its truth is still in the same form as scientific or factual truth, in that it is spoken and passes from one intellect to another by way of words that are common to the two. This is even the case with God, for Jesus testifies to "what I have heard from him." Yet there is another aspect of truth in the fourth gospel, which we may take as the ground of the possibility of the true words: the truth which Jesus *is*. And according to St. John, Jesus was crucified because men hated the truth: he came unto his own and his own received him not.

So if the Hebrew scripture is like champagne in its exuberance and abundance, the New Testament is like the cognac that distills that very spirit into its concentration. The epistles of John distill the themes that I have brought out into utter purity. 1 John 2:3 incorporates the link between knowledge and the commandments with which I began this paper.

> By this we may be sure that we know him, if we keep his commandments.

There is an extra character of reflection in John, for he says not only that we can know God, but that we can be *sure* that we do. And 1 John confirms the link of confidence and belief with truth and knowledge, in words that were to inspire a great discourse of Kierkegaard:

> By this we shall know that we are of the truth, and reassure our hearts before him whenever our hearts condemn us; for God is greater than our hearts and knows everything. Beloved, if our hearts do not condemn us, we have confidence before God.

Finally, in 1 John 4: 7-8 we have the intimate bond forged between knowledge and love:

Beloved, let us love one another; for love is of God, and he who loves is born of God and knows God. He who does not love does not know God; for God is love.

Part Two

The History of the Question

5

Ovid and Courtly Humanism

Kevin McCabe

In this paper I would like to address three questions: First, what does the Roman poet Ovid say about love and love affairs? Second, what influence did Ovid have on the courtly poets of the High Middle Ages? And third, to what extent are the writings of Ovid and the courtly poets a rationalization of the sexual instinct?

The word "love" and the behavior categorized as such is notoriously open to confusion and misunderstanding. Some, such as the poet Baudelaire, have claimed that love is only possible through misunderstanding (*My Heart Laid Bare*): "In love, as in almost all human matters, warm agreement is the result of a misunderstanding. . . ." Perhaps in no other area of our lives are the possible fluctuations between subjectivity and objectivity so great, or the value put on subjectivity so extreme.

As if to illustrate the possibilities of misunderstanding, Horace Walpole tells a story about a young Englishman and three English noblewomen traveling in Italy during the eighteenth century. The ladies involved are Walpole's sister-in-law, Lady Walpole, Lady Mary Wortley Montagu, and Lady Pomfret. Walpole wrote to Richard West on October 2, 1740:

> Lady Pomfret is extremely scandalised with the other two dames, especially with Moll Worthless [Lady Mary Wortley], who knows no bounds. She is at rivalry with Lady Walpole for a certain Mr. X. . . . He fell into sentiments with Lady Walpole and was happy to catch her at Platonic love, but as she seldom stops there, the poor man will be frightened out of his senses

115

when she shall break the matter to him; for he never dreamt that her purposes were so naught. . . . I forgot to tell you a good answer of Lady Pomfret to Mr. X, who asked her if she did not approve Platonic love? "Lord, sir," says she, "I am sure any one that knows me never heard that I had any love but one, and there sit two proofs of it," pointing to her two daughters.

I would like to begin now by citing some passages from Ovid's poetry, which seem to indicate his attitude to the subject. Professor Singer (*The Nature of Love*, 2:30–31) has quoted the classicist Brooks Otis to the effect that Ovid had two conflicting attitudes toward love—that of the witty libertine in the *Ars Amatoria*, and that of the champion of "true love" in the *Metamorphoses*. I hope to demonstrate that the attitudes expressed throughout the Ovidian corpus are essentially the same, and that the *Ars Amatoria*, or *Art of Love*, simply gives a more deliberately provocative twist to sentiments found elsewhere.

One essential difference between love poetry and poetry in general is that love poetry is usually intended for the opposite sex to read. The consciousness of a female audience seems partly responsible for the teasing, provocative tone of much of Ovid's poetry. He himself tells us of the response which he receives from women (*Amores* II.4.19–22):

> Some fair one tells me Callimachus's songs are rustic beside mine—
> One who likes me I straightway like myself.
> Another calls me no poet, and chides my verses—
> And I fain would clasp the fault-finder to my arms.

Since the love poetry both of Ovid's time and of the Middle Ages was frequently written within an aristocratic circle in which the female family members played a large role, female influence as well as a female audience can generally be expected.

Platonic love is decidedly absent in Ovid; in fact, it would be difficult to prove that Ovid had ever read Plato. The only obvious philosophic influence is Lucretius, who is selectively used to highlight the naturalness of sex and the universal power of Venus. It is Lucretius also whose views on sex or love as a civilizing influence on early man are adopted by Ovid. The dogmatic Epicureanism of the great philosopher-poet had subsided by Ovid's day, leaving a nonphilosophic popular hedonism behind. As historian Ronald Syme put it in *History in Ovid:* "Epicureanism was no longer professed, merely practised."

Although various attempts have been made to elevate Ovid's philosophy of love above the level of an educated hedonism, Ovid himself is not very helpful in such efforts. Professor Singer speaks of Ovid's "shallowness of moral insight," and we may suppose that Ovid, like many another candidate for popularity, feels that literary success lies in scrupulously avoiding moral issues.

It is counterproductive for an aspiring author to make his audience feel uncomfortable by raising moral awareness above what his readers readily and customarily feel. Ovid is expert at diverting potentially moral questions into matters of taste, temperament, and grooming; he is a master of surface tension and narrative variety, who quickly whisks his readers away from contemplating the effects of action on character.

Ovid's heroes and heroines tend to behave by instinct and passion, as if they have little independent character. The women of the *Heroides* (Ovid's "Letters from Heroines"), for example, resemble soap opera characters in that they are passive entities to whom things happen. Likewise the rape victims of the *Fasti* and *Metamorphoses* seem to be mere bodies in a landscape who exist to be acted upon. male characters also are not much more individualized in the narrative poems, being usually naive adolescents caught up in simple desires. Such shallowness of characterization aids in circumventing moral issues.

Besides pathetic adolescents, male and female, Ovid's poems commonly contain the character of the older or more experienced seducer, or teacher of love (*praeceptor amoris*), this character may be either male or female, as in the *Heroides*. In *Heroides* IV it is the older woman Phaedra, wife of Theseus, who is attempting to seduce her stepson Hippolytus with the following words (129–36):

> And, should you think of me as a stepdame
>   who would mate with her husband's son,
> Let empty names fright not your soul.
> Such old-fashioned regard for virtue was rustic even in Saturn's reign,
> And doomed to die in the age to come.
> Jove fixed that virtue was to be in whatever brought us pleasure;
> And naught is wrong before the gods since sister was
>   made wife by brother.
> That bond of kinship only holds close and firm
> In which Venus herself has forged the chain.

In *Heroides* XVI it is the Trojan prince Paris who scolds Helen, the wife of Menelaus, about her reluctance to commit adultery (285–92):

> Or do you feel shame and fear to violate your wedded love,
> And to be false to the chaste bonds of a lawful bed?
> Ah, too simple—nay, too rustic—Helen!
> Do you think that beauty of yours can be free from fault?
> Either you must change your beauty, or you must needs not be hard;
> Fairness and modesty are mightily at strife.
> Jove's delight, and the delight of Venus, are in stealthy sins like these;
> Such stealthy sins, indeed, gave you Jove for sire.

It will be noted how Ovid removes adultery from the moral to the aesthetic realm by making shame or scruples a sign of poor education or rustic upbringing.

In the *Ars Amatoria* the poet speaks as the teacher of love in the first person, something that was to give him the character of the "Clerk of Venus" or the "learned doctor of love" in the Middle Ages. In this poem Ovid urges his male readers not to fall prey to rusticity but to press their advantage upon a weakening girlfriend (I.669-74):

> He who has taken kisses, if he take not the rest beside,
> will deserve to lose even what was granted.
> After kisses how much was lacking to your sow's fulfilment?
> Ah! that was gaucheness, not modesty,
> You may use force; women like you to use it;
> They often wish to give unwillingly what they like to give.

Ovid seems to be deliberately provocative in the lengthy passage rationalizing "date-rape," perhaps wishing to draw a cry of protest from his female audience. Likewise in the *Metamorphoses* Ovid teasingly brings in the long-lived prophet Tiresias to give judgment on the question whether men or women get more pleasure from sex. Since Tiresias has had the advantage of a sex change he is able to state positively that women get the most pleasure. All this is a jocular tearing away of the lady's "dernière chemise," so that she lacks any argument to employ against her ardent lover.

Throughout Ovid's poetry there is a sweeping away of any attitudes that might impede sexual passion. The teacher of love encourages women not to worry about physiological matters: the vagina is elastic and resilient (*Ars* III.87-92):

> Study, ye mortal folk, the examples of the goddesses,
> Nor deny your joys to hungry lovers.
> Though they at last deceive you, what do you lose? those joys abide;
> Though they take a thousand pleasures, naught is lost therefrom.
> Iron is worn away, and flints are diminished by use;
> That part endures, and has no fear of loss.

The *praeceptor amoris* indicates that individual tastes are to be cultivated; he himself prefers women over thirty-five because of their greater experience and skill, as well as their eagerness (*Ars* II.663-702). Note that in a poem commending culture in general Ovid's chief criterion here is skill in bed. This passage also may be a wink at the poet's audience, which may well have included prominent "older women."

Commenting on *Amores* II.4, which lists the variety of women who attract the poet, Peter Green writes (*Erotic Poems*, p. 293):

A man who finds so many different women attractive must be drawn, ultimately, by the common factor of their femininity rather than by the individual traits which distinguish them one from another. They may be different to begin with, but refracted through Ovid's gaze they are all alike: all serve the same purpose. Indeed, throughout the poem what Ovid repeatedly anticipates is getting the object of his affections into bed. . . .

Writing as he did in an atmosphere of popular Epicureanism, it was not a problem for Ovid to rationalize sexual intercourse as a worthwhile and adequate goal. According to Cicero, even some early Epicurean philosophers had accepted physical sensations as an adequate test of the *summum bonum*. For Ovid sex is an important ingredient in the good life of the urban sophisticate, which includes poetry, a life of leisure, a cultivated social circle, public and private entertainments, and the arts in general.

According to Ovid, such a life was dictated to the poet by his physical makeup and temperament. As he maintains in an autobiographical poem these factors outside his control forced him to turn away from public life (*Tristia* IV.10.35–40):

The senate house awaited me, but I narrowed my purple stripe:
That was a burden too great for my powers.
I had neither a body to endure the toil nor a mind suited to it;
By nature I shunned the worries of an ambitious life
And the Aonian sisters [the Muses] were ever urging me to seek the security
Of a retirement I had ever chosen and loved.

Love poets are distinguished from the rest of mankind by their soft temperament and gentle nature, as is the poet himself (65–66):

My heart was ever soft, no stronghold against Cupid's darts—
A heart moved by the slightest impulse.

This temperament makes poets unsuited to public life and the professions, but especially susceptible to love.

Ovid professes his innocence in the *Tristia* by maintaining that his behavior is a matter of temperament and, therefore, largely beyond his control: in the *Ars*, written before his disgrace and exile, he states, on the other hand, that the temperament itself is developed by the pursuit of poetry (III.539–46):

Besides, treachery is alien to sacred bards,
And our art too helps to shape our character.
Neither ambition nor love of gain affects us;
The Forum we despise, and cultivate the couch and the shade.

> But we are easily caught, and burn with a strong passion,
> And know how to love with a loyalty most sure.
> 'Tis in truth from the gentle art that our spirit wins tenderness,
> And our behavior is akin to our pursuit.

There were those in Rome who were shocked by Ovid's poetry; otherwise, there would have been no point in trying to be shocking. On the other hand Ovid could feel quite satisfied with himself as a civilizing influence among the rough soldiers and crooked lawyers of the city. He took and enlarged upon Lucretius's idea of Venus or Amor (love) as a power for cultural development, and saw himself and his circle as the enlightened ones. When the emperor Augustus banished him from Rome for teaching immorality, Ovid seems to have been genuinely hurt and surprised. There is virtually no indication in his later poems that he regretted what he had done, or that he could picture himself as doing anything different. Indeed in his poetry from exile Ovid further develops the idea of the beneficial influence of love in society, and the interconnectedness of love, poetry, culture, and sensitive behavior.

If one of Ovid's aims had been to be a best-seller he was certainly successful both in his own lifetime and for centuries afterward. I should now like to consider whether this very Epicurean poet had a substantial impact upon the life and culture of the eleventh, twelfth, and thirteenth centuries in Western Europe. At first sight Ovid would seem an unlikely candidate for Christian Europe to take to its heart.

Professor Singer has raised the question whether Ovid's vogue in the Middle Ages was not due to a misunderstanding of his contents. Noting that Ovid played a special role in the development of courtly love, Dr. Singer adds (*The Nature of Love,* 2:30):

> His works were widely read throughout the Middle Ages and often accepted as authoritative despite their pagan presuppositions. The cynicism in *The Art of Love* was either misunderstood by medieval authors or discounted as subordinate to Ovid's sympathetic concern about the problems of love between the sexes.

Courtly love, like many general concepts, is difficult to define. Professor Singer (*The Nature of Love,* 2:22ff.) includes five criteria as part of his definition of courtly love: (1) the idea that sexual love between men and women is *in itself* something splendid, an ideal worth striving for; (2) that love ennobles both the lover and the beloved; (3) that sexual love can satisfy ethical and aesthetic standards, as well as physical ones; (4) that love pertains to courtesy and courtship, but is not necessarily related to marriage; and (5) that love is an intense, passionate relationship which establishes a holy oneness between man and woman.

It is far from clear that one would find these criteria (except the first) in Ovid unless one were looking for them. As Professor Singer notes, however, Ovid's fictional works, the *Heroides* and *Metamorphoses,* do contain stories of "passion that was mutual, sincere, life-enhancing, and permanent." Greek mythology contains numerous tales about devoted married couples, and in retelling these stories in the *Metamorphoses* and elsewhere Ovid generally retains the element of marital devotion and sometimes even enhances it. Such stories as Cephalus and Procris, Baucis and Philemon, Orpheus and Eurydice, and Ceyx and Alcyone come to mind. And, too, while Ovid delights in tales of seduction and rape, he is extremely skillful in sentimentalizing the fate of the victims, as in his *Heroides.*

Ovid's older contemporaries, moreover, the Roman elegists Tibullus and Propertius, had often adopted a humble attitude toward their mistresses, not unlike that of the courtly lover. While Ovid is not so fond of this humble servant theme, in several elegies he quietly parodies his ardent predecessors in ways that have commonly been misunderstood as expressing his own devotion to his mistress. Ovid also considers the tactic of humble service as one of some practical use in his *Art of Love.*

It is likely, therefore, that medieval readers found enough hints of the courtly love attitude in Ovid to claim him for their own. In general, however, we may say that Ovid supplies much of the raw material for courtly poetry, while it is the courtly poet who provides most of the idealization of love and the mistress. Ovid's chief contribution seems to lie in providing the love stories themselves from mythology and legend, and in supplying a handbook on the nature, stages, and psychology of love affairs. Ovid's works also provide various literary motifs, the love terminology, and literary models for the courtly poets.

As a literary model Ovid may well provide the basic pattern for the courtly love lyric, namely, the eternal triangle of the lover, his mistress, and the mistress's husband. Unlike Ovid, however, the courtly poet is sometimes content to woo his beautiful lady from afar: at times the husband may keep the lady's body, if the poet may have her soul. This medieval humility may have had some relation to the low social status of some courtly poets who were patronized by leading noblewomen of the day. The adoration of the mistress may also owe something to hymns to the Virgin Mary which in their lists of Mary's perfections resemble some secular love-songs. Neither of these factors, however, seems adequate to explain completely the attitudes we find.

On the whole the troubadours' idea of mystical devotion to a married lady is so unexpected a product of feudal society, the Christian faith, and Ovidian literary influence that some have conjectured that a new influx of notions occurred about this time. Denis de Rougemont, in *Passion and Society*, examines the possibility that courtly love was partly inspired by the mysticism of the Cathar heresy, which was strongest in the very centers of Provençal poetry. At the same time the rhetoric, poetry, and doctrines of the contemporary Islamic world, with their Neoplatonic elements, had a definite influence on courtly thought and literature. Other currents, including Celtic and Germanic myths and traditions, also contributed to what de Rougemont called (*Passion and Society*, p. 107) "one of the most extraordinary spiritual confluences in history."

It was certainly difficult for courtly poets to rationalize adultery, or feel comfortable with it in a Christian context. This was especially the case when one attempted to study the subject systematically, as Andreas Capellanus did in the twelfth century in his *Art of Courtly Love*. It is significant that after expounding in dialectic manner on the nature of courtly love in the first two books, Andreas rejects the concept in the third book as incompatible with Christian teaching.

Ovid's own works were condemned by theologians such as William of St. Thierry (ca. 1085–1148), who (anticipating Kierkegaard in *Either/Or*) sees Ovid as representing the natural man who practices neither the life of reason nor, more importantly, the spiritual or divine life. Instead Ovid praises the carnal side of man, and ignores his rational and spiritual self. This corresponds with the view implied in Kierkegaard that Ovid represents the aesthetic level or first stage of human cultivation, fails to attain to the second or ethical level, and has no concept of the third or spiritual level of development.

Ovid provides the literary models and raw materials for courtly love poetry, but little of the idealized picture of love and devotion, and the religious and feudal expression of faith and loyalty the lover feels for his mistress. Many familiar ideas in medieval love poetry can be traced to Ovid, such as the use of tears in winning over one's mistress, the notion that love makes the lover strong, that love is a kind of warfare, and that the lover takes precedence over the husband, as well as advice on bribing servants and keeping one's love secret from friends and others. Some medieval poets, like Ovid, tried to move love out of the moral into the aesthetic realm by approvingly speaking of courting a married lady as *courtois* and blaming the jealousy of the husband as *vilain*. These terms correspond to the Ovidian terms *urbanus* and *rusticus*. In fact, much of the love language of the troubadours is adapted from Ovid's Latin.

The prevalence of Ovidian concepts in medieval literature owes much to the acceptance of the *Ars Amatoria* as a genuine didactic work of merit. Medieval teachers often treated the *Art of Love* as a scientific treatise on the nature and psychology of love. Like Aristotle, Ovid was regarded as an authority, and recourse was had also to the *Metamorphoses* and *Fasti* for matters of astronomy, history, mythology, and science. It may surprise later generations that Ovid's notorious poem, along with some medieval imitations, was used as a school text in the High Middle Ages, and frequently quoted by the clergy. Ovid was also translated into the vernacular, widely imitated or plagiarized, and his teachings surface in various guises and in a variety of genres, including comedy and the verse romance.

It may be significant that the earliest vernacular poet of courtly love was also the closest imitator of Ovid. Guilhem IX, Count of Poitiers, lived from 1071 to 1127; only eleven of his poems survive. These indicate that much of the subject matter, literary form, and even the tone which Guilhem used is indebted to Ovid. Unlike later courtly lovers, Guilhem does not confine his attentions to a lifelong devotion to one lady, nor is he content to view her from afar. As a nobleman he is neither so humble nor so patient as his successors would be. Nonetheless his verses have a freshness, directness, and sympathy with nature which contrast favorably with Ovid's own poetry. For example, the lines beginning "Ab la dolchor del temps novel" (trans. Sally Purcell):

In this mild new season
The woods take leaf;
Each bird sings his Latin
To the new song's melody;
And rightly now a man should take
Whatever gives him most delight.

No scroll or message comes to me
From that place I hold so dear;
I cannot laugh or sleep or dare
To drag myself about, until
I hear from her and know her faith
To be as I would have it be.

Our love is like the whitethorn branch
That trembles all night long upon the tree
In frost and rain until the morning sun
Spills through young green leaves and branches.

I remember still one morning
When we made an end of war,
When she gave me that great gift,
Her loving grace—and sealed it with her ring.
God grant that I may see the day
I hold her underneath her dress!

I do not care that strangers' words
Might part me from my Bon Vezi,

Since I know the words that suit me
In a proverb that says simply:
Swaggerers may boast of love,
We possess it fair and fully.

In this poem Guilhem is clearly deeply involved with love, and on tenterhooks about the faithfulness of his lady; nonetheless his desire is to have his "lady's loving grace," which certainly includes her body. And this leads him to say that he and his lady "possess love fair and fully."

Later courtly poets were much less likely to praise physical satisfaction as, in Donne's words, "the right true end of love." For this reason Ovid is a less direct influence on them. Undiluted Ovid could not easily thrive in an atmosphere of clericalism, feudalism, and devotion. Nonetheless Guilhem's example shows that the medieval use of Ovid was due not to mere misunderstanding, but to a need to adapt Ovid to a different culture and worldview. Guilhem, moreover, was often at odds with ecclesiastical authorities, and, as a prince, could reject their censure of his actions. Other poets of the time commonly saw human love in the light of divine love; even Guilhem sees fit to call upon Jesus in his hour of need, although he rejects the authority of the church.

The poems of Ovid are a product of a "youth culture," and were written at a time when Romans of means could devote themselves to a life of pleasure and the arts. Although there had been at Rome a traditional willingness to allow young men to indulge in youthful escapades before settling down to marriage and a public career, Ovid sees the pursuit of pleasure as a lifelong activity. This relates, for example, to his preference for older women as sexual partners.

In the High Middle Ages, increasing affluence had made it possible for aristocrats to devote themselves to a life of leisure. There was also a growing number of wandering students and young minstrel poets who comprised something like a youth culture. Within these groups there was some acceptance of undiluted Ovidian attitudes.

The extension of these attitudes to the whole of society was strongly opposed by many ecclesiastics, as it went against many basic ideas of medieval society. Some courtly poets themselves severely criticized the life of pleasure, and courtly love itself may be an attempt to moralize and spiritualize the hedonism of aristocrats like Guilhem.

Not only the growth of materialism, but the wide currency of ideas and beliefs of non-Christian origin had contributed to a weakening of Christian patterns of thought and behavior. The heresy of the Cathars with its disdain for the Christian concept of marriage is a relevant example. Nonetheless the power of the Church was still adequate to moderate or even suppress some of these tendencies. It is a regular pattern in medieval life and literature for reflection on courtly love to lead ultimately to a rejection of it on Christian principles. This occurs in Andreas Capellanus, Abelard, and in many poems that end with the hero and heroine entering religious orders.

As in Ovid's own life and work, the problem with courtly love is the attempt to extend it from a period of youth and young adulthood into a pattern for the whole of life; marriage, therefore, becomes an impediment rather than a goal. This inevitably brings courtly love into conflict both with the marriage vows of the secular participants and with the vows of celibacy of its clerical adherents. Courtly love's exaltation and spiritualization of the mistress may be partly to avoid a direct conflict with Christian teachings on adultery; but, since in Christianity the wish to commit adultery is almost as great as in the act itself, such sublimation exists on very shaky ground.

The courtly lovers may point to the ennobling effects of their ethereal love both on the lover and the beloved. In the same way the lovers of young men in Plato's *Symposium* pointed out that love between men will help soldiers to fight better against the enemies of the city. But ultimately concepts of love have to be justified by how well they succeed in their direct effects, not rationalized in terms of possibly beneficial side effects. It may well be that courtly love led to a more sensitive relationship between the sexes, and perhaps improved social relations in general to some extent. Yet in doing so it also introduced social, moral, and spiritual problems and tensions. These very tensions, however, tend to protect the courtly lover from a descent into a mere hedonistic use of sex.

In courtly poetry there is often a freshness, buoyancy, and sense of wonder quite lacking in Ovid. Ovid came at the end of the Hellenistic period in which poets had virtually exhausted all the variations in narrating sexual adventures. Homosexuality, bestiality, incest, and rape were all common themes in late Greek and Roman love poetry. And while Ovid may breathe new life into such stories, his work generally appears to be an attempt to stir up the interests and titillate the tastes of a rather self-indulgent audience.

Ovid's references to the animal world are frequently a mere equation of human sexuality with sex between animals. Throughout the *Ars Amatoria* the poet keeps us mindful that the lover and his beloved are very similar to a bull and a heifer or a stallion and a mare. On the other hand, one of the most attractive elements of troubadour poetry is the simple pleasure expressed in the natural world. The beauty of the world of nature, therefore, becomes the proper background for the beautiful love in the poet's heart. This typical spring poem ("Bel m'es quan lo vens m'alena") is from Arnaut de Mareuil (trans. Sally Purcell):

I love the April wind that breathes
Before the time of May,
When nightingale and jay
Sing all the calm night through,
And each bird goes about
In morning's freshness
Singing in his language
Of pleasure and his love.

And since each earthly thing
Rejoices when the leaves bud
I too remember
The love that gives me joy;
By nature and by custom
I follow Love's happiness
Now that the soft breeze blows
Upon my springtime heart.

She is whiter than Helena,
Fairer than any flower,
Full of courtliness and truth,
Noble, constant, open-hearted,
With white teeth, fine complexion,
And golden auburn hair.
God who made her so supreme
Guard the fairest ever seen!

It would be merciful for her to end
My long sufferings,
To give me a kind kiss
And more as my service merits.
Then we should often travel
That small short path
On which her beauty set me first
And drove my wits astray.

This and many other courtly poems indicate that if courtly love began
with Ovid, it did not end with him. Ovid's poetry helped to stimulate a new
birth of poetry in which Ovid himself was largely outgrown. His poems certainly
spurred medieval interest in sexual adventures, but this interest was eventually
channeled in ways more compatible with medieval religion and society.

Ovid's position as the favorite poet of the High Middle Ages was largely
due to the medieval willingness to read him in their own way for their own
purposes. Ovidius Ethicus and Ovidius Christianus allowed medieval readers
to read the poet's texts in terms of their own moral and religious beliefs.
Though not an attractive approach to us, such readings, like courtly love

itself, allowed the Middle Ages simultaneously to enjoy both the pagan past and the Christian present. And if the mixture was a volatile one, it was perhaps all the more stimulating and fraught with possibilities for that reason. As Professor Singer has pointed out (*The Nature of Love*, 2:31):

> In creating their own kinds of idealization, advocates of courtly love had no need to spurn Ovid's influence completely. In fact . . . Andreas Capellanus's theory of courtly love is virtually a systematic attempt to synthesize Ovidian realism with idealistic elements that derive from Plato and Christianity.

REFERENCES

De Rougemont, Denis. *Passionate Society*, trans. Montgomery Valgion. Rev. ed. London: Faber and Faber, 1962.
Ovid. *The Erotic Poems*, trans. Peter Green. New York: Viking Penguin, 1983.

6

Loving Friendship
According to Thomas Aquinas

Walter Principe

In an earlier essay titled "Affectivity and the Heart in Thomas Aquinas' Spirituality," I had occasion to examine this theologian's thought on love.[1] This essay tried to overcome the all too frequent view of Aquinas as a speculative thinker of powerful intellect and reasoning, but one with little to say about matters of the heart, affectivity, or love. It was a pleasure, then, to see how much attention Thomas Aquinas received from Irving Singer in his work *The Nature of Love,* and to appreciate his many insights into the importance and contribution of Aquinas—even if he found that Aquinas did not answer all the questions he himself was asking about the nature of love.

I cannot hope within this paper to present the thorough analysis of Thomas Aquinas' teaching on love that would be required to comment adequately on Irving Singer's presentation of his thought. The 23-volume *Concordance* to all of Aquinas' writings has approximately 6,500 entries for the noun (*amor*) and verb (*amare*) "love" (nearly 4,000 for *amor,* about 2,500 for *amare*); and about 2,500 entries for "desire" as noun or verb (*desiderium, desiderare*); and over 7,500 for the verb "to will" (*velle*).[2] The nouns "friendship" (*amicitia*) and "friend" (*amicus*)—terms associated with the theme of my paper—together occur over 2,800 times! and this supposedly heady intellectual speaks of the heart (*cor*) nearly 2,300 times, and of affections (*affectiones*) or "affective response" (*affectus*) about 2,000 times. He also has four considerable questions containing twenty-four articles that deal with "delight" (*delectatio*) (1–2.31–

34).[3] And what of "charity," "dilection," "benevolence"? Thousands more texts! It is true that Aquinas is usually engaged in careful intellectual analysis of these terms and the realities they signify, but a sympathetic reader will often sense the intensity of his personal feeling behind his seemingly objective discussions.

In the face of such a mass of material, I propose here to look at a limited number of Aquinas' thoughts on love, friendship, and loving friendship. These, let it be said from the start, may in his view occur in the natural order apart from grace. I should then like to examine the higher, graced mode of love that is charity toward God and others. Finally, I should like to make a few remarks about Dr. Singer's treatment of Aquinas in the first volume of his work, *The Nature of Love*.

1. LOVE AND LOVING FRIENDSHIP

It is interesting and perhaps significant that in his *Summa Theologiae,* Thomas Aquinas presents his longest analysis of love within his treatment of the passions or emotions. Earlier in the same section of this work he had indeed spent some time examining the spiritual volitional faculty, the will: the faculty itself, its motivation, movement, fruition, its choice and other acts (1–2.6–17). But Aquinas saves his analysis of love—and, within it, of friendship-love—for pride of place among the 27 questions, with their 132 distinct articles, devoted to the passions or emotions. As a theologian Thomas is, of course, interested in the good or bad role of the passions in the moral and Christian life. Indeed, one of his important contributions, too often neglected, is his insistence that the passions or emotions share in the goodness or evil of a human moral act and may even increase that moral goodness or evil. Speaking of good acts, Thomas states:

> It belongs to perfect *moral good* that we be moved toward the good not only through our will but also through our sensitive appetite, according to the saying of Psalm 83 (84):3: "My heart and my flesh have rejoiced in the living God": taking "heart" to mean the intellective appetite [the will] and "flesh" to mean the sensitive appetite. (1–2.24.3r)

This passage expresses an important point: even the highest reaches of love can and, one would expect, should be accompanied by passionate feelings. Thomas is no Stoic seeking the sleep of the passions.

These moral considerations are, however, only part of Aquinas' larger considerations of the passion or emotion of love, a consideration that in his treatment expands to include all kinds of love. Thus, in the opening article

(1-2.26.1r), Thomas indicates that one can speak of love as both sensitive (in the sensitive appetite) and intellective or rational (in the will—the intellective appetite). Although in his analyses he often distinguishes these two levels of love, Thomas frequently includes them together in the same texts. Thus it is clear that for him human love is not unfeeling volition but rather includes sensitive affections as integral to its perfection.

In analyzing human love, Aquinas makes an important distinction between "concupiscence-love" (*amor concupiscentiae*) and "friendship-love" (*amor amicitiae*). "Concupiscence" in his usage is a neutral word with no connotation of disorder or sinfulness: concupiscence-love is a movement of love toward an object seen as good—a good that one wishes for oneself or for another. Friendship-love, on the other hand, is directed toward *someone* to whom or for whom one wishes a good. This friendship-love, Thomas says, is love "simply speaking" (*simpliciter*), that is, unqualified love, whereas concupiscence-love is love only in a certain respect (*secundum quid*), that is, qualified love (1-2.26.4r). Aquinas excludes from "the notion of true friendship" Aristotle's category of useful and delightful friendship because to some degree it includes concupiscence-love.[4]

Love is always related to the good and the beautiful, which must be perceived *sensibly* for sensitive love and contemplated *spiritually* for spiritual love (1-2.27.1-2). An important point for Aquinas is that, properly speaking, friendship-love or "benevolence" (*benevolentia*: he seems to equate the two names) is caused by a similitude or likeness between the persons who experience this kind of love. Because they are alike, he says, "the affective response (*affectus*) of one tends to the other as to someone who is one with oneself, and the person wills good to the other as to oneself" (1-2.27.3r); "one who loves another by the love of friendship . . . esteems (*apprehendit*) the person as another self, in so far as the lover wills good to the beloved as to oneself" (1-2.28.1r); the friend is "another self," and "a half of one's soul" (ibid.).[5] An interesting difference between friendship-love and a concupiscence-love that might seem to be friendship-love is indicated by Aquinas: friendship-love interposes nothing between the beloved and the lover, whereas concupiscence-love can lead a person to resist and even hate someone, otherwise a friend, if that person should stand in the way of some good he or she loves (1-2.27.3r).

A rich discussion, which might be called Aquinas' phenomenology of loving friendship, describes the effect of love as the mutual inherence (*mutua inhaesio*) of the lover in the beloved and of the beloved in the lover (1-2.28.2). Aquinas introduces the discussion by quoting a text of scripture that will be significant further on in our paper: "They who abide in charity abide in God and God in them" (1 John 4:16). What is true of charity or love of God, he says, is true of lovers abiding in each other.

Thomas Aquinas sees this mutual inherence as taking place in two ways—

by a cognitive aspect, *apprehensio*, that we have translated as "estimation," and by an appetitive or affective aspect, "complacency" (*complacentia*). With respect to knowledge or *estimation*, the BELOVED is said to be IN the LOVER to the degree that the BELOVED remains in the LOVER'S knowledge or estimation, while the LOVER is IN the BELOVED to the degree that the LOVER seeks to go beyond a superficial knowledge of the BELOVED in order to discover the interior depths of the BELOVED in all detail (1–2.28.2r).

With respect to *appetite,* the BELOVED is in the LOVER by what Aquinas calls a "certain complacency in the [LOVER'S] affective response" (*per quandam complacentiam in eius affectu*): the LOVER delights in the BELOVED or in her good qualities or in the good things he wants for her, his beloved, because he is motivated by his own friendship-love "arising from an interiorly rooted complacency in her as his beloved."[6] Conversely, the LOVER is IN her, his BELOVED, by friendship-love to the degree that he reckons the good or evil that befalls her, his friend, as his own, and reckons his friend's will as his own, "so that it seems as if in his friend he suffers and is affected by [her] good or evil." By thus being identified with her, his beloved, and by judging her experiences as his own, the lover seems to be IN the beloved (ibid.).

This mutual inherence, Aquinas concludes, is found even more completely when friends love each other mutually by a return of love, willing and working for each other's good (ibid.). Such love, Aquinas continues, produces ecstasy. Here he quotes Pseudo-Dionysius the Areopagite on divine love as ecstatic and adds that all love is a kind of participated likeness of divine love (ibid. 3 sc). This love also produces zeal to protect a friend against anything injurious, just as zeal for God leads the lover of God to resist anything against the divine honor or will (ibid. 4r). Further, the passion of love can be so strong in the bodily changes it produces that it may be said to wound the lover (ibid. 5r). When Thomas speaks of the ecstasy experienced in loving friendship, he describes it as happening in two ways: love leads the lover to dwell in *thought* on the beloved so intensely that he loses all thought of anything but her; love produces an *affective response* (*affectus*) that takes him outside himself to his friend because he wills her good and sets about caring and providing for her good (ibid. 3r).

It is true that for Aquinas love of self is first in order and that love for the other person arises from identifying that person with oneself. But as these descriptions of loving friendship show, this identification of the beloved with oneself is no subterfuge for a hidden and perhaps unacknowledged selfishness; indeed, as has been seen, Aquinas states expressly that such a turn of friendship-love back to one's own utility or pleasure would make it a concupiscence-love that would fall short of the notion of true friendship.[7] True friendship-love, on the other hand, leads the lover to delight in, to be concerned for, and to wish well to the beloved in a movement that he dares call "ecstatic"—going outside the self. And it seems to me, as I read Thomas, that I hear echoes of what Dr. Singer calls "appraisal" and "bestowal." *Appraisal* seems to be indicated where Aquinas speaks about the lover's knowledge or estimation of the beloved, and *bestowal* where he speaks of the lover's willing the other's good, inhering in the beloved, and receiving the mutual inherence of the beloved in oneself. It would have been interesting, had Dr. Singer been able to deal with these key articles and questions in Aquinas, to see if he might have found such a correspondence between his thought and that of Aquinas.

It is interesting to note, in addition, that although later on Aquinas will analyze different kinds of human actions in terms of their goodness or evil, at this stage he makes no moral judgment about loving friendships. It would seem, therefore, that what he says applies to all friendships, whether of good persons or not. This judgment is strengthened by the fact that, although Aquinas sometimes applies texts of scripture to human love, he gives no indication in these texts that he is speaking only of a supernatural or "grace" friendship-love. Undoubtedly he would want to say that grace can and should be operative, but in at least one significant passage he asserts that friendship is possible for human beings apart from the influence of grace. Addressing the question whether we can merit eternal life without grace, Thomas maintains that this is impossible because there is a lack of proportion between human nature and eternal life, which consists in the immediate vision and perfect love of God. However, he then continues:

> Nevertheless, we can do works leading to some good that is co-natural to us, such as to work in a field, to drink, to eat, and *to have a friend,* and other things of this sort, as Augustine says in his third reply against the Pelagians. (1–2.109.5r)[8]

In another text Thomas speaks of "natural friendships (*amicitia naturalis*), like that found among relatives:

> Now since love, taken in its universal sense, is directed to the good taken in its common meaning, it must be that any special love whatsoever be directed to some special good object. For example, the natural friendship found among relatives has, as its proper object, the good of nature passed on by one's parents, whereas political friendship has as its object the good of the state. (*Quaestio disputata de caritate*, a. 7r)[9]

2. CHARITY

The notions of mutual inherence of lovers, of each being in the other, and of loving friendship, take on greatly intensified meaning when Thomas Aquinas speaks of the supernatural or graced love that is charity. We have heard him, when speaking of mutual inherence of lovers, quote the scriptural text: "They who abide in charity abide in God and God in them" (1 John 4:16; quoted in 1–2.28.2 sc). Now, when he begins to discuss the supernatural, graciously given virtue of charity, the first question he asks is whether charity is friendship with God (2–2.23.1). But before looking at this, we must enter with Aquinas into the inner life of the Trinity, a life of intimate knowledge and love that is the source of all love but especially of that love which makes possible human friendship with the Father, Son, and Holy Spirit.

The foundation for everything Aquinas says about love, especially the friendship-love that is charity, is the eternally dynamic and ever-present procession of the Holy Spirit from the Father and Son through their love. For Aquinas, when the Holy Spirit proceeds from the Father and Son as the "formal effect" of their love, the Father and Son love not only the divine goodness and each other, but also each human person and indeed all creatures "by the Holy Spirit," Who is Love. Within the Father's and Son's active dynamic mutual love "by the Holy Spirit," each human person is therefore involved as a true, if secondary, object of their love (1.37.2c and ad 3m).

According to this teaching, then, at each moment of our existence we are being known, freely chosen to exist, and loved into existence within the Father's and Son's eternal ecstatic breathing forth of the Holy Spirit of Love. In addition to our being loved into existence as creatures, we receive higher gifts from God's love. Following the teaching of Paul, Aquinas maintains that "the charity of God is poured forth in our hearts through the Holy Spirit, who is given to us" (Rom. 5:5). Aquinas agrees with the Parisian masters of theology, who in common rejected Peter Lombard's position: for him, our charity is simply the person of the Holy Spirit or is at least our being moved by the Holy Spirit immediately, without our charity being an intrinsic modification or habitual disposition of our being.[10] For Aquinas, charity is a created habit or virtue—produced in us by the Holy Spirit and beyond our ability to attain it. It is not some kind of stuff, not some quantified thing; rather, it is a modification of our being, and specially of our will, empowering us to act lovingly toward God and other persons in ways that would be impossible for us by our natural powers. As we shall see shortly, charity and the sanctifying grace from which it flows lead to an indwelling of the divine Persons and a mutual inherence between ourselves and them. It is, therefore, a kind of friendship (*QUAEDAM amicitia*) between ourselves and God (2–2.23.1).[11]

In saying this, Thomas extends the notion of friendship beyond that of Aristotle as well as beyond the natural friendship he spoke of earlier. Not every love includes the notion of friendship, he says, dismissing concupiscence-love for some object because friendship-love exists only when one "wishes well" (*benevolentia*) to another, that is, when we so love someone that we wish good to that person. "Yet even benevolence is not enough for friendship," Thomas adds, "since a certain mutual loving is required because a friend must be a friend to a friend" and since "such mutual benevolence is based on some communication" (2–2.23.1r).

Here Aquinas is daring: there IS "some" communication or sharing on our part with God since God communicates or shares the divine happiness or beatitude with us. This communication or sharing is the foundation for "a certain" friendship; for Thomas, St. Paul confirms this when he says that "God, who is faithful, has called us into the society of his Son" (1 Cor. 1:9). Charity, Aquinas concludes, is a love based on this sharing of God's own happiness (2–2.23.1r). This loving sharing fulfils the word of Christ at the Last Supper: "I shall no longer call you servants, but friends" (John 15:15; 2–2.23.sc).

How can there be conversation or sharing of life with God, one argument asks? By our spiritual life exercised through our higher faculties (the mind), answers Thomas. Already in this life "our conversation is in heaven," as Paul says to the Philippians (3:20)—a conversation with God and the angels. It is an imperfect conversation or sharing of life in the present but it will become perfect in heaven when we shall see God face to face (ibid. ad 1m).

Charity is thus a loving response and a vital sharing of life with God, who (to use Singer's terms) by divine gifts exercises the supreme "bestowal" on those who are divinely "appraised" as creatures freely accepting these gifts. Here Thomas gives few details about this mutual sharing of love between God and us, partly because he has already dwelt at length on the indwelling in us of the Persons of the Trinity and has discussed how this takes place. Earlier we heard him speak of the mutual inherence of friends who love mutually. At the close of his examination of the Trinity, Thomas concludes that the gifts of grace, living faith, and charity so fashion and dispose a person that the Father, Son, and Holy Spirit can and do become present to the person in the way that "a known reality is in the knower and a loved reality is in the lover" (1.43.3). Here we may recall the phenomenology of being-in that we met earlier. In this Trinitarian indwelling, the relationship is between God, the Lover, and the graced creature as the beloved, who by responding to the divine initiative becomes the lover of God, the Beloved.

This being-in or indwelling is not a material indwelling, but one proper to communication between spiritual beings. This spiritual communication is achieved by the most intimate relationships of knowledge and love, whereby the beloved is in the lover and the lover in the beloved. Thomas describes the human person as prepared by God's gifts so that the divine Persons may not only dwell in him or her as in a temple, but even that the human person may "have" or "possess" the Persons, that is, may be able freely to "use" and "enjoy" the divine Persons.[12] Although in this friendship God and the human person are not equals, for Aquinas this makes no difference so long as we are raised by the very gift of God to a level where we can communicate with God through intimate knowledge and love. Although God does not need our loving knowledge, God chooses to receive it and, for Aquinas, this is sufficient for union. In fact, there is no other way that a spiritual union can be established than by the highest acts of the mind. In this way, Aquinas says elsewhere, we most perfectly become images of the Trinity, that is, we express our knowledge of God in our mental "word" and issue forth in acts of love for God, acts of love derived from our mental "word." This procession of a conceptual word and love in us is inferior and yet analogous to the very procession of the Word and Love within God (1.93.8r). This is indeed friendship with and love for the divine Persons.

There would be much to say about the way in which, from this intimate love of charity toward God, there flows into the person an outgoing charitable love for others. This outgoing love consists of one's new "appraisal" of the worth of others because these others are seen as belonging to God, no matter how weak and even sinful they are; it involves as well a new "bestowal" because the love of God poured into the person spreads out to these others. The *agape* that is God's outpouring love becomes, to a lesser but real degree, the *agape* of the person who intimately communes with the infinite *agape* of God through charity, mutual knowledge and love, and mutual inherence. Somehow we are in God as God is in us: "They who abide in charity abide IN God and God IN them" (1 John 4:16). Thomas Aquinas will say that this contemplative union, achieved under the impetus of divine love, gives a delight surpassing every human delight (2–2.180.7r). Yet, he says, the charity that flows from God into the person impels him or her to serve others, to hand over the fruits of this delightful contemplative union through charitable service of others. Perfection finally consists not in the delights of contemplation but in love of God, in conforming oneself to God's good pleasure (2–2.184.1). The loving Trinitarian Friends—Father, Son, and Holy Spirit—urge the human friend to go out and spread their agape to others.[13]

3. REMARKS ABOUT IRVING SINGER ON AQUINAS

Here I should like to bring in a few observations about some points that Dr. Singer makes. In his brilliant and beautiful description of "Philia: Fellowship and Union," he refers to the Trinitarian origins of such fellowship and union, and rightly quotes Thomas as saying that there is no virtuous mean of charity. (Bernard of Clairvaux had likewise said: "The reason for loving God is God Himself; the measure of loving God is to love Him beyond measure.")[14] Dr. Singer spends considerable time examining the ways in which mystics speak about union with God, noting that they sometimes speak of it as happening either through loss of identity or through a very great closeness in which personal identity remains. But I think his questions and observations miss the mark when, after admitting that "their union may even be a fellowship based on reciprocity" and that "the relationship may poetically be called a spiritual marriage," Singer goes on to say: "But God would not be in us literally, or we in God." And in what follows he seems to look for a kind of mutual indwelling by knowledge and love that sounds very material or physical.[15] Aquinas would surely say that the knowledge and love by which persons mutually inhere in one another is their closest possible way of being in each other short of annihilation of one or the other partner. How else can there be union and mutual indwelling with God than by an experiential knowledge and love of God flowing from an intrinsic modification of the very being of the creature through grace—a share in God's own life? I fail to see the "dire difficulties" Dr. Singer speaks of. I wonder if he has not imposed a material metaphor of physical containment on the highest spiritual intercourse.

The same kind of material metaphor affects his otherwise excellent analysis of Aquinas' question whether our charity is the Holy Spirit or whether it is an intrinsic form, a created habit or quality that makes this charity our own.[16] He rightly sees in this discussion one of the fundamental points of divergence between Catholicism, with its transformationist notion of grace, and Lutheranism, with its *simul justus et peccator* (at the same time just and a sinner) and fear of mystical experience. But Dr. Singer lays too much stress on Aquinas' argument from human merit: although it is an important element in the Lutheran-Catholic discussion, it is not the central issue. More important to Aquinas, and distinctive of his position by contrast with Luther's, is the inner transformation of our being through grace, faith, hope, and charity— a sharing in the divine nature—such that, precisely, we can know, love, enjoy, and have converse with the Father, Son, and Holy Spirit already in this life.[17]

Dr. Singer argues that if the Holy Spirit instills a created human habit of love, the Holy Spirit would coerce the human subject and prevent any truly free human response of love.[18] This raises the whole question of the relationship between the causality of God or the Spirit and that of the human agent—between providence and human responsibility, if you will, or between God's gracious activity and human freedom.

Thomas has already anticipated Irving Singer's problem and has given his own answer. Precisely because the Father, Son, and Holy Spirit are so *infinitely,* immeasurably Being, Truth, and Loving-Goodness, they can and do allow created reality a full role in history. Although they wisely and lovingly guide this human role, it really belongs to the creature. For intellectual creatures this means real freedom and real, if relative, autonomy. How can God be the cause of everything (in this case how can the Holy Spirit cause the habit of charity) and yet we remain free? Thomas would identify the source of this puzzlement as a false imagination that we and God are in the same order of being and therefore cause in univocal ways. Rather, he maintains, our very freedom is created and sustained by the very INFINITE power and goodness of God. Utterly BEYOND our creaturely order of activity, allowing us to act freely as second causes or as instruments of the divine wisdom and will, God guides and empowers us without destroying our freedom. It is not as if God has trillions of trillions and trillions of ergs of energy and our free act takes away one erg from God's. No, infinitely transcendent, God causes, and we in our created order cause the one effect, God enabling us to be causes and to be free causes. Thomas treats this question frequently.[19]

Thus there is no coercion when the Holy Spirit modifies our very being, our intellect, and our will by grace, faith, and charity. Human freedom is present first in the very acceptance of this gift and thereafter in its use. A negative confirmation of this freedom is the fact that this gift can be rejected: there is the fact of sin, including the sin against the Holy Spirit.[20] The Holy Spirit's empowering yet freeing presence is well expressed in the way the Vulgate translation speaks of Wisdom: "She reaches strongly from one end of the earth to the other and disposes all things sweetly (*suaviter*)."[21]

St. John of the Cross, that great mystic of union with God, puts the same thought beautifully in his poem addressed to the Holy Spirit:

> Oh flame of love so living
> How *tenderly* you force
> To my soul's inmost core your fiery probe!
> Since now you've no misgiving,
> End it, pursue your course
> And for our *sweet* encounter tear the robe!
>
> O cautery most *tender*!
> O gash that is my guerdon!
> Oh *gentle* hand! O touch how *softly thrilling*!
> Eternal life you render,
> Raise of all debts the burden
> And change my death to life, even while killing.
>
> O lamps of fiery blaze
> To whose refulgent fuel

> The deepest caverns of my soul grow bright,
> Late blind with gloom and haze,
> But in this strange renewal
> Giving to the belov'd both *heat and light.*
>
> What *peace,* what love enwreathing,
> You conjure to my breast
> Which only you your dwelling place may call:
> While with *delicious breathings*
> In glory, grace, and *rest,*
> So *daintily* in love you make me fall![22]

Thomas Aquinas is less of a poet than John of the Cross, but he shows something of this fervor when he comments on the Psalm verse: "My heart has become like melting wax within my bowels." "Melting," he says,

> is also the fruit of love. Before something melts, it is hard and closed in on itself; if it melts, it is poured out and tends away from itself to another. When love comes, a person who was wrapped up in self now tends to another.
>
> This kind of melting can also be explained with reference to Christ as head, for this being melted is from the Holy Spirit and is in the midst of the bosom, that is, in the affections.[23]

The Holy Spirit, for Thomas as for John of the Cross, is the tender Lover who *appraises* us as fit objects of love by reason of our creaturely goodness and our graced condition, and *bestows* on us continual outpourings of divine love in order to dispose us for ever more intimate loving friendship and mutual inherence with the divine persons. Is not this the highest possible exemplification of the analysis of love that Irving Singer has graciously bestowed on us?

NOTES

1. It is in *Spiritualities of the Heart: Approaches to Personal Wholeness in Christian Tradition,* ed. Annice Callahan (New York/Mahwah, N.J.: Paulist Press, 1990), pp. 45–63.

2. See *Index thomisticus: Sancti Thomae Aquinas operum omnium indices et concordantiae,* Sectio II: *Concordantia prima,* 23 vols., ed. Roberto Busa (Stuttgart: Fromann-Holzboog, 1974–1975) s.vv.

3. All references to Thomas Aquinas will be to his *Summa Theologiae* unless otherwise indicated. For this work the divisions are as follows: 1 = *prima pars;* 1–2 = *prima pars secundae partis;* 2–2 = *secunda pars secundae partis;* 3 = *tertia pars.* The subdivisions are first into questions, then into articles within questions and finally

into arguments (1m, 2m, etc.), contrary arguments (sc), main response (r), and replies to arguments (ad 1, ad 2).

4. ". . . In useful and delightful friendship (*amicitia utilis et delectabilis*) a person does indeed want some good for a friend, and in this respect the notion of friendship is preserved. But because the person goes on to relate that good to his or her own delight and utility, it follows that useful and delightful friendship, to the extent it is led to become concupiscence-love, falls short of the notion of true friendship (*deficit a ratione verae amicitiae*). (1–2.26.4 ad 3). Cf. Aristotle, *Nicomachean Ethics* 8.3 (1156a6–21), where the philosopher says that useful and delightful friendship is "incidental" (*kata symbebêkos*).

5. "Another self" is from Aristotle, *Nicomachean Ethics* 9.4 (1166a31–32); the phrase "half of one's soul" (*dimidium animae suae*) is taken from Augustine, *Confessiones* 4.6 (CCL 27.45; PL 32.698), who quotes it from Horace, *Odes* IV.1 3, ed. T. E. Page (London: Macmillan, 1952).

6. In order to translate the texts with clarity, I follow Singer's example and use the masculine for the lover and the feminine for the beloved; these could, of course, be reversed, the lover being feminine and the beloved masculine. As we shall see, for the "mutual inherence" (*mutua inhaesio*) of two lovers, Thomas would require this reversal, the beloved becoming the lover and the lover becoming the beloved. Again, lover and beloved could both be masculine -or both be feminine since for Aquinas friendship is not limited to relations between a man and a woman.

7. See the text given above, n. 4.

8. The reference is to *Hypognosticon adversus Pelagianos et Caelestianos,* 3.4; PL 45:1623. This text is not Augustine's but rather a work written after 435, possibly by someone in the entourage of Prosper of Aquitaine: see *Clavis Patrum Latinorum* no. 381, 2nd ed., ed. Eligius Dekker (The Hague: M. Nijhoff, 1961), and *Patrologiae Latinae Supplementum,* ed. Adalbert Hamman, 2 (Paris, 1960), 1578. They base their statement on G. de Plinval's study, *Pélage: Sa vie, ses écrits et sa réforme* (Lausanne, 1941), p. 372, n. 1 and p. 371.

9. The text continues concerning supernatural love or charity: "Hence charity likewise has a certain special good as its proper object, namely, the goodness of divine beatitude, as has been said in article 4 of this question. Therefore, to the extent that some things are related to this good, they have the characteristic of being loveable out of charity."

10. See Peter Lombard, *Sententiae in IV libris distinctae,* I, dist. 17; 3rd ed., eds. PP. Collegii S. Bonaventurae Ad Claras Aquas (= Ignatius Brady), vol. 1 (Grottaferrata [Rome] 1971), pp. 141–52. For Thomas Aquinas' views see 1 *Sent.* 17.1.1; 2–2.23.2; *De caritate* 1).

11. The *quaedam* is noteworthy as a sign of what I like to call Aquinas' "mental genuflection" before the mystery of God when he is using a created analogy.

12. Answering an argument saying that if the gifts of grace, faith, and charity are the reason for the sending of a divine Person to a human person, the Person is not given, but only these created gifts, Thomas says: "Likewise, we are said to 'have' only that which we can freely use or enjoy. Now to have the power to enjoy a divine person is possible only through the working of sanctifying grace. And yet

in that very gift of sanctifying grace the Holy Spirit is 'had' and dwells in the human person. Hence the Holy Spirit itself is given and is sent" (1.43.3r).

13. See 182.1 ad 3; 182.2; 188.6; 3.40.1 ad 2; *De caritate* 11 ad 6; *De perfectione vitae spiritualis*, ch. 23; *Quodlibetum* 1.14 ad 2.

14. *De diligendo Deo*, ch. 1; in *S. Bernardi opera: Tractatus et opuscula*, eds. J. LeClercq and H. M. Rochais, vol. 3 (Rome, 1963), p. 119.

15. See *The Nature of Love*, vol. 1: *Plato to Luther*, 2nd ed. (Chicago and London: University of Chicago Press, 1984), pp. 227–28: "If God and man are separate spirits, they may conceivably love one another. Their union may even be a fellowship based on reciprocity. Assuming that it is purified of carnal ingredients, the relationship may poetically be called a spiritual marriage. But God would not be in us literally, or we in God. By analogy to human intercourse we may say that spirits enter into one another insofar as they communicate. I know your idea *because* there is something of you that has become a part of me. This language is figurative, however, and needs to be interpreted. Strictly speaking, we do not communicate because we become a part of one another, but vice versa. The idea that you articulate and I understand is not really a part of you that becomes a part of me."

Between purely figurative or metaphorical language and "literally" being in one another (or "part" of one becoming "part" of another) is the proper (and not metaphorical) ontological or metaphysical reality of union through knowledge and love without destruction of personality. Dr. Singer perhaps indicates a certain lack of appreciation of the significance of this level of reality to his problematic when he says (p. 228): "For my part, I have no desire to pry into the ontological bases of mystical union. It is religious attitudes that interest me, and the play of imagination within them."

16. See vol. 1, ch. 14: "Luther versus Caritas," especially pp. 320–23.

17. Thomas teaches, as will Luther, that "grace" is first of all the graciousness of God and that this is the source of all God's gifts (1–2.110.1r); he also teaches, as will Luther, that justification is had only by God's grace and a corresponding faith in us and not by any human merit (1–2.112–13). But he maintains, as Luther will not, that in justification God effects a real intrinsic transformation of the person through the gift of grace, which, he says, "is a certain sharing in the divine nature" ("*quaedam* participatio divinae naturae") (1–2.112.1r; cf. 1–2.110r, 1–2.113.2). He expressly rejects the notion that God's graciousness consists only in "acceptance" of a person or "non-imputation" of sin (1–2.110 ad 1, ad 3), insisting on the interior transformation of the person by the gift of grace flowing from God's graciousness.

Human merit, according to Thomas, is possible only *after* unmerited justification and only within the movement of divine grace flowing from God through Christ (1–2,114).

18. See pp. 322–23.

19. See *De veritate* 22.6,8,9; *Summa contra Gentiles* 3.88–91; *De malo* 3.3 and 6.1; *Summa Theologiae* 1.83.1 ad 3; 1.103.5 ad 2, ad 3; 1.105.4; 1.106.2; 1–2.9.6; 1–2.10.4.

20. See 2–2.14.1–6; 2 *Sent.* 43.1.1c.

21. Wis. 8:1 (Vulgate): "Attingit ergo [sapientia] a fine usque ad finem fortiter, et disponit omnia suaviter."

22. *Songs of the Soul in Intimate Communication and Union with the Love of God* (often called, from the first line, *Living Flame of Love*), in *St. John of the Cross: Poems,* Spanish texts with a translation by Roy Campbell (Harmondsworth, Middlesex: Penguin Books, 1960) p. 45.

23. *In Ps.* 21[22]:15; ad. Parma (1860, rpt. New York: Musurgia, 1949), vol. 14, p. 221.

7

The Marriage of Love and Reason

John R. A. Mayer

I. INTRODUCTION

When Professor Goicoechea first approached me to present a paper on the theme of Dr. Singer's monumental work, he specifically suggested that I should address the topic from the perspective of the section on the second volume of *The Nature of Love* titled "Puritans and Rationalists." Some months later when he came to inquire as to the title of my proposal, I suggested "The Courtship of Love and Reason"; he looked at me askance, and said: "Should you not title it 'The Marriage of Love and Reason'? After all, there is much more tension in a marriage than in courtship." So, I retitled my paper. In it I shall present you with the fruits of my own reflection on the seventeenth and eighteenth centuries, Dr. Singer's account of their attitudes about love, and the role of this section within the larger scope of Singer's intentions for the whole work, and some personal reactions. Nonetheless, the title is still misleading. There was nothing like an enduring marriage between love and reason in the period under consideration; tension there was, however, and a dalliance by reason with love. This dalliance bore such misbegotten notions as "intellectual love" to contrast with "physical love," or "bodily love," where the former was looked at with favor, and the latter repudiated as turbulent, mischievous, transient, and less than noble.

II. AN OVERVIEW OF DR. SINGER'S PURPOSE AND PERSPECTIVE FOR *THE NATURE OF LOVE*

It is perhaps a commonplace to say that words, simple nouns, seem to name a universal, which, however, has many particulars subsumed under it. These particulars, because they each can be designated by the noun, must have something in common. One commonsense way of attempting to pursue an understanding of what a word means is to look at the common features of its many designated particulars, and label these that essence of the particulars which enables them to be designated by their common "name," while the differences among the identically designable particulars would be relegated to their respective "accidental" characteristics. Ever since Plato, however, we have been made aware of the paradox that this cannot be the way of gaining the meaning of a misunderstood term, for if we were genuinely to claim not to know its meaning, we would be unable to select a set of appropriate particulars whose examination would constitute our so-called investigation. Although Plato makes a legitimate point, it is not uncommon to seek the essence of a notion by examining its commonly accepted exemplars to learn more about its nature. This is Dr. Singer's strategy in *The Nature of Love*.

Singer takes us on a rich voyage over Western cultural history, journeying through a diverse and heterogeneous set of attitudes toward love so that our sensibility may be better focused on the possibility of grasping its essence, if indeed there is one. His own suspicion is that instead of a single essence, we shall find a diversity of phenomena named by the same term, "love." His motto could be the transformation of the famous quotation from the Rig-Veda: "The Truth is one, the wise call it by many names" into "The Truth is many, the not-so-wise call it by the same name."

This should not surprise us, since ours is a pluralistic and relativistic age, in which Platonic essences have gone out of fashion. Wittgenstein has helped us to conceive of a substitute for "essence" with his concept of "family resemblance." In his analysis of the word "game," Wittgenstein has shown that if one makes a wide enough list of the exemplars of "game," there may be very few, perhaps no, common properties to all in terms of which each is a "game." Some games, such as solitaire, are very different from others, such as football. Rather, Wittgenstein suggests, a larger, more inclusive list of exemplars will disclose not a set of common properties shared by each and every member, but a kind of "family resemblance" which entitles different particulars with diverse specific characteristics to be subsumed under the term "game." And Singer is convinced that "love" is not different in this respect. In fact, the range of diversities subsumed by "love" is considerable.

I would like to argue that different nouns differ as to the range of contrasts that their subsumed particulars display. Let us contrast, for example, the word "rat" with the word "dog." We can imagine many rats, and these may indeed be individually different. One will be bigger, others, smaller; some may be gray, others brown or white. But rats are rats; and, at least from the common everyday perspective, more rather than less alike. Consider now the word "dog." As we think of what it designates, phenotypically very different particulars come to mind. A German shepherd is very different from a Dachshund, or a Lhasa Apso; a Great Dane is not like either a Mexican chihuahua or a Saint Bernard. Setter, terrier, poodle, collie, spaniel, Newfoundland, Labrador, Afghan, or greyhound. This species, unlike rats, is much harder to reduce to a single, simple grasp. A toy Pekingese and a Doberman pinscher, although both dogs, evoke altogether different associations, feelings, and concepts of functions. I think you will grant the contrast between "rat" and "dog" as nouns, as single names of many diverse particulars.

Now "love" is more like the word "dog" than the word "rat." It has had an interesting and highly contrasting range of exemplifications and associations. Irving Singer is quite aware of this diversity, and is committed to leaving it so. He is not about to "reduce" love to a singular "true" meaning after examining its diverse uses and the various attitudes that peoples, cultures, individuals, and eras have asserted or assumed about it. Rather, in his study Singer draws a variety of axes along which different loves might be ordered, and he will be cautious and reluctant to make any of these axes definitive, and any of their poles exemplary.

Singer's aim is instead to show the fascinating range of difference, of diversity as regards perspectives on different kinds of love. This does not mean to say that he has none of his own. As a matter of fact, he does; and he is, perhaps not surprisingly, a contemporary liberal American. In other words, he has a positive attitude toward physical, sensuous love; he does not want to separate it from either virtue or practical family life; he tries to integrate and harmonize spontaneity and "personal chemistry" with will, responsibility, and commitment; he will not dissuade the intensity and transiency of passion in favor of the value of the enduring, the eternal. Giving and receiving are both important, and yet benevolence needs to balance feeling and impulse, without gaining priority over these. In the larger sense, Singer is interested primarily in interpersonal love at the human, familial, and sexual level, without denying that there is friendship, religious devotion, and other forms of love. He is also clear that there are loveless sexual urges, as well as a sensual love that is not focused on coitus, the physical act of coupling. Thus his preference is to think of the ideal love as an integration of appraisal and bestowing, a striving toward being in love, in contrast with the turmoil and passivity of falling in love, or the comfort and mundaneness of staying in love, with its accompanying libidinal decay.

Given this attitude, Singer will tend to be critical of many alternatives that civilization has presented. Clearly, the will to suppress the physical aspect of love since love is deemed to be sin is a position that Singer will not be sympathetic to; nor does he show sympathy toward the idealization of suffering as the necessary consequence of love, as in the Romantic notion of *Liebestod*. But I must not ramble on about specifics in the total work, but confine my remaining remarks to Singer's treatment of the Puritans and the Rationalists. There is in this both a pure "description" and an implicit "evaluation." Every "description" has norms, in that one selects certain features for attention and ignores other manifestations that are contemporaneous with the exemplars discussed and which also characterize the period. The evaluation and criticism, on the other hand, is often left very *sotto voce,* indirect. Accordingly, Singer's appraisals are often merely inferred, guessed from the tenor of the text. If I have misrepresented him, I hope Dr. Singer will correct me.

So far we have introduced one of the couple, love, whose marriage with reason is the subject of our presentation.

III. REASON

Through a relatively long period of Western cultural history reason has been considered the chief distinguishing feature of the human, in contrast with other animals. It is our rational capacity, so it was claimed, which enables humans to understand the world, to make inferences, and to deduce warranted conclusions from argument. Coupled with this belief that reason is accessible to human beings is the belief that reality is constructed according to rational structures.

But in spite of such beliefs being traceable to Greek antiquity, rationalism does not characterize all of our intellectual history. In the Christian centuries revelation and its authority were generally deemed more important than reason, and the achievements of reason were adjudged according to whether or not these conformed to revelation, as transmitted through the authority of the Scriptures, the Church, and the Church Fathers.

There were also times when a direct intuition, a mystical rapture was considered the most appropriate way of obtaining truth. Mystics and seers were respected as those who could foretell and forewarn. Nostradamus (1503–1566), for example, was so revered, as was Swedenborg (1688–1772).

Rationalism has at least two distinct definitions. The narrower one is the belief that reason, unaided by experience, can arrive at truths. Such a narrow tradition believed that innate ideas were accessible through the inner light of reason, and, therefore, that by means of valid deductive inference a universally legitimate philosophy could be achieved. Descartes (1596–1650), Spinoza (1632–1677) and Leibniz (1646–1716) are the principal torchbearers of this tradition. A more diluted form of rationalism is the commitment to the belief that reality is fundamentally rational, and thus it is apprehensible by means of reason.

We shall argue that Puritanism, an English and American form of Protestantism, was rationalism in the domain of religion, since the Puritans "emphasized the point that a man could arrive at his own conclusions in religion, and opposed a national, coercive, and comprehensive church."[1] John Milton (1608–1674), is closely associated with the English Puritan tradition, in both its political and religious dimensions. He had explicitly written in favor of toleration of heterodox religious opinions such as Socinianism, Arminianism, and the like. Underlying such a plea is the commitment that the right use of reason will explicate the proper meaning of the Scriptures.

IV. THE PURITANS

One associates Puritanism with the rejection of pleasure. The Puritans linked sex and even sexual desire, let alone lustful activity, with sin and man's fall from grace. The Puritan asserts that the properly loving attitude toward God is one of turning away from the world, from beauty and pleasure toward a dour and uncompromising work ethic, conjoined with a hard and simple life, devoid of luxuries, frugal and disciplined. Human nature is deemed corrupt; natural urges and tendencies, misleading; and education is not so much the transmission of information and the empowerment of the natural to full attainment, as the breaking down, repression, and ultimately the total eradication of natural inclinations and urges. The Puritan accepted marriage as the means of procreation, but idealized the procreative act as one of duty rather than delight. The family was a unit, but one designed to provide the collaborative and interdependent prerequisite for each member to serve God unstintingly.

It would seem that the Puritans are at some opposite end of the spectrum from Singer's preferred perspective. This is not altogether correct. Inasmuch as the Puritans are Protestants, and protest even against the high church practices of the Church of England in favor of a more biblically based devotional tradition, they look well upon marriage. In this way they are the inheritors of the innovation championed by Luther, namely that a proper marriage can embody the ideal in which the man-God relationship is well concretized in the temporal world. What is missing with them is the positive valuation of the erotic-libidinal constituent of the marriage bed, which is in Singer's idealization a desirable and appropriate ingredient of the highest kind of love, and an important element of successful marriage.

The principal Puritan discussed by Singer is John Milton. In some sense

Milton is not quite the run-of-the-mill Puritan. In his great work, *Paradise Lost*, both Satan and Adam are presented in a way that cannot but resonate for the reader with sympathy and approval of their species of error and sinfulness.

How does Milton present Adam's fall, his disobedience with respect to not eating the forbidden fruit of the Tree of Knowledge? Not as weakness, being tempted by a seductive Eve to seek the consequences of eating of the fruit as promised by the Serpent. Nor as ambition, to gain God-like knowledge and power. Rather, Adam, realizing that Eve has already eaten of the forbidden fruit, chooses to identify his fate with hers and follows her disobedience to assure their common future. His love of his wife is hierarchically higher than his duty to obey God's edict. Therein lies the Fall as presented by Milton. That it is anything other than the Fall, Milton never suggests. But we, the readers, given our own ethical and religious perspective, tend to find that what constitutes the Fall also constitutes a strength of character, a species of courage and fidelity for which Adam should be praised, not punished.

V. THE RATIONALISTS

Singer presents the philosophical rationalists Descartes and Spinoza as offering a new image of love, a new conception of it. Inheritors of the Puritan disdain of desire, sentiment, lust, and cupidity, the Rationalists posit a new and contrasting love: "intellectual love." This is the exemplary, virtuous love appertaining to "Mind" or "Reason." The appetites of the body, lust, desire, and tumultuous feeling have nothing to do with this pure and worthy "love." Cartesian Dualism, the recognition of two distinct and independent substances, the *res cogitans* or mind, and the spatial, material *res extensa* permit one to separate rather completely the noble variety of love from its ignoble counterpoint.

Indeed, the worldly and cynical successors to these views could then proceed to separate the virtues of marriage from the pleasures of sex. A quiet, harmonious friendship should characterize marriage, while tempestuous and heightened feelings are to be associated with erotic love. It was frequently advised that it is foolish to marry one's mistress, and that an entirely different species of relationship is to separate marriage from those intense, deeply sensuous, and unstable liaisons between men and women that exist outside marriage. By contrast, marriage should be essentially a contract for stability, routine, permanence, and propagation, rather than what characterizes the amorous excesses that give both pleasure and pain to those smitten by sexual attraction to one other.

The words of David Hume are illustrative of the Rationalists period: "Whoever dreams of ecstasies beyond the honeymoon is a fool. Even romances themselves, with all their liberty of fiction, are obliged to drop their lovers the day of their marriage, and find it easier to support the passion for a dozen years under coldness, disdain, and difficulties, than a week under possession and security." Thus Hume advocates *friendship*, "a calm and sedate affection conducted by reason and cemented by habit, springing from long acquaintance and mutual obligations . . . without those feverish fits of heat and cold which cause such agreeable torment in the amorous passion," as fitting marriage.

The cynical Montesquieu also contrasts marriage and carnal knowledge, wittily suggesting that perhaps the reason why a husband ought never publicly speak of his wife is that he may talk of her before people who know her better than he does. Singer cites an eighteenth-century adage comparing a man who marries his mistress to one who first shits into his hat, and then places it on his head.

Thus we see that Rationalists distrust feelings, disvalue passions, even if they recognize that these can be a source of exquisite delight; and while they think of the marriage relationship positively, and can harmonize it with a proper God-man relationship, the price of this acceptance of marriage is its separation from the carnal, libidinal variety of love, so much more central to the late twentieth-century view of the ideal.

The Puritans and Rationalists still suffer, however, in different degree from that basic curse of the Christian heritage in which sex is either the symbol or the prime exemplar of sin and the fall from grace; therefore, they find it obligatory to reject and resent the joys, satisfactions, and ecstasies of the carnal, physical union, which is heightened when coupled with caring, respect, and admiration.

One cannot but exclaim on concluding reading this section of Singer's work, "You've come a long way, baby!"

NOTE

1. *The Columbia Encyclopedia,* 3rd ed., W. Bridgwater and S. Kurtz, eds. (New York and London, 1963), p. 1745.

8

Three Critiques of Schlegel's *Lucinde*

Robert L. Perkins

We are deeply indebted to Irving Singer for his life's work, *The Nature of Love*.[1] Such a comprehensive survey has many virtues, but it also has the vices of its virtues. Thus, I understand it as a guide to the literature and a point of departure for other investigations that will examine the details, fill in some gaps, and in some instances challenge Singer's interpretative judgments.

This paper will attempt to do all three. In order to fill in a gap, I must examine some of the details of Singer's presentation and challenge his interpretative judgment. I will look again at Friedrich von Schlegel's *Lucinde*[2] (1799) to determine whether it does indeed deserve Singer's placement in a chapter on "Benign Romanticism."[3] I shall first recount the import of *Lucinde* in Schlegel's own eyes and briefly mention some details of its contemporary reception. Second, I shall examine Friedrich Schleiermacher's evaluation of *Lucinde* in his *Vertraute Briefe über Friedrich Schlegels* Lucinde (*Intimate Letters concerning Friedrich Schlege's* Lucinde) (1800),[4] in order to try to understand Schliermacher's relation to Schlegel, his own book, and some of the tension in the Romantic movement. Then I shall review two subsequent literary and philosophic judgments of *Lucinde,* those of G. W. F. Hegel and Søren Kierkegaard. Finally, using this material I will evaluate Singer's treatment of *Lucinde.*

Singer, unfortunately, does not fully clarify what he means by the term "benign romanticism." The term apparently is used as a contrast to pessimistic romanticism, but the delineation of it as a concept is brief: "the benign or healthy-minded [romanticism is] a means of eliminating what is negative or destructive in oneself, thereby attaining on earth a maximum fullness of life."[5] This brief remark suggests, however, that the beloved is not at all an end in him/herself, but only a means of the lover's self improvement. Thus Singer's term, "benign romanticism," suggests that love is essentially egocentric and only in a secondary sense mutual or reciprocal. Singer's own characterization of the term suggests that "benign romanticism" may be just an exhilarating and enjoyable form of self-indulgence or self-improvement, at best, or a manipulation of the beloved for one's own benefit, at worst. Singer does not perceive this, I fear, obvious reading of his text.

The matter is made more pressing by Singer's understanding of "appraisal," that is, the act whereby "we assess his or her utility for the satisfaction of needs, desires, appetites, impulses, instinctual desires that affect us in every moment of our lives."[6] The injection of utility with its "hedonistic calculus" sounds crass to the ears of the lover for whom appraisal is more immediate than calculating, more intuitive and passionate than utilitarian, and more joyous than a mathematical problem.

However, more positively, but not entirely consistent with the above, Singer writes "benign romanticism" is "optimistic" in so far as "love [is] an ideal consummation that can be achieved, in one way or another and however imperfectly, within the lives of men and women." Singer contrasts this benign romanticism with a "pessimistic attitude that questions the nature and the likelihood of happy love between the sexes."[7] The examination that follows will raise the question whether Schlegel's *Lucinde* is not pessimistic in precisely this sense. It may well be that the interpretation in this paper fundamentally disagrees with Schlegel's intention, but, if so, Schlegel is not the first author who went wide of his intention and also misled an otherwise perceptive interpreter. With these reservations about Singer's term in mind, I shall turn now to my first task, the examination of Schlegel's own view of his intentions and recommendations.

FRIEDRICH SCHLEGEL'S *LUCINDE*

One cannot limit the critique of *Lucinde* to mere literary matters because Schlegel thought he was presenting a better psychology of the person than that prevalent in German idealism, a morality superior to that of the bourgeois and Christian, and a religion superior to the Christian. Since the book contains these polemics, it can justly be judged by criteria and arguments usually deployed in these areas.

Schlegel sets forth a view of persons which was, to say the least, controversial in the early nineteenth century. He recognized the figure of personal becoming and self-integration that had been a staple of Western cultural expressions since at least Augustine's *Confessions,* but Schlegel does something radically different with the image. For both Augustine and Schlegel the integration of life occurs when the issues of love are resolved. For Schlegel the issue of sexual relations is perhaps even more central to the unity of the person than for Augustine. Augustine, we recall, sublimates his sexual passion to the love of God. By contrast, Julius, Schlegel's hero, attempts to work out his sexual problems by passing from one woman to another, but he does not achieve personal unity until he meets and makes love to Lucinde. Till then he is "seduced by his own imagination" and "[i]n his imagination his whole existence was a mass of unrelated fragments. Each fragment was single and complete, and whatever else stood next to it in reality and was joined to it was a matter of indifference to him and might just as well have not existed at all" (*Lucinde,* 78). The issue for Schlegel is how to reconcile the flux and fragmentation of life with the need for personal unity. Without that unity, we are only fragments of persons lacking a complete human life. However, the relation to Lucinde enabled Julius to become a unified person for the first time, for as he recounted his life to her, "he saw his life as a connected whole" (*Lucinde,* 98), or at least as he so relates to her. Of course, it is a well-known technique of seducers to convince the newly selected recipient of his/her affections that the new relationship is qualitatively different from all that went before. Thus, one is justified in taking Julius's remark with a grain of salt.

One wonders, however, if this achievement of personal unity is permanent or only temporary. Schlegel suggests that this apparent achievement of personal unity is not the last word, for the person is ever changing. "Man's spirit is his own Proteus: it transforms itself and won't account for itself when it tries to come to grips with itself. In the deepest center of life, the creative will produces its magic" (*Lucinde,* 104). There is nothing to suggest that the unity Julius finds with Lucinde will last or that their liaison is permanent. The protean nature of the ego suggests, rather, that the liaison is impermanent. Lucinde is left with child-rearing responsibilities in the country while Julius, justified by his protean nature, goes on his way seeking another transformative liaison elsewhere.

This problem of human nature highlights the conceptual complexity, if not contradictory nature, of the romantic lifeview. The message of *Lucinde* is that there is one man for one woman, and one woman for one man. Nature has established a predestination of one for one, and not just any one, but only one. If one misses that predestined other, then love and life will be incomplete if not tragic. This pretty faith in the predestination of nature is in stark contrast to the romantic rejection of arranged marriages and the social and religious institution of marriage. It appears that the romantics have merely exchanged persons and institutions they do know for a nature that is unknown, at least in any ordinary sense of the verb "to know." There appears to be a complete mystification regarding nature among the romantics, for their views are based as much on emotion as on intellect and method.[8]

At the same time, neither Schlegel's Julius, Mozart's (or anyone else's) Don Juan, nor Kierkegaard's seducer remain satisfied with a single female for long. That Julius wishes to keep his options open is indicated by his scolding Lucinde for her jealousy (*Lucinde*, 72–74). Not only is Julius's devotion to Lucinde an enigma, she is herself also an enigma to the reader.

We cannot be certain that the person Julius writes about is as he describes her. Even in the most expressive moments, Lucinde seems only the creation and extension of Julius' own personality and will, for "he found full harmony only in Lucinde's soul—the soul in which the germs of everything magnificent and everything holy awaited only the sunlight of his spirit in order to unfold themselves into the most beautiful religion" (*Lucinde*, 103). Lucinde even acknowledges that she is only "the marvelous flower of [his] intellect" (*Lucinde*, 126). One can only wonder at the believability of a novelistic character who claims "I don't love you only, I love womankind itself" (*Lucinde*, 61). And we can also express only amazement at a Lucinde who did not run for her life on hearing these words. Julius, of course, "loves himself, Narcissus-like, in her."[9] Unfortunately, the unity of the ego achieved by the encounter with the image of Lucinde created by Julius' ego is also subject to the ego's transformative protean power. Thus neither the relation to Lucinde nor the personal unity founded in the relation is permanent, and as a result, the understanding of love in *Lucinde* is not the unifying passion that it superficially appears to be.[10]

Julius considered himself and his fellow travelers to be superior persons. Unencumbered by the virtue of humility, Julius characterized himself, and to a lesser extent his associates, as "beautiful souls" (*Lucinde*, 55–56). These beauties are set in contrast to the ordinary persons of the common life, the bourgeois and peasant, who work for a living. Julius also "loathed the faintest taint of bourgeois morality" (*Lucinde*, 79). He "disregarded the prejudices of society" (*Lucinde*, 79) and "made it a principle to despise them openly" (*Lucinde*, 87). Julius also claims that Lucinde "belonged to that part of mankind that doesn't inhabit the ordinary world but rather a world that [she] creates for [her]self. Only whatever she loved and respected in her heart had any true reality for her; everything else was spurious: and she knew what was valuable. Also she had renounced all ties and social rules daringly and decisively and lived a completely free and independent life" (*Lucinde*, 98).

Though Julius and Lucinde despise marriage in its bourgeois form, he and Lucinde do respect property rights, for they purchase an estate in the country (*Lucinde*, 108). They despise the city, but they also want to improve the countryside, to make it over into some idyllic utopia (*Lucinde*, 108). The economic basis of life is not accounted for in the novel. It is neither said nor suggested that Julius, whom we have incidentally learned was an artist, ever sold a painting. Thus, the novel displays no historical context, no society, no economic basis, and no political context. A feeling of historical and social unreality haunts the work. The section called "An Idyll of Idleness" praises sloth and demeans labor (*Lucinde*, 63–68).[11] One can only wonder how these beautiful souls sustain themselves. Thinking that they are above the ordinary lot of persons, the romantics, as portrayed in this novel, are actually parasites upon the bourgeois form of life.

Not only did the protagonists think themselves bearers of a superior morality, but Julius also regarded himself as the priest of a new religion (*Lucinde*, 61) and Lucinde as its priestess (*Lucinde*, 126). He specifically mocks elements of the Christian faith, the Virgin and the Incarnate Word. Julius refers to Lucinde as "eternally pure like the Holy Virgin of the Immaculate Conception," who "lacked only a child to make [her] a Madonna" (*Lucinde*, 110). Once Julius understands that he stands at the middle of existence, that the universe is "Julius-centric, " he thinks that he has "found the Word" (*Lucinde*, 102). Julius claims that Wit (intelligence) spoke from the heavens and said, "You are my beloved son in whom I find favor" (*Lucinde*, 62), a gross parody of Matt. 3:17, Mark 1:11, and Luke 3:22.

Indeed, the conception of religious experience and growth in the religion of love is striking. Julius finds his first real passion with a prostitute, Lisette (*Lucinde*, 81–88), and after her suicide and his subsequent numerous encounters with nameless women, he finds an even more consuming love and ecstacy with Lucinde. The sacrament of the new religion, Julius explains, is the sex act, and especially the sex act when the woman is on top and active and the man below and passive (*Lucinde*, 49). The unity of the sexual and the religious in Schlegel is clearly a repudiation of acceptable sexual mores of Germany at the time and a parody of "holy communion" in Christian worship.

Without pity or concern for weakness, pain, illness, and suffering, Julius claims that "health alone" is worthy of "being loved" (*Lucinde*, 57), a phrase with which no Nazi eugenicist would disagree. The anti-Christianity of Schlegel's views is apparent.

THE IMMEDIATE RECEPTION OF *LUCINDE*

It should come as no surprise that the contemporary reception of *Lucinde* was negative. Friedrich Schiller's comment about the novel to Goethe was typical of the literary reception among the giants of the classical age.[12] Schiller wrote to Goethe: "Furthermore this work should not be read through completely since the vapid prattle makes one much too ill. He allows himself everything and he himself declares that audacity is his goddess. This writing is the pinnacle of modern un-form and un-nature."[13] Among Schlegel's close friends in the Romantic circle in Berlin and Jena the reception was ambiguous. Schlegel's doctoral examination in 1800 was a frightful scene with critics of the novel restively objecting to the dissertation and attempting to humiliate the author of *Lucinde*.[14] Friedrich's brother, August Wilhelm Schlegel, wrote a sonnet about *Lucinde* suggesting that the sacred altar of love has its victim, "the noble ardor of the glorious Lucinde." Both Friedrich Wilhelm Joseph von Schelling and Henrich Steffens, whatever their public utterances, regarded the book as an *enfant terrible*.[15] The only member of the tight and mutually congratulatory little circle that took up the defense of *Lucinde* publicly was Schleiermacher.

SCHLEIERMACHER'S "DEFENSE" OF *LUCINDE*

This critical reading of *Lucinde* and brief references to the contemporary response indicate how difficult Schleiermacher's efforts were, for Schleiermacher is, at least officially, a Reformed pastor and as such must uphold the common life and traditional marriage. At the same time, as a Christian theologian, Schleiermacher must include love of the unhealthy and even one's enemy within his views of love. Schleiermacher must also express a theology of the Word understood as self-giving kenotic love rather than tasteless egotism. Schleiermacher's task is made all the more difficult because *Lucinde* was controversial even among its "cultured admirers." The sad truth is, however, that Schleiermacher did not discuss a single one of these issues. He does not object to the gargantuan egotism of Julius, the effete and elitist values in *Lucinde,* its anti-Christianity, the snide condescension toward the bourgeois of which Schlegel and the whole Romantic circle are a part, or the condescension toward the laboring classes upon which the Romantic circle is ultimately parasitic. He has no concern for the areas of existence characterized and discussed by Hegel under the general term *Sittlichkeit* (morality), the civil society and the state. Schleiermacher's ethics is as privatized and quietistic as Schlegel's.

Schleiermacher's response to *Lucinde* is more complex still. He found much in it with which he agreed and much that was contrary to his own instincts and thought. Given the notoriety and anti-Christianity of the book, one can only wonder why Schleiermacher spoke up at all.[16] However, his personal motivations do not concern us. Schleiermacher's *Briefe* is a collection of letters written by Schleiermacher and Elenore Grunow, who in all probability wrote the seventh letter and its appendix. The collaboration between Schleiermacher and Elenore Grunow is complex but need not detain us here.[17]

Schleiermacher's *Briefe* focuses on gender relations and love as these were discussed in the salons of Berlin in 1799 and 1800. In the *Briefe* Schleiermacher affirms the basic intent and success of Lucinde by saying, "Here in *Lucinde* one finds love complete and seamless, with the most sensual and the most spiritual side by side in the same work and in the same characters. Love is expressed most intimately in every expression and in every development."[18] Thus Schleiermacher apparently endorses some of the views of love set forth by Schlegel in *Lucinde*. The novel is, in Schleiermacher's eyes, an advance upon the view that there is an inherent conflict between the sensuous and the spiritual in love. The unity of love, both sensuous and spiritual, is the fundamental agreement between Schlegel and Schleiermacher, but how this works out in life is the source of their fundamental disagreement. In the following, I will attempt to show a few of the many differences between Schleiermacher and Schlegel. The *Briefe,* though a defense of *Lucinde,* is not an unqualified defense.

According to Schleiermacher, Schlegel attempted to overcome the sense of sexual conflict and female subordination so apparent in their society. He was not entirely successful, for he still accepted the idea that love was fundamentally vested in women who then taught men the art of love (*Lucinde,* 47). Continuing to emphasize a sexism of difference, Schlegel writes, "Now he recognized that love—a simple and indivisible emotion for a woman—can be for a man only an alternation and mixture of passion, friendship, and sensuality . . ." (*Lucinde,* 100–101). Still, when love is properly awakened, there is complete reciprocity and a sharing of male and female characteristics and roles in sexual communion (*Lucinde,* 49).

Schleiermacher, by contrast, emphasizes the reciprocal origin of love between man and woman. "Why should love," he writes, "be derived onesidedly from the other? Each love is cause and effect, for love is the return of love, and the reception of love is also a gift of love which will be returned."[19] Schleiermacher's discussion also includes the sensuous, but does not focus so sensationally upon it as did Schlegel in *Lucinde.*

Both Schlegel and Schleiermacher think that persons learn about love as a result of experience. Schlegel, however, apparently thinks that one should and will learn about love only through a series of sexual encounters with members of the opposite sex. Thus we see Julius going through a number of women before he meets Lucinde. His final preparation for the great love is the unrequited love for a friend's beloved (*Lucinde,* 90–96), but this abstention is the exception in his experience. Also, as noted above, the love of Lucinde is not the end of his journey.

Schleiermacher, by contrast, thinks that young people should have an opportunity to meet each other under the careful eye of parents and friends. In these open and free associations they can develop their understanding of themselves, the possibilities and necessities of love, and the variety of persons of the opposite sex. They can also sort out their feelings without commitments and consequences.[20] These meetings are open, public, and based on conversation. Schleiermacher idealizes the contemporary salon as experienced by fully mature adults and recommends that it be used, with appropriate modifications, as a model for the socialization of the young. The encounters are to be chaste, for even coquetry and flirtation would corrupt the free association.[21] Schleiermacher's views of sexual education are thus entirely different from those of Schlegel. That the above description and recommendation is an idealization of the activities of fully mature adults is evidenced by the fact that Schleiermacher regularly met and courted Elenore Grunow, the wife of another clergyman, in the salons of Berlin's upper class. They publicly confessed their love in the seventh and eighth letters of *Briefe*. To think, as Schleiermacher did, that the young can handle their passions and emotions better than mature adults can is, to say the least, unrealistic.

There is, however, realistic common sense offered in Schleiermacher's "Rational Catechism for Noble Ladies," which was inserted as fragment number 364 in *Athenaeum Fragments*. Although the tone would sound patronizing to us today, at the time the fragment was considered radical. Here Schleiermacher recommends that a woman should not create an ideal or hero to be the object of her love. Rather, she should love the person as he is (*Lucinde*, 220). The meeting with persons in an unthreatening and uncompromising atmosphere undoubtedly provides a better opportunity to find the one person whom nature has predestined for us than in the aimless but compulsive wandering and sexual athleticism described by Julius (*Lucinde*, 77-105) in which, as he confesses, his imagination has constantly misled him (*Lucinde*, 78). Indeed, Julius' imagination misleads him not only in love but also in friendship.

In *Lucinde*, Schlegel is not of one mind about friendship. He argues that women are not capable of being true friends, for they are too concentric and lack the capacity of seeing many sides of an issue. Further, women are entirely creatures of love and are incapable of disinterested conversation, while men are intellectual and capable of discursive thought (*Lucinde*, 24-25). Although Schlegel professedly does not mean to denigrate woman by this sexist view, he does nonetheless. He attempts to balance the scales by asserting the priority of love and passion in human beings. But he also relates that Lucinde is a friend, for "[t]here is everything in love: friendship, pleasant society, sensuality, and passion too (*Lucinde*, 76). thus it appears that friendship is possible between men and women, but only when they are lovers. Outside the love relation, a woman is not capable of friendship, for she is too much the creature of love to be a disinterested friend to either male or female. The libido of woman is such that it cannot be controlled.

Schleiermacher and Grunow disagree with Schlegel's characterization of woman: in her letter Grunow argues that as a result of a consuming love, a woman becomes capable of friendship with men (because she has no sexual motives) and women (because she no longer sees them as sexual competitors).[22] Love, then, for Schleiermacher and Grunow, empowers the person, man and woman, to become disinterested friends of members of the opposite sex, the very possibility of which Schlegel had denied for women.

Not only did Schlegel deny the full possibilities of friendship to women, he also had a different psychology of woman from Schleiermacher. Schlegel accepted and modified the view of woman, so widespread at the time, that she was essentially passive, vegetative. Yet at the same time he felt that "in the loveliest situation" woman became active and man passive. In the reversal of traditional sex roles, Schlegel found a "deeply meaningful allegory of the development of man and woman into a full and complete humanity" (*Lucinde,* 49). That is all well and good, but in the development of the novel, Lucinde is left with the role of child rearing in the country while Julius continues to travel and broaden his horizons. The novel fails as a complete picture of the equality of the sexes and the "complete humanity" Schlegel envisioned. Schleiermacher, on the other hand, is more successful in recommending "education" to reverse the miseducation women receive. In the above-mentioned "Rational Catechism" Schleiermacher sees education, not just a reversal of sex roles in bed, as the key to woman's equality and "universal humanity" for both man and woman (*Lucinde,* 220).

These all too brief observations about *Briefe* indicate that Schleiermacher was far from being an apologist for *Lucinde,* although there was much in it with which he agreed. His emendations have many of the same social and class biases that Schlegel had. Still, *Briefe* is an advance, for he better than Schlegel understood what the romantics called "infinite humanity" as inclusive of man and woman and the subtlety of the synthesis of spirit and sensuousness in a person. However, the tempest over *Lucinde* was not stilled by the efforts of Schleiermacher and Grunow. Let us turn now to some episodes in the subsequent history of *Lucinde.*

LUCINDE AFTER SCHLEIERMACHER: HEGEL AND KIERKEGAARD

Schlegel converted to Catholicism in 1808 (at the age of thirty) and did not reprint the novel in his collected works. Neither did Schleiermacher, for very different reasons, reprint *Briefe* in his lifetime. Still, the books continued to be discussed and read.

The most important philosophic criticism of both authors comes from Hegel, who in his *Philosophy of Right* (1821) comments:

Friedrich von Schlegel in his *Lucinde* and a follower of his in the *Briefe eines Ungennanten* [*Letters of an Unknown*] have put forward the view that the wedding ceremony is superfluous and a formality which might be discarded. Their reason is that love is, so they say, the substance of marriage and that the celebration therefore detracts from its worth. Surrender to sensual impulse is here represented as necessary to prove the freedom and inwardness of love—an argument not unknown to seducers.[23]

Hegel's critique is important, for Hegel took sexual relations up into the institution of marriage and placed marriage in an inclusive view of society and politics, a context neglected by Schlegel and Schleiermacher. For Hegel, persons cannot live and flourish outside the social institutions of marriage, civil society and the state. The marriage ceremony is important because it gives status and public expression to the deepest desires and drives of two persons to unite and not simply *be as* one but rather *be* one. "It is in the actual conclusion of a marriage, i.e., in the wedding that the essence of the tie is expressed and established beyond dispute as something ethical, raised above the contingency of feeling and private inclination."[24] Hegel recognizes, even urges, that the marriage ceremony must not be taken as a mere civil or religious requirement, for then the spiritual essence is lost, and the ceremony becomes alien to the marriage. Still, in marriage the self-consciousness of the two parties is expressed as one consciousness, and the mere physical caprice and bodily desires are transmuted. into the mutual recognition of an ethical bond. The passage bristles with critique of the romantic view of the marriage ceremony, for their view is founded upon an ironic appraisal of all social institutions.

Hegel's objections are not just to the humorous superficiality of the "arguments" of *Lucinde* about marriage but, more seriously, he objects to the philosophic import of the irony of the romantics and of *Lucinde* in particular. It is not at all queer to speak of the "arguments" of *Lucinde,* for it is, as Kierkegaard will emphasize, a doctrinaire book. Hegel writes that Schlegel considered irony to be the "principle of subjectivity knowing itself as supreme."[25] The result of such subjectivism or irony, rather than subjectivity, is that the person relates negatively to all social institutions, customs, and usages. The ironist denies the validity and authority of all such limits on his/her inclinations, whims, and desire (*eros*). To Hegel such a viewpoint is arbitrary, for it rejects the ethical institutions of the state, civil society, and family, the totality of which Hegel calls ethical life, *Sittlichkeit.* For Hegel, one cannot opt out of the ethical life, for all life is lived in its terms, even if persons wish to reject those conditions, or, as in ancient tragedy, the various duties come into mortal conflict.[26] Irony and the thought that one may as well ignore the marriage ceremony and the other forms of the ethical life is for Hegel parasitic on the very ethical substance of life that irony undercuts. Moreover, the neglect of the social norms of marriage leave the female and offspring at jeopardy in a world dominated by the sexual fantasies and urges of vagrant males. Public civil and sacred marriage secures the property and education of the children.[27] In his *Aesthetics,* Hegel criticizes the "moral depravity" that is made into "something sacred and of the highest excellence" in Schlegel's *Lucinde.*[28]

In his *Aesthetics,* Hegel does not develop his views of the literary merit of *Lucinde,* or lack thereof, by an aesthetic examination of the literary qualities of its plot, development, or characterization. In matters of literary taste, Hegel favors the classical drama and Shakespeare. In particular, Hegel had a lifelong love affair with Greek tragedy: it both formed the canons of his literary taste and suggested many nuances of his view of ethical life. Aesthetically, it is, no doubt, Hegel's love and understanding of ancient tragedy that causes him to see *Lucinde* as lightweight, frivolous, and obscene. Hegel ironically remarks about "those gentlemen who have had much to say about the 'poetry of poetry' " but whose prose was flat.[29] Hegel then rejects *Lucinde* for both aesthetic and social reasons.[30] Hegel's remarks suggested to Kierkegaard some of his most trenchant criticisms of *Lucinde.* Kierkegaard was urged on, however, by two other treatments of *Lucinde,* by Karl Gutzkow and Heinrich Heine, both of which suggested to him that Hegel's critique was basically correct.

When Karl Gutzkow republished *Lucinde* in 1835, the drama of its first reception was played out again, for he treated it as a defense of free love.[31] Heinrich Heine, in his essay on German romanticism, suggested that though the Virgin Mary may forgive the converted Schlegel for having written *Lucinde,* the muses would not. Kierkegaard followed shortly thereafter (1841) with his dissertation, *On the Concept of Irony with Continual Reference to Socrates,*[32] where he adopts many of Hegel's views of *Lucinde* (*Irony,* 286–301), although Kierkegaard's analysis is a more penetrating and detailed reading than Hegel's.

Kierkegaard makes four interrelated criticisms of *Lucinde.* First, it is *ironic;* that is, it is a hyperbole of the imagination that negates and loses touch with ordinary reality. Second, it is *unethical* for it undermines custom and usage, and licenses a seduction of spirit back into sensuality. Third, it is *irreligious,* for it recognizes no inward infinity. Fourth, and perhaps the unkindest cut of all from a romantic point of view, Kierkegaard urges that *Lucinde* is *unpoetic.* His debt to Hegel and his agreement with Heine are apparent. Although Kierkegaard grants a relative and limited validity to some of what Schlegel affirms about the sluggish and narrow philistinianism in modern marriage (*Irony,* 286–88), he still questions whether Schlegel's cure may not be worse than the disease. The complexity of Kierkegaard's dissertation is that he agrees with Hegel against Schlegel and romanticism, and at the same time agrees with Schlegel against the tame domesticity and docility of spirit in modern society.

The ironic character of *Lucinde* is the fundamental issue in Kierkegaard's criticism. Kierkegaard accepts Hegel's view of modern irony as subjectivism and as "infinite, absolute negativity." He supports this criticism by appeal to Schlegel's view of the imagination. Historical actuality is denied, and the radical freedom of the ironist to define reality and the environment for him/herself is claimed by and for all the "good guys" in *Lucinde*. Schlegel's irony is, then, destructive of the ethical life in Hegel's sense of the term.[33] Kierkegaard goes into vastly more detail in his aesthetic criticism of Schlegel than Hegel did, and nowhere does he better show how very closely he has read the basic Hegelian texts on modern society. Kierkegaard uses *Lucinde* to present what he perceived to be some of the pervasive flaws of modern society.

Claiming that *Lucinde* is a very doctrinaire book (*Irony*, 290), Kierkegaard says, following Hegel, that it is an attempt to suspend all ethics, because Schlegel considers all ethical distinctions to be "mere play" (*Irony*, 289). Kierkegaard adds, "What *Lucinde* attempts, then, is to *annul* all ethics—not only in the sense of custom and usage, but all the ethics that is the validity of spirit, the mastery of spirit over the flesh" (*Irony*, 290). There are two items here. The first is that Kierkegaard recognizes that there is some validity to custom and usage. In the free play of its imagination, romanticism arbitrarily and playfully smirks at long-established custom. Kierkegaard does not for one moment think that all custom is justified or serves well, but he does think that we need to discriminate between what serves well and what does not, and that distinction is not made in *Lucinde*. Schlegel has created a fairy land where, he claims, spirit and flesh are synthesized, but that country does not exist outside a novel. Kierkegaard thinks that Schlegel, in that narrow world, substitutes mere sensuality for the ordered forms of life, imperfect though they may be.

The second issue to be considered under the ethical critique is that Kierkegaard is squarely within the Platonic and Christian tradition that sees the flesh as opposed to spirit. For thinkers in these traditions, there is a series of serious interhuman problems that are envisioned under the contrast of spirit and flesh. For a proper understanding of this opposition it is important to emphasize that for Kierkegaard and the rest, flesh is an image for selfishness, pride, egotism, and sensuality. Again, sensuality is the corruption of sensuousness which is the natural condition of embodied creatures (*Irony*, 291-96) Like many modern thinkers, Schlegel and the romantics do not consider the moral plight of persons. Typically, for the romantics there is no moral issue at all, just a given actuality of desire and any moral concern must be abrogated should it stand in the way of fulfilling that desire. Given the abrogation of the ethical life and historic actuality, Schlegel thinks that the reconciliation of flesh and spirit will occur spontaneously by the active play of the imagination. Thus Schlegel is whimsical and unrealistic when he uses little Wilhelmine as the example of sensuousness (*Lucinde,* 50–53; *Irony,* 289–90). Schlegel seems not to have noticed that sensuousness is not present in a child as it is in an adult, for the child is not qualified by reflection and passion. The outcome of this exuberant but thoughtless view of the complexity of the human situation vis-à-vis one's own sensuousness and other humans, results in the triumph of flesh over spirit, sensuality.

Let us notice now a few of the details of *Lucinde* that Kierkegaard singles out for attention. The complete sensuality of the book is evident in that Lucinde and Julius have no other reality than the sensate, and Julius' greatest dream is to picture himself in an eternal embrace (*Lucinde,* 64; *Irony,* 291).The best-drawn character in the book, he thinks, is the prostitute, Lisette, who has given herself over entirely to sensuality and who as a result suffers such psychological dissociation that she refers to herself in the third person. Prostitution provides a good living by which she is able to practice an otherwise passive and idle life. The problem with this character, from Kierkegaard's point of view, is that Schlegel is not entirely clear about the point he wishes to make through Lisette (*Irony,* 294–96). The characterization of Lisette and other details that could be elicited emphasize the sensuality of the book. The fact that sensuality triumphs over spirit suggests also that the book is not only immoral but also irreligious, and for that reason also unpoetic.

Kierkegaard's third criticism of *Lucinde,* that it is irreligious, is narrowly developed here, but the issue is important for the development of the concept of inwardness or subjectivity in the remainder of the authorship. Because the third criticism and fourth, namely, that *Lucinde* is unpoetic, are so closely related I must summarily treat them together. I shall do this because Kierkegaard writes that the religious infinity is an internal infinity while the poetic infinity is external to the person. Along with this discussion of an inward and an external infinity, Kierkegaard contrasts two forms of "living poetically."

If the ideal is inward, then the person enjoys him/herself. To enjoy oneself is not to have an ideal based on one's relations to something or someone external, but to possess oneself in absolute clarity and infinite transparency (*Irony,* 298). This almost Socratic clarity and self-possession is for Kierkegaard, at this time, synonymous with the religious and will become central to his view of ethical and religious subjectivity.

Not only is *Lucinde* irreligious, Kierkegaard claims, it is also unpoetic. The issue here is more complex than matters of literary criticism. For Kierkegaard, as for the romantics, poetry is vastly important: poetry and poetics have much to do with how we live. However, in Kierkegaard and the romantics we have two competing accounts of poetry and "living poetically."[34] For the romantics, to live poetically is to live in the imagination, fantasy, and possibility. As Kierkegaard sees it, romantic poetry is "a kind of reconciliation, but not the true reconciliation" (*Irony,* 297) with our condition. Poetry does not reconcile us to the historical actuality by changing the lived world or ourselves. At best poetry infinitizes actuality, creating an ideal. However, the ideal may lead to enmity between the subject and the actual world. The characters in *Lucinde,* for instance, are lost in an ideal possibility because they reject historical actuality. The ironist posits a poetic infinity, but it is posited as external to the finite person. However, the person can also become alienated from the ideal he/she has posited because the person, alienated from historic actuality, is unhappy. This unhappiness can then cause the person to reject the ideal itself."[35]

However, if, as Kierkegaard says, the ideal is inward, then the person enjoys him/herself. To enjoy oneself is not to have an external ideal, or an ideal based on one's relations to something external, but to possess oneself in absolute clarity and infinite transparency. This is what it means, for Kierkegaard, to truly live poetically. To live poetically in absolute clarity and infinite transparency is possible only for a person who has an inward infinity.

Finally, Kierkegaard suggests, against Schlegel and every kind of poetic and philosophic condescension toward the ordinary person, the peasant and the powerless, that if living poetically is not possible for all persons, then life is a madhouse. If the possibility of living in absolute clarity and transparency about oneself is not a universal possibility, then despair "is the only alternative to one who is not demented" (*Irony,* 299). To rest transparently in oneself is not the privilege solely of the educated, the elite, or the poet, but is, rather, a possibility for everyone. Such transparency does not result from setting ideals beyond historic actuality and the common life, but by poetic penetration of the actual world. Kierkegaard suggests that it is only in historical actuality that any and all of us can live poetically in a religious sense or fail miserably in our lives.

Later Kierkegaard offers positive and constructive views of love and marriage in the writings of Judge William in *Either/Or* and *Stages on Life's Way* and a detailed analysis of Christian neighborly love in *Works of Love.* Both these viewpoints are critical of the aestheticism of Schlegel's *Lucinde,* though in the last book nothing so tawdry is mentioned. An exposition of the manner in which Kierkegaard handled the issues in those works must be the subject of a further study.

CONCLUSIONS

The three major critics of *Lucinde* share some fundamental agreements as well as significant differences. All three argue, though in very different ways and to different degrees, that there is a lack of ethical sense in *Lucinde.* Kierkegaard in his dissertation follows Hegel in his ethical critique of *Lucinde,* a critique that involves Hegel's whole view of modern society and the state. Schleiermacher urges that Schlegel, for all his good intent, is wrong about relations between the sexes and friendship. All regard Schlegel's views of sensuousness as in some way flawed, though Hegel thinks, probably mistakenly, that Schleiermacher shares the fault. Schleiermacher and Hegel take a nonreligious view of *Lucinde,* the former attempting to keep within the conceptual and aesthetic confines of romanticism and the latter simply extending his secular view of society and human relations. Only Kierkegaard's ethical critique, based in Hegel, ends in a religious understanding of poetry and the person. And only Schleiermacher discusses friendship, which illustrates not only Kierkegaard's dependence on Hegel but also the intensity with which human relations were discussed in the salons of Berlin and thought about within the context of classical philosophy and biblical study in Copenhagen. The author who presented the most sustained analysis of love in all its facets— eros, friendship, and neighborly love—is Kierkegaard.

Following this review, albeit all-too-brief, of three critics of Schlegel's *Lucinde,* one can only be surprised that Singer would think of it as "benign." Singer totally misses the destructive force of romantic irony for the subject and the subject's relations to others. Irony is destructive because, as used by Schlegel, it enables the person to escape from historical actuality into an imagined world of fantasy, possibility, and athletic sexuality. Unfortunately, that escape is into a deeper alienation than the social forms sometimes demand, for it is a self-created and self-imposed alienation. From Hegel's and Kierkegaard's point of view, *Lucinde* belongs in Singer's category of "pessimistic romanticism," though more subtly so than Schopenhauer and the others whom Singer discusses in that category.

NOTES

1. Irving Singer, *The Nature of Love,* 3 vols. (Chicago: University of Chicago Press, 1984, 1987).
2. Friedrich Schlegel, *Lucinde and the Fragments,* trans. Peter Firchow (Minneapolis: University of Minnesota Press, 1971). All references will be to this edition, indicated by the title *Lucinde* and the page number.
3. Singer, *The Nature of Love,* 2:383-93.
4. F. D. E. Schleiermacher, *Schriften aus der Berliner Zeit 1800-1802,* ed. Günter Meckenstock. Kritische Gesammtausgabe 1/3, ed. Hans-Joachim Birkner et al. (New York and Berlin: Walter de Gruyter, 1988), pp. 168-78. All references to *Vertraute Briefe* will be to this edition, identified in the text as *Briefe.*
5. Singer, *The Nature of Love,* 2:298.

6. Ibid., 3:390.

7. Ibid., 2:432.

8. Karl Luethi, *Feminismus und Romantik, Literatur und Leben, Neue Folge,* 26 (Vienna/Cologne, Graz: Hermann Böhlaus, 1985), p. 88. For a brief statement of the romantic view of nature see Marshall Brown, *The Shape of German Romanticism* (Ithaca: Cornell University Press, 1979), pp. 184–85. See also Oskar Walzel's classic, *German Romanticism,* trans. Alma Elise Lussky (New York: Capricorn Books, 1966 [first English edition, 1927]), pp. 51–56, 60–70, 224–47. Schlegel's ideas about mathematics are expressed well in *Ideas* (*Lucinde,* 238). Baader is praised for raising physics "to the level of intuiting poetry" (*Lucinde,* 250).

9. Firchow's comment in *Lucinde,* 24.

10. This interpretation is borne out by the drafts that Schlegel left of the remaining three volumes he proposed to write and which were not available to either Hegel or Kierkegaard. It cannot be determined if Schleiermacher had access to these drafts, brief though they be, or if so, when. See *Lucinde,* 131–40.

11. Schlegel takes up and makes silly, if not pernicious, Friedrich Schiller's ideas about the necessity of play for the complete development of humankind. No one ever made play more important, aesthetically and culturally, than Schiller, and no one ever made play so trivial and narrow as Schlegel. Friedrich Schiller, *On the Aesthetic Education of Man,* trans. Elizabeth M. Wilkinson and L. A. Willoughby (Oxford: Clarendon Press, 1967). Letters 14, 26, etc.

12. Singer mentions several reactions briefly. Singer, *The Nature of Love,* 2: 384.

13. Cited in Martin Redeker, *Schleiermacher: Life and Thought* tr. John Wallhauser (Philadelphia: Fortress Press, 1973), p. 65. No citation given.

14. George Brandes, *Main Currents in Nineteenth-Century Literature* (London: William Heineman Company; New York: The Macmillan Company: 1906), vol. 2, *The Romantic School in Germany,* p. 69. Brandes recreates for us the spirit of the times by tersely repeating many anecdotes and much gossip now mostly forgotten.

15. Cited in Brandes, *Romantic School,* p. 100.

16. Albert J. Blackwell has offered a careful study of the relations between Schleiermacher and his church administrator in "The Antagonistic Correspondence between Chaplain Sack and his Protégé Schleiermacher," *Harvard Theological Review* 74 (1981), 101–121. For the intellectual and philosophic background within which Schleiermacher wrote, see Richard B. Brandt, *The Philosophy of Schleiermacher* (New York: Harper and Brothers), pp. 42–71.

17. For a discussion of this collaboration, see Ruth Drucilla Richardson, "Toward a New Assessment of Schleiermacher's 1800 *Vertraute Briefe über Schlegels Lucinde* in *Papers of the Schleiermacher Seminar,* American Academy of Religion, 1989 Annual Meeting, pp. 59–73. My treatment of Schleiermacher in this section is dependent upon this essay, her dissertation, "Friedrich Schleiermacher's Weihnachtsfeier as Universal Poetry" (Drew University, 1985), p. 937, and her article, "Schleiermacher's 1800 "Versuch über die Schaamhaftigkeit": A contribution Toward a Truly Human Ethic," in *Schleiermacher in Context: Papers from the 1988 International Symposium on Schleiermacher at Herrnhut, The German Democratic Republic,* ed. Ruth Drucilla Richardson (Lewiston: Edwin Mellen Press, 1990), pp. 65–108. This last article is one of the most perceptive

on the *Frauenfrage,* or "woman question," in the eighteenth and nineteenth centuries. Two other major reviews and evaluations of *Briefe* are: Paul Kluckholn, *Die Auffasung der Liebe in der Literatur des 18. Jahrhunderts und in der deutsche Romantik* (Tübingen: Niemeyer, 1966), pp. 343–463. Wilhelm Dilthey, *Leben Schleiermachers* (Berlin: Walter de Gruyter & Company, 1970), 1:496–516. For a listing of shorter treatments see Richardson, *The Role of Women in the Life and Thought of the Early Schleiermacher 1768–1806* (Lewiston: The Edwin Mellen Press, 1991).

18. *Briefe,* 150. All translations are my own.

19. Ibid., 199. The translation is certainly not literal, but it is correct so far as meaning is concerned.

20. Ibid., 186.

21. Ibid., 188.

22. Ibid., 208–209, See Richardson, "Assessment," pp. 65–66 and "Schaamhaftig-keit," pp. 89–98.

23. G. W. F. Hegel, *Philosophy of Right,* trans. T. M. Knox (Oxford: Clarendon Press, 1958), p. 263 (an addition to paragraph 164). The additions to Hegel's text were inserted into the first posthumous edition of the text of 1833 from student notes at Hegel's lectures. Knox took the additions out of the main text and put them in an appendix. For an excellent recent interpretation of Hegel's view of sex and marriage, see Rudolf Siebert, "Hegel's Concept of Marriage and Family," in *Hegel's Social and Political Thought* (Hegel Society of America, The Papers Delivered at the Biennial Convention of 1976), ed. Donald Phillip Verene (Atlantic Highlands: Humanities Press, 1980), pp. 177–214. See also Robert L. Perkins, "The Family: Hegel and Kierkegaard's Judge William," *Hegel Jahrbuch* 1967, pp. 89–110. Recently David Farrell Krell has given a more critical reading of the basic texts in *Right* in his "Lucinde's Shame: Hegel, Sensuous Woman, and the Law," in *Hegel and Legal Theory,* ed. Drucilla Cornell, Michel Rosenfeld, and David Grey Carlson (New York: Routledge, 1991), pp. 287–300.

24. Hegel, *Right,* #164, p. 113.

25. Ibid., p. 102. See also Robert L. Perkins, "Hegel and Kierkegaard: Two Critics of Romantic Irony," *Review of National Literatures* 1 (1970): 232–54.

26. Ibid., pp. 114–15. See also his comments on *Antigone* in *Hegel's Aesthetics* tran. T. M. Knox (Oxford: Clarendon Press 1975), pp. 221, 464, 471, 564, 1163, 1213.

27. Ibid., pp. 116–22.

28. *Hegel's Aesthetics,* p. 508.

29. Ibid., p. 858.

30. The passage in which Hegel praises the brothers Schlegel is laced with sarcasm. He alludes to the "miserable philosophic ingredients" of their aesthetics. They also came "alongside" the philosophic idea, but "alongside" is a miss, and a miss is as good as a mile. See *Hegel's Aesthetics,* p. 63, for Hegel's irony against the ironists.

31. *Schleiermachers Vertraute Briefe über die Lucinde* mit einer Vorrede von Karl Gutzkow (Hamburg: Hoffmann und Campe, 1835). Reprint: Lewiston: Edwin Mellen Press, n.d.

32. Søren Kierkegaard, *The Concept of Irony with Continual Reference to*

166 Part Two: The History of the Question

Socrates, ed. and trans. Howard V. Hong and Edna H. Hong (Princeton: Princeton University Press, 1989), hereafter referred to in the text as *Irony,* with the page number.

33. Throughout this whole section on *Lucinde* Kierkegaard uses *Saedelighed,* the Danish equivalent of Hegel's *Sittlichkeit,* with all the distinctions to *Moralität* that Hegel intended.

34. For an elaboration see Sylvia Walsh, "Kierkegaard, Poet of the Religious," in *Kierkegaard on Art and Communication,* ed. George Pattison (London: Macmillan, 1992), pp. 1–22, *Living Poetically: Kierkegaard's Existential Aesthetic* (College Park: The Pennsylvania State University Press, 1994). See also Hans Dierkes, "Friedrich Schlegels *Lucinde*; Schleiermacher und Kierkegaard," *Deutsche Vierteljahrschrift für Literaturwissenschaft und Geistesgeschichte* 57 (1983): 431–49.

35. This analysis of the alienating power of the ideal appears to be an unconscious application of Hegel's phenomenology of the unhappy conscience on Kierkegaard's part.

9

Kierkegaard's Philosophy of Love

Sylvia Walsh Perkins

In the preface to the first edition of *The Nature of Love,* Irving Singer rightly observes that "in the last sixty years or so the analysis of love has been neglected more than almost any other subject in philosophy."[1] While his own three-volume study makes a major contribution toward remedying this deplorable situation, it is sometimes superficial in its treatment of philosophers selected for the study. This is especially true of the nineteenth-century Danish philosopher Søren Kierkegaard (1813–1855). Although Singer rightly notes that Kierkegaard "writes book after book about the nature of love" (Singer, 3:38), his thought receives only twelve pages of consideration in a chapter shared with and devoted mostly to Tolstoy and Nietzsche. In this paper I propose to rectify this imbalance and to reverse the priority Singer gives to Nietzsche, who wrote comparatively little about love, by providing a more thorough—though by no means comprehensive—analysis of Kierkegaard's philosophy of love. As a result I hope not only to demonstrate the importance of love in Kierkegaard's thought but also to secure his rightful place as a major thinker and perhaps the most significant modern Christian philosopher in the history of the philosophy of love.

As indicated in Singer's comment on Kierkegaard quoted above, love is a major theme in Kierkegaard's writings. It forms a central concern of the pseudonymous works *Either/Or, Repetition,* and *Stages on Life's Way* and is integral to other of Kierkegaard's writings. In the pseudonymous works one can discern several different philosophies of love being worked out consistently with the aesthetic, ethical, and religious lifeviews of the authors to whom Kierkegaard ascribes the writings. Although these contribute in important ways to the formation of Kierkegaard's philosophy of love, the views they set forth cannot be unequivocally identified as his own. For that we must turn to a later work, *Works of Love* (1847), a collection of Christian discourses published under Kierkegaard's own name and thus indisputably representing his own point of view. This work constitutes by far the most important treatment of love in Kierkegaard's thought. As I have claimed elsewhere, it is "perhaps the most deeply reflective of all Kierkegaard's writings and surely one of the most profound meditations on love ever written."[2] Unfortunately, however, Singer allots only two and a half pages to it, regarding it as one of Kierkegaard's "religious tracts that need not detain us long" and quickly concluding that the book is "too remote from human experience to be convincing" (Singer, 3:45, 48). That such an estimate constitutes a gross misjudgment of this work is one of the points I shall seek to establish in this paper. Concentrating on *Works of Love,* my analysis will center on the dialectical identification of Christian love and self-renunciation in Kierkegaard's thought, with its consequent implications concerning the relation between human love and divine love, self-love and self-renunciation, neighborly love and erotic love and friendship, and finally love and suffering.

LOVE AND SELF-RENUNCIATION

Kierkegaard was first and foremost a Christian thinker, and thus in his philosophy of love he sought primarily to clarify the nature of Christian love. In *Works of Love* Kierkegaard understands Christian love in a traditional manner as involving love of God, one's fellow human beings, and even oneself, but as he sees it, Christian love must be distinguished from a merely human conception of love and understood in terms of its dialectical expression in self-renunciation. The dialectical relation between Christian love and self-renunciation is such that the first is not possible without the second, for Christian love *is* self-renouncing love.[3] Part of the problem Kierkegaard wishes to address in *Works of Love* consists in his belief that Christian love and self-renunciation have been confused with and subsumed under purely natural, pagan, universal-human and worldly conceptions of love and self-renunciation. A common error, he points out, is to regard Christian love as the highest expression of human love. Kierkegaard agrees that Christian love is the highest form of love, but in his view it is not the highest in direct continuity with purely human forms or expressions of love. Rather, Christian love is qualitatively different from, even the opposite of, merely human love and is distinguished by being placed against, not on, the comparative scale with natural, pagan, purely human and worldly expressions of love (WL, 122–23). Far from being the highest expression of merely human love, it constitutes an offense to that understanding (WL, 70–11). Natural or merely human forms of love consist in immediate, spontaneous feelings or inclinations toward others such as erotic love and friendship. Christian love, too, is a passion that is grounded in inwardness, but one that seeks expression as action rather than as mere feeling. Christian love is what it does, i.e., it is a passion or form of inwardness that reduplicates itself inversely in outwardness and thus is known by its fruits, the works of love.[4] Although works do not provide any direct or unconditional demonstration of love, they at least indicate indirectly the presence of love. Still, one must believe, for one cannot know, that such works are expressions of love. Belief in love is possible, Kierkegaard thinks, only when one is a loving person oneself (WL, 33). By abiding in love one is able to recognize love in others, and one's own love becomes recognizable in the same manner. The important task, however, is not to seek recognition but simply to produce the fruits that manifest love, which make it knowable even if it cannot be unequivocally known.

Christian love is also distinguished from natural, human, and pagan forms of love by the fact that it is eternal, whereas these other forms of love are essentially transient, perishable, and subject to change even if change does not occur. For this reason temporal forms of love are always uncertain and require continual reaffirmation of their existence between lovers. Christian love, by contrast, is love that has won not merely continuance (*Bestaaen*) without change but continuity (*Bestandighed*) and security through endurance amid change (WL, 46). Continuity is gained by love's having undergone the transformation of the eternal so as to become consciously grounded in the eternal through the Christian command to love. Christian love is thus a passion that is no longer simply immediate or spontaneous but one that has become a matter of conscience and duty.[5] When love is a duty it is forever decided that one shall love and that love shall abide.[6]

The qualitative heterogeneity of Christian love from merely human or pagan forms of love is most evident in the latter's view of what constitutes genuine love and self-love. As Kierkegaard understands it, paganism rejects self-love in favor of erotic love and friendship, which are regarded as genuine expressions of love inasmuch as they are passionate preferences for other persons (WL, 65–66). In his view, however, even erotic love and friendship are secretly forms of self-love. He points out that even when pagan love devotes itself to another and admires that person the relationship has the effect of turning back to the lover's advantage, for just as the loved one is the lover's object of admiration, so the lover forms the beloved's object of admiration in return (WL, 67). To relate oneself to others in such a way as to expect or require reciprocity in love and to make demands upon them, to use them or try to get something from them, Kierkegaard contends, is really self-love.

In Kierkegaard's view, then, it is the selfishness in erotic love and friendship, not the immediacy or spontaneity as such, that Christianity directly opposes and excludes (WL, 65). Christianity presupposes that persons naturally love themselves. It thus sets out to do away with selfish self-love, using natural self-love in such a way as to rid it of selfishness by requiring that one love one's neighbor as oneself. Selfish self-love is mastered by reduplication, that is, by the duplication of oneself in the other as neighbor. Erotic love and friendship also involve reduplication, Kierkegaard admits, but quite differently from what takes place in Christian reduplication. For in erotic love and friendship duplication of oneself in the other means that the beloved becomes one's "other-I" (WL, 66–69). It is not really the other person who is loved but oneself as projected into and benefiting from the relation. Erotic love and friendship culminate in two becoming one in the creation of "a new selfish self" (WL, 68). In contrast to this, Christian reduplication involves reduplication of oneself in the neighbor in such a way as to transform love for oneself into love for the other. Every demand in the relationship is placed upon oneself rather than upon the other, and one desires for the other what one would have desired for oneself. In Christianity, therefore, one regards the other not as an "other-I" but as a genuine "other-you" who is distinct from oneself and who is loved first and foremost not on the basis of preferential love but because that person is a human being like oneself.[7]

In Christian reduplication, therefore, one renounces oneself, or more accurately, one renounces self-love in the form of selfishness or egocentricity in oneself by loving others as oneself. Only Christian reduplication is real duplication, Kierkegaard's claims, for selfish self-love cannot abide two, and even in its projection to the other it essentially maintains a single concern for itself (WL, 37–38, 69). The "as yourself" in the Christian command, however, implies two, that there is another whom one loves just as one loves oneself. At the same time it also implies that self-renunciation in Christian love does not entail a total renunciation of oneself but only a renunciation of selfishness. Christian reduplication, in fact, produces a proper form of self-love. As Kierkegaard understands it, Christianity is not opposed to love of self *per se* but only demands that one love oneself in the right way, that is, in a way that does not, for example, squander one's time and energy in vain or frivolous activities or give in to despair and self-destruction (WL, 35, 39). If one cannot do this, then neither can one love one's neighbor. Kierkegaard explains:

> To love oneself in the right way and to love one's neighbor correspond per-
> fectly to one another; fundamentally they are one and the same. When the
> law's *as yourself* has wrested from you the self-love which Christianity sadly
> enough must presuppose to be in every man, then and then only have you

learned how to love yourself. The law is, therefore: you shall love yourself in the same way as you love your neighbor when you love him as yourself. (WL, 39)

In Kierkegaard's view, Christianity also preserves erotic love and friendship, but the requirement is that we must express neighborly or spiritual love within and in addition to these relations. To love only selectively and to call this "loving one's neighbor" is to make Platonic and erotic special relations the highest and to confuse them with Christian love. First and foremost one must love all persons as neighbors. For Kierkegaard the category of neighbor is equivalent to that of human being, which is the fundamental qualification of every individual (WL, 142). The Christian rule, according to Kierkegaard, is that "what is eternally basic must also be the basis of every expression of what is special" (WL, 141). Being a friend, beloved, or spouse is a "narrower definition" of one's position in a special relation (WL, 142). Every special relation must be informed by the broader conception of the other party as a neighbor. Thus, while one certainly loves one's mate differently from the way one loves others, the difference is not essential, since fundamentally one loves one's mate as one loves others, that is, as a human being or as a neighbor (WL, 142). If one does not love one's spouse, beloved, or friends as a neighbor, then one does not love one's neighbor. For to love one's neighbor, as Kierkegaard understands it, is to love all persons without exception and to love them first and foremost as human beings, which we all are equally. A person's particularity or distinguishing characteristics are secondary and cannot serve as a basis for making that individual an exception to the Christian command of neighborly love (WL, 142).

As Kierkegaard sees it, therefore, the Christian task is first of all to love all persons on the basis of our common humanity without making any distinctions between them. This means that one must learn, as it were, to "shut one's eyes" to the differences between persons, to become "blind" to them and to "look away" from them (WL, 79, 80). Christianity does not literally do away with distinctions but seeks instead to make us victorious over the temptation of distinctions by teaching us to lift ourselves above them (WL, 81, 83). Nor does it attempt to reduce everything to one distinction as does "well-intended secular striving," Kierkegaard claims (WL, 82). In his view, earthly likeness (*Lighed*), or the establishment of one social condition or class for all, is not the same as Christian equality (*Ligelighed*) (WL, 82). Christianity "allows all distinctions to stand," he argues, "but it teaches the equality of the eternal" and locates the decisive change in the way one views distinctions (WL, 82–83). For the Christian, distinctions between persons begin to "hang loosely," enabling that which is common to all persons, their essential humanity, their "eternal likeness," to show through (WL, 96). Then, while making no distinction between those whom one will love, one must at the same time make infinite distinctions between them. That is, one must love each according to his or her own individuality or personal differences (WL, 252–53). For Kierkegaard this consists primarily in helping persons become authentic selves or individuals by enabling them to become independent and stand on their own as individual selves before God. This is, Kierkegaard says, "the greatest, the only benefaction one man can accomplish for another" (WL, 258–59).

GOD AS THE OBJECT OF LOVE
IN CHRISTIAN TRANSFORMATION

Central to the possibility of Christian love or self-renunciation is the requirement that one allow the God relation to penetrate and become a middle term in every love relation. In Kierkegaard's view, Christianity recognizes only one kind of love—spiritual love—and insists that this "lie at the base of and be present in every other expression of love" (WL, 144, 146). Before God the lover learns what it means properly to love oneself, to love the beloved, and to be loved in return. Earlier in *Works of Love* we have seen that Kierkegaard defines proper self-love as love for self that excludes selfishness. Later on he further qualifies this definition by adding that the "true idea" of what it is to love oneself is to love God (WL, 113). In Kierkegaard's view God is the only proper object of love. This does not mean that one should become occupied solely with love of God or that the love of others is effaced by one's individual relation to God. On the contrary, as Kierkegaard understands it, the true conception of what it means to love another person is to help that person to love God, and, vice versa, to be loved means to be helped by another human being to love God. Since, in Kierkegaard's view, "love is God" and "God is love" (WL, 27, 74, 124, 335), this means that the true object of every genuine love relationship is love itself. Christianity seeks to transform every love relation into sacrificial love, that is, to help each party learn to love rather than seek to be loved in and through their relation. Christian transformation consists finally in being made wholly into an active power in the service of God or love, of becoming dedicated to the well-being of others rather than to one's own self-elevation and promotion in the world.

In Kierkegaard's view, this is how Christianity proposes to spiritually qualify and transform erotic love and friendship. It does not seek the discontinuation or modification of special relationships, but rather desires to inform all human relationships with a third dimension by making God or the neighbor a middle term in them.[8] In his view, all human love is fundamentally grounded in divine love and contains the possibility of manifesting that love by consciously centering personal relations in God, thereby bringing about a transformation of love. This change which Christianity brings about in love relations is internal rather than external in form. Externally everything remains the same, but it has been inwardly purified, sanctified, and made new (WL, 145). This is the paradox of Christian transformation, that love is the same yet infinitely different, old yet marvelously new. Christianity seeks to change all forms of love into spiritual love, but it allows the outward distinctions between these forms to persist, simply requiring "the transformation of infinity" to take place in them (WL, 139). Christian transformation, then, is a transformation of one's former mode of existence in the world. Christianity does not require one to cut oneself off from one's former relationships and flee the world but rather to express Christian love in the context of one's ongoing relationships in the world. In Kierkegaard's view, Christianity's goal is to bind the temporal and the eternal, to make the temporal a reflection of the eternal, not to negate or exclude it (WL, 24, 96).[9]

This ethic of transformation has the effect of significantly qualifying the Christian dialectic in relation to the immediate, natural, pagan, worldly, and merely human conceptions of love. While Christianity stands uncompromisingly opposed to these conceptions in their unqualified selfish forms, the intent of the dialectic points beyond mere differentiation and opposition to an eventual or ultimate union of the natural and the spiritual, the temporal and the eternal, the human and the Christian through the transforming power of self-renouncing love. Unlike some analyses of love that distinguish between various forms of love such as *eros, philia,* and *agape* (e.g., Nygren, C. S. Lewis, Tillich, and Singer), and in certain perspectives, most notably Nygren's, which regard eros and agape as unalterably opposed to one another, Kierkegaard recognizes only one genuine form of love, which is spiritual or Christian love.[10] In his view, spiritual love is not separate from or higher than natural forms of love such as erotic love and friendship, but rather an altruism or concern for others that comes to expression precisely in and through those forms of love when the element of selfishness has been eradicated from them (WL, 59, 70).

LOVE AND SUFFERING

Finally, an account of Kierkegaard's philosophy of love would not be true or complete without some consideration of the element of suffering in Christian love. In his view Christian love always involves "double danger" and the possibility of offense on the part of others as well as oneself, inasmuch as it involves a different conception of love than is normally held. Serious consequences may result from the attempt to mediate one's temporal relationships with Christian love. Thus the possibility of suffering is always present in love and becomes, in Kierkegaard's later thought, the inverse sign of love by which it becomes indirectly recognizable in the external world. Although reciprocity in love would seem to be an ideal in human love, spiritual love, Kierkegaard claims, does not depend on it and may even express itself in ways that could appear to the other as hatred rather than love. This is just the point where outright collision between the divine conception and the merely human conception of love develops, and where Christian love must be expressed and made recognizable through a second form of self-renunciation. If to love another person means essentially to help that person love God, the extreme implication of this is that if only one party in the relation understands this, then that person may need, as it were, to hate the beloved out of love, even break off the relationship so as not to permit the beloved to reciprocate love as if one were God or meant everything to the beloved. In the context of love, this is what Kierkegaard understands by Christ's teaching that the Christian shall, if necessary, hate father and mother and loved ones. Christianly understood, such an extreme action is not really hate—Kierkegaard says "such atrociousness is far from Christianity"—but it would be regarded as such by others (WL, 114).[11] From the world's point of view, to call such an act the expression of love and to sacrifice one's own happiness and that of the beloved is sheer madness. Thus the double inversion develops, namely that precisely what Christianity regards as the ultimate expression of love is looked on by the world as self-love and unkindness, while conversely what the world regards as genuine love Christianity considers to be the expression of self-love. There is, then, an infinite difference between the divine and human conceptions of love. What the world understands and approves as sacrificial love is, Kierkegaard claims, a kind of personal sacrifice of a portion of one's selfishness for the sake of the community (WL, 123). As he sees it, however, this is nothing more than the subordination of personal selfishness to a larger group-selfishness, and does not constitute true sacrifice because it seeks and has as its reward the approval of society. In Kierkegaard's view, true sacrifice has no reward, or rather, it has as its reward precisely the opposite of what could be expected through the performance of sacrifice. For the Christian discovers that as a reward for love one is sometimes hated by the beloved and abominated by the world. But voluntary submission to being hated and scorned in return for love is precisely the decisive distinction of Christian love and the "double mark" of self-renunciation (WL, 189). The Christian not only expects opposition from the world but "knows in advance that this will happen and chooses it freely" (WL, 188). In the purely human expression of self-renunciation one gives up one's own selfish desires, longings, and plans, but with the expectation that for doing so one will become appreciated, honored, and loved by the world (WL, 188). In *Judge for Yourselves!* Kierkegaard cites as an example of this the medieval practice of self-denial in which men were accorded worldly esteem for their acts of sacrifice.[12] The Christian concept of self-renunciation, by contrast, is to give up one's selfish desires, longings, and plans in order to work disinterestedly for the good and then, further, to submit by free choice to being abominated, scorned, ridiculed, and perhaps even executed, for this action (WL, 188). From the world's point of view, however, to be willing to be forsaken and treated in this way is stupid and insane. It hardly warrants admiration and approval.

Thus Kierkegaard cautions: "if your ultimate and highest purpose is to have life easy and sociable, then never have anything to do with Christianity. Flee from it, for it will do the very opposite: it will make your life difficult and do this precisely by making you alone before God" (WL, 127). He even advises ministers of the gospel that they should be prepared to preach against Christianity, if need be, so as to warn people of the dangers to expect in becoming a Christian instead of enticing them to Christianity by a fraudulent depiction of the Christian life (WL, 190–91). Christianity, Kierkegaard thinks, should not be directly recommended to people; on the contrary, sermons should open with the possibility of offense contained in Christian existence (WL, 191). The common practice in the preaching of Christian love, however, is to leave out the added danger that if one ventures to express such love in one's relations to others it will go hard for one in the world (WL, 185). In Kierkegaard's estimation such a presentation of Christian existence is deceptive and false. Opposition between Christianity and the world is essential, not accidental (WL, 187). If one ventures to express Christian love unconditionally in one's relations to others, then opposition from the world will surely result, since the Christian and worldly concepts of love are converse and qualitatively heterogeneous. Thus Kierkegaard says that the Christian who gets through life without any opposition should be suspicious of himself (WL, 187). One must at least expect and be willing to accept opposition, not enter upon the Christian life with the thought of avoiding it and leading a happy life as a consequence of one's decision. The earnest Christian does not seek to avoid danger but willingly chooses it. A Christian does not seek worldly happiness in Christianity but conversely chooses to become unhappy—doubly unhappy—by constraining self-love and then, as a reward for not acting like the crowd, by reaping the world's ridicule, hatred, and scorn (WL, 196).

Kierkegaard's definition of Christian love and self-renunciation in terms of double danger thus has the effect of significantly qualifying his understanding of love. The Christian conception of love posits an ethical task, making it a duty to love and to make every sacrifice in order to help others become loving persons too. Whereas the worldly person's aim is to have life made easy and happy, Christianity makes life difficult, dangerous, and unhappy. At the same time, however, in coming to love God and neighbor, one finds true meaning in life and truly lives. In the conclusion of *Works of Love* Kierkegaard imagines the beloved apostle John as saying:

> "the commandment is that you *shall* love, but when you understand life and yourself, then it is as if you should not need to be commanded, because to love human beings is still the only thing worth living for; without this love you really do not live; to love human beings is also the only salutary consolation for both time and eternity, and to love human beings is the only true sign that you are a Christian"—truly, a profession of faith is not enough. (WL, 344).

CONCLUSIONS

It is this strong conviction of the ultimacy of love in the form of spiritual or Christian love for God and other human beings, I would contend, that makes Kierkegaard's philosophy of love so deeply profound and so eminently important for the construction of a modern as well as a postmodern theory of love.[13] To be sure, Kierkegaard presents an idealization of love that is extremely high and uncompromising, perhaps to an unbearable degree for most human beings, but it is tempered by an equally strong doctrine of grace and forgiveness in the realization that no human being other than Jesus Christ— who in Kierkegaard's view is not merely human but the God-man—can express the Christian life of love fully and boundlessly. That does not exempt us, however, from assuming the ethical task of striving to fulfill it. In the definition of this task Kierkegaard delineates a perspective that tackles the age-old problem of selfishness or narcissism in a way that exposes its presence even in those expressions of erotic love and friendship where it is presumably overcome.

Although Kierkegaard does not discuss the issue of sexuality in relation to love as directly or centrally as we might wish in *Works of Love,* certainly there are profound implications in his thought for the expression of sexuality in love and vice versa. For as we have seen, Kierkegaard does not reject sensuousness in favor of a noncorporeal expression of spiritual love but rather seeks to transform the expression of sensuousness or erotic desire in human relations so as to eradicate the element of selfishness in them. In contrast to Irving Singer, who concludes in his own attempt to formulate a modern theory of love that appraisive love—that is, love of others on the basis of their appraised value or utility in relation to our own interests or needs— is a crucial ingredient of love" (Singer, 3:396), Kierkegaard believes in the possibility of human self-transformation via a relation to the eternal that does away with selfishness or self-centeredness while preserving individual self-identity and an authentic form of self-love. Like Singer, he rejects any notion of a "shared identity" or communal "ours," which in Kierkegaard's view constitutes only an augmented form of self-love (WL, 249; cf. Singer, 3:406–417). But unlike Singer, who rejects any form of transcendentalism in favor of a naturalistic account of love, Kierkegaard views human love in the context of the divine, which for him constitutes the only true object of love. One of the chief criticisms Singer brings against both Platonic and Christian concepts of love in the first volume of his trilogy on love is that they advocate a transcendent idealization of love in the Good (Plato) or in God (Christianity) as the object of human love, with the consequence that love of persons is either neglected or used merely instrumentally as a means to this higher end (Singer 1:84, 343–63). Assuming that this criticism is justified in the cases of Augustine, Aquinas, and Luther, the three giants of Christian thought against whom Singer principally makes this charge (and that is certainly a debatable contention which space does not permit me to challenge here), I want finally to suggest that part of the profundity and importance of Kierkegaard's position lies in the way he deals with this problem. Since for Kierkegaard God is identified with love, and God or love itself is projected as the object of human love relations, it would appear that he, too, is subject to Singer's fundamental criticism of Christian views of love. But Kierkegaard's position is immune to this charge, I think, on at least two grounds. First of all, for Kierkegaard a genuine love of persons is secured on the basis of the Christian doctrine of human equality, which requires the recognition of human value bestowed upon all persons by God, not merely upon a human bestowal or creation of value in the love of selected individuals as Singer would have it (Singer, 1:3). Second, since for Kierkegaard love is the object of love relations, love for the other person comes to expression precisely in helping that individual become an independent and loving person. As the true object of love, God is not conceived as a transcendent entity that directs us away from love of persons in the world but rather is understood in a relational context as the transcendent ground and matrix of love within which love of all persons is affirmed and expressed in the world. For Kierkegaard, then, love of God and love of persons are integrally connected; one cannot have the one without the other.

In these and other ways, Kierkegaard has plumbed the depths of love to a degree unmatched in modern literature on love. While there are shortcomings and limitations in his thought, as is true of every other philosopher of love, Kierkegaard has much to offer for our individual edification and scholarly reflection on the nature of love.[14]

178   Part Two: The History of the Question

NOTES

1. Irving Singer, *The Nature of Love*, 3 vols. (Chicago: University of Chicago Press, 1984 (vols. 1 and 2) and 1987 (vol. 3), 1: xi. Hereafter references to this work will appear in parentheses in the text as Singer with the volume and page numbers.

2. See Sylvia I. Walsh, "Forming the Heart: The Role of Love in Kierkegaard's Thought," in *The Grammar of the Heart: New Essays in Moral Philosophy & Theology,* ed. Richard H. Bell (San Francisco: Harper & Row, 1988), pp. 234–56. This article also contains a bibliography of other recent secondary studies on *Works of Love.*

3. Søren Kierkegaard, *Works of Love,* trans. Howard and Edna Hong (New York: Harper & Row, 1962), p. 67. All subsequent references will be to this edition, cited in the text as WL with the page number.

4. Thus it is not sufficient, and even promotes the very confusion Kierkegaard hopes to dispel, to characterize Christian love simply as hidden inwardness. Whereas true religiosity is identified in *Concluding Unscientific Postscript* as consisting in hidden inwardness which can find no satisfactory outward expression of its pathos, in *Works of Love* Kierkegaard claims that Christian love, though ultimately hidden in inwardness, is not "such a hidden feeling that it is above bearing fruit or such a hidden feeling that the fruits proved nothing for or against" (WL, 31).

5. By becoming consciously based on the eternal love does not lose its immediacy but rather becomes a new form of immediacy after reflection or a "second immediacy," a phrase that does not appear in *Works of Love* but is used in several other works by Kierkegaard. On love as duty and second immediacy, see my article, "Forming the Heart," pp. 242–46.

6. Kierkegaard recognizes that it is still possible for an individual to "fall away" from love, in which case that person becomes guilty in relation to the one who is forsaken. But in his view, "the true lover never falls away from love," even if, in an external sense, the relation to the beloved is broken. An excellent example of this is Kierkegaard's own love relation to Regine Olsen, to whom he broke an engagement to marry but whom he never stopped loving. For further discussion of the problem of falling away from love, see my article, "Forming the Heart," pp. 242–43.

7. On Kierkegaard's view of genuine alterity see also my article, "The Philosophical Affirmation of Gender Difference: Kierkegaard versus Postmodern Neo-Feminism," *Journal of Psychology and Christianity* (special Gender Issues number) 7, no. 4 (Winter 1988): 18–26.

8. The notion of a third factor in love relations appears very early in Kierkegaard's thought, for he writes in his journal in 1837: "All true love is grounded in this, that one loves another in a third" (*Søren Kierkegaard's Journals & Papers,* ed. and trans. Howard V. Hong and Edna H. Hong [Bloomington: Indiana University Press, 1967–78], 3: 2380).

9. Kierkegaard's thought is frequently misinterpreted as calling one away from temporality and finitude. For example, K. E. Løgstrup in *Opgør med Kierkegaard* (København: Gyldendalske Boghandel, 1967) charges that Kierkegaard does not offer any observation on what is required in action by individuals in their milieu or temporal situations, only the action which eternity outside of all temporal and worldly

requirements demands of the individual (p. 133). Similarly, T. W. Adorno, in "On Kierkegaard's Doctrine of Love," *Studies in Philosophy and Social Science* 8 (1940): 413–29, accuses him of being "socially conformist," of leaving the world to the devil, and of advocating a "fictitious, merely inward doctrine of equality" severed from social concern and insight. While it is true that Kierkegaard does not provide a "social ethic" in the form of a specific program for the implementation of the Christian command to love in society, one is not relieved from the duty and responsibility of implementing the command to love in one's everyday life. This is not made easy, nor does Kierkegaard attempt to tell us specifically how to do it, because in his view there is no direct and unconditional expression of love and self-renunciation in outward forms.

10. Cf. Anders Nygren, *Agape and Eros,* trans. Philip S. Watson (New York: Harper & Row, 1969); C. S. Lewis, *The Four Loves* (New York: Harcourt Brace Jovanovich, Inc., 1960); and Paul Tillich, *Love, Power, and Justice* (London: Oxford University Press, 1954).

11. K. E. Løgstrup manifests precisely this sort of misunderstanding in his work cited in note 9 above. He accuses Kierkegaard of turning love into hate, of transforming it into something evil and isolating the beloved, whereas, in Løgstrup's opinion, love that is really for the neighbor's sake would do and say everything in order to win the neighbor's acceptance (pp. 144–45). From Kierkegaard's point of view, however, this way of proceeding would turn the relation back into selfishness and would not have the best interest of the neighbor at heart, whereas in true sacrificial love one is willing to sacrifice everything, even one's own positive relation to the beloved, for the sake of the beloved's highest good.

12. Søren Kierkegaard, *For Self-Examination* and *Judge for Yourselves,* ed. and trans. Howard V. Hong and Edna H. Hong (Princeton: Princeton University Press, 1990), p. 205.

13. For an attempt to formulate a postmodern expression of the altruistic life of self-denying love and compassion for the Other, see Edith Wyschogrod, *Saints and Postmodernism: Revisioning Moral Philosophy* (Chicago: The University of Chicago Press, 1990). Typical of postmodernism, however, is the negation or rejection of the concept of self in the affirmation of an excessive desire for the Other that leaves no room for personal individuality or particularity in the form of a fixed identity or ego on the part of the one who loves or in the Other who is the recipient of love. Over against this extreme expression of altruistic love Kierkegaard's thought offers a more dialectically balanced position affirming both the self and the other, an authentic form of self-love as well as unbounded self-renunciation in disinterested love for the other.

14. For an indication of what I perceive as some weaknesses in Kierkegaard's views on love, see my article "Forming the Heart," p. 248. See also other studies on Kierkegaard's view of love cited in note 2 of that article.

Part Three

Contemporary Formulations

Part Three

Contemporary Applications

10

Through a Glass Darkly: Freud's Concept of Love

Pat Duffy Hutcheon

"Is all this really necessary?" asked George Santayana after his first in-depth encounter with existentialism. This rhetorical question occurred to me as I read Irving Singer's meticulous analysis of Freud's sexual theory of love. Surely a century of opposing evidence from biology, physiology and experimental psychology should have laid Freud's fanciful speculations to rest by now! On second thought, however, I realized that more than scientific falsification will be required to wrest the roots of Freudianism from the worldview dominating modern culture. Thoughtful discussions by philosophers such as Singer—who share some of Freud's premises and interests—may have more influence than compelling evidence ever can on those matters of sentiment, faith, and metaphor which, in the end, determine our commitments and beliefs.

THE FOUR FACES OF LOVE

Singer's thesis is that Freud's theory of love, although multifaceted and evolving throughout his lifetime, was of one piece. The implication of this would seem to be that one cannot justifiably select some aspects of the theory while rejecting others, as Freud's followers and intellectual descendants have tried to do. Here Singer seems to be signaling an intent to raise fundamental questions about the entire edifice. He begins by explaining that Freud sought, and believed he had found, a unitary principle determining the entire course of human development. He thought this was a principle springing from deep within the instinctual wellsprings of human nature.

Singer feels that a major source of confusion in Freud's work is the fact that he referred to love in four different ways. He apparently viewed it as (1) a fusion of sexuality with affection or tenderness, (2) libidinal energy—both "aim-inhibited" (and thus available for culture-building tasks) and directed toward its original pursuit of a love object, (3) Eros (the life instinct driving all humanity), and (4) the total life force comprising Eros *plus* an aggressive or death-instinct.

Singer then discusses these four senses in which Freud speaks of love. In the first case he notes that Freud attempted to locate the roots of love in the sexuality of the newborn infant, as it suckles at the mother's breast. In the process, the child supposedly attains a confluence of satiation, for both hunger and sensuality are satisfied in that experience. Freud claimed that this initiates the onset of affection toward what is, at one and the same time, the child's first sexual love object and its crucial source of sustenance. All subsequent development is driven and defined by the vain attempt to reunite these twin aspects of love. The child's first sexual satisfactions are therefore experienced in the bodily functions necessary for self-preservation, according to the theory. Only eventually—as the sexual focus turns from the nose and throat to the anal area and then (with puberty) to the genitals—does the goal of species reproduction become uppermost.

Singer presents two conclusions regarding this particular aspect of the psychoanalytic model. He credits Freud with the insight that all human attributes (including sex) are in some way developmental, but he disagrees with the entire explanation of the process and of the central, predetermined role of sex within it. Says Singer, "The most that Freud could infer from his scenario of human development is the idea that a great deal of adult sexuality includes traces of affective occurrences that belong to the individual's earlier life."[1]

Singer next tackles the notion of love as "libido": a quantifiable energy required to keep the human engine operating. According to Freud, libido ". . . seeks to force together and hold together the portions of living substance."[2] Singer maintains that libido is not at all the same as Bergson's *élan vital,* in spite of Fromm's opinion to the contrary. He quoted Freud on the organic and adaptive nature of libido, to show that at no time did he forsake his biological model. Singer's conclusion regarding Freud's use of the libido is that it merely amounts to ". . . an 'idealization': a bestowing of importance upon an aspect of life that particularly quickens and enthralls his imagination."[3] Singer could have added that the problem with an idealized construct masquerading as scientific theory is that it is incapable of generating hypotheses that can be tested by experience; and that it is singularly impervious to the influence of disconfirming evidence in any case.

Freud's subsequent introduction of "Eros" into his theory of love has proven even more confusing to most readers. Singer is no exception, although he correctly recognizes that, for Freud, its source was in the innate sensual/affectional conflict within the very nature of sexual development. Freud had begun to speculate about the phenomenon of "narcissism," and felt the need to make room for it in his theory. He had wondered how exaggerated self-love could be explained solely in terms of the libido's unceasingly unrequited quest for a fusion of the sensual and the affectionate. Clearly the fact of narcissism demanded the existence of a powerful ego instinct as well as a love instinct!

Singer points out that Freud eventually decided that both instincts could be explained in terms of sex—the difference being that the ego instinct turns inward toward itself as the sex object, while the other is actually an *object* instinct, i.e., it seeks satisfaction from other objects. According to Singer, at this point in Freud's thinking, he decided that what was by now a considerably enlarged concept of libido would henceforth be designated as "Eros."

Singer notes that Freud acknowledged the apparently mystical overtones of the latter, and its similarity to Plato's original concept. Nonetheless, he concludes that Freud's Eros does not represent a detour into vitalism, as Erich Fromm and Herbert Marcuse have maintained. He would probably agree that Freud's version of Eros resembles some sort of engine of biological life—fueled by chemically inspired libido energy and nothing more. Singer concludes: "The universal love that Freud calls Eros does not progress toward stages of greater spirituality."[4]

The fourth face of love in Freudian thought involves yet another irreconcilable conflict. This time it is between the twin impulses toward love and hate arising from the libido driving Eros. In later life Freud had reluctantly recognized an instinct for aggression in human beings which he considered at least as powerful as love. In an attempt to incorporate this new instinct into his theory, Freud suggested that humans, having emerged from inorganic matter, are programmed to return to it. All life (represented by Eros) was now defined in Freud's model by the resulting struggle between the life urge that strives to maintain the individual and the death wish seeking to maintain the species at the cost of the individual.

Critics and followers alike have sought to identify in Eros the notion of a generalized love of humanity. Singer disagrees with this, and rightly so. Freud always claimed that the concept of universal love as a motivating force or realizable ideal was highly dubious. He thought that any culture that encourages the love instinct to operate without restraint is setting itself up for the unbridled reign of hate as well.

In summing up this aspect of the theory, Singer notes what he considers to be Freud's regrettable tendency toward dualism. Moreover, Singer is troubled, he says, by "the fact that Freud's speculations about Eros and the death drive are inherently chaotic, even confused."[5]

Singer is also critical of Freud's essentialism. There seems, however, to be some confusion on this point. For me, essentialism is indicated by a tendency within the idea system toward reification of descriptive or explanatory categories—thereby treating these mental constructs as concrete phenomena and subsequently substituting them for the very entities they were originally designed to clarify. This brings the search for understanding of the subject of inquiry to a crashing halt, while opening the door to endless speculation unhampered by any requirement of objective observation or testing.

Freud was undoubtedly one of the most striking examples of this tendency ever visited upon an unsuspecting world. To read his letters and many of his works is virtually to step into Looking Glass Land. One is confronted with a darkly mirrored reflection of a territory peopled not with descriptions of problems to be solved or regularities to be documented, but with concrete, living entities locked in endless combat for the soul of man: "Oedipus complex," "penis envy," "castration complex," "libido," "sadistic-oral fixation," "genital phase," "narcissism," "the death wish"—the list seems endless.

Singer, however, does not refer to any of these. He goes on to discuss Freud's pessimism, and traces it to the influence of the darker currents within German Romantic idealism. He describes Freud quoting Schopenhauer's parable about freezing porcupines who shuffled to and fro seeking warmth and comfort until they had achieved some sort of standoff. Singer says that whereas Schopenhauer saw this as an example of the coexistence of love and hate in human nature, Freud drew a stranger lesson. His conclusion was that humans cannot tolerate too much intimacy.

But why bring love and hate into it at all? Why the unnecessary anthropomorphism? For me, the entire story merely demonstrates how widespread is the lack of understanding of the process of evolution. What about applying the much simpler idea of adaptation to environmental demands—to the point where a "developmentally stable strategy" has evolved for the porcupines: something that constantly occurs in human sexual behavior as well?

THE IMPACT OF CULTURAL PAROCHIALISM
ON FREUD'S CONCEPT OF LOVE

It is somewhat surprising that Singer does not mention the significance for Freud's work on love of the social environment that formed his worldview. It is impossible to appreciate the one-sidedness of Freud's concept of love without recognizing him as quintessentially a creature of nineteenth-century German culture. Like most of his peers, Freud was paternalistic and authoritarian in the extreme. Typically Victorian in his prudishness, he was nonetheless so obsessed with sex that, in his early practice, he diagnosed every neurosis presented to him as a case of *coitus interruptus*—invariably attributable to some failure on the part of the woman.

Women's rightful place in the scheme of things is made clear in numerous passages such as the following in *Contributions to the Psychology of Love:* "We regard it as a normal reaction to coitus for a woman to hold a man closely in her arms . . . at the climax of gratification, and this seems to us an expression of her gratitude and an assurance of her lasting thraldom to him."6 In fact, Freud's strange physics of the libido seems less a *human* theory than a strictly *male* one. For example: "Since man has not an unlimited amount of mental energy, he must accomplish his tasks by distributing his libido to the best advantage. What he employs for cultural purposes he withdraws to a great extent from women and his sexual life."7

Freud meant well, and some of the therapies derived from his model may have been helpful. However, no appraisal of his concept of love can legitimately ignore the crimes perpetrated against females in the name of the theory. Beginning with the botched operation on poor Emma, from whose nose Freud's friend Fleiss tried to wrest her sexual demons; through all the desperate women whose complaints about rape were disbelieved; to the legion of dedicated mothers who have been blamed for their sons' homosexual practices, neuroses, drug addictions, and suicides; to the toddlers accused of seducing their adult abusers—wherever the dark and distorting shadow of the mirror fell, the suffering of women has been incalculable.

Freud's Looking Glass entities had a disturbing way of escaping into the world of human experience. Freud's sexual theories of love have plowed a deep and lasting furrow through the currents of twentieth-century Western thought, leaving in its wake a society obsessed by sex, ambiguous about love, and newly armed with a pseudoscientific justification for bias against women. A major legacy of Freudianism is the belated recognition that ideas do indeed have consequences—especially those taught as "essential" Truths defining an eternal human Psyche.

FIVE CRITICISMS

In the end, Singer seems to have raised five major objections to Freud's theory of love. These are what he perceives to be: (1) its empirically and logically unwarranted doctrine of child development as inherently sexual in form and content, (2) its emphasis on a kind of normative essentialism rather than the pluralism that Singer himself prefers in sexual affairs, (3) its dualism, (4) its conceptual confusion, and (5) its inadequacy due to an exclusive focus on "evaluation" to the neglect of the aspect of "bestowal" developed by Singer in his own works on love. I will discuss each of these assessments in turn, indicating the extent of my agreement or disagreement.

Beginning with the last, I believe that Freud did include within his theory something similar to Singer's concept of bestowal. In *Civilization and Its Discontents,* Freud explained how *a small minority of people* do, in fact, achieve the ability ". . . to make themselves independent of their object's acquiescence by transferring the main value from the fact of being loved to their own act of loving: they protect themselves against loss of it by attaching their love not to individual objects but to all men equally. . . ."[8] This seems to describe a human capacity for bestowing love as distinct from either the present sensation of value associated with receiving it or the valuing associated with selecting a love object.

The conceptual confusion apparent to Singer is considerably obviated once the philosophical premises informing Freud's work are taken into account. There *is* logic relating and making sense out of his entire structure, but it is a logic now largely invalidated and (one would hope) increasingly foreign to modern thought. It is the Hegelian logic of the dialectic, which I intend to discuss in some detail a little later.

I think Freud's dualism is likewise more apparent than real. If one means by dualism a belief in the existence of two realms of reality corresponding to the old mind/body and sacred/secular division; or a belief that human beings are different in *kind* rather than degree from other animal species— Freud has to be judged innocent. There are just too many indications throughout his writings of what Singer himself has called his relentless commitment to a "mechanistic" biology.

Singer's accusation of essentialism raises many intriguing questions. In the first place—as in the case of dualism—I have a problem with his definition. Singer says, "By essentialism I mean the belief that there is a single structure that defines the instinctual being of men and women."[9] He views Freud's idea of a fixed progression of developmental stages programmed within the human instincts as objectionably essentialist. But surely this is an empirical proposition requiring either confirmation or falsification, and not to be written off because one objects to the idea as being too biologically deterministic. It is not a matter of aesthetic or political preference, nor does it depend on whether philosophical essentialism or pluralism is the order of the day.

Clearly, Singer prefers an explanation of sexual development and orientation that relies more on environmental than biological programming. He is probably right, but Freud was perfectly justified in presenting his instinct theory as a possible scenario. The problem with Freud's proposition is not its contention but that he expressed it as a doctrinaire postulate to be proven by circular logic, rather than as a tentative hypothesis requiring confirmation by evidence.

Singer's negative assessment of Freud's exclusive focus on sex as the defining element in human development from infancy onward is scarcely debatable. It is possible, however, to appreciate some of Freud's observations and to recognize behavioral patterns identified by him without accepting his bizarre *explanations* for those regularities. B. F. Skinner has done a masterful job of giving Freud credit for these while explaining them in a much simpler and more commonsense way. For example, Singer suggested that what Freud called the Oedipus Complex would no doubt disappear with the advent of equality for women. The asymmetrical relation of the female parent was probably at the root of it all, combined with a culture in which punishment was paramount. "Is it possible," asked Skinner, "that the so-called Oedipal relations to mother and father are simply mythical representations of positive and negative reinforcement? The boy longs, not to sleep with his mother, but to be close to the one who positively reinforces his behavior, He longs, not to kill his father, but to escape from or destroy one who punishes."[10]

THE NATURE OF HUMAN NATURE

For a number of reasons I am unable to agree totally with Singer's depiction of Freud as a dualist and essentialist. As previously mentioned, it is possible that we attach somewhat different meaning to the two terms. For me, essentialism and dualism are the defining characteristics of a current of thought bequeathed to Western thought by Socrates, Plato, and Aristotle—and reformulated in turn by Descartes, Kant, and Hegel. It continues to prevail as the dominant worldview. To a considerable extent Freud was, indeed, a captive of this way of thinking.

An example of Freud's peculiarly anthropomorphic brand of essentialism is the way he referred to Eros. "In no other case does Eros so clearly betray the core of his being, his purpose of making more out of one."[11] At times it almost seems as if Singer, too, has been seduced into the same way of thinking, as when he writes, in apparent seriousness, "The question that Freud finds most puzzling and therefore most fruitful for analysis is why the two types of Eros fail to cooperate, why . . . [they] do not jointly create a civilization that provides happiness for those who participate in it."[12] The obvious answer is that they do not exist! Freud created a fictional Janus-faced entity designed to explain the human condition, and then discovered that what was implied by it did not accord with experience. So he struggled with his own imaginary problem in his own imaginary territory. But let us at least refuse to wander with him on the far side of the mirror.

Singer would have been quite warranted in criticizing Freud's propensity for reification as essentialism. But I think that he is not so warranted in the claim that he actually makes. Singer seems to assign the essentialist label to Freud's attempt to seek commonalities or regularities in human nature. This definition could reduce all the findings of social science to the level of Platonic pronouncements of immutable human essences. Singer may be revealing existential or phenomenological leanings here. Sartre, for example, was so firmly embedded in the essentialism of the very Romantic idealism he imagined himself to be rebelling against, that he was unable to conceive of any version of human nature other than some absolute picture in the mind of the God he rejected. So he assumed that there could exist no such thing as a nature common to human beings.

But, of course, there is another—nonessentialist—way of viewing human nature. Biologists would explain that, while each individual phenotype is indeed unique (because genetic programming and experience differ from person to person), the underlying genotype is relatively stable and amenable to study. Similarly, from the point of view of the social science that Freud was endeavoring to pioneer, psychosocial *processes* are likely to be the same wherever they occur. We are all aware that digestion and reproduction are similar the world over. Why not certain aspects of sexual development and associated psychic or behavioral complexes?

The problem with Freud is not that he looked for patterns in the words and actions of his patients, and sought to explain them. There was nothing wrong with his *objective;* it was in the implementation that he went astray. Surely Singer is not suggesting that Freud, as a would-be scientist, was wrong in seeking out regularities that transcend the uniqueness of the individual! With what does social scientific inquiry deal, if not with commonalities in the nature of human nature?

FREUD AS A DIALECTICAL "SOCIAL DARWINIST"

It is impossible to understand Freud's concept of love without an awareness of the philosophical systems that both inspired and limited him. We need to know that he considered his instinct theory to be the only credible extension of Darwinism into the realm of psychosocial and cultural affairs. Above all else, Freud saw himself as an evolutionary theorist, one destined to complete the Copernican evolution. As he explained it, Copernicus had destroyed geocentrism, and Darwin had done the same for the illusion that humanity was somehow different from and sovereign over all the rest of creation. Freud believed that his theory had accomplished a similar undermining of the illusion of "free will," or belief in the sovereignty of the human ego. This was the goal that drove him. This was the challenge that required his theory to remain monist in the Naturalistic sense, and demanded from him—not the habits of the free-floating speculative philosopher, but those of a scientist.

In this claim Freud was demonstrating the extent of his own egoism, for there were others more deserving of the mantle of Copernicus. Nonetheless, in his contribution to our understanding of the motivating power of subconsciously retained remnants of previous experience (if not of race memory), Freud did indeed make a significant contribution to social science.

From the beginning, however, Freud's work was flawed by three serious errors concerning the nature of evolution. Like his contemporary, Herbert Spencer, Freud never really understood the mechanism of natural selection. A related error involved his captivation with Darwin's notion of sex selection and his subsequent distortion of that aspect of evolution. A third had to do with his failure to recognize the implications of the Darwinian revolution for the concept of organic and psychosocial causality.

Few people even today fully comprehend Darwin's crucial insight about the nature of organic causality, as distinct from the push-pull (or "mechanistic") operation of cause and effect at the inorganic level. Darwin had demonstrated how, once life emerged, natural selection operated according to an after-the-fact causality, whereby the *consequences* of the organism's lifetime of environmental forays feed back into species' future by determining which organisms will live to reproduce. Freud, intent on applying the rules of Newtonian physics to the contents of the psyche, missed entirely the implications of this revolutionary breakthrough.

He was handicapped as well by the teleological perspective dominant in the culture of his time. The older idea of a Great Chain of Being was still prevalent, even in biology. Non-Darwinian evolutionists still thought that evolution had to be aiming *toward* some predestined goal and inherently *progressive* in its unfolding.

Freud made a fatal error concerning the key evolutionary concept of sex selection. Darwin had suggested that because reproduction is so crucial to the evolution of the species, the process (as well as appendages and behaviors) by which individuals attract potential mates must be of great significance. Freud transferred this idea from the species to the level of the organism. He postulated that if sex drives species formation it must be the innate force energizing individual development as well!

Another mistake followed from Freud's failure to understand the nature of natural selection. He was probably influenced here by Herbert Spencer, whose works on biology, psychology, sociology and ethics were widely distributed during the last decade of the nineteenth century. Like Spencer, Freud thought that characteristics acquired during an individual's lifetime were somehow fed back into the evolutionary process, so that aspects of culture (or "civilization") were inherited in some mysterious way along with biological propensities. Spencer developed an extremely sophisticated theory concerning this process, which was later taken up and built upon by Jean Piaget. Compared to these, Freud's model was crude in the extreme. But it had the advantage of being seductively appealing to the human imagination and desire for melodrama.

Freud decided that instincts had to be the repositories of all the past experience of the human race. And because he saw species reproduction as the "aim" of evolution, and sex its energizing force, he reasoned that experience could only be stored in some sort of sexual form. Only sexually relevant bits of species information would be sufficiently useful to be passed into succeeding human psyches by means of inherited biological instincts.

At this point it was necessary to employ the concept of the "unconscious." Freud knew that the conscious ego had no awareness of much of what actually motivated its actions. He decided that the unconscious layer of the psyche must be a vast storehouse of the earlier defining sexual experience of the human race, and that aspects of this might possibly be revealed to our consciousness through dreams and inadvertent comments and behaviors.

We now understand that there is no possibility of the inheritance of race memory or any messages from an individual's current life experience. Modern biology has demonstrated conclusively that genetic instructions follow a one-way street. But cherished dogma dies hard, and it seems to take more than scientific knowledge to storm the bulwarks of "true belief."

Two characteristics of the social science of Freud's time also helped to lead him astray: both were attempts to imitate physics. Today, with our more sophisticated understanding of the nature of scientific inquiry, we would call these "scientisms": procedures with the surface *appearance* but not the appropriate conceptual base, rigorous data-collecting methods or the disciplined attitude of science. One of these was a widespread tendency to look for universal, immutable *laws* governing individual development and successive forms of society. This was usually combined with the teleological outlook bequeathed by certain of the Enlightenment thinkers and revived by Kant. The other was a preference for defining social phenomena as discrete categories or as flows of energy: both assumed to be readily quantifiable. Marx's theory demonstrated both of these tendencies. So, too, did Freud's. Both thinkers were convinced that in adopting these approaches, they were being scientific.

FREUD AS A DIALECTICAL THINKER

There was yet another misleading philosophical premise shared by Marx and Freud—one that Freud seems never to have acknowledged. It was the Hegelian dialectic. Only by fitting Freud's concept of love into a dialectical framework does it begin to assume a sense of inner cohesiveness and logic. In the absence of a recognition of the dialectic as an organizing principle Freudianism is indeed the confused muddle of discordant ideas referred to by Singer. However, we need to be warned that interpreting Freud's theory in terms of the dialectic does not make it more credible; it merely renders it understandable.

Singer thinks that Freud's propensity for dividing everything in two makes him a dualist. But a passion for dichotomizing is not dualism! In the usual sense of the term Freud was at least as materialistic as Marx. What the famous Freudian dichotomies represent is, instead, the thesis and antithesis of the dialectic. The clue is that with each, there was the expectation of an inevitable synthesis to a more advanced stage.

Freud began in a fairly traditional manner by recognizing two basic instincts of hunger and love. He eventually came to see these as representing the self-preservative or ego instincts on the one hand, and the sexual instinct—functioning to reproduce the species—on the other. He believed both are manifested in a force driven by hunger for nutrition and for sex. The force energizing and synthesizing these drives, Freud called the libido.

Freud saw an inevitable conflict between the ego instinct and the sexual instinct. "For, in human beings, it may happen that the demands of the sexual instinct, which of course extend far beyond the individual, seem to the ego to constitute a danger menacing his self-preservation or his self-respect. The ego then takes up the defensive, denies the sexual instincts the satisfaction they claim, and forces them into those bypaths of substitutive gratification which become manifest as symptoms of a neurosis."[13] Neuroses, then, result from the wrong kind of resolution of the conflict rather than from a healthy synthesis of the two opposing forces.

Indeed, the process of child development begins with a condition of synthesis. In the beginning of its development, according to Freud, the libido is directed toward itself; it *serves* the ego. This is the primitive synthesis of egoism or childhood narcissism into which the infant is born. There is a fusion of sensuality and affection as the child satiates both forms of hunger at the mother's breast and in the ministrations of other loving family members. Gradually, as the sexual instinct turns away from the child's own body for sensual pleasure, and toward other objects, the essential conflict between ego and sexual instincts comes into play.

Freud claimed that in healthy development, the ego finds it necessary to redirect the operation of the powerful sexual instinct in order to achieve its own goals. It gradually accomplishes this by inhibiting the aim of the sexual instinct and thus directing its energy to other, ego-controlled ends. Affectional and nonsexual family bonds are formed, and then these are extended to friendships and to bonding within successively larger communal groupings. Coincident with this, a new and higher-level synthesis is being formed in terms of an encompassing *mental* form of sexual energy called the libido. The latter comprises both "aim-inhibited" energy and energy directed toward the original sexual end, in the person of an external sex object.

It is this sublimation of the sexual instinct and the diversion of libido to the service of other goals that makes society and culture possible, according to Freud. All is still not clear sailing, however, for yet another conflict hovers on the horizon, ever ready to assert itself. There emerges an opposition to the libido in its task of preserving the organic substance and binding it into ever larger units of organization. Freud explained this as an antithesis to libido which seeks to dissolve all the organic and social units and reinstate their previous unorganized (or inorganic) condition. It is a death instinct—but whether or not Freud believed it to be anti-evolutionary is not clear. He was ambiguous about the exact nature of this drive toward death. Sometimes he seemed to be viewing it as an essential aspect of the process of evolution, because of its function in removing the individual from the scene once the cause of reproduction has been served. At other times Freud spoke of it only in terms of the eternal conflict between aggression and bonding, or between love and hate within the human psyche.

Freud rehabilitated Plato's concept of Eros in order to posit a higher synthesis of the instinctual forces driving the evolution of human civilization: an all-encompassing life force capable of enveloping and riding herd on both the libido and the aggressive or death instinct. He described cultural evolution as ". . . the particular modification undergone by the life process under the influence of the task set before it by Eros and stimulated by Ananke, eternal necessity; and this task is that of uniting single human beings into a larger entity with libidinal attachments between them."[14]

Freud's was a vision of hate and love forever in opposition within a temporary cease-fire established by Eros—and in a psyche that had now expanded to take in the whole of human culture! He died with little confidence in the ultimate achievement of his hoped-for synthesis. Santayana accused Freud of having moved from the scientific search for objective knowledge to a "pan-psychism" that rejected altogether any attempt at objectivity. In the end, Freud's "psyche" had indeed become the crucial defining essence of all humanity: one giant Eros astride a world forever doomed to *coitus interruptus.*

NOTES

1. Irving Singer, *The Nature of Love* (Chicago: The University of Chicago Press, 1987), p. 108.
2. Ibid., p. 111.

3. Ibid., p. 110.
4. Ibid., p. 112.
5. Ibid., p. 119.
6. Sigmund Freud, "Contributions to the Psychology of Love," in *Freud: On War, Sex and Neurosis* (New York: Arts and Science Press, 1947), p. 231.
7. Sigmund Freud, "Civilization and Its Discontents," in John Rickman, ed., *Civilization, War and Death* (London: The Hogarth Press, 1953), p. 72.
8. Ibid., p. 45.
9. Singer, *The Nature of Love*, p. 130.
10. B. F. Skinner, *Notebooks*, ed. Robert Epstein (Englewood Cliffs, N.J.: Prentice-Hall, 1980), p. 353.
11. Singer, *The Nature of Love*, p. 142.
12. Ibid., p. 143.
13. Sigmund Freud, "A Difficulty in Psycho-analysis," in *Freud on War, Sex and Neurosis*, p. 15.
14. Freud, "Civilization and Its Discontents," p. 72.

11

Love's Moral and Religious Implications: Irving Singer's Trilogy

John Nota

Ama et fac quod vis: "love and do what you want to do." Let me apply this so often abused advice of St. Augustine to explain what I intend to say in this paper.

I have a special love for philosophy and, to be more specific, an even more special love for a philosophy of love. So I am interested in philosophers who wrote about love, including Max Scheler, Gabriel Marcel, Otto Bollnow, Edith Stein, Pitirin A. Sorokin, Paul Tillich, Erich Fromm, Herbert Marcuse, G. Madinier, Maurice Nédoncelle, Maurice-Edouard Blondel, and Vladimir Solovyev. I was excited to hear about Irving Singer's three volumes on *The Nature of Love* and, given the length of the volumes, I started to look for my favorite philosophers and the way the Singer dealt with them.

It is a bit unfair to point to philosophers who are missing, especially because Professor Singer mentions that he cannot be complete (1:44); however, *amicus Plato, magis amica veritas*: Plato may be my friend, but the truth is a greater friend. Singer describes in the first chapters of volume 1 his own a priori definition of love as "bestowal and appraisal" and with this definition he approaches the many artists, philosophers, theologians he is dealing with to arrive at the construction of a new philosophy of love, a "contemporary humanism 'more suitable' to our modern age" (1:44). So I think that it is not unfair but fair to the phenomenon of love, to make my own selection and elaborate the philosophy of love of Max Scheler (1874–1928). This may help make readers aware of certain aspects that are lacking in Singer's descriptions. I will also take the opportunity to mention the misunderstanding of Scheler's philosophy by Singer and Anders Nygren[1] and to clarify, within the context of this philosophy, the fundamental misunderstanding regarding autonomy and heteronomy, especially in the philosophy of love of Thomas Aquinas.

Scheler wrote very often about love. I am going to limit myself to the period from 1898-1921, so as to avoid Scheler's new ideas of the metanthropological period. The most important publications about love within the period we are concerned with are: *The Nature of Sympathy*, "Ordo Amoris" (published in the *Nachlass* and in an English translation in *Selected Philosophical Essays*), and *Ressentiment*.[2] The titles of these works make it clear that "love" is much more to Scheler than an empty word. He is a phenomenologist and speaks from the experience of love: he has lived the phenomenon of love and deeply thought about it, in order to arrive at the knowledge of the essence of love. The only way to understand Scheler's philosophy of love is to experience it along with him. The outsider may be right in quoting words, but will never understand.[3]

The starting point of Scheler's philosophy of love is the man Scheler himself, from whom follows his *Menschenbild,* or image of man. Scheler acknowledges a diversity within the unity of a human being, the most important aspect of which is the level of the spirit, i.e., the *person* in its concrete form. Scheler rejects, in his understanding of person, the notion of a static substance, although he likes to talk about act-substance. Person, according to Scheler's way of thinking, is a unity of acts. Within this unity the emotional sphere holds the primacy. Under this heading come acts of feeling, the so-called spiritual sensing of values, and also loving and hating. Further analysis reveals that there is again on this level a primacy of love and hate, where love ultimately plays the more basic role, because hate is at bottom a reaction against some form of wrong love. In "Ordo Amoris" Scheler writes: "Our heart is first of all destined to love" ("Ordo Amoris," p. 126). I might use this phrase as a summary of Scheler's entire life, with all its fallings and risings.

Now, the person is a concretization of spiritual acts. Hence love, as the act of the person, is itself spiritual. Because of the complexity of human beings, we must also speak of love on the level of the psychical and the vital, but not represent such values as the pleasant or the useful. Of course, you may say that you "love" cheesecake or blueberry pie, but here our way of speaking does not adequately represent the phenomenon. Genuine love always presupposes a dynamic in the direction of higher values, but such movement is lacking when the intentionality is directed to the nonpersonal. All one really means to say is that cheesecake or blueberry pie is very "tasty." The value involved here is the pleasant. I hope that is what Dr. Singer means when

198 Part Three: Contemporary Formulations

he says that we should love inanimate things as ends in themselves (1:352). Now you may enjoy a glass of wine better than a glass of beer, but does this make wine object of my love as my final end? If I am an alcoholic, the answer is yes, but there are still some more implications which I shall be discussing later.

For similar reasons Scheler has even less appreciation of any talk of "sensual love." When love is expressly sensual or sexual, it is not directed to a person but only to the enjoyment of a certain aspect of a person, with the person then being used simply as object or means of enjoyment. In the terminology of our time, the person is a mere sex object. Such an attitude, in which the other person is not respected but degraded, cannot be called love in the strict sense. It is true that sensual or sexual love can be an accompanying aspect of spiritual love, as it normally is in a full-fledged human love relationship in marriage, but sensual love by itself cannot be called love.

In "Ordo Amoris" Scheler describes the double infinity that exists within a human being: the infinity of sensual love, which always wants more because "This water makes you more and more thirsty, the more you drink it," and the infinity of spiritual love, which finds no end to its happiness and therefore wants to give more and to immerse itself ever more deeply in its happiness ("Ordo Amoris," p. 113f.). In letters of 1924 to his wife Marit Furtwängler, Scheler contrasts his *love* for her with his *passion* for, as well as his *comradeship* with, Maria, his third wife. Thus Scheler's philosophy of love is bound up with his own life's experiences in a very special way.

The clear distinction between passion and love also makes it impossible for Scheler to interpret love exclusively as a sublimation of libido. Freud and other naturalistic thinkers err in their estimation of the phenomenon of love not only because they give a mistaken explanation in which a true aspect is turned into the totality, but, first and foremost, because there are certain aspects of the phenomenon which they simply do not see. They do not notice, for example, that in the evolution of life and of humanity—Scheler repeats this point any number of times—completely new acts can sometimes appear and indeed do appear. This happens with a leap, as it were, and therefore it cannot be explained as a gradual development. Love on the level of the psychical and love in the sphere of the spiritual (especially the holy) differ in essential respects from love in the sphere of the vital and sensory, and thus may not be explained away as illusory.

In the final analysis love and hate cannot be defined. Yet it is possible to let them be seen as "primal phenomena."

Love is a movement that proceeds from the lower value to the higher, a movement in which the higher value suddenly rises up. This movement must not be viewed as a striving on the part of the lower to go higher in the sense of something wanting to realize itself, of desiring something and wanting to obtain it. Love is not concerned with the realization of value, although there does dwell within it a dynamic toward the higher.

Scheler here distances himself radically from the Greeks as he describes it in his famous article on ressentiment, in which he, a long time before Nygren, places eros and agape against each other. Within the Greeks' male-dominated society where the principle of *agon,* or struggle, is dominant and all movement has to be seen against the background of the cosmic movement of the eternal recurrence, Eros is a movement from the lower to the higher, from the imperfect to the perfect. For the sake of consistency it is then maintained that God does not love and that Eros is not a god. In the *Symposium* Plato tells us, through Socrates-Diotima, that Eros always remains conscious of his origin, his birth out of Poverty and Abundance, and is always a transition from nonbeing to being, from lack to possession, without ever being able to achieve genuine rest in what is obtained. Eros remains identified with desire. Aristotle's god, likewise, does not love; he is only the *object* of love and striving. With all their high philosophical acuity, then, the Greeks did not know of a God who loved. (Scheler does not go, like Singer, into Plotinus's idea of Eros, which, according to some texts, admits of a more nuanced interpretation).

The wondrous thing about Christianity is that it has reversed love's movement: we can speak of a reversal in direction here. Since God has consented to become man in the Incarnation, it is clear that love is not a desire and lack. Instead of a striving for what is higher, love now becomes a bowing to what is lower. In this act of lowering, this losing oneself in all others, both good and evil (for they are all worthy of love), we discover that loving means becoming like God (*Ressentiment,* pp. 84ff.). The fact that this love loves evil and not only the good confuses Singer and Nygren. They think that this is a kind of *romantic love,* but the real point is that the object of God's love, and man's love with him, is *God's creation,* a creation that cannot "sin away" its fundamental goodness and so always contains an aspect that is lovable. As Scheler expresses it: this love is directed to the kingdom of God, whatever way you want to explain it. Indeed, Scheler exaggerates when he writes that it is better to commit the external act of sinning than to become frustrated and full of ressentiment by the desire for sin, but that is not the real issue here.

I want to develop more fully this concept of love more deeply than Scheler experienced it and reflected on it. But it may be helpful to contrast it first with Singer's concept of love, see how he criticized it from his point of view, and give my own opinion about this criticism.

Basic to the Christian concept of love are the elements of:

1) *giving,* instead of trying to receive;
2) *forgiving,* even of enemies so that love is not limited to a group of

family, tribe, race, friends, or compatriots, although they are certainly included in this universal love which is as wide as God's creation and comprises even the deceased and the subhuman world; and

3) *redeeming* by God: self-redemption is for Scheler an absurdity, a contradiction in terms.

Singer, who describes Christian love pretty well in his first volume, admits that he is an outsider and does not take part in it (1:314). Moreover, he wholeheartedly disagrees with it. Singer dislikes the giving, has his misgivings about forgiving, rejects redemption as demeaning (1:310), and even doubts whether a Christian lover is able to love fellow human beings or, for that matter, anything at all except God.

First of all, Singer is against the giving aspect. This may surprise you, because I mentioned at the beginning of this paper that his a priori definition of love consists in love as bestowal and appraisal, but his bestowal seems to presuppose the existence of the beloved and to coexist as an addition to a reality that is independent. For Singer God cannot be love. "For love is an attitude, or an ideal, or a phenomenon, or a category of analysis. How then can love be a person, or a person be love?" (1:358). How can I be myself when I owe my being to somebody else? The problem for Singer, I think, is that he is so thrilled by the idea of autonomy that he does not see that autonomy does not exclude heteronomy. He only accepts an absolute autonomy: a creature is not free, because it owes its existence to God. He might have received a better understanding from listening to Max Scheler and especially to Maurice Blondel about the unity of autonomy and heteronomy. But he quotes St. Thomas Aquinas, who disagrees with Peter Lombard's opinion that charity in a human being is the Holy Spirit (1:319ff.). Thomas says without any rancor that Peter Lombard had this opinion "because of the sublimity, the grandeur of charity, but, when you think well enough about it, then his solution is at the expense of charity. . . . For it is necessary that the human will be moved by the Holy Spirit to love in such a way that the will itself is also the cause of this act of love."[4] According to Thomas the greatness of God's love shows itself in letting his creatures be themselves: "To strain the perfection of creatures is to strain the perfection of the divine power."[5] God does not force his divine grace upon us, so that we may participate in it. And once you accept his gift, you are still the cause of our human graceful actions. I do not have the experience that being grateful for an achievement will diminish me as a person; nor do I think that the receivers of Academy Awards are all simply hypocrites when they say that they owe so much to their parents, husband, wife, or director. Sometimes they mention God. This is not a denial of their own effort and success. God is not a competitor with man. You may think that I am exaggerating in ascribing this to Professor

Singer, but just read his overreaction to St. Augustine's well-known statement, more pastoral than metaphysical, that one should not *frui* (enjoy) but *uti* (use) God's creation, and that one should not be attached to the passing world as if it would last forever. Singer answers by saying that one should never use a person as a means to an end, one of the great statements of Kant's *Critique of Practical Reason*. Every follower of Augustine would agree with that. But, Singer continues, the subhuman world should also be loved as an end in itself. Here we are back at the enjoyment of the glass of wine as an end in itself. It is great for the alcoholic, but the question may be asked, is being an alcoholic so great? The problem is that there is an order in values, an order in my love; put otherwise: some realities are subordinated to the being of the person, even when they are lovable, enjoyable, and asking for respect. And the human person is certainly an end in itself but still subordinated, together with the community, to the Person of persons, to God. This final end does not take away the importance of the *finis intermedius*, i.e., the intermediary end. On the contrary, it guarantees it. To love finite reality as God's creation does not destroy my love for my fellow human beings nor my loving care for the subhuman world. It makes everybody and everything more precious, touched by the hands of God (1:334ff.).

To forgive is a second essential aspect of Christian love. In this context I was told a story about the former mayor of New York City, Ed Koch. I do not know if it is true or simply apocryphal, but it illustrates my point. Mayor Koch once was asked why he did not forgive a certain person who had hurt him. Koch's answer was: I am not a Christian!

Singer writes that forgiving in the Tanakh or Hebrew Scriptures was reserved only to God (1:261ff., 285ff.). He certainly makes a right point here, but perhaps one may suggest that, just as God in ancient Judaism is a loving and giving God, full of mercy, so there are at least signs that he would like others to do the same and forgive. Think, for example, about Ezek. 16, where Jahweh, the giving and forgiving bridegroom, gives everything to the foundling Israel, makes her his bride, and renews his covenant with her forever notwithstanding her infidelity. Singer himself mentions the story of Jonah, who is reprimanded by Jahweh because he is sorry that Niniveh is going to be saved. There is also the example of David and Absalom.

But it is true: when God becomes man, then God's forgiving love is present on this earth. First in Jesus, later in Stephen, the deacon-martyr, and so it is being continued in our own days: my relative and fellow philosopher, the Dutch Carmelite Titus Brandsma, who died in Dachau, and my friend the phenomenologist, Jewess, and Carmelite sister, Edith Stein, who died in the gas chambers of Auschwitz. Both prayed for their enemies, the Nazis. Singer thinks that the arguments in the parables of the New Testament and the writings of Thomas Aquinas and others are not very stringent (1:350f.). I think, however, that the existential argument of Christ and his followers lies behind Thomas' reasoning, and this should always be the way to understand his position.

Redemption is the third aspect of Christian love, closely related to giving and forgiving, because the source is always the love of the Person of Christ the Redeemer. I have already mentioned that, according to Singer, redemption is demeaning; Singer even thinks that Christian *agape* is basically suicidal (1:309). To quote Singer here: "To the Christian . . . nature and time are consecrated to the devil" (1:308). In the redemption Christ takes nothing from the world other than its sins (1:310). Singer thinks that according to medieval Christianity, man could redeem himself with God's help, and that Luther denied this. My opinion is that there is some confusion here between Manichaeism, a Catholic and a Lutheran concept of redemption, and Singer's misunderstanding of the issue.

First of all, according to the Catholic faith, nature and time are *not* consecrated to the devil. God created the world, and it was good. Of course, in sinning humankind succeeded in spoiling this original goodness, but never completely. Humanity, nature, is wounded but not corrupt. Sin lies in breaking the union of love, and so the world is a broken world. But God restored this union in Christ, who appeals to the freedom of each human being to cooperate with him. Nobody is forced to be part of this union, it is just an appeal, an invitation. In this limited sense you may speak about coredemption, insofar as the Redeemer does not redeem us automatically, not without our cooperation. Christian love consists in giving, forgiving, coredeeming. If one can redeem oneself, one does not need redemption or Christ the Redeemer. But once you are united with Christ, you will still try to do something about the reality of this broken world.

Excuse these theological reflections. But my topic is the moral-religious implications of love. Singer deals with the issue, and I have to mention that in the second volume of *The Nature of Love* Singer writes a beautiful paragraph on "the most lovable of medieval saints," St. Francis of Assisi, and his love for all God's creatures. Still I do not think that Francis, in singing the "Canticle of the Sun," was able to give much thought to "the Platonic symbol of the Good," but that his real inspiration was: *Amor not amatur*—Love does not receive love in return" (2:54f.).

Let me now return to Scheler's philosophy of love. This dynamic power of love, as described in his "Reversal of the Movement of Love," is the supporting ground of the emotional life of the spirit to which Scheler assigns such a special place. But we must be extremely careful when we start talking about love. Love is a phenomenon set apart, and it must be distinguished from all other acts that fall within the sphere of the emotional. Just as value-feeling cannot be reduced to cloudy thinking or some process of sensory perception, so love cannot be reduced to any form or feeling, knowing, or willing. Spinoza's definition of love as "pleasure accompanied by the idea of an external cause" is for Scheler simply nonsense, taken as it stands. Love is not simply a feeling that is in turn caused by something else. Therefore, Scheler also regards "empathy" (*mittfühlen*) as different from love.

Love is not necessarily directed toward the other; a person can also love him/herself. Moreover, love is not a feeling or sensing in the sense of a function, an accepting (*aufnehmen*); it is an act, a movement. Love is not an answer but a spontaneous act, even in the case of reciprocal love. Empathy always presupposes feeling in the other with whom one empathizes, but in the case of love this is not essential. Empathy has its foundation in love and ceases where there is no love, but the reverse is not the case.

To desire good for someone is not yet to love him or her.

Love is directed towards a person and toward personal values, and in the final analysis it must not be conceived of along the lines of benevolence. This cannot apply at all to such objects of love as art, knowledge, and beauty. It would be laughable, Scheler points out, to be benevolent toward God. Naturally, when we love a person, we will also wish him or her well, but this is a consequence of love and is not love itself. Moreover, love as such does not seek to realize something or to achieve something in connection with the other. "What is the mother trying to achieve when she looks at her sleeping child with eyes full of love?" Scheler asks in *The Nature of Syumpathy*, p. 141.

Striving and desiring can be consequences of love or can accompany love, but they are not love itself. Those who strive come to rest when they attain what they are after, but love does not know such satisfaction. It remains the same—and even grows by the act of loving. Nor does Scheler care to hear anything about "Fulfilling one's love obligations." Love cannot be bound by obligations, for then it degenerates into good deeds or benevolence. Therefore, Kant was wrong in removing love from the sphere of moral action. One could well have a moral value without first founding it in an (outward) duty. Moreover, all duty is ultimately founded in love.

Now that I have given this necessarily schematic and all too brief sketch of Scheler's extensive phenomenological analysis, I may perhaps join him in offering a circumscription that sums up these analyses. This circumscription is again taken from *The Nature of Sympathy*: "Love is the movement wherein every concrete individual object that possesses value comes to the value that is highest for it in accordance with its ideal destiny or in which it attains the ideal values-essence that is proper to it" (p. 161). I have modified the translation somewhat). This circumscription is deliberately formulated in such a way that it disregards the value-bearer, who is here primarily the person (strangely designated by the German *Gegenstand*, or object) and is applicable to the many sorts of love, with the first differentation being love for oneself and love for the other.

In *Formalism* one finds a formulation that is perhaps somewhat more enlightening: ". . . it is not essential for the love act that it direct itself to a value by way of response *after* the sensing of the value or *after* having given its preference to this value. No, the love act much more plays the proper role of the discoverer in our perceiving of values —it alone. It is, as it were, a movement in the course of which new and higher values are raised up, values which are still wholly unknown in connection with this entity. Thus the love act does not follow value-feeling and the acts of preference but rather precedes them as pioneer and leader" (*Formalismus*, p. 275; my own translation).

With this I arrive at the next step in my exposition. What especially concerns me in this context is the relation between love and value-feeling. Love and hatred are not identical with value-feeling but provide the foundation for it, as they also do for knowing and willing. V. J. McGill, who makes of Scheler a forerunner of the Nazis, reproaches him also for not giving any love cognitive function. This is based only on McGill's confusion of the phenomena[6]. And the English translator of *Vom Ewigen im Menschen* (*On the Eternal in Man*) believes he is doing the reader a service by maintaining that "love is knowledge."[7] The interesting thing is that Scheler's essential intuition is that love is *not* identical with knowing. His patient listening leads him to such respect for reality that he is able to analyze interlaced phenomena with great precision and care. Love is bound up very closely with feeling and knowing, but it must still be distinguished from them if we are to aid confused and unjustified conclusions.

The complex value a priori is built up out of love as its deepest ground— "the mother of the spirit," as Scheler says in "Ordo Amoris," p. 110. Following upon it are the "acts of giving preference" (*Vorziehen*) and "thinking less of" (*Nachsetzen*). Here Scheler distances himself from Franz Brentano. In the confrontation of values we determine how high or low values are determined by means of specific acts of "giving preference" and "thinking less of," acts that are not to be equated with love and hatred, which is what Scheler accuses Brentano of doing and what I am afraid I must accuse Professor Singer of doing. What happens here is not yet the making of a choice; it is only an "appraisal," led by love, but not love itself. Moreover, love itself is directed not to the value but to the bearer of the value. "I do not 'love' a value but something that is valuable." The task of love is to make the value known through acts of giving preference and thinking less of and to make it manifest for feeling. How much love is to be distinguished from feeling is apparent from this consideration, that it belongs to love's essence that there is more to what is being loved than what the lover now feels. Love makes everything more beautiful insofar as it makes visible that which no one suspected was there, and always creates new possibilities in order to make it possible to penetrate further into the realms of values, the realm of love.

Love is not blind; to suppose that it is would be to confuse it with sensual passion. Love allows us to see and makes visible what was hidden. Hate makes us blind in that it makes it impossible for us to find the values. In this sense love is truly creative, for in every area of values it knows how to penetrate more deeply into the realm of values. Thus love of the holy knows how to enter more deeply into the essence of the divinity and is able to learn more from God about God. Love does not stand still by the value that at this moment is present to the feeling of the one who loves; it is constantly pressing for more. It moves from the value to the bearer of the value, like a pioneer continually making new discoveries in the domain of values. More concretely, if we love someone we do not say: "I love him (or her); I know him or her through and through." All too quickly this may become: "I've seen all I want of him (or her)!" Love is dynamic, and in its dynamism love (together with hatred) determines the realm of values for a particular person.

When we consider this primacy of love above all other acts in the person, we would do well to bear in mind that Scheler means to connect this love with a religious background. As I mentioned earlier, he discovered this way of loving, of giving oneself, or, to speak metaphorically, of bending down from the heights to the depths, in Christianity and especially in the person of Christ. This personal element in love is so important to Scheler that he writes that in pantheism no love is possible because there is no distinction between persons. Through the Incarnation we discover that persons become themselves by losing themselves in God.

God himself is love. So is his being as Creator. The person who loves must therefore "put the sources of his soul in contact with the primal source of all being that is only static in itself," and then his loving becomes a "loving with and in God." Because God is the first in love, all loving is a loving toward and in God. The consequences of this view are very important and are also drawn by Scheler. Love toward God is the love of God, he maintains. But what typifies God's love is his love of human beings. Therefore, love for God means love for humankind.

The acts of human beings and of God are certainly to be distinguished, but they are identified in content. Therefore, one cannot love God without at the same time loving his fellow human beings—indeed, loving all creatures and the whole world. It would be a contradiction if anyone were to try to make such a distinction. Creator and creation cannot be separated from one another. I mentioned earlier that Singer has strong reservations on this issue. Scheler gives him even more reason to disagree in maintaining that love for the human being is possible only through love of God.

In the first years of his second period (about 1912), Scheler was very negative toward philanthropy, or what Singer calls humanitarian love, characterizing it as a repressed hatred of God, but later in the same period he became more open toward the notion of humanism, even if it is not explicitly paired with love for God. In essence Scheler continued to maintain that the two loves must be one and cannot be separated.

Because of the possibility of loving, human beings are elevated high above all that cannot love. They bear something divine within them, because they love with God's love. In the years after *Formalism* this point is worked out more explicitly. The human being, standing in the midpoint of the world, must join God in redeeming all things. Only God is love in the full sense; the human being *is* not love, for his person must win love and so become him/herself. Yet Scheler writes: "Man is not first of all a thinking being or a willing being but a loving being (*ens amans*)." What drives a human being is love, as a gift of God. The ultimate goal is that there be "a maximum of love upon the earth."

The task of human beings is the task of a moral being and it becomes "as much as possible . . . to love the things as God loves them." Therefore, their love must be properly directed, for the purpose is to find the true *Ordo amoris* which is the kernel of both the world order and the divine order. Here I come back to Scheler's personal problem, which is at the same time the problem of human beings in his time and in ours, namely, what the proper order of values is in love, so that human love can go together with love in God. That would be the topic for another paper, but in the meantime I would recommend the movie *Awakenings*, based on the book by Dr. Oliver Sachs. In the patients of the psychiatric ward the person is hidden, as Scheler would say, and they are dealt with by the medical staff as vegetables. However, the new psychiatrist, Dr. Sayer, is able to wake them up from their sleep with carefully chosen medicine, prompted by his love for the person in each one of them.

NOTES

1. Anders Nygren, *Agape and Eros* (Philadelphia: The Westminster Press, 1953).

2. Max Scheler, *Formalism in Ethics and Non-Formal Ethics of Values* (Evanston, Ill.: Northwestern University Press, 1973); *The Nature of Sympathy* (Hamden, Conn.: Archon Books, 1974); "Ordo Amoris," in *Selected Philosophical Essays* (Evanston, Ill.: Northwestern University Press, 1973); *Ressentiment* (New York: Schocken Books, 1972). Future references to these texts will be to these editions.

3. John H. Nota, *Max Scheler, The Man and His Work* (Chicago: Franciscan Herald Press, 1983), p. 37.

4. *Summa Theologiae* II.II.23.2.

5. *Summa contra Gentiles* III, 69.
6. V. J. McGill, "Scheler's Theory of Sympathy and Love," *Philos. and Phen. Res.* 2 (1941–42): 273ff.
7. *On the Eternal in Man* (Hamden, Conn.: Archon Books, 1972), pp. 215f., n. 2.

12

Inauthentic and Authentic Love in Sartrean Existentialism

Thomas Flynn

It may seem odd to begin with the inauthentic. After all, is not the very term parasitical on a positive conception, to which it attaches either as negation or at least as privation? Should we not discuss love first in its authentic mode, the better to draw the contrast with whatever inauthentic forms may attend it?

In the case of Jean-Paul Sartre, I believe it is inappropriate to do so. After all, he is noted for the phrase, "Hell is other people," the Hobbesian tone of which is not very optimistic about interpersonal relations. And his famous phenomenological description of the "look" (*le regard*) in *Being and Nothingness* exhibits an ontology of the visual that seems to justify the thesis commonly ascribed to him that all human relationships are basically sado-masochistic. So it would seem that Sartre's apparent pessimism about love requires that we begin with the inauthentic and consider whether authentic love is any more than an abstract ideal, another "futile passion" to plague human reality.

After rehearsing the better known passages in Sartre's phenomenological ontology that militate against even the most basic concept of love as mutual well wishing (*amor benevolentiae*), I wish to consider other loci that offer us a concept of love which contradicts the one we usually associate with his work. I shall conclude with thoughts on the significance of this paradox in Sartrean existentialism as well as with several observations about what theorists like Irving Singer might learn from Sartre's phenomenology, his politico-economic philosophy, his aesthetics, and his social ontology regarding a more adequate account of the phenomenon of love. In addressing Singer's reading of Sartre, I am attending to the most thorough attempt thus far to locate the existentialist in the broader context of the history of the concept of love in Western philosophy.

I

Sartre's most famous discussion of love occurs in *Being and Nothingness,* in a section entitled "Concrete Relations With Others."[1] There he describes the "two primitive attitudes which I assume confronting the Other" (BN, 363), namely, the attitude of assimilating the other's freedom as such (which reaches its extreme in masochism) and that of simply objectifying the other's freedom so that it retains its character of freedom (the extreme of which is sadism). In either case, the point of the relationship is not to destroy the other freedom but to possess it. Destruction of the other's freedom would, in fact, be loss of my own *identity* (being-in-itself), which the other's freedom has imposed upon me and yet kept tantalizingly out of my reach.

A basic, irreducible dimension of human reality, for Sartre, is its being-for-others. The presence of other subjects is a contingent fact that I experience as alienation, though strictly speaking I do not "know" it, for knowledge is objectifying and it is precisely as subject, not as object, that the Other is experienced by me in my alienation. As Sartre's well-known discussion of the "look" seeks to establish, this experience of my being an object for the Other subject yields "an absolute and self-evident fact, but a contingent fact" (BN, 363), one not deducible from the ontological structures of consciousness itself. Sartre sees the failure of each of these attitudes as moving us to the other in a motion that is circular, not dialectical, but enriching at every turn. And he insists, "we can never get outside the circle" (BN, 363). Let us examine the phase of these revolving relations that Sartre calls "love."

At the outset, we must note that love belongs to the same cluster of relations as the masochistic attitude, whereas sexuality pertains to the sadistic group. The lover, in Sartre's view, wishes to assimilate the other's freedom. Since the basic relation between consciousnesses, for Sartre, is one of looking-looked at, the lover must seduce the other's freedom by exaggerating his/her own status as being-looked-at, by making himself/herself a "fascinating object" (BN, 372).

Sartre had previously described a fascinating object as one before which I feel as nothing, one which I raise in absolute relief on a background of emptiness that I likewise constitute (BN, 177). He seems to have in mind

the Husserlian concept of immediate evidence, to which he adds a characteristically dramatic touch, as well as Rousseau's pantheistic intuitions of
"melting" into the universe. But in the latter case Sartre cautions us not to
neglect that "nothing" which separates the knower from the known and allows
the universe to appear as a phenomenon in the first place (BN, 177–78). (Sartre
would have difficulties similar to Singer's with the "idealist" theories of love
as "merging." But he would not accept Singer's alternative, as we shall see.)[2]

"By seduction," Sartre observes, "I aim at constituting myself a fullness
of being and at making myself *recognized as such*" (BN, 372, original emphasis).
I effect this by acts that point in two directions, inward and outward: inward
toward a pseudosubjectivity wherein I aim toward a seemingly infinite series
of possible acts that constitute my objective, unperceived being (what Irving
Singer would call "Proustian realism" [*Nature*, 3:292]); and outward toward
the world, which I present to the beloved as necessarily mediated by me.
I present myself to the beloved as infinite depth and as encompassing world;
in both cases as unsurpassable. Of course, the other's freedom must give its
consent by recognizing itself as a nothingness before the plenitude of my being.

But if love is fascination, not all fascination is love. The loss of myself
in the object that some experiences of evidence seem to entail, scarcely suffices
for a relationship of love. What is required in addition is that the beloved
him/herself project being loved. In other words, that the beloved try to capture
the lover's freedom by acts of seduction as well. In sum, "to love is in essence
the project of making oneself loved" (BN, 375). This is love as ideal, as illusion,
as a "game of mirrors" analogous to the pure "reflection-reflected" of Sartrean
consciousness.

One may well ask: Why this endless dance of seduction/fascination? Why
can't the two lovers simply express their affection as they lose themselves
in something "bigger than both of us," as they say in the movies? The answer,
as we should expect, is ontological. It is the nature of Sartrean consciousness
to be *non*self-identical, that is, to exist as a relationship of internal negation
to all others and to its very self. "Man is free," Sartre observes in a lapidary
phrase, "because he is not a self but a presence-to-self" (BN, 440). Freedom
as presence-to and not identity-with implies otherness. There is no direct action
on another freedom. As Sartre explains in his essay *Anti-Semite and Jew*,
we can act only on the other's situation, not on his/her freedom.[3] Fortunately,
we do not have to discuss the problematic relation between freedom and
situation in this scheme. It is enough to point out that this is the context
out of which Sartre can use a word like "demand" (*exige*) to denote the relation
between lovers that excludes reciprocity, as in the following quote:

> Each of the lovers is entirely the captive of the Other inasmuch as each
> wishes to make himself loved by the Other to the exclusion of anyone else;

but at the same time each one demands from the other a love which is not reducible to the "project of being-loved." What he demands in fact is that the Other without originally seeking to make himself be loved should have at once a contemplative and affective intuition of his beloved as the objective limit of his freedom, as the totality of being and the supreme value. Love thus exacted from the other could not *ask for* anything; it is a pure engagement without reciprocity. Yet this love cannot exist except in the form of a demand on the part of the lover. (BN, 375)

Reference to a "contemplative and affective intuition" in this passage indicates Sartre's less than rationalistic approach to the love relationship. And his introduction of the beloved as "supreme value" seems to counter Singer's claim that "at no point does [Sartre] consider instances in which the lover bestows value upon the beloved" (*Nature*, 3:298). For even in the alienating relations of *Being and Nothingness* there is a contemplative and affective intuition," presumably a direct intentional relation, of the beloved as "supreme value."

Now I believe Singer could respond that the value mentioned by Sartre in this passage is purely instrumental, not intrinsic, that it is a means to my achieving the impossible goal of founding my own consciousness. Moreover, the love context is typically masochistic: I wish the Other to regard me, her beloved, as the supreme value (and vice versa).

While I agree that the question of any intrinsic values in Sartre's philosophy is problematic (though I believe that freedom is one such), I would argue that it is the beloved *as constitutive* of my in-itself-for-itself, not merely as an extrinsic means toward its achievement, that forms the "supreme value" Sartre speaks of. This, of course, would seem to imply that my ideal, my identity and godlike self-coincidence, requires the Other and that the individualist Sartre is committed *nolens volens* to an *interpersonal* ideal. I think this is indeed the case as soon as we admit the de facto presence of the Other on the horizon of Sartrean consciousness. In other words, the Sartrean "human reality," even in its vintage existentialist phase, is not as atomistic as is commonly believed. To be sure, its interpersonal dimension is a contingent fact, dependent on the fact of the other's presence. But so, too, is the existence of human reality itself. Still, to develop this claim would lead us deeper into Sartre's social ontology than the scope of this brief essay allows.

The demand-response relationship mentioned in the lengthy quote given above will continue to function in Sartre's social ontology constructed in the *Critique of Dialectical Reason* in the 1950s. It does so in the analysis of an agent and the "objective demands" of a social situation, that of the industrial capitalist, for example, responding to the exigencies of the "iron law of wages." It functions likewise in what I have called elsewhere the "command-obedience" concept of authority operative in Sartre's political theory.[4] But we should note that in all these examples it is a question of *alienated* relationships; the agent is laboring under the aegis of seemingly insuperable otherness. If alienation is to be evacuated from interpersonal relations for Sartre, "alterity," as he terms it, must be either overcome or rendered innocuous.[5]

In *Being and Nothingness* as well, the context is one of alienated freedom. Human reality is fundamentally the futile passion to coincide consciously with itself, to be a conscious thing, to be God. This drive infects the love relationship by seeking to capture the freedom of the Other, whose objectifying gaze holds the key to my identity. As Sartre observes: "Here we encounter the true ideal of love's enterprise: alienated freedom. But it is the one who wants to be loved who by the mere fact of wanting someone to love him alienates his freedom" (BN, 375).

The love relationship is a perpetual play of mirrors which can last as long as neither party considers the other a mere object, simply a means or instrument to his/her ends. Should that occur, the game is over, the illusion shattered. We are returned to the normal world of practical concerns.

This ideal of the love relationship as alienated freedom, that is, as reified nothingness, as an identity that is nonself-identical, is exemplified in many of Sartre's plays, novels, and short stories. It obtains, for example, between Annie and Roquentin in *La Nausée*. Each is attempting to achieve Sartre's ideal of love as alienated (objectified) freedom; each is destined to futility.[6]

But there is a certain modification of Sartre's pessimism concerning love manifest in his play *The Devil and the Good Lord* and in his brilliant introduction to Jean Genet's collected works, *Saint Genet: Actor and Martyr*. In the former, it is the faithful love of a woman, Hilda, Sartre's equivalent of Camus' secular saint, that enables the chief protagonist, Goetz, to transform hatred into love—by pushing hatred to its extreme. ("I wanted pure love: ridiculous nonsense. To love anyone is to hate the same enemy; therefore I will adopt your hates.")[7] The point is not to achieve a union of freedoms where alienation is absent; it is to embrace that *otherness-within-unity* as consciously as possible. The unity, in this case, is the common project of the Peasant Rebellion, and the otherness is the impossibility of overcoming the nihilating function of consciousness. As Goetz says to Hilda at the height of their relationship, "You are myself. We shall be alone together" (DGL, 146).

In his study of Jean Genet, Sartre offers us a detailed example of authenticity in the young man who "chooses" to be the thief others have objectified him as being in order to turn the tables on their objectifying power. He pursues this reversal by seducing them into the strange hell of the imaginary where he is the Lord of Nothingness, an interpretation Sartre repeats in his study of Flaubert's "choice" of the imaginary, though in this case an inauthentic choice.

It is the association of love with *generosity* in this work that marks a significant advance in Sartre's understanding and moves it closer to the authentic. Hilda's love was faithful but not generous: she helped others because, as she said, she needed them. In Sartre's Jean Genet, no doubt an imaginative creation, we have the consummate artist whose works are acts of freedom addressed to other freedoms who choose to realize the aesthetic object or not as they see fit. But the very production of the art work is a generous act, one that proffers a *gift* to whoever encounters it properly. Speaking of Genet, Sartre remarks: "In his private life, he attains at least the virtue that resembles him, generosity, *his* virtue. I for one rate this virtue rather high, because it is in the image of freedom, as Descartes realized. But let us not forget that it is freedom refracted through the feudal world."[8] In other words, the gift confirms us in the illusion of possessing; it does not liberate us from it.

What is lacking in the gift relationship to make it authentic, what keeps it in the orbit of *Being and Nothingness* is the absence of *positive reciprocity* in these acts. Sartre enunciated the root problem in interpersonal relations when he said that reciprocity, equality, mutuality between consciousnesses was impossible: "The essence of the relations between consciousnesses is not *Mitsein* but conflict" (BN, 420). It is no exaggeration to say that the evolution of Sartre's understanding of love turns on his growing sense of the social possibility of positive reciprocity between agents. In *Being and Nothingness* this was impossible, chiefly because of his commitment to a visual model of interpersonal relations. But soon thereafter Sartre began to appreciate both its possibility and its necessity. The locus for his discussions is ethical—Sartre was always a moralist—but it was in his unpublished notes for an existentialist ethic that he most directly addressed these issues. Let us examine them more closely.

II

The *Notebooks for an Ethics* are the pages Sartre filled in preparation for the ethics he had promised would follow *Being and Nothingness*. Published posthumously in 1983, they offer a view of Sartre's concept of love that contradicts in many aspects the one commonly attributed to him. Yet in those reflections Sartre remains tied to the looking-looked at ontology of his previous work. The incompatibility of his evolving notion of interpersonal relations with the social ontology of *Being and Nothingness* is the source of many of the tensions that characterize these notebooks. Let us examine several of the more telling passages.

On the concept of the gift, for example, Sartre continues to acknowledge the possibility that conferring a gift on another may be a form of enslavement, not an act of liberation. He cites the Potlatch, an American Indian festival at which gifts are distributed, as such a practice and adds that "the Potlatch has a structure analogous to that of love."⁹ But he immediately acknowledges the basic *ambiguity* and instability of the Potlatch and of the gift in general: it may serve as an act of friendship and solidarity or as one of defiance and enmity. Each party to the relationship has an implicit ("nonthetic," Sartre calls it) awareness of this ambiguity and the relationship changes as the interpretation of the other party's intention varies (NE, 376).

What is it that enables the agent to proffer a gift that liberates, not enslaves? Although space will not allow us to elaborate the claim, there is an increasing sense of the category of objective possibility operative in the *Notebooks* and especially in the *Critique of Dialectical Reason* (1958). It reinforces Sartre's thesis, mentioned earlier, that we cannot act on another freedom except indirectly, by changing his/her situation. In the present text, Sartre reflects on the reason for optimism in the midst of seemingly inevitable social alienation: "At least as a rubric, as an ideal directive," he allows, "one can conceive of an absolute conversion to intersubjectivity. This conversion is *moral.* It presumes a political and social conjunction (namely, the suppression of classes and of the State) as its necessary condition, but this suppression is not sufficient" (NE, 406–407).

Given the tentative and hypothetical nature of the reflections gathered in these notebooks, it is not surprising to find sketched here thoughts that will dominate Sartre's next major theoretical enterprise, the *Critique of Dialectical Reason.* For example, he adopts Malraux's term "apocalypse" to express that moment when individuals will break free from the alienating domination of the Other. In words anticipating the "spirit of '68" Sartre writes:

> Such is the true historical dialectic. Its three terms are: [a] given Alienation, Apocalypse, and alienation of the Apocalypse. One sees that the moment of human effort is the Apocalypse. The reversal of *Praxis.* The Alienation of this Apocalypse occurs dialectically and without the concurrence of responsible wills. So the human moment, the moment of ethics [*la morale*] is that of the Apocalypse, that is to say, [the moment] of the liberation of oneself and of the other in a reciprocal recognition. Paradoxically, it is also most often the moment of violence. . . . Celebration, apocalypse, permanent Revolution, generosity, creation—behold the *moment of man.* The Everyday, Order, Repetition, Alienation—behold the moment of the Other than man. There can be no freedom except in liberation. An *order* of freedoms is inconceivable because it is contradictory. (NE, 414; F, 429–30)

The ambiguity as the interpersonal is underscored: "The real human relationship among freedoms is *always* present and always alienated. There is always *both* recognition and subjugation" (NE, 414). But Sartre is now aware of the positive reciprocity that he had overlooked earlier:

No love without that sadistic-masochistic dialectic of subjugation of free-doms which I described [elsewhere]. No love without deeper recognition and reciprocal comprehension of freedoms (a missing dimension in *B[eing and] N[othingess]*). However, to attempt to bring about a love that would surpass the sadistic-masochistic stage of desire and of enchantment would be to make love disappear, that is, the sexual as a type of unveiling of the human. *Tension* is necessary to maintain the two faces of ambiguity, to hold them within the unity of one and the same project. As soon as one loosens the ambiguity, duality takes over again. There is no given synthesis to be achieved. It has to be invented. (NE, 414–15; F, 430)

This acknowledged ambiguity of love (the inevitable tension between the sexual and the benevolent), while allowing a positive dimension overlooked in *Being and Nothingness,* seems to leave us with the advice given by Sartre's Genet: to have the courage to "go to the limits of ourselves in both directions at once" (SG, 599).[10] This is, indeed, the image of authentic love as Sartre portrays it, but it is the picture of authentic love in an inauthentic society (to paraphrase Reinhold Niebuhr). It is the love between individuals for whom love is both necessary and impossible (to paraphrase *Saint Genet*). It is a Sisyphean undertaking that has abandoned hope of pacific possession either of oneself or of another.

Finally, in the *Notebooks* Sartre suggests the ideal of love that might be possible in a classless society: a generosity without possessions, a gift of oneself in absolute freedom. As he formulates it: "The ego *exists to lose itself:* it is the Gift. Reconciliation with Destiny is generosity. In a society without classes it can also be love, that is, the project undertaken confident that freedoms evaluated as such and willed as such will take up and transform my work and therefore my Ego, which will thus lose itself in the absolute dimension of freedom" (NE, 418).

This linking of love with *mon oeuvre* reminds us that in an alienated society and perhaps elsewhere, "the true relation to others is never direct: [it occurs] through the intermediary of the work. [The work] is my freedom implying mutual recognition. " Sartre reflects, "Yet one loses oneself in giving oneself. Generosity. Love. [We have] a new relationship between my For-itself and my For-others: by means of the work. I define myself in giving myself to the other as an object which I create that he/she may return this objectivity" (NE, 470; F, 487; cf. NE, 500). Throughout Sartre's writings, the paradigm of this generous act is artistic creation. To write is an act of generosity, an act of confidence in other freedoms, a risk of communication between freedoms valued as such. Although the spirit of possessive individualism may intervene to short-circuit this undertaking, its fundamental thrust remains to offer us hope that in more equitable circumstances such a project might succeed.

But it would be a gross misrepresentation of Sartrean theory to imply that simple change of socioeconomic conditions could bring about authentic love. A fundamental change on the part of the individual, what he calls in a famous footnote in BN a "radical conversion," is required as well. Although I cannot elaborate the nature of this conversion here, its nature is likewise sketched in the reflections of the *Notebooks*. Briefly, it entails a "purifying reflection" by which I "choose," in the Sartrean sense of fundamental "choice," to live my love in the *anguished tension* between my previous acts and my real possibilities for the future. This is love as "doing" (*faire*), not as "being," and it introduces the temporal dimension to the ontological aspect of freedom already discussed (NE 475, 477).

Sartre is now able to describe "what *loving* signifies in its authentic sense. I love if I *create* the contingent finitude of the Other as being-in-the-midst-of-the-world by assuming my own subjective finitude and by *willing* this subjective finitude, and if through the same movement that makes me assume my finitude/subject, I assume her finitude/object as being the necessary condition for the free goal that she projects and which presents itself to me as an unconditional end" (NE, 501; F, S16). As Sartre explains, "this vulnerability, this finitude, *is the body*. The body others. To unveil the other in her being-in-the-midst-of-the-world is to love her in her body (NE, 501; F 517). This leads Sartre to give us what is perhaps the most advanced of his descriptions of love, "an original structure of authentic love," namely, "to unveil the Other's being-in-the-midst-of-the-world, to take up this unveiling, and to set this Being within the absolute; to *rejoice* in (enjoy) it (*s'en rejouir*) without seeking to appropriate it; to shelter it in my freedom and to surpass it only in the direction of the Other's end (*fin*) (NE, 508; F, 523–24).

Note that in this case as with the artwork, I enable the other to reveal his/her freedom by responding to the demand-appeal which that freedom in its vulnerability constitutes. I have come to the point of respecting the other freedom as noninstrumental or as coinstrumental, of enabling it to pursue its end which is compatible with my own.

III

Let us now address the paradox posed at the outset of two Sartrean concepts of love. We can then determine how Sartre might strengthen Singer's account of the nature of love as we critique the latter's reading of these Sartrean texts.

The evolution of Sartre's concept of love in the few years between BN and the *Notebooks* is indicative of changes in his philosophy overall. This is a crucial period in Sartre's philosophical development, when he comes to realize the importance of properly social categories for understanding the human condition. His challenge is to discover a means of incorporating the existentialist concepts of spontaneous freedom and individual responsibility into the categories of social causation, rights and duties, institutional roles, and the like. If he is to reserve a place for the positive reciprocity and mutuality of love in the midst of economic scarcity and racist practices, it must be in a manner that "historicizes" the phenomenological descriptions of BN. In other words, these last must be seen as describing interpersonal relations in an alienated society. The glimmer of hope shining forth from the *Notebooks* presumes the possibility, at least, that such oppression and exploitation might someday come to an end. The contradictory character of these two works (the descriptions of authentic love and positive reciprocity in the *Notebooks,* for example, which BN dismisses as impossible) is lessened by this "contextualization," but it leaves us suspicious of Sartre's perspicuous hindsight in this regard.

Secondly, Sartre's continued reference to the subject-object relation reveals the tension generated by his continued use of the looking-looked at model of interpersonal relations. Another model is called for and the word for it, "praxis," is uttered once in the *Notebooks* but never exploited. Only with his exchange of praxis for consciousness in the *Critique* is Sartre able to generate a viable social philosophy and by implication a plausible theory of love.

Thirdly, the truly social aspect of the love relationship, as distinct from its simply interpersonal character, is at least alluded to by means of the claim in *Notebooks,* which contradicts that of BN, that "love and hatred are oaths" (NE, 476). Again, it is a matter of Sartre's sensing the inadequacy of his analysis in BN without realizing the source of the difficulty: a failed model of social relationships based on a visual concept of consciousness.

One may question why Sartre did not publish these notebooks, but it would be inaccurate to say that he repudiated the concepts of love and related topics which he formulated in these pages. Many of these ideas recur throughout his subsequent writings. And they approximate the position he expressed on love and the ethical in the famous Benny Lévy interviews toward the end of his life.[11] And what can a theorist like Irving Singer, who obviously respects Sartre's writings, learn from them as he reflectively pursues "the nature of love"? As I mentioned at the start of this discussion, Sartre can instruct us on this topic from several perspectives; as phenomenologist, as socioeconomist, as aesthetician, and as social ontologist. These are areas where Singer's critical analyses of Sartre seem to miss their mark. Let us conclude this essay with a brief consideration of each.

First, Sartrean phenomenology necessarily entails a certain value-bestowing dimension in every act that it describes. Consciousness for Husserl is essentially meaning-giving and Sartrean consciousness is no exception. All conscious acts share in the fundamental project that individuates the agent. It is from this perspective that they endow their objects with meaning-value, a nuance proper to existential phenomenology. So there is no such thing as value-free consciousness, much less value-free knowledge, for Sartre. As we saw earlier, the lover "constitutes" the beloved as "supreme value." No doubt the nature of this "value" is problematic in Sartre's larger theory, but that remains to be investigated along with the nature of Sartrean love in general. I have tried to sketch the lines along which such inquiry might be pursued. In any case, Singer's criticism of the Sartrean lover's failure to "bestow value" on the beloved is misdirected. What it should address is the character of that bestowal. In the *Notebooks,* at least, it is not merely instrumental.

Sartre's socioeconomic theory instructs us about the nature of love *in concreto.* The *Notebooks* refer to the socioeconomic conditions for authenticity and consider them necessary, though not sufficient, for the advent of genuine love. To the extent that it ignores the social dimension of the love relationship, Singer's analysis seems excessively abstract. Sartre's, on the contrary, is concrete in the Hegelian sense of being more fully determined in its historical conditions. As he moved from abstract to concrete freedom in his later work, so did his analysis of the love relation "thicken" after BN. If there is one broad criticism that I would direct toward Singer's masterful three-volume study in general and his reading of Sartre in particular, it is its tendency to overlook this socioeconomic dimension of love as "lived." No doubt, the philosopher must maintain a certain degree of abstractness under pain of losing professional identity. But what one abstracts from is indicative of a certain understanding of the profession and, I would argue, of one's social and political commitments as well. Sartre was the paradigmatic *philosophe engagé.* It is not inappropriate to address this essential aspect of his treatment of the question of love, even if only to explain why one considers it irrelevant.

Next, by the cluster of concepts that include demand-appeal, generosity, and revelation-unveiling Sartre connects the *communicative* dimension of love with what he has written about the artwork. From the very first, Sartre was a philosopher of the imagination. Anyone who would analyze, much less reconstruct, Sartre's implicit theory of love must address the role of the imagination in his works. In particular, they must reflect on the important parallels that he draws or implies between the beloved's body as *oeuvre* and the artwork which mediates freedoms without objectifying (alienating) them. Singer does not pursue this promising line, even though he shows himself sensitive to the imaginative dimension of the love relationship.

There is more to be learned from Sartre's social ontology, especially from his analysis of the mediating Third and the group-in-fusion, than Singer has thus far gathered. He repeats the standard criticism that "Sartre's philosophy never manages to explain how *interpersonal unity* can be the powerful experience that it is for many people" (*Nature,* 3:331). On the contrary, I would insist that Sartre's close scrutiny of the experience of "the same" and of "here" in group action in the *Critique,* for example, where everyone is "the same" as I and the locale of each is "here" for my practical concerns, is both subtle and insightful. It grounds ontologically the psychological experience of the friend as *alter ego*—precisely the kind of "interpersonal unity" that Singer notes is such a powerful experience for many people (ibid.). And Sartre's use of the concept of the mediating Third in that same work maintains a delicate balance between wholism and individualism in social ontology, respecting the "synthetic enrichment" of individual praxis that group activity entails without dissolving everything in a collective fog.[12]

Finally, Singer would benefit from reflecting on what Sartre writes in the *Notebooks* about love and hate as "oaths" (NE, 476) as well as from his discussion of the category of the "practico-inert" in the *Critique.* The latter elaborates the phenomenon of our sedimented past praxes returning to limit, deflect, and sustain our present activities. But this applies as much to linguistic events like saying "I love you" as it does to physical deeds like the abuse of our environment. The love relationship can easily be analyzed from this perspective, especially the phenomenon that Singer aptly distinguishes as "staying in love." And the relevance of Sartre's understanding of love as oath to staying in love is even more obvious.

But it would be improper to conclude without acknowledging the accuracy and depth of Irving Singer's analysis and critique of Sartre's position in the third volume of *The Nature of Love.* As I read Singer's remarks after preparing my own, I was struck repeatedly by the thoroughness with which he addresses the subject. If the same level of scholarship pervades the rest of these three volumes, I thought, this is a truly remarkable opus. Having now read much more of that work and listened to several authoritative reactions to other portions, I am convinced of its philosophical significance. *The Nature of Love* is indeed a *tour de force.*

NOTES

1. Jean-Paul Sartre, *Being and Nothingness,* trans. Hazel H. Barnes (New York: Philosophical Library, 1956), 361–412, hereafter cited as BN.

2. See Irving Singer, *The Nature of Love* (Chicago: University of Chicago Press, 1966–1987), vol. 3, *The Modern World,* 293–301, 406–18, and *passim,* hereafter cited as *Nature.*

3. See Jean-Paul Sartre, *Anti-Semite and Jew,* trans. George G. Becker (New York: Schocken Books, 1948), p. 148.

220   Part Three: Contemporary Formulations

4. See my "An End to Authority: Epistemology and Politics in the Later Sartre," *Man and World* 10 (1977): 448-65.
5. As in the "free alterity" of the group-in-fusion. See the *Critique of Dialectical Reason*, trans. Alan Sheridan-Smith (London: New Left Books, 1976), pp. 366ff.
6. Joseph H. McMahon describes this aptly in his *Humans Being: The World of Jean-Paul Sartre* (Chicago: University of Chicago Press, 1971), pp. 48-50 and 250n.
7. Jean-Paul Sartre, *The Devil & The Good Lord and Two Other Plays*, trans. Kitty Black et al. (New York: Vintage Books, 1960), p. 145, hereafter cited as DGL.
8. Jean-Paul Sartre, *Saint Genet: Actor and Martyr*, trans Bernard Frechtman (New York: New American Library, 1963), p. 578, hereafter cited as SG.
9. Jean-Paul Sartre, *Notebooks for an Ethics*, trans. David Pellauer (Chicago: University of Chicago Press, 1992), p. 376, hereafter cited as NE. This is a translation of *Cahiers pour une morale* (Paris: Gallimard, 1983), cited as F when my own translation is used.
10. In his commentary on these Sartrean texts, Singer notes a similar tension. See *Nature*, 3:319ff.
11. See "L'Espoir, maintenant . . ." *Le Nouvel Observateur*, No. 800 (March 10, 1980): 19; no. 801 (March 17, 1980): 52; and No. 802 (March 24, 1980): 55. English translation with some omissions in *Dissent* 27 (Fall 1980): 397-422.
12. I develop these notions in my "Mediated Reciprocity and the Genius of the Third," in Paul Arthur Schilpp, ed., *The Philosophy of Jean-Paul Sartre*, The Library of Living Philosophers (La Salle, Ill.: Open Court, 1981), pp. 345-70.

13

Caring Love and Liberty: Some Questions[1]

Marvin Kohl

What is love? To what extent, if any, does it (or a central form of it) require that we "help" a beloved by intervening in, or interfering with, her or his life? In other words, is there a kind of adult relationship[2] where the possibility of a closer relationship is not ruled out by one of the parties and where the relationship requires or permits a form of what I shall call *moderate paternalism,* i.e., a form of assertive caring, without control? I will suggest that there is an empirically manifested type of relationship, whereby if X loves Y, X must cherish and desire the well-being and happiness, the welfare of Y; and that, given the constituents of this relationship, X is required to help Y in certain circumstances if that help proves necessary. I shall call this relationship *benevolent* or *caring love.*

I

It is tempting to begin by saying that, given a commonsense understanding of the relationship between love and liberty, if X loves Y, X often has the right to interfere with Y's right to self-determination. So stated it may seem obvious, since it is widely believed that there is a kind of love that requires helping those we love if that help proves to be necessary, and futhermore that this provides much of the grounds for the right to intervene in their lives.

I confess that I am unable to give an adequate analysis of this entitlement. Perhaps it is true that loving generates an overriding right to seriously intervene sometimes in the lives of others. Perhaps it is also true that the rights of the lover to choose between alternative courses of action or goals without being restricted by external authority must bow before the so-called rights of the beloved. But "rights" talk adds a moral dimension that is, at best, notoriously untidy. I do not wish to compound the difficulties by adding to what is already a historical intellectual quagmire.

Alan Soble suggests that the demanding and intelligent reader, after surveying much of the literature on love, "might conclude the area is a mess, the idea is a mess, probably love itself is a mess."[3] There is no quick and easy way to tidy up this mess. But we may be able to clean up part of it, albeit a small part, by avoiding adventitious additions, especially the question of rights. For it is one thing to argue that if X loves Y, X often has the right to interfere with Y's right to self-determination. It is another to lower our intellectual sights and be content to better understand why love often requires intervention—perhaps even coercion. It is the second question that will be the focus of this paper.

II

What is there about the nature of caring love that appears to justify paternalistic behavior? A simple answer is that there is a central sense of love whereby love means caring and caring means helping when help is needed. In other words, the answer seems to be that when we care about someone, we care about that person's happiness and well-being, or what I shall call his or her welfare.

If this is true of caring, it seems to be yet more evidently true of love. Of course, this is an arguable leap. But if there is an underlying argument, one formulation may read; if X cares about Y, X is concerned about the welfare of Y. However, if X loves Y, X is deeply concerned about the welfare of Y (that is, more actively disposed, or more committed, to help Y) and largely—but not only—because of this X will intervene in Y's life if that action, in the context of Y's life, is necessary to protect an important good or prevent a serious harm. Thus if Barbara loves George and if, unknown to George, his life is immediately threatened by deadly force, then Barbara (given the usual caveats about the limits of reasonable action) is required to help George, especially if she is the only one in a position to do so. The rough but fundamental intuition is that death is typically a great, often *the* greatest loss; that the greater the threat, the greater the need to protect a beloved against it.

Let us consider a more contentious example. I deliberately use it because I do not believe that the commitment of the lover to the beloved is limited to cases of protecting against threats of death or, more generally, to the protection of only physical welfare. Suppose George's stance on abortion is actively pro-life. Suppose that Barbara is convinced that this will destroy his political career. Now if Barbara loves George, if Barbara is deeply concerned about his well-being, as well as what makes him subjectively happy, then aside from general moral duties or the special duties she may have, Barbara seems to be obliged to intervene in George's life, say, by reminding George forcefully that his stance on abortion may undermine his important career goals. This example may be illuminating, but it is not unproblematic. First of all, neither Barbara nor George knows (in any strict sense of the term) whether his abortion stance will prove helpful or harmful. Second, what Barbara is purportedly protecting is not a basic physical need but an important career goal. Finally, it raises "the how much intervention is warranted" question. Barbara seems content with supportive confrontation. Should she be more coercive? Does love, in this and essentially similar cases, allow or require greater intervention? If so, how much?

III

Let us return to the main argument. It may be thought that it misses its mark. True love, we may be told, requires that if X loves Y, X must accept Y as he or she is. This essentially means accepting the values and habits that are important to Y. So, if George has deep convictions about the wrongness of abortion and Barbara truly loves George, Barbara must not interfere with that stance.

Is this true? Does love demand, or even suggest, complete acceptance? That is to say, does love require that we accept a loved person completely as he or she is?

A positive answer to this question may involve a confusion between agapeic (or unconditional) love and nonagapeic (or conditional) love. I say "may involve a confusion" because I do not wish to deny that there are special circumstances in which the preferred thing is to love unconditionally. Nor do I wish to deny that conditional love requires commitment to the welfare of the loved object.

To love someone in a most central sense of nonagapeic love is to be emotionally attached to and generally take delight in the contemplation of that person and want his or her good. Accordingly, if X loves Y, X must cherish and desire the well-being and happiness of Y. I have called this kind of caring, benevolent or caring love in order to distinguish it not only from other kinds of love but also from even minimalistic forms of (what Robert Sternberg has called) consummate love.[4]

Here, however, it seems that even fair-minded opponents may be upset. They may suggest that benevolent love is a matter of degree and that at its most fundamental level only concern and well-wishing are required. If X benevolently loves Y, X must cherish and desire the well-being and happiness of Y, but X need do no more than wish Y well. Evidently, some thinkers would approve of the cultivation of this kind of affection, but would not recommend the cultivation of a more caring love. They may urge that benevolence in terms of well-wishing is enough. Now it may be admitted that, while all caring love is a form of benevolent love, not all benevolent love is caring love. What appears to be common to both is that they involve a direct concern for the good—that is, the happiness and well-being of another person. However, the rough but essential difference between benevolent and caring love is that the former is often limited to inert concern while the latter involves, by its very nature, active concern. Someone who wants a relationship of reciprocal caring love will generally be frustrated by, or dissatisfied with, a relationship where the other is content with well-wishing and inert concern. Imagine, for example, Barbara loving George caringly and George loving Barbara only in the more limited sense in which I use *benevolence*.

What the latter means is that there is often a conflict between what is in a person's best interest and what he or she wants. Someone, for example, may want to overeat because gluttony has become an essential condition for his happiness. But it does not follow that gluttony is a condition of well-being. Similarly, someone may want to smoke cigarettes because this habit has become a compulsion and he or she feels happier smoking than not smoking. But few would want to argue that this behavior is conducive to anyone's physical well-being. Similarly, if George's stance on abortion is self-destructive in some important way, it is difficult to understand—*ceteris paribus*—why, if Barbara knows this and loves George, she does not act accordingly.

Exactly how Barbara should go about interceding is difficult to say. There is an interesting body of evidence to indicate that attempts to change one's partner significantly in a loving relationship often signal the breakdown of that relationship. Diane Vaughan suggests that uncoupling begins when one of the partners starts to feel uncomfortable in the relationship and that it ends when that unhappiness is both explored and acted on.[5] The line between beginning to end a relationship and attempting to improve it may be a thin one. But there seems to be a vital difference between the attempt to change the behavior or values of a loved person because it primarily serves one's own perceived good and the attempt to change that person because one is primarily committed to his or her welfare. Caring love, if I understand it correctly, requires that when we interfere with the values or lifestyle of a beloved, we do so only because we intend and foresee their welfare, not because we solely or predominantly are aiming at our own. Indeed, it is true that relationships typically involve a complex mix of these feelings and motivations. Nonetheless it seems odd, if not counterintuitive, to say that X loves Y in this sense, yet X completely accepts Y's self-destructive behavior.

This position may seem to some offensively paradoxical; conseqently they may think it desirable to abandon it and substitute an agape notion of love. Here we may observe, first, that it is quite consistent with agapeic love to say that X loves Y only if X unconditionally accepts the qualities or features of Y or accepts Y regardless of her or his qualities, if by *acceptance* we mean to view or deal with the other with affection, without any criticisms or conditions. That is to say, there is one kind of agapeic love where all that seems to be required is that we bond and be committed to the other without any conditions (or, perhaps, significant conditions).

Biblical scholars suggest that this kind of commitment has its prototype in the love "manifested by God, and therefore it must be spontaneous and unmotivated, uncalculating, unlimited, and unconditional"[6] Similarly, Irving Singer regards agape as being wholly nonappraisive love, where we are to love more or less as God loves, remembering that "God loves all creatures regardless of how worthless they may be in an appraisive sense. . . ."[7] If, then, we seek agape love, we must accept the beloved exactly as he or she is. If George is a glutton and smokes and if Barbara loves George in this agapeic sense, then Barbara must accept the gluttony and the smoking. If George's stance on abortion is self-destructive and the nature of Barbara's affection is commitment without any conditions, then she may be bound by her love not only to accept but to support George's stance on abortion.

To be clear, then, we must particularize the kind of love we are talking about and at least distinguish between agapic (unconditional) and nonagapic (conditional) love. Even so we have not got rid of the problem, for we are still faced with the stark choice of being an agapeic or nonagapeic lover. Nor, for that matter, is the nonagapeic view free of the problem of paternalism.

IV

I may illustrate this by returning to George's life and the notion whereby if Barbara loves George, Barbara must cherish and desire the well-being and happiness of George and, although committed to George, it is not an unconditional love. Now the nature of commitment and the role it may play in the various kinds of love is not an easy one to understand. According to Sternberg:

> The decision/commitment component of love consists of two aspects—one short-term and one long-term. The short-term aspect is the decision to love

a certain other, whereas the long-term one is the commitment to maintain that love. The decision to love does not necessarily imply a commitment to that love. Oddly enough, the reverse is also possible, where there is a commitment to a relationship in which you do not make the decision, as in arranged marriages.[8]

Thus, a decision to love another is not a necessary commitment to love him or her throughout life. This is easy enough to understand. But it does not help us with the more difficult question.

What exactly does having a commitment mean? For Sternberg it seems minimally to mean making a decision to love a certain other but not necessarily making a commitment to maintain that love. Yet it is not at all clear what "making a decision to love" signifies. It does not seem to mean the state of arousal Sternberg calls passion, since it is unusual, if not odd, to say that a person decides and, thereupon, has a feeling of attachment toward another. Unlike Singer, Sternberg does not distinguish between the appraisal and bestowal elements of love. What Sternberg perhaps should say is that loving a person minimally means according that person a preferential status that is unearned in any appraisive sense;[9] that it is having a profound primitive affinity, an affinity richer than mere liking for that person; and that it implies a decision to maintain or nurture that feeling but not necessarily the intimacy or the relationship.

The last-named notion, is, however, perplexing. After all, if X has a profound primitive affinity for Y, an affinity richer than mere liking, then why would X not want intimacy or a relationship with Y? Sternberg, by way of a partial answer, suggests that not all love is acquisitive. Contrary to a venerable philosophical and literary tradition, it is possible for people to love without necessarily directing their longing and desire to the possession of that human object by whom one expects to be made happy. In other words, having the passion in itself does not necessarily *cause* the wanting of intimacy or possession of the love-object in question. Nor does the having of passion in and of itself illuminate the nature and limits of a commitment to care for a beloved. Sternberg tells us that one can be smothered by love, that a lover, among other things, can care too passionately or possessively. But he does not suggest the rules of a reasonably caring relationship, which is not exactly the same as providing rules for successful relationships.

Jan Narveson's argument[10] for relationships based primarily on self-interest, even in outline, is a complex one. I will not pretend to do it full justice here. Narveson agrees that there is a contrast between the idea of what is in one's interest and what one wants. But he suggests that this cuts across another contrast, that between what X thinks Y's interests are and what Y thinks they are. Imagine Barbara *thinking* George is interested in having a caring love relationship, where George thinks he is not. Or imagine George *thinking* Barbara would be a better person, in the sense of caring about her own well-being, if she retreats from having a caring relationship with George. Narveson asks whether the attempt to change these interests is motivated by love or really by self-interest. The answer, I believe, is that in some cases it is motivated by love, in some cases by self-interert, and in some cases by a combination of the two. Here I would follow Carol Gilligan and say that love and self-interest are not necessarily incompatible and what is required is a kind of education that stresses different ways of imagining the self in relationship, a kind of education which encourages inclusive problem solving.[11] However, this is probably a feeble reply to those who have plausible theories of the self and self-interest, or to those who have selves which, given their present nature, cannot become caregivers in relationships.

One might argue that these distinctions and facts merely illustrate the relationship between one kind of love and what I have called moderate paternalistic behavior. Men and women do not have to love in a caring way. Yet surely it does not follow from this alone—from the diversity of the kinds of love or even from the fact that a person can love another merely by having a profound emotional affinity for that person—that human beings are justified in having life plans devoid of caring love. To discuss this fully would carry us too far beyond the range of this paper. But we may perhaps note that a libertarian may plausibly argue that if the price of full autonomy is to have a life plan devoid of caring love, then that is the price one must pay. However, this has to be argued, since caring love is a source of the fullest satisfaction known to human beings and typically is considered the primary emotional good.

To sum up, there is a kind of love that requires a form of paternalism. It is a kind of conditional affection I have called caring love. For X to love Y, in this sense, X must cherish and desire (in the sense of being actively concerned about) the well-being and happiness of Y. Given the constituents of this relationship, X is required to help Y in certain circumstances (given the usual caveats about the limits of reasonable action) if such help proves necessary even if that help involves intervention. Remaining issues include a fuller analysis of how liking, intimacy, and commitment are related to caring; more carefully distinguishing between caring as a constitutive element and caring as an obligation; having a clearer understanding of how conflicts between the subjective happiness and well-being affect how a lover should care about the welfare of the beloved; and the extent to which agapeic love can be successfully mixed with, or serve as an ideal for, its nonagapeic counterparts. These issues deserve a detailed examination, one that must be reserved for a future date.

NOTES

1. This is a revised version of "Love and Liberty," a paper presented at the *Free Inquiry* Conference on Humanism and Liberty, Boston, November 4, 1990. Although I do not share Jan Narveson's self-interest theory of relationships, I am indebted to him for several valuable suggestions.

2. By limiting my analysis to adult love, I hope to reduce the need of addressing the question of caring for others, especially children, by helping them grow and actualize themselves. Contrary to a venerable tradition, children seem more vulnerable to paternalism, especially its more subtle or suffocating forms, because they are in the process of self-determination, of forming their own values and ideals. I am not suggesting that in adulthood or even in late adulthood this process is necessarily complete. I only wish to suggest that many adults seem less vulnerable to control and more capable of protecting their own values and life plans.

3. Alan Soble, "Analyzing Love," *Philosophy of the Social Sciences* 19 (1989): 493.

4. My characterization of caring love largely follows Bertrand Russell (*What I Believe* [London: Kegan Paul, 1925], pp. 28–42). Robert Sternberg, on the other hand, maintains that there is a cluster of human relationships which can be measured and better understood by using (but not only using) scales of liking and love. Sternberg suggests that love can be understood best in terms of three components: intimacy, passion, and decision/commitment. Using these components, he distinguishes eight kinds of love, including consummate love. Consummate love (i.e., the combination of all three components) seems to be akin to what I have been calling caring love. The difficulty is that what is purported to be consummate love is a matter of degree and is, therefore, not necessarily consummate. The reason seems to be that intimacy and commitment, in themselves or when they are only minimally present, are not synonymous with caring and being strongly disposed to help actively. See Robert J. Sternberg, "The Nature of Love," *Journal of Personality and Social Psychology* 47, no. 2 (1984): 312–29; "Liking Versus Loving: A Comparative Evaluation of Theories," *Psychological Bulletin* 102, no. 3 (1987): 331–45; *The Triangle of Love* (New York: Basic Books, 1988).

5. Diane Vaughan, *Uncoupling: Turning Points in Intimate Relationships* (New York: Oxford University Press, 1986), p. 13.

6. Anders Nygren, *Agape and Eros,* trans. Philip S. Watson (New York and Evanston: Harper & Row, 1969), p. 91.

7. Irving Singer, *The Modern World,* vol. 3 of *The Nature of Love* (Chicago and London: University of Chicago Press, 1987), p. 391.

8. Sternberg, *Triangle of Love,* p. 46.

9. Singer, *Nature of Love,* p. 393.

10. Personal correspondence, November 29, 1990.

11. Carol Gilligan, "Remapping the Moral Domain: New Images of the Self in Relationship," in *Reconstructing Individualism: Autonomy, Individuality, and the Self in Western Thought,* ed. by Thomas C. Heller et al. (Stanford, Calif.: Stanford University Press, 1986), pp. 237–52.

14

Singer's Idealization of Love: A Postscript

Marvin Kohl

"Caring Love and Liberty" was written in order to raise questions about the limits of paternalism and autonomy. I confess that I was unable to give a fully adequate analysis of these questions. Moreover, I have said relatively little about why caring love is preferable to weaker forms of benevolent love. There seem to be similar difficulties or questions with respect to other kinds of love, especially those in which the decision to love does not necessarily imply a commitment to help the beloved. But in so far as caring love is a subspecies of benevolent love, the former may be characterized as follows: in order for X to caringly love Y, X must cherish and desire (in the sense of being actively concerned about) the well-being and happiness of Y. This active concern involves a commitment to help Y when this help is necessary to protect important goods or prevent serious harms. Given the constituents of this relationship, X is required to help Y in certain circumstances if it proves necessary even if that help involves intervention. In other words, there are situations in which a love of this kind requires that one seek to alter the beloved in ways that are contrary to his or her own inclinations and desires. The caring nature of this love also requires that, when we interfere with the values or lifestyle of a beloved, we do so only because we intend and foresee his or her welfare, not because we are aiming at our own, or have some other overriding goal. From this perspective, to have reverence for a person as an end, not as a means, involves a concern about his or her welfare, and this is a larger concern than one limited to what a person may or may not consent to.

I share in the admiration commonly accorded to Singer's historical analysis and, largely because of this, I had hoped to be able to avoid a direct attack on his theory. However, it is not difficult for me to see, in retrospect, why Singer responded critically to my paper and has requested a less oblique analysis.

Polemic in philosophy often forgets the product and loses itself in battle. A view too commonly held is that, because explanations of love in relation to sentiments such as hatred, anger, benevolence, and caring are difficult to provide, it is prudent for philosophers of love to be content with disputation. There also is a tendency to stress the work a philosopher has not done rather than the work he has done. This, I hope, explains my initial reluctance to focus upon Singer's scattered statements about autonomy. In addition, there is a tendency, at least in analytic circles, to overlook the value of Singer's history of the philosophy of love, his analytical ingenuity and the importance of his insights into the nature and role of ideals.[1] For Singer himself limits the goals of his trilogy. Originally, it was limited to the task of drawing a distinction between two types of valuing—appraisal and bestowal—and explaining how each is relevant not only to love but also to the philosophy of love in the ancient, medieval, and modern world. He does not purport to offer a philosophical description of love in relation to other important sentiments. Nor does he pretend to offer a theory of love with developed arguments as to why we should accept another as he is in himself or as he happens to be, assuming that is what the beloved wants. But this claim forms a thread that runs throughout Singer's writings. Early in his study Singer suggests that a lover "will feel an intimate concern about the continuance of good properties in the beloved and the diminishing of bad ones." But in the same context where he raises the question of helping the beloved realize her potentialities, Singer adds, "assuming that is what she wants."[2]

> Appraisal without bestowal may lead us to change other people regardless of what they want. . . . But this is not a loving attitude. . . . In loving another person, we respect *his* desire to improve himself. In offering to help we do so because he wants to be better than he is, not because *we* think he ought to be.[3]

Similarly, I find Singer's reply to Russell Vannoy not fully satisfying.[4] For one thing, the notion of having love accept the other *only as she wants to be* while also being concerned, not merely about her "indefeasible autonomy," but also about her multidimensional welfare needs, is problematic. For another, Singer's purported explanation seems to exacerbate the problem. To say that "in itself bestowal adds nothing to the appraisive value of the beloved." that bestowal "devotes itself to creating value *beyond* appearance," and to conclude that "love is indeed an acceptance of another as she is in herself"—to my mind, isolates and mystifies the notion of bestowal.

To sum up: The negative claim is that *the bestowal of love does not seek to alter the object in ways that are alien or contrary to its own inclinations and desires.* The stronger claim is that *neither in the bestowing of, nor in being in, love is there warrant for intervention unless such an action is consented to.* It is not entirely clear from his writings which position Singer holds. But, given the conference discussion, I suspect it is the latter.

Singer seems to be a libertarian. Common to most variants of libertarianism is a core commitment to the inviolability of the individual and relatively unencumbered private property and autonomy rights. For the libertarian love may be important but what is more important and the overriding good, is the dignity and autonomy of the individual. Notice that Singer seems to believe not merely that appraisal may lead us to change other people regardless of what they want, but that in loving another person we should *only* respect his desires to improve himself. If we offer to help, we should do so *only* because he wants to be better than he is. Philosophically, what is objectionable is not that Singer is or appears to be a libertarian. For a libertarianism successfully explicated is an initially plausible alternative to other theories. What I find objectionable is that Singer systematically criticizes other thinkers for their unsupported idealizations but fails to provide the rational grounds for his own. What I find most disconcerting is the impression (perhaps adventitiously generated) that Singer is describing a neutral naturalism but one in which libertarian preferences, nonetheless, appear as self-evident truths.

Professor Singer correctly distinguishes between the type of joint dependence that is basically demeaning because each attempts to use the other selfishly, and the type of relationship defined in terms of interdependence. The former is a condition of mutual enslavement. But the latter, Singer writes, is a desirable mutuality.

> As an expression of interpersonal needs, their love will cause them to rely on one another and to that extent they will be dependent. But their dependence will no longer feel the same, and indeed it will not be the same: it now belongs to a relationship in which each wants the welfare of the other rather than merely wanting selfish benefits. It is therefore a mutuality they can freely accept.[5]

Advocates of caring love also oppose the kind of enslavement that sounds more like pathological than healthy love. Like Singer they also cherish a relationship in which each wants (but not only wants) the welfare of the other. But appreciating the autonomy of a beloved is not necessarily the same as never intervening in their behalf unless one has consent. And one tends to become suspicious of Singer's kind of "autonomy talk"—not only because it seems to reflect a male story as opposed to a woman's story of love, but because it fails to recognize that when it comes to a pluralistic welfare perspective, autonomy is not always trumps.

Dignity and autonomy *are* necessary conditions of the good life. An individual is said to have dignity to the extent that he or she has reasonable power to control important aspects of his or her own life. But dignity as self-possessed control does not require having total power; rather it consists in having reasonable control over the significant aspects of one's life. It consists in having a broader notion of welfare, one that understands that the best of personal relations is based upon caring for others *and* the enhancement of their dignity. For it is one thing to completely shatter the autonomy of an individual or irreparably damage his or her sense of self-worth. It is another to intervene without incurring such damage, especially if one does so only in vitally important matters and on the basis of fairly compelling evidence that it is really in behalf of the beloved's best interests.

Researchers are finding that the sense of being in control, and the desire for such control, are crucial aspects of the healthy and happy personality. Describing a study of convalescent home residents, Daniel Goleman writes that "increasing the sense of control among elderly men and women living in convalescent homes made them happier, increased their alertness and—perhaps most dramatically—lowered their mortality rate, over a period of 18 months, by 50 percent, compared with residents in the same homes who did not get the experiences of increased control."[6] Similarly, David Myers maintains that happy people believe they have personal control and choose their own destinies. He quotes, with favor, a survey reporting that "having a strong sense of controlling one's life is a more dependable predictor of positive feelings of well-being than any of the objective conditions of life we have considered."[7] "Although the behavioral sciences," Myers writes, "are sometime accused of undermining traditional values, the verdict of these studies is reassuring: people thrive best under conditions of democracy and personal freedom."[8] Obviously, the role played by a sense of control is a vital one. But this in itself is not an argument for never intervening in the life of a beloved. Nor do these studies remotely suggest that control is a sufficient condition for happiness and well-being. The fact that the welfare of an individual also involves meeting basic physical needs and developing traits such as self-esteem, optimism, and extroversion indicates that human beings often have to trade off some welfare considerations in order to obtain others.

Even if we admit that respect for a person qua person is paramount, it does not follow that we should accept a person as he or she wants to be. For a person typically has a future as well as a past and a present. Just as it seems to be incomplete to say that we should only love a person for what he or she can be, it seems incomplete (and misleading) to say that we should only love a person as he or she wants to be, if reliable evidence indicates that what that person wants is contrary to his or her welfare in some deep and important way. Unless a person is completely blasted by the infirmities of existence or is at death's door, he or she always has a future offering a potential for growth. Respect for a person involves respect for this potential. Expressed differently: love for another person does not seem to be limited to caring for his or her "present self" but extends to the future and often involves considerations of a better or improved self. A person who caringly loves bestows value, not merely by caring about the present and immediate interests of the beloved, but also by caring about his or her long-range interests and growth potential.

Singer may object. He may urge that the inclinations and desires of adults, at least, *always* should be trump. But without argumentation, this is just libertarian presupposition or dogma. It assumes adults are much more rational than they really are and that they are *always* the best judge of what is in their own interests. This is not the place to parade the contrary evidence. But the literature on weakness of will and the nature of decision making, especially the studies of Ainslie and Kahneman and Tversky,[9] indicate that the beliefs of men in general are not formed on purely rational grounds.

I have suggested that much, if not the heart, of this dispute has to do with contrary views about the nature of welfare. There is a tension between believing that a lover ought to accept her beloved only as she wants to be and believing that lover ought to be actively concerned about her multi-dimensional needs. The issue, therefore, is not welfare versus nonwelfare concerns. It is much more subtle, having to do with whether a narrow notion of welfare in which autonomy is always dominant is preferable to one in which other needs or interests may be dominant. I have suggested that there is a kind of love the constituent nature of which requires that, in some situations, welfare interests other than autonomy take precedence. Aside from the question of whether I have created or described a commonly held ideal of love, there remains the intriguing question of how to rationally choose between these competing notions.

It would be both unfair and ungrateful to end without again acknowledging the value of Singer's analysis of the role of ideals. Rejection of Singer's libertarianism is compatible, I believe with a judicious acceptance of the process of idealization that, typically accompanies what lovers do to their beloved and also what philosophers do when they formulate theories about the nature of love. It is a matter of common experience that confusion and mistaken doctrine are sometimes connected with the failure to distinguish between prescriptive theories involving normative definitions and those which do not. Yet it may be part of the process of conceiving uplifting and transpersonal ideals not to label them as such in order to avoid the process and perils of justification. Singer appears to be a lover of a libertarian ideal. He may suffer from the afflictions of this love; but, for Singer, that may be the chaff not the wheat. The wheat may have to do with the pervasiveness and importance of idealization. Thus Singer writes:

> Idealization is not limited to our relations with human beings. It also occurs in philosophical reasoning. It almost seems to be a constant in the history of philosophy, particularly the philosophy of love. Whether they are defining the attitude or the ideal of love, whether they prefer a love of persons or things or ideals, whether they speak as self-conscious moralists or quasi-scientists—in almost all cases, philosophers have *created* one or another ideal of love by giving criteria abstracted from their own experience. However objective their analyses, they idealize what matters most to them as human beings surrounded by their own emotional bestowals.[10]

NOTES

1. This is not the place to extol the virtues of Singer's theory of ideals. It is a theory that begins in the trilogy and matures in his *Meaning of Life: The Creation of Value* (New York: Free Press, 1992). This book contains one of the best analyses of ideals. It includes such gems as:

> For most people there is virtually no experience—not even a highly pleasurable one—that will seem meaningful unless it can be justified in terms of an ideal one has chosen. (p. 92) . . . [And that] throughout the varied pursuits that make a life significant, what remains constant is the growth of meaning when this involves creations of values in service of transpersonal ideals. (p. 117)

2. Irving Singer, *The Nature of Love*, vol. 1 (New York: Random House, 1966), p. 9.

3. Ibid., p. 11.

4. Irving Singer, *The Nature of Love*, vol. 3 (Chicago and London: University of Chicago Press, 1987), pp. 403–404.

5. Ibid., p. 412.

6. Daniel Goleman, "Feelings of Control Viewed as Central in Mental Health," *New York Times*, Tuesday, October 7, 1986, C 1 and 11.

7. David G. Myers, *The Pursuit of Happiness* (New York: William Morrow, 1992), p. 113. Quoted from Angus Campbell, *The Sense of Well-Being in America* (New York: McGraw-Hill, 1981), pp. 218–19.

8. Myers, *The Pursuit of Happiness*, p. 115.

9. See George Ainslie, "Specious Reward: A Behavioral Theory of Impulsiveness and Impulse Control," *Psychological Bulletin* 82:4 (1975): 463–96 and his "Beyond

Microeconomics: Conflict among Interests a Multiple Self as a Determinant of Value," in *The Multiple Self,* ed. by Jon Elster (Cambridge: Cambridge University Press, 1988), pp. 133–75; Daniel Kahneman and Amos Tversky, "Prospect Theory: An Analysis of Decision Under Risk," *Econometrica* 47:2 (1979): 263–91, and their "The Psychology of Preference," *Scientific American* 246 (1982): 160–73.

    10. Singer, *The Nature of Love,* 1:42.

15

Can Scientists Make Love?

Stanley G. Clarke

About eight years ago, I read an article in a reputable science magazine titled "Love Is Blue." Here it was claimed that love could be identified with a certain chemical that photographed blue under certain standard conditions. Although, I was not at the time in a love-depleted stage of life myself, I was filled with a momentary sense of optimism for others. "Scientists can make love," I exclaimed. But, alas, being a philosopher, my mind was soon consumed with questions before I could even tell my love-starved friends the good news. What, I worried, would love be like if blue dye-injected persons did not express their state lyrically in the languages of love: sweet talk, poetry, and song? Whatever love is, it is too intimately related to its expression to be identified with anything that might not lead to the appropriate sort of expressiveness. And I mean not something that could be neutrally described as "behavior," but an expression of meaning through metaphorical language indicating a different way of being.

There is a tension in all of us that the ambiguities of the question "Can scientists make love?" brings into focus. Many of us will have a secret hope that there might someday be love clinics in the same sense as there are reproduction clinics today, where technology, and not talk therapy, would be the means of renewal. Yet we have a strong tendency to deny that scientists will ever make love just because of the other obvious, voyeuristic sense of the question. That is, "Can scientists be poetically engaged with their lovers in a manner that will bring erotic fulfillment?" It is just this expressive side of love which we are sure scientists cannot make as professionals although

236

they may be exceedingly proficient amateurs. And it is also this expressiveness of love which has brought some to question whether scientists can make love in a third sense—namely, can they make a model, a theory of love? Irving Singer gives one answer to this question: "We are nowhere near the point where scientists can expect to formulate a unified comprehensive theory. But we are making progress and there is no need to despair about future possibilities" (3:345). This is an answer I wish to challenge.

In this paper I hope to ease some of the tension about these ambiguities by providing an intellectual framework within which I think answers to the above questions are best formulated. I also hope to go some way in showing what scientists can and cannot do and why. Briefly, my answers will be as follows. Since I am not much of a voyeur, whether scientists can fulfill themselves erotically is a question to which I am content to answer, "Probably." More seriously, I will try to show that parts of love are such that scientists could in principle technologically make them. All the same, we cannot turn to science for a comprehensive theory of love just because love is, in the end, a process that is historical and not strictly natural.

To set the framework in which love should be discussed, I think that it is profitable to return to the Aristotelian pursuit of determining how to categorize objects of inquiry. We should ask, "What sort of a thing is love?" in a general sense, of course, love is a certain kind of capacity, or disposition. More particularly, however, we need to know what kind of capacity by looking at the sort of way in which love is manifest.

Much discussion about love is conducted in a manner that assumes that realized love is a state for which one can attempt to give a definition in terms of something like necessary and sufficient conditions. The debate between Singer and Alan Soble on how appraisal is to be characterized in relation to love seems to me to be a case in point. Singer claims that appraisals are necessary conditions for love but not constituents or part of the definition (1:13). Soble argues that they must be seen as constituents (Soble:23). To my mind, the argument between these two is marred by assuming that love is a state.

If love is categorized as a process, that particular type of debate between Singer and Soble is shortcircuited and will move to substantive issues such as the role of appraisals in love. A process is a series of events which has a beginning, a middle, and an end. A process need not be what I would call a rigid process, such as the process of fermentation, which begins in one way only, with a specific developmental structure resulting in only one goal. There are things we would call "processes" which are multi-originated and multi-ended. Education, for instance, would be one such process. It may begin in different ways and we have no agreed-upon end of education, but all would accept that some goals are achieved. Love is analogous to education in these ways.

The grounds for categorizing love as a process are good Aristotelian ones of looking at the sorts of questions one can ask about love. Basically, the fact that we can ask about beginnings and fulfillments of love indicates that we are speaking of a process. However, we also describe love as something that takes time, is never complete at any moment, and has a direction in that different moments cannot change their place in time without changing the identity of that love. Love, like education, is a process that has many origins and many goals.

One of the implications of taking love to be a nonrigid process is that it shows that the search for a definition of love in terms of necessary or sufficient conditions is out of place. Singer, as we have already seen, uses that terminology in his account. And Soble who does not attempt to provide a definition of love, still assumes such a framework. When he specifies some derivative features of love, he writes:

> Conceiving of personal love as axiomatically, constitutively, or by definition constant, exclusive, or reciprocal, or insisting that only genuine personal love is any of these is a mistake: these features must be viewed as derivative. (Soble:17)

Accounts of processes, especially nonrigid ones, move us out of the search for necessary conditions. This is because the name of a process can legitimately be applied even when only parts of the process have occurred. The beginning of education is education just as any other part of the process is, and the same is true of love. The search for necessary conditions tends to encourage one to identify love with only one part of the whole. Furthermore, various stages of a process can be abnormally caused by starting the process at the middle or near the end. In this case, the search for necessary conditions that would appear in a definition cannot but fail. Thus, the best we can hope for in the description of a process is the identification of what normally occurs and how the elements are normally related. This means that we should turn away from conceptual analysis and look at what various accounts of love—biological, psychological, historical, and interpretive—reveal. Such a framework will displace the question of whether love is erosive (requiring appraisals) or agapeic (needing only bestowals) from one of definitional doctrine to a search for whether there are such roles in the process of love. The same love might be both erosive and agapeic if love is a process. The goal of our understanding would, then, have to be discovering how these elements are related.

In the end, I shall argue that love is a historical process. Its historicity is largely what accounts for its being a nonrigid process and an inappropriate candidate for a comprehensive scientific theory. However, that does not imply that science can tell us nothing about love. There can be processes within processes and some of these may be amenable to a scientific account.

Assuming that love is a process, I hope that we can now answer quite clearly the question of what science can tell us about love. First of all, it is worth looking at one scientific account of the emotions which implies that a comprehensive scientific theory of love can be given. This is the theory of social constructionism. It is broadly, at least, a scientific theory in that it appeals to social causation by explaining the occurrence of emotions in terms of their role in attaining social goals such as preserving morality or supporting culturally approved values. There are two versions of social constructionism: strong and weak. The strong version asserts that emotions are intrinsically functional and depend for their existence on serving a social function (Armon-Jones:61). This version seems implausible in that studies of emotion in infants and animals would appear to justify the claim that there are some nonsocialized emotions. I agree with Claire Armon-Jones in her article "The Social Functions of Emotion" that the weak version is the more plausible thesis. This version is that social function is the main determinant in the existence and explanation of a significant class of emotions (Armon-Jones:61). On this view, love would be a plausible candidate for a constructionist account.

Although I would not reject an explanation of some emotional phenomena by social function, we need to be clear about what is required by such an explanation. And this will show us how this explanation is limited with regard to emotion, especially love. Explanation by social function is not the same as explaining the occurrence or spread of some practice by appeal to education. In the latter case, the goals can be vague and the practices for reaching them relatively plastic, leaving significant room for creativity, and therefore unpredictability, in their exercise. Explanation by social function, on the other hand, to be scientifically supportable, requires that the social function, as well as the role of the emotion in attaining it, be clearly specifiable. This can be achieved only in cases where emotions are rigidly structured. They are set for attaining a specific goal by a specific route. And, of course, there are emotional phenomena of this type. One example from Armon-Jones's paper makes this clear. "Hatred of Jews" appears to be a paradigm for functional explanation of the weak version. Although hatred may have many natural features, the main determinant of hatred of Jews would appear to be social function. As Armon-Jones writes:

> For example, while "anti-semitism" was based on the belief that Jews are bad, this belief was itself crucially related to the value imposed by Nazis upon the Aryan ideal. Here it can be argued that the "hatred" in question was not merely warranted but was regarded by members of the Nazi com-

munity as a desirable response in its role of vindicating the Aryan ideal and the agent's commitment to, and endorsement of, this value. This role of "hatred" is substantiated by the fact that agents were condemned, and in some cases punished, for failing to express strong contempt for Jews. (Armon-Jones:72–73)

Here we have a rigidly structured emotion. Its object is both abstractly and rigidly described in the terms "Jewish" and "evil." The possible expressions of the emotion are narrowly constituted as well—exhibiting contempt and doing harm. Here both the goal and the role of the emotion are clearly specifiable in a manner that suits explanation by social function. Since hatred tends to be rigidly structured, it is open to the influence of social determination.

Many emotional phenomena are not rigidly structured and simply aid in bringing into play certain types of intelligent, and thereby flexible, behavior in certain contexts. Fear, for example, can be rigidly structured, especially in the case of phobias. However, there are many instances of people being motivated to deal responsively and creatively with danger. In the case of love, the situation is similar. The goals of love and the motivated behavior of lovers are too open, flexible, and unpredictable to satisfy the requirements of functional explanation. This is not to deny, however, that some loves may best be explained by social function. There are social stereotypes of love that are sometimes manifest all too directly in the lives of some lovers, but that is exactly when we throw the motivation of these lovers into question. Some loves may be social constructs, but we judge them as being deficient just insofar as they are. We make this judgment on the basis of ordinary love which is open and flexible in a manner that is not susceptible to explanation by social function. Thus, I think it is clear that social constructionism does not afford us a comprehensive theory of love.

Sociobiology, however, is taken by some to be a more promising route to a scientific account of love. Initially, the relevance of sociobiology seemed to be more a threat than an aid since it appeared to rule out the possibility of genuinely altruistic behavior in humans. More recently, there is general agreement that this is not so. Laurence Thomas, in *Living Morally,* makes the case quite clearly that sociobiology is committed to a connection between unwitting altruism and unwitting selfishness. However, this does not imply that motive altruism is biologically impossible. Singer comes to the same conclusion on different grounds: ". . . the sociobiologists can only establish that self-sacrificial behavior *frequently* serves to protect one's genes" (3:359).

However, sociobiology can be pushed further. Both Laurence Thomas and Sydney Mellen have formulated rather speculative theories to show that love is actually biologically selected for. In the case of Thomas, the love in question is what he identifies as parental love which is transparent, whereas

Mellen gives an evolutionary backing for a type of romantic love (Singer, 3:365). I will concentrate mainly on Thomas since I am not as interested in the soundness of their speculative claims as I am in understanding what sort of things such theories would tell us about love. To understand this, Thomas's focus upon transparent love is significant. According to him, transparent love is one

> . . . that consists of a concern for a person's well-being and is not tied to the person's performances. This is unconditional love not because one may never cease to have such love for an individual, but because there is no belief about that individual's behavior, performances, or what have you, that constitutes a conceptual bar to so loving that person, there is nothing a person can do, nothing a person can become, that would cause one, on conceptual grounds, to cease loving him. (Thomas:60)

Thomas's argument that such love has been biologically selected for is basically the following. Psychological security is basic to the survival of humans. Parental love that is transparent is conducive to security in the child. Thus, transparent parental love serves directly a survival need and is plausibly thought to have been selected for.

This argument leaves something to be desired, since the fact that a feature of human beings serves a survival need does not prove that that particular feature was selected for. That feature may be a socially developed form of some more general capacity for which biological selection operated.

Nevertheless, an interesting issue arises here about the sort of motives that can most plausibly be given a biological grounding. It would seem that these would have to be motives that are, in the language of cognitive science, "cognitively impenetrable." Types of mental activity are cognitively impenetrable when they cannot be directly affected by changes in one's beliefs and attitudes (Fodor:47–101). Reflexes would be the clearest examples of cognitively impenetrable behavior. No matter how much I trust you not to touch my eyeball, I am still going to blink when you point your finger close to my eye. Perception, too, appears to contain some levels of activity that are cognitively impenetrable. Could you see my blue pen as green, for instance, just by changing your beliefs and attitudes? The feelings of hunger and thirst are examples of motives that appear to be cognitively impenetrable. You can, perhaps, turn your attention from them, but you cannot change them directly by manipulating your own beliefs and attitudes.

We can now formulate two important questions given the distinction between cognitively penetrable and impenetrable mental activity: (1) Does sociobiology apply plausibly only to the impenetrable? (2) if so, what does that imply about Thomas's case for the biological selection of transparent love? The answer to the first question is that to the degree that any mental item is penetrable, it is open to the influence of thought and, therefore, judgmental decision in a manner that leaves the behavior of that item indeterminate, hence explainable in nonbiological terms. If cognitive impenetrability is a requirement for what can be biologically explained, what is the status of transparent love?

Laurence Thomas, at least, is not clear about the status of such love when he comments:

> What I have called transparent love, or something very much like it, is thought to be one of the defining features of Christianity. And observe that while the Christian commandment to love one's enemies is regarded as exceedingly difficult, doing so is not ruled out on conceptual grounds. (Thomas:60)

A love that can be commanded is, of course, a cognitively penetrable love and is not capable of biological explanation. However, this comment about Christian love does not really square with Thomas's account of transparent love which, I think, implies that it is cognitively impenetrable. You might recall that transparent love is such that ". . . there is nothing a person can do, nothing a person can become, that would cause one, on conceptual grounds, to cease loving him" (Thomas:60). Furthermore, when Thomas turns to explain how parental love generates love in children, he appeals to the principle of reciprocity which is that ". . . we become disposed to act favorably toward those who art favorably to us" (Thomas:83). This is a principle which is characterized as operating without cognitive mediation. Of course, one will cognitively process how one is going to deal with the tendencies this disposition raises in one, but that is processing *about* the disposition, not *within* it. So it seems to me that Thomas should characterize the transparent love which he wishes to ground biologically as a cognitively impenetrable mechanism, or module. Humans are such complex creatures, however, that the activation of transparent love does not determine one's behavior. We can decide to kill our loves, just as we might drown our sorrows or suppress our appetites. None of this is done directly by changing beliefs, but indirectly by employing other causal means such as different environments, alcohol, or pills.

I am still not convinced of the sociobiological account of specific capacities such as transparent love. Nevertheless, the important thing in this context is to realize that, even if true, sociobiology does not provide us with a comprehensive theory of love but explains the continued existence of some elements of the whole complex process of love. More importantly, it raises the question of whether there might be many modular aspects to love— mechanisms which are cognitively impenetrable but which generate products that are taken up into the whole love story. I think that recent work on emotion makes this plausible and indicates one of the main areas in which science can be of theoretical and practical help in understanding love. The other main area is describing the developmental and structural relations between emotions which operate regardless of how we think about them.

Many are tempted to take "falling in love" itself as a mechanism that would satisfy this project. However, I think that would be a mistake. Falling in love is itself a complex state which can take time and be changed significantly by critical reflection. However, we would be too hasty if we jumped to the conclusion that there are no mechanisms involved. Progress in the study of falling in love will require the sort of detailed analysis of the phenomenon that generated progress in study of emotions through facial expression. In fact, there are some plausibly mechanistic activities connected with falling in love. These include fixation of attention, wanting to be near the beloved, and imaginative embellishment. For anyone who has been in love, these elements will at least seem to be cognitively impenetrable ones. Although I can learn to deal with each, that is done by manipulating myself and my surroundings so as to try to cause a change in them. It is not by directly thinking myself out of any one of them. If science can tell us anything about love, it will be partly about such mechanisms as these.

The other area in which science appears to be capable of contributing to understanding emotions, love in particular, is that of structural relations between them. For example, as Jon Elster writes:

> The cessation of an emotional state—be it positive or negative—does not simply bring us back to the earlier emotional plateau. Rather, it tends to generate another emotional state of opposite sign. Consider a person who has just discovered a lump in her breast and is extremely anxious. Upon hearing from her doctor that there is no possibility of cancer, her mood for a while turns euphoric before she returns to an affectively neutral state. (Elster:65)

These sorts of structural relations are also likely in the case of love. Singer reports the view of Melanie Klein that love and hate are dialectically related so that you cannot have one without the other (3:353). Although Klein's theory may not be strictly scientific, post-Freudian theories like it, along with personal experience and historical accounts, suggest that a generalization linking love and hate upon some structural basis is probably sound. Awareness of such structural relations will help people get rid of such unrealistic and self-defeating ideals as a love life with only happy emotions.

It is not my business here to give the content of a scientific account of these various aspects of love. I argue only that science can give an explanation of these sorts of elements and features of love. Understanding these items as natural ones that simply happen to us and can be accounted for by science is part of a humanistic understanding of love of the sort that Singer describes as his goal. It allows humans to live less guilt-ridden lives and to refrain from running from them before their time is up just because they exhibit features that are there naturally. Nevertheless, science can only provide us with accounts of these various, relatively mechanistic aspects of love. It cannot give us a complete theory of love, and that is because love is not only a process but a historical process—the feature to which we shall now turn.

Irving Singer tends to find the limitations of scientific accounts of love in the bestowals which he takes to be its defining feature. This is because they involve the use of imagination to be creative and invent new values. Partly because I think the notion of bestowal is itself one that applies only within certain historical formations of love, and partly because it is not obvious that psychology will be unable to give a scientific account of creative imagination, I prefer to explain the limitations of science here by an appeal to certain features of love as historical.

The two features that I will mention are contingency and dynamic interaction. Contingency characterizes love in that accidentally generated coincidences can be significant determinants in the course of any love. This contingency works at the very beginning in that you simply happened to meet this particular person. But it also continues through the process of loving. It just happens that you are depressed about other events in your life at the moment that you happen to see your love interest again. And it just happens that your love takes your demeanor to be about that love. Everything would have gone smoothly but for the fortuitous coincidence of two different causal sequences. Love is, through and through, day by day, riddled with contingency. That is what makes the beginning, process, and fulfillment of love radically unpredictable and scientifically intractable. The second feature is that of dynamic interaction between the two lovers. Amelie Rorty describes this feature in "The Historicity of Psychological Attitudes."

> There is a kind of love—and for some it may be the only kind that qualifies as true love—that is historical precisely because it does not (oh so wonderfully) rigidly designate its object. The details of such love change with every change in the lover and the friend. . . . Having been transformed by loving, the lover perceives the friend in a new way and loves in a new way. (French, Uehling, Wettstein:402)

Describing the historicity of psychological attitudes in general, she writes:

These psychological attitudes are identified by the detail of the narrative of the interactions between the subject and the object, interactions that also individuate the persons involved. (ibid.:402)

The changing identities of both the loves and the lovers also make any attempt at a scientific theory of such processes impossible. The generalizations that we can make are severely limited by these transforming identities.

These historical features of love guarantee that no complete, or even general, scientific theory of love will be forthcoming. Nevertheless, significant historical writing about love can help us understand it in a general way. I would like briefly to show how Irving Singer has done some of this sort of historical writing even though he does not characterize it in that way.

When Singer gives his account of three states of love, he characterizes what he is doing as describing three states of experience:

Much of what we mean by romantic passion is exemplified by the experience known as "falling in love." But we must contrast two other states, both compatible with marriage, which I shall call "being in love" and—staying in love. (3:383)

"Experience" is a tricky word here. For Singer and his pragmatist approach, it includes both psychological states and actions. This inclusive use of "experience" tends to blur the fact that actions have a historical character and, I think, this is what permits Singer to be so hopeful about a comprehensive scientific theory of love. Seeing love as experience, he ignores its historicity and, therefore, intractability for science. However, if we look at how Singer describes being in love and staying in love, it is clear that he is sketching stages of a historical process. They are not just descriptions of psychological states since they involve actions. Singer indicates how activities are involved in these stages:

Being in love begins the process of reorientation, the actual making of the new world. (3:384)

And, with respect to staying in love, he writes:

Consider the bond between a man and woman who have spent many years in each other's company, each attending to the other's needs with recurrent and reciprocating concern. (3:388)

The only state that Singer discusses in purely experiential terms is "falling in love," which he describes as follows:

Falling in love is volcanic. It is a phenomenon of great emotional stress. (3:384)

This seems to me to be mistaken. Even falling in love is just one stage in the history of a love and itself includes actions and not just experiencing—though it may, of course, begin by the activation of some of those love modules, or mechanisms, mentioned earlier.

To support my case, I will appeal to the sensitive rendering of love's blossoming in Turgenev's novelette *First Love*. The description of Vladimir's first seeing of Zinaida is as follows:

The young men offered their foreheads so eagerly, and there was in the girl's movements (I saw her in profile) something so enchanting, imperious and caressing, so mocking and charming, that I nearly cried out with wonder and delight, and should, I suppose, at that moment, have given everything in the world to have those lovely fingers tap my forehead too. My rifle slipped to the grass; I forgot everything; my eyes devoured the graceful figure, the lovely neck, the beautiful arms, the slightly dishevelled fair hair under the white kerchief—and the half-closed, perceptive eyes, the lashes, the soft cheek beneath them. . . . (Turgenev:26)

Neither Turgenev nor the character Vladimir identifies this fixation of attention as "falling in love." It takes a few days of activity before Vladimir is ready to talk about the beginning of his love, or his falling in love.

From that day my "passion" began. What I experienced then, I remember, was something similar to what a man must feel when first given an official post. I had ceased to simply be a young boy; I was someone in love. I say that my passion began from that day: and I might add that my suffering began on that day too. (Turgenev:52)

"Being given an official post" is the analogy Turgenev uses to elucidate the falling in love which begins Vladimir's new passion. This analogy indicates that even falling in love is not just an experience but has the complexity of taking on a role. Such taking-on is an action that can be done all at once or gradually, intelligently or stupidly. And however one falls in love, that falling will exhibit history and not just feeling.

Singer's classification of the states of "falling in love," "being in love," and "staying in love" are best understood as a classification of three historical stages of the process of love. They are the same sort of historical terms as Kuhn uses in describing science as containing stages of crisis, revolutionary science and normal science. Writing about love in these terms is just like writing any explanatory history and can be justified in the same manner.

Given that science cannot give us a comprehensive account of love, it is to such histories and to literature that we must turn. Literature will give us pictures of what we may choose to realize historically. They may be harmful and oppressive pictures if they take no cognizance of the humanity that must realize them—a humanity that must accept its own passivity exercised through psychological mechanisms of various sorts, including those that are near the heart of love.

REFERENCES

Armon-Jones, Claire. "The Thesis of Constructionism." In Rom Harre, *The Social Construction of Emotion*. Oxford: Basil Blackwell, 1986.

Eibl-Eibbsfeldt, Irenaus. *Human Ethology*. Aldine de Gruyter, 1989.

Elster, Jon, *Nuts and Bolts*. Cambridge: Cambridge University Press, 1989.

Fodor, Jerry A., *The Modularity of Mind*. Cambridge: MIT Press, 1983.

Malatesta, C. Z., and C. E. Izard. *Emotion in Adult Development*. Beverly Hills: Sage Publications, 1984.

Rorty, Amelie. "The Historicity of Psychological Attitudes: Love Is Not Love Which Alters Not When It Alteration Finds." In P. French, T. Uehling, and H. Wettstein, *Midwest Studies in Philosophy X*. Minneapolis: University of Minnesota Press, 1986.

Singer, Irving. *The Nature of Love*. 3 vols. Chicago: The University of Chicago Press, 1966, 1984, 1987, respectively.

Soble, Alan. *The Structure of Love*. New Haven: Yale University Press 1990.

Thomas, Laurence. *Living Morally*. Philadelphia: Temple University Press, 1989.

Turgenev, I. S. *First Love*. Harmondsworth, England: Penguin Classics.

16

Male and Female in the Modern World*

John Mitterer

INTRODUCTION: THE CORE PROBLEM

In this paper I shall consider aspects of the relation of male and female in the modern world. This topic is is so broad, so important and so intimidating; it calls for the "grand view." Appropriately, I began by reading through parts of Irving Singer's (1984a, 1984b, 1987) own wonderful and masterful sweeping philosophical history, his three-volume series, *The Nature of Love*. As I did so I despaired of having much to add. It is not, as I realized, that I was unfamiliar with many of the issues; I am as enmeshed as anyone in trying to work out these matters in the context of my own life. What I hadn't done was to try and work out my own "grand view." As I tried, I found it very difficult to "step back"; what follows here is a sketch of the progress I have made so far.

As I see it, no literate and thoughtful person today could miss the central problem with which modern men and women are confronted. Roughly put, most people today think that the old ways in which men and women have traditionally related, with men dominating women based on arguments of biology, social upbringing, or what have you, are no longer viable. In this paper I shall use the phrase "psychology of domination" to refer to the thoughts and emotions of men and women who still relate this way. Furthermore,

---

*Nora Baboudjian's insight and patience were invaluable in the formulation of the ideas presented here.

most people agree that men and women need new ways to relate which center around equality rather than dominance. I will use the phrase "psychology of equality" to refer to the thoughts and emotions of men and women who relate this way. In this paper I shall agree with the modern view that male-female relations have too often been based on a psychology of domination and that we need to better develop a psychology of equality. What I wish to discuss here is the prospect of successfully making the transition from old to new ways; from dominance to equality-based relationships. Will it be hard to do? What, exactly, needs to change?

By way of an overview, I will look at this central problem a little more closely. I shall go on to propose that Irving Singer's historical treatment has laid bare the incredible depth of the problem. As I see it, he shows that the dominance of men over women has its roots in Christian thought, which is itself based on Greco-Roman thought. These particular "grand views," or systems of thought, are what Richard Rorty (1989) would refer to as "metaphysics." Roughly, I will argue that we need to "deconstruct" these metaphysics in order to dismantle the underpinnings of our psychology of domination. Only then will the way be clear for the fuller development of a psychology of equality. I will then go on to consider whether the attempt to articulate *any* metaphysics, which is the aim of much philosophy as it has classically been defined, may itself be part of the problem rather than of the solution. In other words, my concern is that the search for the final, correct "grand view" may actually spawn a psychology of domination. I shall close with some reflections on aspects of an alternative approach to the problem of men and women in the modern world. The key feature of this alternative approach is that we will have to "grow up," to give up metaphysics. In Richard Rorty's (1989) terminology, we need to become "ironists" on the premise that we will never find *the* final vocabulary. Our new psychology will have to stand up on its own as a naturalistic, humanistic psychology of equality.

One can begin by asking why the bad old days were bad old days, especially for women, but, I think, for men as well. I, for one, think that the history of the treatment of women leaves no doubt that the bad old days were indeed bad. I also tend to agree with such thinkers as Shulamith Firestone (1970) and Elizabeth Rappaport, who go so far as to argue that men and women will not be able to love authentically until sexual equality is achieved. In my terminology, authentic love is possible only within a psychology of equality. While the thoughts and emotions of the psychology of domination may be important to study, that psychology will not include the thoughts and emotions of authentic love.

Most often, considerations of why men dominated women have organized themselves around the great polarities that have been at the core of study about human nature through the ages. Here the great polarity is that between humans as animals and humans as divine or above nature. The modern incarnation of this great polarity is the nature-nurture controversy.

On the nature side of the issue is the biological proposition that we are what we are because of our genetic makeup. Simplistically put, on this view men are dominant because they are animals that have evolved to be so. Male dominance, then, is an animal characteristic. It could be because they are adapted to control territory (including females) or to aggressively hoard female reproductive capacity for themselves. Similarly, females have evolved to select the most fit mate and then to stay at home and have babies. The sort of evidence adduced in favor of the nurture side of things is usually derived from the animal kingdom. We are told that this is how it works with chimpanzees, or gibbons, or elephant seals. Another common line of evidence is to hold out the universality of the traditional male and female roles as evidence of their underlying genetic base.

On the nurture side of the issue is the (usually) social proposition that we adopt roles in life, including sex roles, because we have learned to do so. On this view, it is our social climate which perpetuates traditional sexual roles as mothers and fathers consciously and unconsciously pass on those roles to their daughters and sons. Proponents of this viewpoint usually argue that human nature, in some way, transcends the purely animal. For example, according to Shulamith Firestone (1970:10), Simone de Beauvoir says: "Humanity is not an animal species, it is a historical reality. Human society is an antiphysis—in a sense it is against nature; it does not passively submit to the presence of nature but rather takes over the control of nature on its own behalf."

I do not wish to take up here either side of the nature-nurture debate in its usual form. Nor do I think we are going to find the answer to the sorts of problems we are considering by dichotomizing. It isn't either/or; rather, I would want to argue that nature and nurture are dialectically entwined. From a humanistic naturalistic perspective, everything that we are is part of our nature, the animal and the divine, the cruel and the sublime. Even our nurture is part of our nature. Alternately, everything that we are is part of our nurture, even our nature; we have evolved into social animals that pass on our species knowledge through social communication.

And it is in the communication process that I think much of the answer lies. According to Ernst von Glaserfeld (1984:27), Giambattista Vico in 1710 suggested that, "As God's truth is what God comes to know as he creates and assembles it, so human truth is what man comes to know as he builds it, shaping it by his actions." This is an early formulation of the constructivist view which holds that we create the reality of our daily experience; we create our truth out of the fabric of our everyday life. Richard Rorty (1989), in *Contingency, Irony, and Solidarity,* suggests that the language that we speak, the vocabulary that we use to think about the world, is central to the *creation* of the world of our experience. He describes our language in a Wittgenstinian way as being a tool which we use to craft our experience.

And where do our everyday vocabularies come from? From the broader social and linguistic context which itself is embedded in the frameworks or metaphysics of our times. So it is the core ideas as articulated in overarching frameworks such as "philosophies" and "religions" that undergird the social creation of the "reality" within which the socialization of the individual structures his or her biology. And it is to the history of these ideas to which I now wish to turn.

THE HISTORICAL ROOTS OF THE PROBLEM

Irving Singer begins his three-volume work with a distinction between appraisal and bestowal, a distinction that forms a cornerstone of his approach to love. Says Singer: "I start with the idea that love is a way of valuing something" (1984a:3). Here he is speaking about views of love which hold that "love searches for what is valuable in the beloved" (1984a:3) or that love "creates value in the sense that it makes the beloved objectively valuable in some sense" (1984a:3). He then goes on to assert that in love the lover goes beyond mere appraisal: "Love supplements the human search for value with a capacity for bestowing it gratuitously" (1984a:14). For Singer, then, love must involve some combination of appraisal and bestowal, a basically positive appraisal enhanced through a creative bestowal of value on the beloved: "love would not be love unless appraising were accompanied by the bestowing of value" (1984a:10).

Throughout all three volumes, Singer documents the tendency of philosophers to treat love as an idealizing process. For example, he discusses the Platonic tendency to treat love as transcending the loved to reach the universal good. George Santayana, a modern exponent of the Platonic approach, has said: "If a man falls in love with a fair-haired woman, he does so because his heart has been captured by the ideal of a perfect blonde. It is this ideal object, not the woman 'in her unvarnished and accidental person' that the man truly loves" (1984a:26).

At the other end of the spectrum, Singer shows how Freud's treatment of love reductively idealizes the love object as self-love to be derived from the mother. Of Freud's approach he says: "According to Freud, all love is reducible to a desire to be loved: every interest in another object is just a circuitous device for satisfying self-love" (1984a:29). And, of course, only the mother ever really satisfied, every other object only approaches her as the ideal.

The main body of Singer's work considers what has been written about love across the ages. He uses the notions of appraisal, bestowal, and idealization to reveal the ever-changing richness of conceptions of love. It was in reading about these changing conceptions of love that I found myself enthralled; Singer has provided an important source for anyone interested in the topic of love. And it is here that I found what seems like striking evidence that ideas about love, as they have been expressed through the ages, often imply a psychology of domination:

As I see it, a major root of a psychology of domination can already be found in some asymmetries in the philosophy of the Greeks, particularly Plato and Aristotle. Their ideas formed a part of the foundation of early Christian thinking, which in turn undergirded medieval and romantic conceptions of love. I believe that today we still mostly struggle along with this intellectual heritage, although the philosophical support for it no longer remains.

Singer treats the philosophy of Plato as a key component of the Western philosophy of love, and I agree. Greece of the fifth and fourth centuries can be considered as having discovered abstract thought; in cognitive psychology, we speak of metacognition, our ability to reflect upon our own mental processes. The Greeks arguably invented metacognition. Plato, reflecting upon the abstractive capability of the human mind, invented the "forms"; Aristotle reflected upon the inferential capability of the human mind and invented logic.

For Plato, as revealed in his famous metaphor of the cave, intellectual reflection makes it possible for the philosopher to transcend the imperfect and misleading world of the senses and appreciate the world of the forms. Forms are eternal, unchanging, and essentially perfect. They are "reality," not the illusions of everyday experience. Any particular oak tree is imperfect but the form underlying all oak trees is ideal. Plato treats love in the same way. Love is not an appreciation of the imperfect world we live in; rather it is an appreciation of a form. In this case the form is the "greatest good." All love, for Plato, can be seen as striving toward the greatest good, or simply the Good. Of course, given the Greeks' anti-female bias, only men are deemed likely to find it so the love men have for women is less developed than the love of males for other males. But ultimately, in loving a woman or another male, a man is really just trying to transcend human imperfections to reach the disembodied Good.

I believe that the Platonic conception of the forms and hence the Platonic conception of love is fatally flawed. Plato imagined an ideal: the eternal, unchanging world of forms. What he did next is the cardinal error of Western philosophy: he reified the forms, imagining that they actually existed. He projected them out of his mind and into nature. Rather than love the man who imagines the most perfect forms, Plato loves the forms themselves. He does not see that they are only ghosts projected from a mind. He does not love the mind itself, he loves the ghosts. Here, of course, I reverse the polarity in Plato's image of the cave; I uphold the earlier "dark" philosopher who asserted that you can never step into the same river twice.

This reification has remarkable consequences. It leads to a split between the mind and the body. Thought is good, emotion is not good. Love, if it is to be an approach to the Good, must be intellectual not emotional, Platonic not sexual. Men do the thinking, women do not; love of men for women is a degraded form of love; love women have for men hardly counts at all. When modern women complain that modern men are not in touch with their emotions, part of what they are complaining about can be traced back to Plato's error of reification.

Aristotle didn't help things either. His logic, lauded as such a magnificent human achievement (and it certainly is that), was also reified. It was assumed that if one could only think logically, then one could directly appreciate the truth. Mathematical deduction became the ideal method for knowing the truth (i.e., appreciating the forms). As a consequence, nonlogical forms of cognition and knowing became devalued. We know now that what Aristotle achieved with his logic was a partial formalization of human thinking. These were some rules we could use in our thought. Using these rules, however was never sufficient to reach the truth. Logical arguments might nevertheless be false.

To summarize, then, the Greeks gave us a split; an asymmetry between our minds and our bodies. Our minds were better than our bodies; our thoughts superior to our feelings, ideals better than the flux of experience. Love was conceived as an intellectual appreciation of an ideal. One result of these developments was a schism between intellect and emotion which left the intellect unchecked. Philosophers were doomed to abstract from the flux of experience; to objectify by underconstruing; to fail to love flesh-and-blood women. And objectification always has been a deep part of the psychology of domination.

These Greek asymmetries formed part of the undergirding for Christian thinking. For Christians, God is eternal and perfect. Man is temporal and imperfect. The relation between man and God is asymmetrical. Some asymmetry is to be found in most, if not all, religious traditions and is often attributed to our fear of the unknown universe and our desire for a cosmic parent to protect us from it. But the Christian form of the asymmetry, I believe, can be traced back, in part, to Plato and the world of the forms. Because of the reification of forms, God can be imagined and then projected up into heaven. Then our psychodynamic desires can be projected up at him. Without this reification, I think the Christian conception of God would be rather different. While a perfect being could still be imagined, this act of imagination, in itself, would not make anyone believe that He or She actually existed. When we reify God as all-powerful, all-loving and all-important in our lives, then we make the love of God central and again treat the love of men and women as derivative, as degenerate, except as the love of men and women transcends their own imperfections (or sinfulness) and is aimed at God.

As I see it, a psychology of domination must inevitably flow from this Greek-influenced conception of God because the determining factor must be the asymmetry between God and man: God is perfect, man is not. God loves completely or actually *is* love; man cannot love completely. This asymmetry is laid bare by Singer's analysis of four key facets of Christian love: *eros*, *agape, nomos,* and *philia*.

Eros flows from man to God. For the Greeks, eros was a form of love which manifested itself in a striving for, or a movement toward. For Plato, the object of eros was none other than the greatest good, which could be appreciated only by the intellect. The Christianized version substitutes an anthropomorphic, personalized God for the greatest good. Humankind was doomed to strive toward God but to be unable to reach him; we could never bridge the gap between the imperfect and the perfect. And we could never be satisfied with the imperfect love of man and woman.

But eros was asymmetrical. God did not need man nor did God strive toward him; God was perfect and therefore did not need to strive toward anything. As the greatest good just was, the forms just existed, so God simply was. He did not strive for erotic union with man (I am aware that one could argue the opposite: God created man out of a need for completion himself; but this is an unusual and mystical argument that is germane to the thinking of very few people).

For Christians, God does love man, although not in the erotic sense of striving toward. Agape flows from God to man. The early Jews saw God as choosing them to be the recipients of his attention, for reasons never clearly articulated in the Old Testament. This conception of a downward flow of God's grace, often as manna from heaven, can only be conceptualized as largesse. Agape, in this form, is also asymmetrical. God can bathe man in grace; but man can never do the same for God because God doesn't need any more grace and because man usually doesn't have enough grace even for himself.

The third component of Christian love is nomos. The story of Job reveals how God requires not only adherence to His laws but a submission of the will of man to His own. Thus, by subverting his will completely, man signals his love for (submission to) God. Nomos is clearly asymmetrical (since God cannot submit to man) and quite obviously implies a psychology of domination.

The final component of Christian love which Singer articulates is *philia* (see Singer 1984a:200–202). Philia, or brotherly love, can pass only between equals. God is not equal to man; he loves man more than man can love him so there can be no philia between man and God. But of Jesus, Singer says: "Born of a woman, practicing the ministry of life, dying the death that all men face, being a scapegoat for human sins, Christ effects an idealized equalization between God and man. The highest puts itself on the same footing as the lowest, as symbolized by Christ's eagerness to associate with moral outcasts." In this way, love of God can be philia. Unfortunately, it does not work; for Protestants this is scandalous. Christ descended to save us, not be equal to us. As Singer notes (1984a:202): "But if friendship was impossible, how else could man raise himself into the love of God? To which Luther replies: he cannot."

So the concepts making up Christian love are centered around the attempt of imperfect mortals to imagine love for and love from a perfect immortal. I believe that relations between men and women were often imagined on a simple analogy: God is to man as man is to woman. Thus woman is dominated by man and must depend on his largesse, as man relies on God's agape. Woman must strive toward her man, like man must erotically strive toward God. At the same time, woman must submit herself to man's will as man must submit himself to God's. Man and woman cannot love filially because they are not equal.

I will spend little time on courtly and romantic love except to agree with Singer's characterizations. For him, courtly love sought, but failed, to elevate human love by reconciling it with religious love. Romantic love also never escaped from idealism. Of the romantics Singer says: "From Plato and the Neoplatonists they [the Romantics] inherited the search for purity in love which transcended ordinary sexual experience, true love being an ideal relationship that rarely appeared in the empirical world. From Christianity— particularly the ecstatic mysticism of writers like St. John of the Cross, St. Teresa, Jan van Ruysbroeck, Meister Eckhart, Jacob Boehme, and others— they appropriated the notion of an interpersonal love that enabled the lover to partake of divinity. In courtly love they saw an attempt to justify an intimacy between men and women that was comparable to religious love."

To summarize to this point: I believe that Singer's history reveals that the psychology of domination is undergirded by a metaphysic dating back to the Greeks. This metaphysic includes a belief in a timeless, perfect realm as well as the belief that the intellect can open this realm up to us. From Christian thinking, this metaphysic has elaborated the notion of an asymmetric love between God and man. The subsequent development of the ideas of courtly and romantic love seems never to have escaped from this metaphysic.

PHILOSOPHY AS THE PROBLEM:
COMMENTS ON THE PHILOSOPHICAL APPROACH

I would like to begin this section with a few comments about the framework Singer uses in *The Nature of Love*.

Throughout his work, Singer shows an admirable resistance to the tendency to idealize love. In his third volume, he says: "I emphasize human nature because the tradition that treats love as somehow originating in a transcendental realm beyond our own seems to me defunct and unacceptable when taken literally" (1987:369). Where Singer sees idealism being involved, if at all, it is as follows: "The meaning of love is to be found in our propensity to create ideals that liberate us from reality while manifesting our adherence to it" (1987:369).

I also applaud Singer's insistence that love should not be understood as beyond the human, as metaphysical. As his history amply shows, this conception of love has been all too common, and, as I have argued, leads to a psychology of domination. Likewise I agree with Singer that love (authentic love?) is primarily anti-idealistic: a contextualized, historicized response of one existentially located human being to another, subject to all the vagaries of time and space.

On the negative side, I would just like to note that the distinction between appraisal and bestowal; an objective valuation and a subjective creation of "added value," is difficult for me to understand. I think cognitive psychology reveals that we are always bestowing, always experiencing in our own terms. In other words, the notion of objective valuation is troublesome.

Also, I find that Singer has been too analytic for my tastes. While he does vary his approach, he most often can be read as treating love as a "unary" relation. He regards love as something flowing from the lover to the loved. As a minor point, Singer always casts "the lover" as a he and the "loved" as a she. He claims it is just convention (1984a:6), but I don't believe him. When I try to reverse some of Singer's wording, I find it difficult to sustain his claim. He tends to treat male as active and female as passive throughout. Has he, at least in these volumes, unconsciously bought into some of the mapping of the relationship of God:Man onto Man:Woman?

A treatment of love as a unary relation is problematic in the modern world where we need to move away from asymmetry to symmetry. As I shall argue later, symmetry is best seen as cybernetic or a dialectic. The loving relation is not unary but binary—not an action but an interaction, a dance or a dialectic. I was quite surprised to find that Karl Marx had it this way: according to Singer (1987:68), Marx "insists that love must be reciprocal and that it must show itself in a concrete relationship between individuals responding directly to one another: 'Love only can be exchanged for love, trust for trust, etc. . . . If you love without evoking love in return, i.e., if you are not able, by the *manifestation* of yourself as a loving person, to make yourself a *beloved person,* then your love is impotent and a misfortune.' " Perhaps, to use Singer's vocabulary, love is a reciprocal bestowal which it is best not to analyze any further.

Beyond the details of Singer's framework, as I began to grapple with these issues, I became increasingly concerned that there may be a fundamental problem not only with the "grand views" of the Greeks or the Christians, but with the whole business of finding grand views. I guess I have been influenced a bit by Richard Rorty (e.g., 1989), who has argued that there is no grand view other than what we project "out there." Perhaps all metaphysics is a reification of what we think or wish to believe. If this is true, then the idolization of thought rather than emotion as a method for divining the "truth" is an oversimplification, an ignoring of emotion and action as alternate ways to appreciate the "truth" of experience.

Perhaps all metaphysical philosophers are doomed to fall into a psychology of domination because authentic love requires more of a stress on emotion and action. Abstracted from real men or women by their overemphasis on the intellect and the world of thought rather than of feeling and action, metaphysical philosophers might be fated to abstract, analyze, and objectify. One school of psychologists even have a label for such a personality type: they call it a "schizoid type."

While I have been a bit whimsical in making this point, I must stress that I am nevertheless serious. I worry that an overemphasis on the intellect makes authentic love difficult if not impossible to achieve. I should note that usually, according to psychodynamic theory, a schizoid type develops from a chronic denial of painful emotions, not from a deliberate stress on the intellect.

Another difficulty I have with philosophy of the "grand view" variety is that it may have little to offer by way of any guiding psychological principles. John Novak (1991) recently put it quite clearly when he said that the real question should not be "What is love?" but rather "How can I be more loving?" The answer may involve much more than intellectual abstraction.

In discussing the sexual experience, Michel Foucault (1978:57) claims that we are the only major society that has failed to develop an *ars erotica.* He says, "In the erotic art, truth is drawn from pleasure itself, understood as a practice and accumulated as experience; pleasure is not considered in relation to an absolute law of the permitted and the forbidden, nor by reference to a criterion of utility, but first and foremost in relation to itself; it is experienced as pleasure, evaluated in terms of its intensity, its specific quality, its duration, its reverberations in the body and the soul."

Instead we have a *scientia sexualis.* Foucault claims that the last several centuries have seen an assimilation of sexuality to discourse. We began to talk more and more about sex. For Foucault, this talk was not intended to repress sex, but rather to express it within the categories of the newly emerging bourgeois society. Sex needed to be regulated and channeled. This was achieved through making it discursive; which is presumably why we are bombarded, to this day, with writing about sex.

As Foucault (1978:78) himself expresses it: "We have placed ourselves under the sign of sex, but in the form of a *Logic of Sex*, rather than a *Physics*. We must make no mistake here: with the great series of binary oppositions (body/soul, flesh/spirit, instinct/reason, drives/consciousness) that seemed to refer sex to a pure mechanics devoid of reason, the West has managed not only, or not so much, to annex sex to a field of rationality, which would not be all that remarkable an achievement, seeing how accustomed we are to such 'conquests' since the Greeks, but to bring us almost entirely—our bodies, our minds, our individuality, our history—under the sway of a logic of concupiscence and desire." To this I can add only that if we have failed to develop an erotic, sexual art, have we for the same reasons failed to develop an art of love in the fuller sense as well?

WHAT IS OUR ALTERNATIVE?

I wish now to turn to alternatives. If we need to move away from our past reliance on "grand schemes," on metaphysics, and even away from an exclusive reliance on the intellect that produces those grand schemes, then what can we look to for an alternative? I must stress that the alternatives I offer here should not be thought of as alternative metaphysics from which to derive a psychology of equality. It is clear that some of the mythopoetic tradition can be used to inform a psychology of domination. Rather, I suggest that these alternatives be seen as useful only as far as they provide insight into a psychology of equality. Here I offer (in no particular order of preference) a few possibilities:

First, as I have noted earlier, we need to develop cybernetic approaches to love. The view Singer propounds is more linear than I would prefer; it is too analytic. The minimal analysis may more profitably be cybernetic—a dyadic interaction, or a dialectic. One-way appraisal or bestowal is a bit weird. If it is unrequited, is it love? It is bestowal, certainly, as Singer defines it, that makes the world go round. But it must be mutual bestowal: the joint creation of a life together, a shared dance, a tapestry woven by more than one, a story written by more than one.

Second, we can look to the East. Joseph Campbell tells the story of an exchange at a conference on religion held in Japan. A social philosopher from New York says to a Shinto priest that he has observed many ceremonies but still doesn't understand Shinto. He asks, "I don't get you. You don't have any ideology; you don't have any theology." The Shinto priest thinks for a time and responds, "You are right, we don't have any ideology; we don't have any theology; we just dance." Mervyn Sprung (1987) has recently offered a clear exposition of Eastern thought which suggests just this: that we need to move away from our sole reliance on reason to establish truth— that sometimes what we need is the "magic of unknowing." Psychologically, what this would do is to quiet the mind so that the heart and the body can have their say. A healing of the rift between body and mind would be enabled and a fuller love between men and women might result. I feel, more than I can clearly express, that this is the direction in which we must move if we wish to attain to a psychology of equality. This is because a psychology of equality must be based on a full and mutual response between two people.

Third, we might profit from a more psychological, rather than philosophical, approach. We would not seek to treat psychology as another philosophy but rather as a method for deepening our experience of ourselves and others. What I am getting at here is that a philosophical approach to matters of human relations attempts to treat them as one more verbalizable topic. It is as if merely articulating the issues constitutes an understanding. This, however, could not be farther from the truth. Philosophical methods are likely ineffectual in getting at the heart of essentially psychological matters. No matter how much Freud's psychoanalysis is described as a "talking cure," the talking has very little to do with philosophy.

The alternative psychological methodology, whether psychoanalytic or not, is rather different from philosophy. An excellent example is to be found in a book by Augustus Napier, *The Fragile Bond,* about maintaining love after marriage. There Napier argues that clusters of associations awaken "in us feelings that become so charged and intense that they literally change what we are experiencing." For Napier, associative clusters follow not logical but experiential principles. An experience with a woman can trigger an associative cluster which relates to how a man experienced his relationship with his mother. This largely unconscious relation can then condition how he treats the woman. The conscious understanding of how these unconscious clusters operate is a prerequisite to the construction of an authentic relationship.

Fourth, we might do well to consider alternative approaches to the human sciences, beyond the hypotheticodeductive ideal of the physical sciences. One alternative approach is the narrative approach (see, e.g., Donald Polkingholme, 1988), which begins with the assumption that humans tend to organize their experience of the world into narrative form. It is important to recognize that this is an alternative to philosophical analysis since philosophical analysis most often relies on the principles of logic for ensuring the coherence of philosophical argument, whereas narrative structure need not at all be logical in this sense.

Two episodes may follow one another in a narrative without any (obvious) logical implication.

I note here that the best worked-out form of the narrative approach is the novel, and also that Singer does incorporate insights expressed in the form of novels into his history of love. Here, however, I wish to uphold the value of a form of the narrative approach which I call the mythopoetic approach. This approach recognizes the power of myth and the efficacy of poetry in delivering mythic insight. Pre-Platonic Greek mythology is one rich source of mythopoetic inspiration as is the New Testament, where it deals with the narrative of the life of Christ and especially with the parables (I note here that a psychology of equality can be derived from the ethical principles articulated in the Bible without any commitment to the metaphysic outlined primarily in the Old Testament). Yet another source of mythopoetic inspiration is in pre-Christian and "pagan" traditions. It is as an illustration of the value of this source that I wish to turn to a discussion of a recent book by Robert Bly (1990), *Iron John: A Book about Men.*

According to Bly, the gods and goddesses, the kings and queens, the wild men and wild women, used to enrich our world. But they have been dead for a while now, and no one takes their myths, their fairy tales, and their hearth stories seriously any more. It also used to be that older men, guided by this ancient knowledge, initiated boys into manhood. But this practice has been lost and now boys grow up alone, often very distant from their fathers—or any other model of manhood. That, as a consequence, modern men have lost their strength and their potency, and have become "soft males," is the key premise of this book.

Only a man like Robert Bly, a masterful poet, attuned as he is to the mythopoetic realms pioneered by the likes of Carl Jung and Joseph Campbell, would dream of going beyond merely documenting his case. Bly is actually determined to bring them all back to life—all those gods, queens, and especially the "Wild Man." In doing this, he assumes the role of initiator; he becomes Merlin, the wise sage who helps the young prince in his quest, and helps us all to become men.

Bly achieves this remarkable goal through an insightful and often brilliant analysis of a wonderful fairy tale, the story of Iron John, which was first written down in 1820 by the Brothers Grimm. He distinguishes eight episodes in that story and guides us in reading these episodes as a "map" to follow in our growth to manhood. At each step along this psychodynamic journey, Bly links key elements from the story with a rich variety of mythological traditions ranging from ancient Greece to modern New Guinea. In the process, Bly's scholarship makes it clear that this is no idiosyncratic reading; he is onto something important and universal.

The story of Iron John begins with the discovery of a frightening Wild

Man deep beneath the surface of a pond located somewhere on the edges of a kingdom. In this beginning Bly says: "When a contemporary man looks down into his psyche, he may, if the conditions are right, find under the water of his soul, lying in an area no one has visited for a long time, an ancient hairy man." Buckets are used to empty the pond and reveal the Wild Man who is then taken to the castle courtyard, locked into an iron cage, and named Iron John." We each have to "do bucket work," to encounter the Wild Man in us. Bly comments: "Welcoming the Hairy Man is scary and risky, and it requires a different son of courage. Contact with Iron John requires a willingness to descend into the male psyche and accept what's dark down there. . . ."

A little further on in the story, the king's son is playing in the courtyard with his golden ball. It gets away from him and rolls into Iron John's cage. When the boy asks for the ball back, Iron John says he will return it only if the boy lets him out by stealing the key to the cage from under the pillow of his mother, the queen. The golden ball represents "the unity of personality we had as children," and the rolling of the ball into Iron John's cage shows us that "a man can't expect to find the golden ball in the feminine realm, because that's not where the ball is." We cannot become men only by developing the feminine in us.

The boy does eventually steal the key from under his mother's pillow and then goes off into the forest riding on the shoulders of the Wild Man. As Bly says: "Freud, taking advice from a Greek play, says that a man should not skip over the mutual attraction between himself and his mother if he wants a long life." Boys *have to* make a symbolic break with their mothers. They also *have to* be welcomed into manhood by their fathers and the other older men, to be taken off into the woods on their shoulders.

It is this part of *Iron John,* about the estrangement of boys from older men, and especially from their fathers, which is the most touching. "Both male and female cells carry marvelous music but the son needs to resonate to the masculine frequency as well as to the female frequency. Sons who have not received this tuning will have father-hunger all their lives." Without the father's help, or the help of some older male, the boy may never find the Wild Man, may never bucket him out, may never steal the key from under his mother's pillow, may never ride off on the Wild Man's shoulders, may never meet a Wild Woman, may never really become a man. Seen in this way, *Iron John* can be seen as a call for all older men again to take up the task of helping their boys become men.

The thoughtful man and woman may be concerned that *Iron John* is a call for males to return to the crudeness of the past. Bly thinks not: "I speak of the Wild Man in this book, and the distinction between the savage man and the Wild Man is crucial throughout. The savage mode does **great** damage to soul, earth, and humankind; we can say that though the savage man is wounded he prefers not to examine it. The Wild Man, who has examined his wound, resembles a Zen priest, a shaman, or a woodsman more than a savage "When we understand our maleness we do not become abusers of women; rather we become powerful partners of modern women who have already begun to free the Wild Woman in themselves. We become kings for our queens, lovers for our beloved; we are no longer afraid to give her wild flowers. Bly's mythopoetic reading of the story of Iron John leads him to explicate some of the conditions under which a psychology of equality can develop, conditions that recognize the strengths of both men and women.

CONCLUSION

At the risk of being accused of having lapsed into complete fuzziness, of having completely given in to "New Age" or mystical thinking, I would like to close by summarizing and extending the ideas I have developed here. These ideas may not be terribly new, but I think they need airing once more: The old Western worldview is in trouble. Philosophy has deconstructed itself and in the process has laid bare its strengths and limitations. Many people today think that we need to go beyond the way we have been to find a new way to approach our existence. They think this because they are afraid that if we go on in the same way, we will destroy ourselves and our planet.

I have spoken in this paper of the need to find a way of allowing the sexes to coexist in symmetry, of moving toward a psychology of equality. Along the way, I have wondered whether we need to grow beyond Western metaphysics and even to recognize grand linear, idealizing thinking as being part of the problem. In its place, I would put more feeling and pragmatic, cybernetic, psychological narrative. I have wondered if the mythopoetic approach embodied in the work of Carl Jung, Joseph Campbell, and our mythological tradition offers an alternate route. Robert Bly was offered up as an example of a recent writer taking that route to find a better grounding for men. Implied in his approach was a more balanced approach to male-female relations.

I cannot help wondering if a switch from a psychology of domination to one of equality might not have implications for more than how men and women get along. After all, in our daily speech we talk of Mother Nature. Are humans "Man" as a counterpoint to nature as "Woman"? Do the same dynamics which drive asymmetry in male-female relations also drive them in our relation to the natural world? We often hear the term "the rape of nature" as a way of describing the dominance we have shown over it. If we could become more balanced, as we reconstrued male-female relations, perhaps our relationship with nature would also change from old to new, from one of dominance to one of coexistence with "her." We certainly need a new approach as we drive ever more species into extinction, and pollute the planet to death.

A key feature of the alternate approach I have been exploring here is the need for us to find cybernetic balance; a steady state. We desperately need to develop a steady-state approach to economics which tells us that all is going well if we *haven't* grown (or shrunk). We also desperately need to develop a steady-state approach to politics—an approach many hoped would emerge from the ice age of the cold war, a politics that says it is good for the nations of the world to eschew war.

So, am I a New Ager? Perhaps partly. In the vocabulary of this paper, New Agers are exploring a psychology of equality in their relations to other people, to animals, and to the planet. They are driven to this exploration by their horror at the barbarity of the psychology of domination. (I note parenthetically that it is not the horror of the death of other people which drives New Agers most strongly. Images of oil-covered cormorants hurt much more since they portend the immanent death of our planet.) I tend to share with New Agers their conviction that we had better develop a psychology of equality, for the future of life on Earth hangs in the balance.

Unfortunately, most New Agers are still "grand view" philosophers; to use Richard Rorty's (1989) term, they are "metaphysicians" who think that final answers to the deep questions can be found. They are searching for a metaphysics of equality to undergird their conviction that a psychology of equality is the only way to go. To its credit, this search has resulted in an implicit recognition that the underpinnings of our traditional values will not do. The New Agers recognize those underpinnings as constituting a metaphysic of domination. I believe that this is why their search has led away from the Christian metaphysic to Eastern philosophy and to pre-Christian pantheism.

Richard Rorty (1989) has made me an "ironist." I no longer think that I am going to find a metaphysic of any sort at all. However, this doesn't stop me from trying to understand as best I can. It only means that I shall never be confident I have got the last word. I am reminded of something I believe that St. Augustine said, which goes something like this: "Shallow-witted philosophers are constantly seeking after truth while we Christians can rest assured in the certainty that we have found it."

To the extent that I am a shallow-witted ironist, I am not a New Ager. Ancient theories of why crystals focus energy hold no more than historical curiosity for me. Eastern philosophy and pre-Christian pantheism are of interest only as inspirations in my search for a psychology of equality. I seek to be an ironist who realizes that our past metaphysic has spawned a destructive psychology of domination. I think we now face the task of constructing a

264   Part Three: Contemporary Formulations

new psychology of equality without the luxury of an underlying metaphysic.
I tend to distrust New Agers because I am worried that they will seek to
establish a new metaphysic which will inevitably spawn a new psychology
of domination. I think all metaphysics are dangerous; I don't want any "green
Ayatollahs."

I suspect that we have to go it alone in the universe, that we have to
be "grown up." Likewise, our new naturalistic, humanistic psychology of equality
will have to stand up on its own. I close by returning to Shulamith Firestone
(1970) and Elizabeth Rappaport, who worry that men and women will not
be able to love authentically until sexual equality is achieved. If I am right
in my conclusion that sexual equality will be achieved only when we can
find a naturalistic, humanistic psychology of equality, we still have quite a
bit of work ahead of us.

REFERENCES

Bly, Robert. *Iron John: A Book about Men.* Reading, Mass.: Addison-Wesley, 1990.
Firestone, Shulamith. *The Dialectic of Sex.* New York: William Morrow & Co., 1970.
Foucault, Michel. *The History of Sexuality.* Vol. 1: *An Introduction.* New York:
    Vintage Books, 1978.
Napier, Augustus Y. *The Fragile Bond.* New York: Harper & Row, 1988.
Novak, John. Personal communication, 1991.
Polkingholme, Donald E. *Narrative Knowing and the Human Sciences.* Albany: State
    University of New York Press, 1988.
Rorty, Richard. *Contingency, Irony, and Solidarity.* Cambridge: Cambridge University
    Press, 1989.
Singer, Irving. *The Nature of Love.* Vol. 1: *Plato to Luther.* Chicago: The University
    of Chicago Press, 1984a.
———. *The Nature of Love.* Vol. 2: *Courtly and Romantic.* Chicago: The University
    of Chicago Press, 1984b.
———. *The Nature of Love.* Vol. 3: *The Modern World.* Chicago: The University
    of Chicago Press, 1987.
Sprung, Mervyn. *The Magic of Unknowing: An East-West Soliloquy.* Peterborough,
    Canada: Broadview Press, 1987.
Von Glaserfeld, E. "An Introduction to Radical Constructivism." In P. Watzlawick,
    ed., *The Invented Reality: How Do We Know What We Believe We Know?*
    (Contributions to Constructivism). New York: W. W. Norton, 1984.

17

Evaluating Sexual Love:
A Prologomenon to Postromantic Inquiry*

John McMurtry

Irving Singer's three-volume interpretative narrative of ideas, *The Nature of Love,* is the most comprehensive and erudite literary overview of the subject in the English language. As such, it provides us with an ideal background for analysis of what is missing in the vast history of ideas about love, in particular in subjectivist commentary on love of which Singer's work is an exemplar.

What is lacking in Singer's study of love is an adequate basis in the biological and the social-structural conditions within which sex-love and choice of sex-love take place. Considerations of love as a relationship of perilous physical possibilities, of sexist power and dominion, or of proprietary control and repression do not figure in Singer's account. What is also missing, relatedly, is any clear principle of value by means of which we can tell the good from the bad in love, and be guided by our code.

In this analysis of love, I will begin by accepting as love whatever linguistic practice recognizes as love. Usage confers legitimacy on wholly different and incompatible meanings of love, from "altruistic devotion" to "bodily addiction," from universal concern to private obsession. If there is a unifying sense to

*This paper was originally prepared for presentation during The 2000 Years of Love Conference, Brock University, Ontario, February 1991. I am grateful to the participants in this conference for their comments, and to G. A. Cohen, David Goicoechea, and Irving Singer for their suggestions.

these meanings, I will not seek it. The evaluation here will not be in terms of what is and is not love, but of what it is for love to be good or of value, and what it is for love to be bad or of no value.

Professor Singer says of love that the "source of love . . . is idea about love" (p. xiii). . . . "Love is never elicited by the object in the sense that desire or approbation is. . . . When love happens it happens as new creation of value" (p. 13). . . . [Love is] above all an artifact of the human imagination (p. 22). . . . "Love . . . [is] a way of bestowing value *upon* the object, taking an interest in it regardless of how good or bad it may be (p. 90)."[1]

Professor Singer's concern, as these citations show, is with the subjective bestowal of love rather than the objective bearing or value of love, with love as a creation of value, not something that itself needs to be evaluated. He even goes so far as to say in volume 1, a position he modifies in volume 3, that: "it is the valuing alone that *makes* the value" (p. 5). I will take the opposite approach here. The point of my analysis is to move beyond the subjectivist concept of love Singer's study paradigmatically bears to the underlying structures of power and precipice within which love must struggle to exist, whatever the ideations of its experiencers may be. The concern of my analysis will then be to introduce a principle of universal value which can be applied to these objective structures and problems of love to guide us through them in a good way rather than an idea-hypnotized way.

The focus will be on sexual love. Sexual love may pose the profoundest natural and social problems we face personally in life, and certainly generates some of the most unbalanced and disabling behaviors of which humanity is capable. Underneath its creative, often hallucinatory, bestowals of value lie organic dangers and socially structured denials of human realization that the subjectivist view tends to overlook.

THE PATRIARCHAL STRUCTURE OF TRADITIONAL SEX-LOVE RELATIONSHIPS

Feminists have made us aware of the dominance of the patriarchal structure of conventional sex relations over almost three millennia in all the major cultures—in particular, in the relationship of marriage, where until recently in the developed West the woman was obliged to consent to an inviolable and permanent commitment to "obey" her husband "until death do you part," in whatever situations confronted their "one body" in the course of their lives as, essentially, subject and subjected.

The patriarchal structure of love, of course, classically governed father and child and master-servant relations as well, and found its ancient basis in the recognized *patria potestas* (paternal right) by the *paterfamilias*, i.e., family patriarch, to beat, to abandon, or to put to death any member of his household. The venerable idea of a "rule of thumb," which we still conventionally deploy as a metaphor for acceptable practical standard, refers to the approximate thickness of the rod or whip with which a husband could rightfully flog his wife. Women's more or less absolute dispossession of power within the relationship of love, marriage, and civil society over most of world history is too well known to belabor here. Suffice it to say that from Confucian China to nineteenth-century Europe, it included prohibition from holding property; exclusion from positions of responsibility or independent employment outside the home; requirement of unconditional submission of the woman to husband, father, or other male family member; deprivation of civil rights, and so on. Such a structure of one-sided power and powerlessness within the accepted and established man-woman relationship—akin in its nature to the relationship of master and slave, which still structures love-images today—can hardly be ignored if one is to understand "the nature of love" that lives within its confines. Yet literary and philosophical accounts of love within this power structure routinely ignore its determinations, presuppose it as a given order of existence, and indeed often sanctify its bonds as divinely ordained. We find the same idea of love in the larger cosmos in the relationship posited between Almighty God and the lowly human subjects over whom He rules as Love and they, His helpless adorers, in turn worshipfully serve. I confess I am sometimes tempted to wonder whether the bestowal of love so valued by Singer, and frequently compared by him to the divine effulgence of God, is not ultimately grounded in this patriarchal tradition. That is, bestowal of attributes on a loved one entails the power to grant or withhold these attributes at will. Recognition of a loved one's worth, in contrast, leaves the existence of this attribute as something belonging to the other's own being—not something one bestows on the other as a gift. The latter operation seems to be patriarchal power endowed with a benign face.

The patriarchal ideal of love is by no means dead, even in the presence of feminist politics and power. A woman is typically an object of male love because of her seductive weakness and innocence, her dependency, her submissiveness to male achievement and power, and her possession as a beautiful appendage. One might be eruditely deferential to this ideal and to the knightly virtues of the strong man protecting her fragile beauty from the harsh outer world. I do not know that the idea-created love so valued by Singer ever rules out this structure of ardor, mutual passion, and delight. But at some time we must get underneath even imaginative creation within the patriarchal form and ask ourselves whether this underlying traditional structure of love is not, in truth, bad—a detriment to the autonomy and growth of the woman, and to the breadth and vitality of the love relationship itself.

There are, in sum, two major steps to be made beyond the type of analysis proffered by Professor Singer: first, to recognize the patriarchal infrastructure within which traditional love of all sorts has been typically confined and, second, to subject this structure and its manifest variations to some hard evaluation in terms of its reductive effects on human capability.

THE PRIVATE-PROPERTY STRUCTURE OF LOVE

The proprietary structure of love also admits of a nonpatriarchal form, one of egalitarian reciprocity. Here both the man and the woman relate to the other as a private possession, with rights of exclusive access and control conferred on each by their mutual possession. The "bond" or "wedlock" here is, ideally, wholly symmetrical, and each relates to the other as an equal, that is, equally bound within the other's territorial enclosure or agreed-upon possessory right.[2] This deep property structure of love is widespread across human society, and has come slowly to replace the patriarchal system and its traditional relationship of one-side domination by the man. It is, for example, quite normal in this current period of Western civilization for neither man nor woman to be in a position of dominion over the other, but for each instead to equally possess the other as "my own," "my one and only," "my precious," and so on. This relationship of mutual property-hold over one another's being can often be total in its claim on the other's life, even its past, so that no access by another to any aspect of the loved one's existence can pass unnoticed or not be a potential site of jealous vigilance and concern (a possessiveness which *Othello*'s Iago exploited, and which drove Angel Clare to abandon Tess of the d'Urbervilles to her ruin). Whatever the range of domain held within such a mutual ownership arrangement—whether confined to the intimate regions of the lover's life or totalized as possessory relation to the entirety of the beloved's existence—it is a relationship akin to private property, because it supposes the right to *exclusion of all others* from the possessed regions, from normally clothed body parts to facial expressions to ideas communicated in conversation—even to private thoughts.

    Most of the love relations celebrated in popular music and culture, as well as in Professor Singer's learned study, seem to presuppose the private-property structure of love in *some* form as the natural order of the world. Perhaps it is. But then again most of the conficts over love arise precisely because this containment of it within a possessory relation is *not* felt as "natural," but is experienced as suffocating and repressive. From the rebellion of the archangel against the all-loving Lord, or the child against the possessive love of the parent, or the notorious struggles within the possessive relationship of romantic love, we find a recurrent pattern of deep conflict and rebellion against this underlying, and usually unmentioned, property structure of love.

So there is surely some need to reflect critically on this traditional form, not just assume it as a given with which creative bestowals can flourish in hot-house style. Might not the tragedies of *Othello* and of *Tess of the D'Urbervilles,* or of Hester Prynne in *The Scarlet Letter*—or indeed of *Paradise Lost*— be more deeply understood if we critically examined this monolithic presumption of love as a possessory relationship? Might not these be literary symptoms of a profound problem in our assumptions about the "mine and thine" structure of love? Not at all, so far as I can see, for Professor Singer, whose accounts seem to work consistently within this presupposition. And not for most of us who understand this given order as a cornerstone of acceptable morality.

As with the long presupposed patriarchal structure of love, so with the mutual property structure of love that has progressively succeeded it, two basic steps of analysis are required. The first is to acknowledge the presupposed structure and its determination of love's possibilities, and the second is to evaluate it critically. It may be that its assumed morality is in the end justified, but we need to be aware that it is there before we can know that it is justified, and we need also to understand the principle of value by which we can appraise it before we can know whether it is of value, or disvalue, or, more likely, an unexamined mixture of the two.

THE HEALTH ECONOMY OF LOVE

By "the health economy of love," I mean the three basic physiological implications of the traditional sex-love relationship:

1. pregnancy and/or birth *or* prevention of both;
2. disease to one or both partners in consequence of sexual intercourse *or* prevention of disease;
3. incapacitation of normal faculties by long- or short-term "lovesickness" *or* no incapacitation and mutual empowerment by the love relationship.

Subjectivist ideas and theories of love are by their nature above the strictly physiological dimensions of sex-love and its pathological possibilities. I do not know that any reference to sexual disease, a basic problem of sex-love for centuries in the West, and intimately related to its taboo limits, once occurs in Professor Singer's study. It is an impolite subject, not mentionable in the highest literary circles or with proper philosophical removal from the world. Yet it could hardly be more basically important to human life and decision in our world, as we are learning today with such lethal clarity from AIDS. It needs the attention of those who would understand the nature of love in more than its lily-white forms.

Then there is the problem of unwanted pregnancy and reproduction. This *is* a topic of literary interest here and there throughout the great tradition Professor Singer considers, but only as an incident of scandal and a presupposed occasion of social downfall, disgrace, permanent scars, and danger. When in this tradition is pregnancy not presupposed in this way, and left at that with no further questioning or analysis? Yet here, too, the problem is one deserving some philosophical reflection. Consider, for example, the bastard Edmund in *King Lear,* one of tragedy's greatest villains, and implied as such by Shakespeare in virtue of his birth out of wedlock as "Nature's offspring," a mutant for conventional order whose treachery is accepted as a product of his illegitimate origin. He is, if we take the matter deeper, a pathological symptom of a dichotomous structurizing of human birth; good and wonderful news if the reproductive cycle is within marriage, bad and possibly murderous news if this cycle occurs outside the conventional structure. Why is this? We will find no answer in Singer's subjectivist approach, does he even pose the question. He views love as ultimately a creation of value by lovers. The whole underlying world of physiological reproduction and social classification and repression is taken as the given order of the world. What is of interest to this subjectivist approach is how people *imagine* what is going on within this prefixed structure of reality. This does not take us very far. Nor does it enlist our human responsibility to evaluate our conventional ways of coping with such processes and structures. Nor can it, consequently, ever pose to us a problem of doing something about them to better their hold, or to release us from their deformations. In short, this approach leaves us up in the air.

The issue with sex-love is not just an issue of lovers' and literatis' experiences of it, and the endless interpretations and transformations of this subjectivity. It is more problematic than that. Sex-love reaches into the depths and breadths of the human condition in ways we overlook when we isolate and idealize it, and do not see that the entire condition of human survival is implicated in its workings.

I suggest that the first and most basic problem of sex-love is that it breaks or penetrates the very membrane of life, that ever-present dividing line between physical self and other that does not normally admit even a tiny foreign particle for a moment without catastrophic consequence to its existence.

Even the apparent exceptions here, food and water, are normally mediated by a host of protective filters of custom, preparation, choice, and trial before they are admitted into the body. The self's protective membrane is at work everywhere to maintain its thin envelope of life. The problematic begins with the fact that this membrane is the primary line of defense of life which sexual action seeks to penetrate. Every erotic move—and there are countless numbers and variations—has this penetration as its inner theme. Prior to the progressive physical passages into the other's body, beginning and continuing, interest-

ingly, with the orifice that consumes, there is normally the foreplay of mutual yielding up of each other's social defenses and finding common life in
words. This is the communion of language expressing and developing a joining
of thought and desire which, if the love is good, grows past the climactic
moments of shared organic being to a far wider field of shared human existence.
Sex-love, however, can be adequately understood only if its existential ground
in body interpenetration is understood, and the ultimate stakes of life and
death involved here are comprehended.

Sex-love is at its poles of possibility a risking of death or compounded
life, or disease or expansive health—and the entire literature of love *reflects*
these themes in creative metaphor. To miss this underlying ground of the
creative expressions of love, is to love in a shadow world of ideas without
bearings in the organic beings that we are. We cannot tolerate anything less
than the most exacting care in the breakage of life's membranes of individuation
and existence. Biotic love must accompany subjective love as its embodied
base, or the ideation and so often misrepresentation going on above the body
may be more or less ruinous.

Once we understand the life-and-death, health-and-disease stakes underlying sex-love, we are also much better able to understand historical ideas
about it. The rarefication of these stakes is made manifest in love's conventional
literary metaphors of sickness and dying, of heroic vitality and rebirth which
dominate ideas of sex-love from the ancient Tantrics to Wagner. This is not
to say these ideas are any the less creative or beautiful for their having a
life-base to express.

Not only the creative ideas and expressions *of* sex-love, but also the age-
old and variant taboos *against* sex-love are given their explanatory base when
we move to the membrane of life as the ground of our analysis. Given the
ultimate stakes of sex-love on the organic level—and these are poles of a
range of possibility, not another either-or dualism—the historical social taboos
and restrictions fencing in sex-love become functionally intelligible. These, too,
however, are taken as societal givens by Professor Singer and most literary
and philosophical commentary on love, despite their apparent oppressiveness
and absurdity to more culturally critical minds. Yet once we lay bare the
underlying problems and dangers of sex-love's breaking of the very lines of
organic defense and life, then we can see that these taboos and restrictions
serve a very useful function. They constitute a kind of unconsciously evolved
social defense of these delicate defining lines between organic self and Other,
an extracutaneous wall of protection that rings around the extremely sensitive
and vulnerable human organism a second, social layer of defense. Given the
spontaneous powers of the sexual urges, which in our species are polymorphous
and year-long in their drive, and given at the same time the distinctively sensitized
skin and openings of our body's interface with the world, the strict barriers

of social prohibition against impulsive breakings of the membrane of life are understandable as a survival strategy of human society in all its variations. Once we recognize that we love from within these diaphanous envelopes of life which sex-love can dangerously invade if not very carefully regulated, then we can understand the *responses* to this our human condition, whether in the death-courting ideas of love poetry or the iron regimens of social taboo. From this recognition we can then begin to develop conscious value-bearings to guide us, and not remain unmoored in the stratosphere of literary creations disconnected from the bodily world, nor trapped inside blind social customs which imprison sex-life within crude and unconscious taboo.

The other basic level of organic reality ignored by subjectivism is the elemental reproduction drive itself. This is the organic base of sex-love's overwhelming urge toward creative joining, life's primeval longing to reproduce itself. Even loin-focused realists have been inclined to overlook the ultimate function of this longing to bear children. I do not know that the significance of children in the love relationship has any place in Professor Singer's study. The point here as elsewhere is not to *reduce* sex-love subjectivity to a mere biological function, but to give it its *natural* creative basis so we can understand better what is expressed and created *from* it. We only understand the overflowing power and exuberance of sex-love attractions, as well as the life-and-death stakes of the future it resonates within our experience, when we ground our subjective phenomenology of love in the deep creative currents of Nature from which it springs. This does not diminish the imaginative expressions and transfigurations which artistic sensibilities interpret and derive from this underlying natural base; it simply provides them with their real foundation. This is of hermeneutic value because it gives us the natural rationale of the mad frenzy of sex-love which otherwise may seem insane. As Shaw, for example, suggests in *Man and Superman,* in a reverse sexist way, the most basic vital motivation known to us is the urge of life to go on living beyond the limits of our skins, in the seeds of new human life we plant or nourish. That we recognize the ultimacy of this primeval longing as the nature of our condition as organic beings, puts the inflamed desperation and impetuosity of love so often mythicized by creative art into the larger perspective of Nature as a whole. Madness in love is no longer so irrational and distressing when it is thus grounded.

On the practical side of morality, the reproductive stakes of sex-love are of the greatest importance in understanding the conflicts, jealousies, social disaster, and personal anguish that can arise out of sex-love which is not consciously regulated by a guiding value. We are dealing here with the possible takeover of the woman's entire body by a growing organism within her for a fixed cycle of months, and the birth into the world of the claims of another, long-helpless human being. We are confronting the underlying cause of all the historical love problems of abortion, infanticide, bastards, orphans, fallen women, unwanted children, parental abuse, and ultimately the nature of the social fabric itself. If these are not concerns of sex-love's subjectivity—and where *are* they concerns for critical evaluation in the tradition of Singer's accounts of sex-love subjectivity?—then commentary on the so-called nature of love may be not only theoretically denatured but ethically insensible.

As with the problems posed by sex-love's other natural processes and consequences, Professor Singer passes this one by. He leaves the actual moral restraints and judgments here to the operations of established social prescriptions and prohibitions to whose order, it seems, we are not to be "disloyal" in the structure of our thoughts about love.[3]

CONNECTING NATURE AND CONVENTION: TOWARD IMAGINATIVE SEX-LOVE RESPONSIBILITY

Interestingly, there are systematic connections between the natural and social structures of sex-love, which can together account for the unconscious formation of conventional codes. We have already discussed the connection between the immunological membrane of human life and the care that must be taken to ensure against pathogenic invasions of this protective membrane, a care that has been unconsciously institutionalized in sexual taboos across human societies. A similar connection exists between these taboo prohibitions and the elemental sexual drive for reproduction—with sex codes functioning as a socially evolved protective wall against unwanted pregnancies and births in the community, loss of family lines and stability, eruption of primary-emotion conflicts, and so on. In both cases, because sex-love involves such great stakes in its consequences, these conventional regulations surrounding it have been central to the function and survival of past social formations. It is here that we can see a cunning of reason to patriarchal orders of sex rule, as well as to the private property structure of monogamy and its variants. Both kinds of sexual control serve to rule out the serious problems which the unregulated primordial sex-drive can give rise to. Without understanding their protective function, sex taboos may be uncritically presupposed as givens of the world's order or, from a more questioning perspective, seem repressive impositions on human freedom. Under deeper analysis, however, it becomes clear that these proprietary orders of sex love by their nature systematically limit the right of sexual access (i.e., to one person or none), and thereby select against pathogenic invasion, unwanted reproduction, and the other basic threats to human well-being which might occur if the exuberant sex-urge is not confined within recognized fences of control. These limitations also might be seen to work to prevent patently subjective disorders associated with the gauntlet of "falls," "faints," "entanglements," "heartbreaks," "dyings," "sicknesses," "conquests," "devastations," and "breakups" associated with sex-love's deep realignments of organic and emotional structures.

Yet there is something dehumanizing about accepting property lines around people, and in submitting to external prohibitions that are not consciously given to oneself. But if one is not to defect to such dehumanization and unfreedom, where is one to draw the line in sex-love? There is little in the endless philosophical and literary stories of love, or in Professor Singer's story of stories, to adequately ground us here. Yet there must be developed controls of some sort on what is a potentially life-and-death matter. What value can we believe in here that is not mere subjective construal or conventional proprietary presupposition, but takes full moral measure of the deep stakes involved?

It has long haunted historical judgment of sex-love that it is bad *in itself.* This is because of the great temptations and problems it causes, so great that they remain largely unspeakable for conventional value judgment. Even the great sages (Or should one say the great sages in particular?), Buddha, Socrates, Jesus, and Spinoza, seem to have avoided these great pitfalls of sex-love by renouncing it altogether in a spiritualized purity of abstinence. This is no solution for Professor Singer, who healthfully affirms the profound joys of sex-love. But we need deeper groundings and critical reflections on the objective structures at work here. Those prescribed for us by status quo assumptions do not suffice.

It is the axiomatic nature of all value that what is good is *what enables a more inclusive range of being,* and what is bad is what *reduces this range of being*—of thought, of experience, or of action. At first blush, increase of sex-love relationships might seem to be commended by this principle of value, and this is indeed the inner logic of the radical free-love position. Free love is good, it is implied, because it liberates us to participate as widely and deeply as possible in sex-love's delights. Although the radical free-love position, along with other "unseemly" matters, is not one that Professor Singer elects to feature in his sedate narrative, it deserves our attention, since we are being constantly solicited by countless commercials and images inviting us to be seduced into the arms of an endless array of alluring sex-partners (albeit only in the company of marketed commodities).

As soon, however, as one brings to consciousness the underlying life-and-death stakes that are involved in the sex-love relationship, from the problem of bodily health and survival on up to personal anguish or disintegration, one can see that there is a great danger in attending solely to the subjectivity of the lovers. If one is not merely to ignore these underlying problems and recline in mentations within conventional norms, on the one hand, or carelessly indulge a free-love gambol of unseen perils, on the other hand, one needs to mediate the mind-altering power of the sex urge with a more grounded and self-regulating value approach. In fact, what may *seem* to be good in sex-love relationships is very often bad in virtue of reducing the range of human beings—by communicable pathogens, unwanted pregnancy, or complications in trying to prevent it, conflicts over vital time for more productive activities, and emotional imbalance and exhaustion.

A way of meeting these problems by other than mere imaginings about love is to be openly conscious of their possibility in all sex-love relationships, and to attend to their prevention by one's actions. Such concrete responsibility is incumbent on any mature exercise of freedom, but depends on the clear recognition of these infrastructural and objective problems of love before it can be exercised. Here is where the creative imagination so prized by Professor Singer in sex-love subjectivity is of critical importance: in transfiguring the sex-urge to love that raises in the imagination not only the object of its desire, but the full spectrum of organic problems, sociostructural repressions, and personal incapacities posed as pathological possibilities through sex-love actions. The requirements of imaginative empathy and thinking through here are vast in their interest and implications. They take us far beyond the conventional egocentricity of the sexual drive, as well as beyond the bestowals of value on one's love, and relate us to the larger universes of nature and society as a whole. Nothing less than the exercise of this creative responsibility is adequate to the scope and depth of the problematic presented by sex-love's implications.

Only if mediated by this consciousness of sex-love's wider bearings do the lines of good and bad, of enabling versus disabling action in sex-love, become clear. One cannot make any a priori pronouncements here, because the objective circumstances of sex-love are notoriously complicated. But what one can safely say is that *unless* there is such a sex-love responsibility employing the full capacity of imaginative exploration of the possible problems attending sex-love action, the action is bad. It is bad to the extent that there is a failure of such life-protective thoughtfulness. This is true not merely because of the deep processes of life-reconstitution sex-love sets into motion, posing organic, social, and personal dangers and potentials that will otherwise be unseen. Even aside from the possibility of grievous impairment of capacity as a consequence of unconsidered sex-love, there is the intrinsic reduction of thought, experience, and action which thoughtless behavior entails *in itself.* By contrast, imaginative sex-responsibility deepens and broadens the scope of thought and experience by its very nature; it is a good in itself. A choice to forfeit this extended range of intrinsic being is a self-diminution. It also bears in its wake a loss of connectedness with another, the very other with whom one is entering into deepest intimacy. There is a sad incoherence and reduction of being here that is painfully exposed by Lawrence Ferlinghetti's next-morning realization that "she had bad teeth and didn't like poetry." Reductive sex-love is bad for our own inward life prior to its objective dangers to health and well-being.

It is not as if this principle of telling the good from the bad were repressive. Imaginative sex-love responsibility generates a more inclusive range of being in its own right, and thus takes us far beyond the sexual relationship itself to a natural and social sharing of being which can, as the poets recognize, be all-embracing in its reach. There is no question of disaffirmation of sexuality here, only a question of sensitizing it to the wider scopes of life and existence implicated by it: that is, affirming sexuality inclusively, not reductively.

Are we then to sacrifice the exhilarating vitality of exuberant "flings" and "passionate affairs" to a moralistic mind? These are not necessarily excluded by the proposed principle of value. It may well be that sex-love responsibility can affirm these leaps into the vortices of life as ultimately generating a greater scope of being. If thoughtful reflection reveals no objective problems for the parties concerned, and they are agreed as to the nature of their relationship as one that is not destructive to life or happiness, these sex-love moments may be good in their positive extension of experience into fresh intensities of being. Moreover, they may endure in memory as accessible experiences, epiphanies that deepen the reach of human existence. Perhaps they may also be touched with a painful nostalgia or yearning to share again. For the principle of value of more inclusive being, such pain is not bad. It becomes bad only when it disables us. Pain that reduces us, that narrows our emotional life into fixation of fear of loving in the future may be what causes many people to reject the "fling" or "affair." Judgment here depends on the persons involved and the objective parameters of their organic and social lives.

Where imaginative sex-love responsibility decides that the choosing of sex-love is a disabling option after all things have been considered—perhaps only on the grounds of prior commitments to time with loving others who count on it—still this does not mean the repression of love's possibilities. Already in thought an inner world of shared beings has been entered and explored. Love is still love that remains "at a distance." If this does not diminish one's being by obsession—although obsessive love at a distance can be very creative, as we know from Dante's love for Beatrice—then it is of value for the increased scope of care and correctedness it has generated. A contributory factor to this more inclusive being may be the created value bestowed on the loved one, the overriding value in Professor Singer's account. But one need not bestow value to create it. The universe of value increases wherever any more encompassing range of thought and experience has been opened. The beauty of the "love at a distance" possibility is that none of the life-and-death problems associated with sex-love on the embodied plane can occur—not even the problem of competing demands on one's time, because there is no requirement to be in more than one spatiotemporal location simultaneously. Imaginative love precludes no possibility, including that of one day acting on the attraction. This possibility is better for the fuller awareness of all that this action may involve. The inward life of humanity is indeed miraculous in its creative possibilities, and Professor Singer is right to have given great importance in his account to its value.

Where we differ fundamentally is on Singer's understanding of the transformative capacity of love only insofar as it *bestows value on the loved one*. The shortcoming of this position is that it narrows the universe of value-creative possibility in love to what is bestowed on another by the lover. It thus overlooks the far wider range of value-creation generated by the very act of *taking into consideration* all the being and circumstances of the other and oneself which connect one to the greater creative powers of nature and society implicated in any sex-love relationship. By this opening to the larger creative world not seen by the bestowal focus, life as a whole is transfigured by the animating energy of erotic interest. It creates, by the very imagination of all that is implicated by the sex-love connection, a new ground of being and possibility. This more encompassing creative power of love seems to me quite lost to Professor Singer's analysis. The most profound misunderstanding I am aware of in his study, of the philosophy of Rousseau, is a symptom of his closure to it. The interior realm of natural and social connectedness that is everything to the theory of Rousseau—thinking in terms of the common interest—seems to be little or nothing to the individualist subjectivism of Singer.[4]

THE PROBLEM OF BESTOWAL

By his emphasis on the lover's bestowal of value on the loved one, Professor Singer seems to have set aside a primary requirement of imaginative sex-love responsibility, which is to consider what tells *against* the value one has perhaps misleadingly or foolishly bestowed on the loved one. As we know, "love can be blind," harmfully blind, and it may need nothing so much as a widening exploration of what contradicts sex-love's heated valued bestowals. I am not endorsing a theory of Judaic desert or Freudian reductionism, which I think are highly rejected by Professor Singer as too mean-spirited. I am arguing rather for a responsible social imagination which inwardly explores all that may shed light on a sex-love interest, both prior to and during its issue in action. The value that should guide us is that of enabling a more inclusive range of being in the world. If the sex-love possibility clearly works against this value's realization—as it often does—then it and the bestowals associated with it should be declined as bad love. For example, you might feel a sex-love attraction toward another whose life, on deeper consideration, will flourish only if a full-time or long-term commitment can be made to your love. If love is not able to make such a commitment because of existing objective facts, such as another such relationship, then to act on this sex love possibility would be wrong; however, it may, without disbabling effect, be enjoyed in one's imagination, broadening one's inner life without hurt. Conversely, one may be drawn to make such a commitment to another who will by all accounts, despite great sexual attractiveness, diminish one's productive powers or will over the long term because of an uncaring disposition toward one's life work. It would be bad as well to pursue this sex-love interest. Erich Fromm's deepest comment above love, that it is "an expression of *productivity*,"[5] is one that supports the way of evaluation proposed here. If love makes possible a more embracing scope or depth of being, then it is good. If it reduces or narrows life's range, then it is bad. So also for loving bestowals on another of perceived value. If this promises to energize thought, experience, or action into new dimensions, then it is to this extent good. But it may not. It may be pure selfishness *à deux*, indulgence in mutual delusion at objective cost to the world. Then it is bad. Professor Singer indicates no principle of value by which we can recognize these problems.

Of course, these are complex matters requiring the entire attention of imaginative sex-love responsibility to find adequate bearings. Creative considerateness reverberates outward from the focal relationship to the wider natural and social world within which the sex-love possibility occurs. Here we return to the first and main point, to the need for the creative capacities of erotic interest to move far beyond the immediate domain of the loved one to the greater universe of organic and social life implicated in the possible or actual relationship. There is a world of value significance to be considered here, as the "boundlessness" of love experience intimates to us.

"True love" is, in fact, a long process, not a sudden act or realization (although much can happen in a very short time as measured by the clock). Love is a shared being, for good or for ill, that with sex-love involves a throwing open of the body itself, past its normal defense systems on all levels, and with various life-and-death possibilities. It is a shared being that touches one's organic survival and reproduction as well as the familial and communal fabric beneath its subjective flights of imagination, which must be linked to these objective depths to be of general value. It is an ongoing choice toward the good or the bad, the inclusively enabling or disabling, from the first urges of joining, to the consideration of possibilities, to the decision to act, to the ever more broadening, or narrowing, path of life's being. In truth, sex-love is but a deeply energizing site for a way of existence whose value or disvalue is decided in accordance with how inclusively capacitating or incapacitating its choices are not only to the lovers, but ultimately to the larger world their love both incorporates and recreates in its microcosm. It is a kind of nature-driven "chemistry" of new ontological bonds, involving great stakes of being and value on all levels in its closing or opening of the possibilities it bears.

AFTERWORD

In consequent discussion and correspondence, Irving Singer has raised three major objections to my critique of his evaluation of love. I will report these as best I can, and reply to each to clarify my position.

The first issue has to do with my characterization of Professor Singer's approach as "subjectivist" since he holds that he has in fact sufficiently emphasized the objective elements of love.

I understand his point as follows. In my emphasis on the "bestowal of value" in love, which Singer argues, in volume 1 of *The Nature of Love*, is that which "creates" and "makes the value" of love, "regardless of how good or bad its object may be" (pp. 13, 22, 90), he does not think that I adequately take into account volume 3 of his study. Here, from pages 390 to 400, Singer explains that he intends to acknowledge the "appraisive element as an ever-present constituent of love." While insisting that there must be some giving or bestowal of value in love or it "assumes the parameters of a business association," Singer makes it clear, as he does not in his earlier volumes, that he thinks appraisal is a "crucial ingredient" in the "causation of love." By appraisal he means: assessing the loved one's "utility for the satisfaction of needs, desires, appetites, instinctual drives that affect us every moment of our lives."

I agree with Professor Singer that I need to make clear what I mean by "subjectivist." When I have done so, it will become evident why I think what he calls "the appraisive element of love" and "bestowal" qualifies as "subjectivist."

There are two sense of "subjectivist" which I intend when I use the term:

1. Value in general depends on an evaluator's creation or recognition of it (as opposed to value or disvalue inhering in something *independently* of anyone's idea of it: for example, the inherent value of life over death or sight over blindness).

2. Appraisive value depends on the loved one's "utility for the satisfaction of [the lover's] needs, desires, appetites, [and/or] instinctual drives" as opposed to such "appraisive value" having to take account of what is or is not of value *beyond* the satisfaction of the needs or desires of the lover: for example, the value of the love relationship for wider circles of concern such as the upbringing of children or contributions to the well-being of the larger human community.

Singer's concept of love as essentially "bestowal" of value is subjectivist in the first of these senses, and radically subjectivist to the extent that its concern is with the lover's *creation* of value in the loved one. Singer's introduction of "appraisive" value in volume 3 is subjectivist not in this sense but in another—in its confinement of value to what the loved one does for the lover alone. In neither case does the realm of value extend further than the circle of lovers. While I do not reject the importance of these subjective elements of love, I do think that we need to take stock of the underlying social and biological structures of love as well as the objective implications of sex-love relationships beyond the lovers if we are to adequately understand sex-love's overall meaning and value.

The next and related main issue arising from my critique of Professor Singer's study has to do with my concern that he has ignored sex-love's fundamental problems of patriarchal power, property-structured affection, unwanted pregnancy and children, and physical disease. Since Professor Singer does not, of course, recommend that we deliberately create these problems, except perhaps that of possessiveness, which he appears to think is a "drive," and since, moreover, he considers feminist literature, and specifically the issue of male dominance, at the end of volume 3 (pp. 419–25), Singer thinks it "unfair" that I have criticized his work on the grounds that he does not deal with these basic problems.

My reply is that Singer misses the point of what I am arguing. As I take pains to point out, I criticize Singer's philosophical narrative not on the grounds that he asserts or defends the desirability of any of these disabling undersides of sex-love, but because he does not raise them as issues at all.

Philosophical inquiry, as I understand it, lays bare and critically examines underlying general structures of our being and valuing, in a way that at best emancipates us from a merely conditioned presupposition of them. But when one looks to Professor Singer's rich tapestry of ideas about love since Plato, we find that these basic underlying structures of being and valuing with which I am concerned in my critique—patriarchal power, proprietary love relations, and biological health and reproduction—are never exposed as problems in his study, or even taken into account. Since these are deep and objective problems that have bedeviled sex-love since time began, I hold that they should be addressed by any account that pretends to philosophical adequacy.

Professor Singer might reply that the problems to which I am referring are "sociological" rather than "philosophical." But this will not do. As generalizable and underlying problems across the human condition that are subject to our interpretation and critical evaluation, they are paradigmatically philosophical issues. Philosophy, it is true, has certainly been reluctant to address them, embodying as they do principles of social order and power. But this is all the more reason why they need to be exposed to philosophical reflection.

What about the issue of patriarchal power which Professor Singer feels he has dealt with in his section on feminist writing at the end of his volume 3? In fact, the concept of patriarchy is not mentioned by Singer. In his brief discussion of feminist ideas (3:419–25), Singer says that he has difficulty in understanding what Shulamith Firestone means by "incorporation or absorption of another being." He then argues that although "male dominance" has been a factor in the history of love, and although "women have often identified with the aggressor and acquiesced in their social enslavement for reasons of love . . . radical feminists . . . ignore the possibility that a woman's love for a man can be a liberating experience, while a man's love for a woman may convince him that neither she nor any other member of her sex should be treated as an inferior creature." Singer does acknowledge that "men may dominate women as a whole while singling out an exceptional female who can even become a goddess to them," but he concludes that men in their love still "experience the joy of bestowing value gratuitously. That is a human faculty which is not limited to either sex."

Here we can see that even when Professor Singer is obliged to confront an underlying objective structure of power or pathology, his romantic viewpoint continues to avoid and to gloss over the problem. He moves the discussion around to the human capacity to "bestow love," even while acknowledging that this love is conferred within a structure of "social enslavement."

To be fair, I think this propensity to omit mention or interrogation of deep issues of power and pathology is endemic to a long tradition which Irving Singer so synoptically explains to us.

The final issue Professor Singer has raised in response to my critique is on the question of a *guiding value* in love. He objects to my criticism that his study lacks value bearings, affirming that he clearly espouses the value of "pluralism." This value does emerge explicitly in his study (3:434), where he refers to his "pluralistic approach." But a "pluralistic approach" is not an authentically guiding value, because it does not enable us to choose between opposing courses of action: for example, between being acquisitive and possessive in love, or open and nonpossessive. Pluralism by its nature confers moral legitimacy on different and opposed forms of thought and action without proposing any grounding value to choose among them. In this way, it cannot, in principle, give us those general value bearings with which my critique is essentially concerned. It, therefore, provides no answer to my criticism.

It may be because a "pluralistic approach" does not provide us with a way to choose between different kinds of love that patriarchal and proprietary forms of love, and the many pathologies generated by these and other undiscussed infrastructures of sex-love, are not laid bare or critically evaluated by Singer. They may remain insulated from his exposure or challenge because they do not cross any deeper value he has, or at least speaks from, in this work.

This is why I proposed and argued for some deeper value-bearings in my critique: so as to provide us with those basic footholds of judgment we require to address these profound problems with which sex-love has been afflicted since time immemorial. Without any such value grounds for critical evaluation, we are left without a coherent standpoint from which we can recognize such problems *as* problems. They can continue undetected in our analysis, with no end to or even understanding of their presupposed hold, because we have no principle of value whereby we can bring them to light and seek to resolve them.

With the help of the general value I propose and work from in my critique, these fundamental issues of sex-love can be identified as the problems they are, and can be critically assessed and perhaps resolved by its guiding principle of evaluation. I try to explain the way such an approach would work in the body of my paper, and so I will not try to reiterate it here. It will be obvious, however, that patriarchy's one-sided structure of power, or the possessory control of another's life, or people's disablement by unwanted reproduction or by sexual disease, are all in basic violation of the guiding value I propose, and are readily exposed as such by its principle.

The question that may remain is, can this principle also justify, as Professor Singer has suggested, "rape, murder, lying, sadism, etc."? This may seem a perverse question, but it has been posed by others whose criticism I also respect, and so I will briefly answer it here. It is logically impossible that the principle of value I advocate, in which the good is to enable more inclusive ranges of thought, experience, and action, could ever justify any of the vicious acts brought up by Singer. This is because all these acts can be shown very clearly to reduce or to eliminate the range of being of those they victimize—whether it be totally (by murder), as extremely as possible consistent with life (by rape, sadism), or variously depending on the circumstances (by deliberate deception or lying). The only way in which the proposed principle of value could be misread as allowing for these or like acts is by illicitly confining its coverage to the circle of the self, which is precisely what its principle of inclusiveness rules out.

Although I am critical of Irving Singer's vast study, I cannot easily think of any recent work in philosophy that I have more richly enjoyed. Its resonant knowledge of Western ideas of love over 2,500 years, its graceful clarity of explanation, and its textual mastery of the ideas it narrates are a continuing delight and encyclopedic source. This is a work which is a great act of love in itself, though perhaps of a different kind than Professor Singer has envisioned.

NOTES

1. Irving Singer, *The Nature of Love*, vol. 1 (Chicago: Chicago University Press, 1984). Professor Singer has objected to the attribution "subjectivist" for these statements on the grounds that volume 3 places more emphasis on "appraisal in love than these citations from volume 1 indicate. Whatever the consistency of Singer's position, the underlying objective problems I identify in this analysis at no place emerge as issues of concern in his account, whether he is talking of lovers' "bestowals" on or "appraisals" of each other.

2. For a fuller analysis of the private-property structure of the conventional monogamous relationship, see McMurtry, "Monogamy a Critique," *The Monist* 67, no. 4 (1972): 588–600.

3. Professor Singer says in a summarizing statement:

Where courtly love resembled a faction that wants the state to remain strong but with power transferred to itself, Romantic love is more deeply disloyal. It either renounces political ambition and emigrates to a new world of passionate adventure or else it undermines the status quo by presenting it as an inauthentic shadow of some transcendental state that will eventually recognize the majesty of love. (Singer, *The Nature of Love*, 2:488)

4. Singer says: "The general will [of Rousseau] differs from the will of all citizens in being *that part of each man's self-love (amour de soi)* which harmoniously coincides with the self-love of everyone else . . . predicating the principle of justice upon a rational estimate of *how to secure one's own good* [my emphases]." Singer, *The Nature of Love*, 2:336 and 339. Rousseau, in contrast, holds that the nature of moral citizenship is to think in terms of the common interest, *not* one's own particular interest, which is overcome in the "common self" created by the social contract. (Jean-Jacques Rousseau, *The Social Contract*, book I, chapters 6, 7, 8, 11; book II, chapters 1, 2, 3, 4.)

5. Erich Fromm, "Selfishness, Self-Love and Self-Interest," in *Man for Himself* (New York: Holt, Rinehart and Winston, 1947).

Part Four
Special Problems

18

Love in *Don Giovanni*

Marc Widner

Who, or what, is Don Giovanni? Romain Rolland has postulated a close connection between the hero-villain and the composer who immortalized him in music:

> If one studies Don Juan a little closer, one sees in his brilliance, his selfishness, his teasing spirit, his pride, his sensuality, and his anger, the very traits that may be found in Mozart himself.[1]

This statement cannot leave the informed Mozartian indifferent. If one removes oneself from the subject matter of the Don Giovanni tale, it becomes clear that the qualities referred to in Rolland's statement surface time and time again in descriptions of history's great creative artists. The acidic side of Mozart's personality is revealed in its least subtle form by the composer's correspondence with his father. This is amply demonstrated in this passage from a letter of August 22, 1781:

> I will not attempt to describe the mother. Enough that it was an effort to prevent myself laughing at her at table. You know Frau Adlgasser, and this is a worse case of the same sort, only *médisante* into the bargain—stupid and malicious. The same with the daughter. If a painter should want to portray the devil to the life, he should have recourse to her face! She is as fat as a farm wench, sweats in a way to make one sick, and goes so scantily clad that one can read as plain as print: "Pray, look here!" True, to look is enough to strike one blind. . . .[2]

It should be acknowledged that some recognition should be given to the fact that Mozart lived in an age when it had suddenly become acceptable to express one's highly subjective reactions, at least in written form. There is nevertheless something approaching barbarism in this absolutely unquestioning rejection of the human beings. It is not easy to reconcile this with the perfection in musical taste and craft attained by Mozart the composer.

Is Don Giovanni, then, merely an inflated abstraction of one side of the brilliant creative artist? I refer here to Mozart's frequently observable tendency—arising out of wilfullness, necessity, or both—to insulate himself from the complex of behavioral rules that keep society in good working order. Dr. Irving Singer has observed:

> But in *Don Giovanni,* passion is always directed toward something Mozart values very highly: freedom to express one's natural playfullness, to take one's pleasure as one wishes, to sport with sounds and words and deeds and people, and in general to enjoy the sensuous aggressivenesss of an emancipated male.[3]

Let us accept that all composers worthy of the name sport with sounds and people, whether these people be the characters in their operas, or simply their listeners. How do Mozart's musical personality and craft rise to the challenge?

One of the best sources of information lies in the score of the Piano Concerto in D Minor of 1785, which bears many interesting parallels to the *Don Giovanni* of 1787. The use of the dark and moody minor mode for the showy and public medium of the concerto is comparatively rare in the eighteenth-century period of composition which we refer to as the Viennese period. In fact, only two of Mozart's twenty-seven concerti use the minor mode. The D minor of the concerto becomes, in *Don Giovanni,* the D minor suggestive of evil and damnation. The opera opens with this D minor, and, some two hours later, more of the same will accompany Don Giovanni's descent into the abyss. The treatment of rhythm at the start of both the concerto and the opera's overture bears close examining. Both feature extensive syncopation—the simultaneous playing of rhythmic figures whose respective pulses are out of synchronization with each other.

EXAMPLE I. Mozart, Piano Concerto in D Minor, K466 Mvt. 1, bars 1–6

EXAMPLE II. Mozart, *Don Giovanni,* Overture, bars 11–14

This disturbed rhythmic language provides an instant feeling of darkness and disquiet, reinforced by the tendency of both works to exhibit a tension-building, chromatically rising thrust early in their expositions.

EXAMPLE III. Mozart, Piano Concerto in D Minor, K466 Mvt. 1, bars 8-13

EXAMPLE IV. Mozart, *Don Giovanni,* Overture, bars 23-26

Both these segments fulfill largely similar purposes. They set a stage, defining the other dramatic limits within which the characters will operate.

In the opera, these are the seven characters who participate in the drama of one man's destruction through his evil behavior. Paradoxically, Mozart's characterization fulfills all the standard requirements of eighteenth-century comic opera. The higher classes are represented by characters aptly described as "serious"—Donna Anna, the noblewoman in pain over Don Giovanni's slaying of her father (the "Commendatore") in a duel; her husband-to-be, Don Ottavio, who patiently waits for marriage as Anna grieves; and lastly Donna Elvira, the partly tragic, partly hysterical woman unfortunate enough to have taken Giovanni's seduction seriously. Zerlina and Masetto, lower-class counterparts to Anna and Ottavio, will also feel the whirlwind of Giovanni's reckless behavior as the fickle and inconstant Zerlina almost succumbs to the womanizer's advances. The group of "comic" characters is rounded out by Leporello, Giovanni's sidekick and servant, whom one easily imagines being as opportunisitic as his master. Squarely in the middle of this cross-section of society sits Don Giovanni, the evil seducer who is dragged down to hell as punishment for his absolute rejection of morality and authority.

It is small wonder that these sharply contrasted and archetypal characters, not to mention the musical delineation which they receive at the hands of Mozart, have caught the imagination of opera lovers since 1787. It is equally fascinating to observe the composer's ease in exploiting his gift for characterization within strictly instrumental forms.

Turning back to the concerto, one can virtually identify the "persona" of the hurt noblewoman Donna Anna at the piano's first entrance:

EXAMPLE V. Mozart, Piano Concerto in D Minor, K466 Mvt. 1, bars 77–85

As so often happens with Mozart, this clear and strong "affekt," or feeling, dissolves just as clearly into a flourish under the pianist's fingers, reintroducing the tormented music witnesssed earlier, but in which the piano soloist now participates.

Further down the road, a musical about-face awaits. Assuming a musically successful performance, these coy, gently turning phrases, playfully exchanged between winds and piano, should catch us off guard. Abruptly, D minor is gone, yielding to F major, one of Mozart's sunniest keys. This is the F major of Zerlina's aria "Batti, batti," "Beat me, beat me, dear Masetto," in which she attempts to soothe her jealous husband-to-be Masetto, who cannot easily accept the flirtatious nature which Don Giovanni so easily elicits from her.

EXAMPLE VI. Mozart, *Don Giovanni:* "Batti, batti," bars 1–6

All this music, both in the concerto and the opera, is really Zerlina through and through—gently twisting and turning, peeking this way and that, and all with such a beguilingly innocent exterior. We are only too happy to be taken in by these short, elementary, repetitive phrases, presented in a prevailingly diatonic musical vocabulary. One should note the obvious and audible contrast with the rhythmically tense and chromatically charged material heard earlier.

Returning to the concerto, one can probe more deeply into the notion of Zerlina's music. It is as though, freed from text and characters, Mozart's gift of musical characterization asserts itself even more forcefully. Cute at first, this music erupts into gently mocking laughter, before ingratiating itself even more fully with a creamy, sliding motion in the left hand (measure 123). This upward glide in the left hand leads into juicy, mellow chords capped by a bit of frothy virtuosity in the right hand. Yet Mozart's cleverness has not yet ceased—a hint of minor mode (left hand, measure 126) conveys that this personage can feign seriousness as well.

EXAMPLE VII. Mozart, Piano Concerto in D Minor, K466 Mvt. 1, bars 120–129

This crystal-clear, rapidly paced change in the emotional tone of the discourse, within the same musical sentences, typifies the very essence of Mozart's art. In fact, there is no emotion at all, but merely its stimulation.

A look at the endings of both works provides another obvious but noteworthy parallel. The sunny closing moments of the concerto find us a universe away from its dark D minor beginnings. A similar eradication of all hints of the world of D minor marks the ending of the opera. The remaining characters have come on stage to tie things up and to assure us that their lives, each in its own way, will proceed apace. A final summation occurs, featuring a series of imitative entries in which it is stated that, "Here is an end we all shall face." This fugato style, in which successive voices imitate each other's music, reflects the formal, noncommittal Mozart, capping a big construction with a sturdy, "learned" style.

Upon hearing this ending, one quickly begins to ponder the world without Don Giovanni. There is no problem for Leporello, who will head for the nearest tavern, to find not only a new master but indeed a better one; Donna Anna will exact one more year of patience for Don Ottavio before their relationship can be consummated in marriage, so that time may heal the wound of her father's death. As does Dr. Singer, so would I completely discount the views of those who speculate that Anna is hobbled by some feelings of leftover attraction toward Don Giovanni.[4] All this, both music and text, clearly informs us that Don Giovanni's most interesting attribute is his triviality, his ultimate inability to influence those who come into contact with him. He is a playboy, an outstanding loser who does not understand things until it is too late. The come-uppance that he receives is perhaps the most valuable theme of the opera. The various conventions, manipulations, and behavioral abuses surrounding the notion of love which this opera displays serve to set up this theme. Striking also is the strong undercurrent of fatalism—the characters are notable for their lack of evolution during the course of the opera. They will all follow their preordained paths right to the end. Donna Elvira will head off to the nunnery where she belonged all along, Don Giovanni's abuse of her feelings notwithstanding—the strutting, angular, and graceless phrasing of her ario "Ah, fuggi il traditor," "Beware, the traitor lies," has made that abundantly clear. There is neither nobility nor self-possession in this anguish. Zerlina and Masetto will return home to feast further, and the rough and ready male chauvinist world to which Zerlina has unwittingly accepted to pay her dues lies clearly in wait. The more we look for it, the more love is remarkably absent as a genuine, going concern in this opera.

What of the notion of manipulation? We may bank on Don Giovanni's aptitude for manipulating women, or Zerlina's manipulation of Masetto, or even Donna Anna's possible manipulation of Ottavio. But if these people end up as prisoners of destiny, who is manipulating whom? It would be helpful to return to the Piano Concerto, where it was demonstrated that the clarity of feeling was matched by the impermanence of the same feeling. Mozart is possibly unrivaled in musical history for his ability to change the emotional tone of the discourse, even while maintaining a semblance of absolute wholeness and logic in each phase of the progession. What more fertile field of endeavor for so manipulative a composer than the Don Giovanni tale, with its cynical view of human pretenses and follies?

It is now time to answer the question raised at the very beginning of this essay. *Don Giovanni*—not the character, but the opera—is a clear projection onto the stage of Mozart's own creative and psychological world in the closing years of his life. The composer revels in the awareness of his own technical brilliance, his mastery of the art of stimulating feeling through music. At the same time, Mozart conveys his realization that all these manipulative powers are irrelevant once one considers "the end we all must face." A composer's ability to completely transcend himself, his topic, and indeed his art, has rarely been more clearly demonstrated than in *Don Giovanni.*

NOTES

1. Romain Rolland, *Essays on Music,* ed. David Ewen (New York: Dover, 1959), p. 245.
2. *The Letters of Mozart and His Family,* ed. Emily Anderson (New York: St. Martin's Press, 1966), p. 760 (translation slightly altered by this author).
3. Irving Singer, *Mozart and Beethoven: The Concept of Love in Their Operas* (Baltimore and London: Johns Hopkins University Press, 1977), p. 69.
4. Ibid., pp. 55–59.

19

Irving Singer and
The Goals of Human Sexuality

Ric Brown

SINGER'S PLURALISM

Irving Singer's exciting new brand of sexology is one that argues for the necessary combination of the rigor and precision of scientific method and experimentation with the sensitivity of the humanistic tradition in acknowledging that there are genuinely irreducible human differences.[1]

In *The Goals of Human Sexuality*,[2] Singer sets out to investigate the nature of the male and female orgasm, arguing that this is worthy of our serious consideration because it exposes the major goals of human sexuality. This is important for Singer since these goals are far from being uniform or self-evident.[3] The orgasm, he says, is not always the same ". . . either as a physiological process or as a psychological event" (p. 8). Some sexologists such as Kinsey and Masters and Johnson profess that an orgasm is an orgasm, that all orgasms are and must be essentially the same, regardless of who has one, when they have it, where they have it, or by what means. Masters and Johnson, for example, ". . . insist upon an underlying uniformity of physiological response not only in male and female human beings, but also all other mammals" (*Goals of Human Sexuality*, p. 22).[4] Rather than define "orgasm" simply in broad and vaguely psychological terms, or take the restrictive and equally unsatisfactory route of defining "orgasm" exclusively in physiological terms, Singer offers a new, pluralistic alternative. It attempts to account for

295

the fact that some women have the requisite physiological responses but no feeling of orgasm or sexual satisfaction, while others have the feeling of orgasm without the physiological responses that Masters and Johnson would demand. According to Singer, Masters and Johnson ". . . have limited themselves to a definition that falsifies the actual diversity of physiological and psychological events which make up the female orgasm" (*Goals of Human Sexuality*, pp. 31–32). Because sexual satisfaction has both a physiological and a psychological component, Singer argues that it is entirely possible for a woman to be satisfied in only one or the other component, or perhaps in both.[5] This conclusion accords with what women themselves report if you listen to them rather than rule out in advance what they have to say because it does not reflect some ideological prejudice.

> Instead of thinking that orgasms are all alike but women evaluate them differently, it seems more reasonable to assume that evaluations differ because different women, or the same woman on different occasions, have different predilections among physiological responses which are available to them. (p. 34)

This is the reason why Singer's study emphasizes difference, diversity, and plurality in sexual response and why he argues so strongly against any kind of essentialist sexology which claims that a single description of all orgasms must be true or it cannot be categorized as an orgasm at all. Singer outlines his task as follows;

> We must ask ourselves . . . whether the orgasm is a single entity or a diversity of responses referred to by a single word, whether it is similar for male and female, whether it is the most important consummation, and whether it is or is not the goal for all sexual experience that people have considered successful and wholly satisfying. (p. 25)

Only by understanding the diversity within the nature of the orgasm itself can we recognize the diverse goals of human sexual response.[6] What is most important for Singer's thesis, though there may be some reason to question his success in this regard, is that in principle each type of orgasm is deemed to be just as normal, healthy, and valuable as any other type of orgasm.

In *The Goals of Human Sexuality,* Singer draws our attention to Freud's *Was will das Weib?* question. "The great question that has never been answered and which I have not been able to answer, despite my thirty years of research into the feminine soul, is 'What does a woman want' " (p. 89)?

It seems to be Singer's negative attitude toward essentialism which makes him in favor of a pluralistic approach to the question of human sexuality.

By "essentialism," Singer means ". . . the assumption that in all sexological matters there must be a single, basic, uniform pattern ordained by nature itself . . . (p. 15). Singer criticizes Freud's "What does a woman want?" question because the question itself assumes that ". . . there is one thing which all women want simply *by virtue of* their being women" (p. 89). Freud is by no means the only sexologist Singer thinks is guilty of an essentialist bias, which is predicated on two mistaken beliefs: that there is a single, universal human nature and that there must therefore be a single essence to all human sexuality,[7] a single goal that is appropriate to it and which ought to be prescribed to everyone as the mature, normal, and natural goal. In opposition to essentialism, Singer believes ". . . there is no sexual nature of a uniform sort, no unitary sexual instinct, no universal goals or culminations . . ." (p. 156).[8] In place of essentialism, Singer advocates sexual pluralism, which he defines extensively as,

> . . . the refusal to assume in advance that nature prescribes a unitary model for male and female response, that there is any one norm which could indicate how all men and women must behave in order to function properly, that there is a unique mode of consummation that satisfies male or female sexuality, that there is a universal condition which constitutes or structures sexual response in all people on all occasions, or that there is a single instinct or biologic system basic to all human sexuality. (pp. 15–16)

SENSUOUS AND PASSIONATE

Although Singer is sensitive to the fact that there are as many differences and variations in human sexuality as there are individuals, the differences can be conveniently classified under two major systems of sexual response, namely, the sensuous and the passionate. After making his analysis of these two modes, Singer will relate them to two characteristic types of sexual expression, including different kinds of orgasms, each providing a correspondingly different kind of satisfaction (see p. 79).

Jointly, the sensuous and the passionate represent the ". . . different and possibly irreducible forms of sexual response that exist in different men and women on different occasions, or at different times in a person's life . . . (p. 9).

Singer describes sensuous sex as calming, relaxing, easygoing, delectable, even quieting to the nerves. The sensuous mode is the innocent enjoyment and pleasure which we take in the body as it is experienced by means of our sense modalities. Singer tells us that the sensuous "can be approached as an artistic activity designed to maximize and prolong human pleasure" (p. 57), and adds that the ". . . sensuous aspect of human sexuality must surely approximate what monkeys and apes enjoy while being groomed by one another" (p. 49), although we may do it more cleverly or intellectually. However, the sensuous appears to be an end in itself as well as a means. Singer says,

> The sensuous then operates not only to stimulate desire and to create pleasures that come from its arousal, but also to direct libidinal interests toward a final release that takes them beyond sensation. Without the mediation of the senses, people would not exist for one another. But their *affinity* to each other is more than merely sensory. (p. 51)

The affinity that Singer has in mind is something which appears to belong exclusively to the passionate mode. The passionate is described in terms of burning desire, gnawing tension, and savage hunger for the other person; an urgent and compelling need, a craving and a yearning for the other person involving ecstatic abandon. Only passionate sex is so intense and so meaningful "... as if ... [two persons] sought to merge their bodies as well as their minds" (p. 119). Passionate sex

> ... requires a *yearning* for the person one is with, a *craving* to penetrate her and to be penetrated by him, a *striving* for the deepest contact, a *need* for emotional union that enables each to participate in the other, to appropriate the other, and possibly to give oneself as well. (p. 59)[9]

In the passionate mode orgasms tend toward very powerful cathartic emotions.[10]

Although the sensuous and the passionate define two distinct sexual attitudes that are conceptually separable in theory, in our lives they seem to be intertwined, like lovers perhaps, as if they required one another for mutual maintenance. Singer claims, for example, that, "The sensuous induces sensory awareness, which may then be experienced as passionate yearning; the passionate impels the sexes into each other, and this may lead to sensory gratification as well as emotional ecstasy" (p. 52). The passionate would not happen at all without at least some measure of the sensuous, because the sensuous is what makes all human sexual experience pleasurable and enjoyable by arousing the sexual appetite.

At the same time, Singer claims that there would be nothing particularly sexual, or meaningful, about sensuous activity per se if it were not relating us passionately to some other human being. It is the passionate mode which "... contributes a sense of importance that cannot come from the sensuous alone" (p. 49). It is the passionate "... which enables us to *care* about other people, to want them and want to be wanted by them" (p. 61). It is the passionate which provides "... that vital urgency without which we could not identify with fellow creatures struggling like ourselves in a world we never made" (p. 61). Indeed, according to Singer, ". . . without the impetus of passion, a purely sensuous society could not mold those affectionate bonds which ordinarily belong to the very concept of a person" (p. 61). By arguing that it is the passionate which is conducive to personhood, Singer appears to put the passionate and the sensuous modes of human sexuality on a very uneven field and it may already indicate, in some fashion, what to expect about the real value of these two sexual modes.[11]

VULVAL, UTERINE, AND BLENDED ORGASMS

Having outlined the two major systems of sexual response, Singer then correlates the passionate and the sensuous modes to two distinct types of sexual expression. They express themselves differently both in terms of behavioral manifestations and types of orgasm. In this endeavor, Singer has rejected the Freudian terminology of "clitoral" and "vaginal" orgasms, finding their use both ambiguous and laden with value judgments.[12]

It is Singer's contention that female orgasms are not always the same, physiologically or psychologically.[13] Contrary to Masters and Johnson's opinion, Singer argues that ". . . in focusing on orgasms that *do* involve vulval contractions, Masters and Johnson have neglected every other kind of climax which many women would be likely to call an 'orgasm' " (p. 68).[14]

Singer maintains that the vulval orgasm is characterized by voluntary, rhythmic contractions of the orgasmic platform, induced either with or without intercourse, manifesting itself behaviorally by panting or hyperventilation. It depends in large measure on the strenuous pelvic movements of the female: ". . . the free and spontaneous moving of one's body serves as a likely prerequisite for the sensuous. . . ." (p. 120). The crux of the matter is that, "There is reason to believe that vulval orgasms are consummations in which the sensuous predominates. . . ." (p. 79).

The uterine orgasm is characterized by measurable emotional changes (a catharsis) but lacks precisely the involuntary contractions of the orgasmic platform which Masters and Johnson have identified with orgasm per se. Uterine orgasm is manifested (if not, in part, actually caused by) apnea, an involuntary holding of the breath caused by laryngeal displacement and tension.[15] The orgasm results when the breath is explosively exhaled; it is immediately succeeded by a feeling of relaxation and sexual satiation" (p. 72). Uterine orgasm occurs only with sexual intercourse because it requires that a thrusting penis actually buffet, jostle, or otherwise beat the uterus. Singer makes this point most candidly when he states that, ". . . no woman needs to be hurt or beaten with a stick, although many women love to be 'beaten' with a penis once in a while. Lacking this, they may become disagreeable and scornful" (p. 147).[16] Because uterine orgasm can only be induced through coitus and then only with the prerequisite peritoneal or visceral stimulation,[17] it requires a kind of penile thrusting which is strong, accelerating, and deep but relatively brief. The pelvis of the female must also remain motionless. The crux of the matter is that ". . . uterine orgasms have a special dependency upon the passionate" (p. 79).

Singer also describes a third type of orgasm, namely, the blended orgasm which is felt to be deeper than a vulval orgasm and emotionally satisfying like a uterine orgasm though linked to brief and repetitive apnea and contractions of the orgasmic platform.[18] "Many women, probably most, find that even under extremely favorable conditions they rarely if ever achieve blended orgasms" (p. 114). What might be important about blended orgasms is that they harmonize the attributes of vulval and uterine orgasm.

SEXUAL MORES AND INHIBITIONS

Singer recognizes two distinct systems of sexual mores, two different behavioral patterns for sexual intercourse, each having its own distinct orgasmic goal. It is his belief that, ". . . human sexuality always occurs within one or another system of inhibitions which create sexual energies in some respects while also destroying them in others" (p. 132).

There is something in the nature of human sexuality itself which might be responsible for continuously renewing the "internal warfare" (p. 52) or conflict between the sensuous and the passionate modes of sexuality, a warfare manifesting itself in the two distinct sexual mores. Certainly, ". . . something very profound impedes a satisfactory harmonization" (p. 53) between the two spheres. Singer contends that some elements of sexual repression or inhibition probably depend on inner or organic restraints built into the nature of a specific sexual response. Removal of these inhibitions would damage the specific sexual response. What, then, are the two different sexual mores?

The first is constituted by variety in sexual techniques, which are all designed to maximize the pleasure and enjoyment of sexual stimulation by means of a prolonged foreplay before effecting sexual intercourse. This sexual practice maps the sensuous form of sexual encounter culminating in the vulval orgasm because the ". . . sensuous approach creates circumstances most conducive to vulval orgasms . . ." (p. 114). This sensuous eroticism is basically free from any sexual inhibitions defining "inhibition" as ". . . a vague disinclination toward a particular erotic technique on some occasion, or merely as a preference for another, or direct type of behavior" (p. 108) on another.

The second of the sexual mores is characterized as simple-and-direct coition mapping the passionate sexual encounter which culminates in the uterine orgasm because ". . . the simple-and-direct is a pattern that considers inhibitions to be a natural and indispensable ingredient in lovemaking" (p. 107).

Singer trusts that some sexual inhibitions are in effect "biologic cues" which direct sexual activity toward one or another goal. For example, "the simple-and-direct approach shortens the interval between intromission and ejaculation, just as it shortens the period of foreplay. Perhaps this procedure, Singer suggests, including many of the inhibitions which it entails, serves a biological purpose" (p. 178). There may be an instinctive reproductive pattern which reflects those times (within a woman's menstrual cycle) when she most desires simple-and-direct coitus. Such passionate sex also requires that the pelvis of the female remain motionless in order for uterine orgasm to occur, emphasizing, as Singer claims, ". . . the receptivity of the woman—and probably her acceptance of a biological role in which she submits to the possibility of reproduction—rather than search for sensuous pleasure" (p. 120). The frequency of the missionary position for sexual intercourse may reflect ". . . something in the nature of man's sexual need which not only conduces to, but even requires, a fairly rapid ejaculation" (p. 151).

The requirement for sexual privacy follows from the fact that a woman may experience sensory disorientation, a dulling of the senses, or even a loss of consciousness following uterine and blended orgasms. Women who experience this variety of orgastic consummation naturally seek privacy because of their heightened vulnerability.[19]

There may even be ". . . some biological significance" (p. 121) in the fact that men do not know which particular system of sexual response (passionate/uterine or sensuous/vulval) any given woman wants on any given occasion, if this lack of knowledge on the man's part adds to a woman's attractiveness, mystery, and charm.[20]

HARMONY OF THE SPHERES

Singer announces that there is a new challenge facing men and women today as the old barriers that used to restrict sexuality thus disappear, giving us the freedom to enjoy sexual experience any way we choose. The challenge, however, is to discover "positive sexual experiences," that is, those sexual encounters that are sensuously delectable as well as passionately intense and meaningful. Perhaps our acceptance of the sensuous and uninhibited mode of sexuality in our own time (due in large measure to Masters and Johnson, Shere Hite, and Dr. Ruth) is just such a "wholesome reconciliation" (p. 49) of the two conflicting sexual modes. But can the sensuous and vulval and the passionate and uterine modes of sexuality really be harmonized? And if they can, does anyone need to harmonize them in order to have a satisfactory sex life? (see pp. 52, 65).[21]

We are reminded that blended orgasms combine both the passionate and the sensuous; therefore, almost by definition, they seem to be able to provide at least one obvious means for harmonizing the two systems. But, Singer warns, ". . . harmonization may vary considerably from one occasion of successful love making to another" (pp. 153–54). And even though the blended orgasm can harmonize the sensuous and the passionate, it is not evident that this is the route anyone ought to take apart from the fact that blended orgasms are rare.[22] But why bother to harmonize them at all, even if that possibility exists, especially when Singer himself laments that, "Harmonization between the two modes of sexuality is probably unavailable to most people on most occasions. And even when it is available, it may not always be preferable to the satisfactions that accrue without harmonization" (p. 154). In the strongest possible terms, Singer declares that ". . . a priori there would seem to be no basis for preferring one [sensuous/vulval or passionate/uterine] over another, for setting up a model that would apply to all of the diverse situations in which men and women find themselves, or for insisting that only a perfect blend of the sensuous and the passionate can provide the optimal orgasm" (p. 134).[23]

EVALUATION

Singer says that we should not depreciate the vulval orgasm or consider it in any way inferior to the uterine orgasm acknowledging that for any number of encounters, vulval orgasm may acutally be considered both optimal and ideal. Indeed, many women are said to have no need for anything else.

From the perspective of *The Nature of Love* (3:376), Singer summarizes his earlier analysis of *The Goals of Human Sexuality* as follows: "My analysis of the sensuous and the passionate sought to be pluralistic, recognizing both as viable human attitudes and *favoring neither at the expense of the other*" (emphasis mine).

I am somewhat skeptical about Singer's avowed normative neutrality or evenhandedness when he claims that one should not think that the sensuous is inferior to the passionate: "In isolation from the other, neither system need be considered more or less natural or basic or definitive of sexual response as a whole" (p. 106). Nevertheless, Singer does ask ". . . whether or not there may be advantages in each of the behavioral patterns . . ." (p. 107), and the advantages he discloses indicate that Singer has a clear preference for the passionate mode.

Singer gives a strong impression that there is either something important lacking in vulval orgasms or something important which can only accompany uterine orgasms when he confirms that a "woman who has a vulval orgasm may sometimes find the event singularly unrewarding. She may require something else, or something more, out of sexual inexperience. . . . (pp. 99–100).[24] In one of several pieces of evidence that Singer culls from Malleson, who quotes a female two-type patient (i.e., a woman who has the capacity to experience more than one type of orgasm though at different times), we find the following: "Of women who can reach it [orgasm] from either area it is found that the inner climax [uterine] is generally—but not quite always—*the one most valued* (p. 104, emphasis mine). Similarly, Singer quotes Doris Lessing who exclaims that there ". . . can be a thousand thrills, sensations, etc., but *there is only one real female orgasm* and that is when a man, from the whole of his need and desire takes a woman and wants all her response" (p. 146). Lessing is obviously equating the only one real female orgasm with the uterine orgasm. And again from Malleson: "The inside climax [uterine] comes from *loving,* but the outside one [vulval] is just animal feeling" (emphasis mine). Singer then asks the question, "Would other two-type women agree with this statement, and if so, cannot the word 'loving' be analyzed further" (p. 80)?

Recognizing that, in Singer's opinion, Malleson remains the "most rational and most unbiased of all authorities in the field," Singer goes on to quote yet again from another Malleson case study: "I *love* with the internal one [uterine orgasm], the outer [vulval orgasm] is just sheer pleasure" (p. 104, emphasis mine). Unless we give sheer sensual pleasure and love equal value, uterine orgasms appear to come out ahead. Indeed, Singer continues, "There is some reason to believe that passionate orgasms in the female of the sort that we have been calling uterine and blended are thwarted if the woman cannot trust and admire her mate at the moment of coitus" (p. 146). Singer sees the need for these "positive evaluations," which thus far include love, trust, and admiration, only for passionate, uterine orgasms and not for sensuous, vulval orgasms. Only the passionate requires some form of emotional corroboration such as a tight or firm sexual embrace. The sensuous requires a different technique best described as gentle, light, delicate, and rhythmic. The choice appears to be between "Row, Row, Row Your Boat" or Mahler's "Resurrection" Symphony.[25]

Are both modes of human sexuality really equal (though different in kind) or is one more equal, that is, more advantageous, more attractive, more promising, more rewarding than the other? Uterine and blended orgasms are, after all, "terminative and *fully satisfying*" (p. 153, emphasis mine).[26] Singer's most damning attack on the theory and therapy of Masters and Johnson lies in the fact that in their exclusive encouragement of the sensuous side of human sexuality, they promote and encourage only vulval orgasm. Singer agrees wholeheartedly that the sensuous side with the vulval orgasm should be promoted, although Masters and Johnson's exclusive endorsement of the sensuous/vulval entails, for Singer, "a deflection from that ecstasy, that eager bursting forth, which only the passionate can provide" (p. 152).

"If I didn't love you, would I be doing *this*?" It is unnecessary to explain what "this" is though we want to ask whether the "this" ought to be passionate rather than sensuous sex given the relationship between passion and caring, trust, admiration, ecstasy, emotional catharsis, personhood, and, dare I say, "love." But what makes the question "If I didn't love you, would I be doing *this*?" an appropriate target for humor (however unfunny it may be) is that the answer can point toward either sensuous or passionate sex and have nothing to do with love whatsoever.

From the point of view of *The Goals of Human Sexuality,* Singer says that love only ". . . refers to the *manner* in which we relate to other people, *how* we are sensuous or passionate toward them" (p. 41). While to love another person passionately requires both love and passion, passion itself is no guarantee that there is any love (see p. 43), because passion and love are not the same thing and not necessarily connected. Sex can be, and often is, passionate without being loving, while love can be sexual without necessarily being passionate. Similarly, there is nothing in the nature of the sensuous that would either necessarily preclude or include love. "When it effects a mutality of enjoyment, the sensuous belongs to a loving attitude no less than the passionate—and whether or not it is accompanied by the passionate" (p. 43).

There is, however, a vital and important connection between passion and love because, Singer claims, ". . . without standards of value the phenomenon of passion could not exist" (p. 64). "There must be something in valuation itself which engenders the passionate" (p. 65). So Singer concludes that although the passionate cannot be reduced to the drive for sexual intercourse and orgasm, intercourse and orgasm are nevertheless characteristic of sexual passion because they themselves ". . . presuppose a craving to unite and a feeling that it is *important* to do so. Passion would not arise unless the desired person, or the activity of uniting, or both, were cherished by the lover as something *worthy* of his desire" (pp. 64–65).

CONCLUSION

Have I been entirely fair to Singer by pushing the connection between passionate sex and love? Not entirely. Singer does make it clear that the conditions necessary for passionate sex are not incompatible with rape (see p. 192). Indeed, Singer says that, "Both [the sensuous and the passionate] may be equally loving, equally a giving of oneself, equally pleasurable, and equally desirable. Each may be misused" (p. 135). Love is not necessarily connected with either sensuous or passionate sex. Each sexual mode may be ". . . selfish or loving, bestial or humane" (p. 145).

> In many cases at least, the fast and forceful ejaculation belongs to a passionate attitude which may or may not satisfy the woman and which may or may not be sadistic, but which authentically belongs to man's aggressive nature in a way that none of the magnificent delights of sensuousness can approximate (p. 151).[27]

How then do we go about creating new ideals and alternatives within the parameters of human sexuality, ideals, and alternatives that will afford us the opportunity to fulfill ourselves as unique individuals? Singer's single demand is that such ideals must be sensitive to individual sexual inclinations as well as individual preferences. I think this is where the strength of Singer's pluralistic approach discloses its inherent impotence. Because pluralism is so sensitive to every individual's unique needs, it renders itself unable, not to mention unwilling, to make any genuine suggestions to anyone, apart from something that is too general, too vague, or simply too tentative to serve as any real directive or guideline for an improved human sexuality. As Singer says, "We may argue for a society which is more sensitive to differences in sexual response, and we may encourage people to find their satisfaction through any behavior which does not harm others; but we cannot enunciate general principles that would enable an individual to choose a life which is most suitable for *him* (pp. 157–58). So, ". . . we can only make tentative suggestions. And no one can foresee the outcome of future investigations" (p. 158).

> Faced with the diversity of authentic responses which pluralism suggests, the reader may not find that he knows how to improve his sexual response even if he understands it better. Of course, he may not feel any need to change. Some people will continue to prefer the sensuous or the passionate to the exclusion of the other; and some will seek to harmonize them occasionally but not often, or at different times and in different ways. It is always possible that such choices will be mistaken, however, and I am not confident that what we have said thus far provides the assistance that most people will require in order to choose the life which is best for them. (p. 154)

A NEW BEGINNING

What light does Singer's trilogy shed on the relationship between the two modes of sexuality and love as we have uncovered it in *The Goals of Human Sexuality*? At the end of the trilogy, Singer summarizes *The Goals of Human Sexuality* in two scant paragraphs (3:376) and then confesses,

306   Part Four: Special Problems

... there is a major difficulty that my earlier writing failed to confront. Assuming that I was right in suggesting that sexual love could be either sensuous or passionate, or both in some combination, was I justified in thinking that passionate lovers tend to rely on simple and direct behavior that sensuous lovers spurn or consider less important? (3:376-77)

In *The Goals of Human Sexuality,* Singer claimed that the passionate and the sensuous each contribute to their own particular kinds of sexual expression. The two dispositions, however, *may* contribute to their own particular kind of sexual love but, as we saw, it is not necessary for either of them to do so.

... I was distinguishing between the sensuous and the passionate without assuming that either would have to be accompanied by love. There was no claim that passionate response would necessarily be an example of love. (3:377)

The simple reason for any possible confusion about the relationship between sensuous or passionate sex on the one hand and love on the other for those having read only *The Goals of Human Sexuality,* is that Singer does not make any explicit connection in *The Goals* between them. The concept of the "passionate" does require some further development as Singer himself suggests. What follows is a thumbnail sketch of his improved scheme.

In *The Nature of Love,* Singer sets about to "analyze sexual love anew" (3:37) and, in doing so, actually redefines (rather than simply refines) the concept of the "passionate." However, he does not build his own modern, unified theory of love from the ground up. He begins first by using the bricks of Grant's account of sexual love. While Grant argues that sexual love is exclusively amorous emotion in contradistinction from two other elements, Singer argues that sexual love must have all three components either simultaneously or ". . . at least at various times within the erotic relationship" (3:373).

The first component is sexual impulse, drive, instinct, or desire characterized as a libidinal craving, organic hunger, or physiological demand for sexual gratification through genital contact. Since it is directed solely at the satisfaction of a genital urge through physical and sensory pleasure, this criterion can be met rather indiscriminately and without any care or concern whatsoever for the well-being of another person.

The second component is benevolent concern or care which one may have for another person and for his or her interests and welfare. It is characterized as altruistic, compassionate, and tender and is obviously possible within an entirely nonsexual relationship.

The third component is what Grant refers to as "amorous emotion." Though decidedly both a sexual and emotional relationship, it cannot be reduced to the sexual impulse because it is directed, very selectively, toward a person's aesthetic qualities, attributes, or traits (e.g., beauty) rather than toward genital activity per se. It is characterized as selfishness, jealousy, and possessiveness.

By combining all three components in dynamic interaction, Singer claims that sexual love requires some benevolent attitude toward the person who is sexually desired ". . . as a necessary condition for there to be love supervening upon sexual impulse" (3:375). Sexual love, *in nuce*, ". . . is sexuality in a state of harmonization with tenderness and aesthetic delight" (3:375).

After contrasting romantic passion (a dynamic search for interpersonal unity as the means for happiness) and married passion (a lasting interdependence), Singer generates out of the former the notion of "falling in love" and out of the latter the motions of "being in love" and "staying in love." Being in love is shown to harmonize the other two. But they each represent different kinds of passion and logically interdependent types of love. And added to this, Singer conjectures that there is every reason to believe that male and female sexual love (as sketched above) are undoubtedly different as well (see 3:424–25). It is apparent that Singer's universe has become increasingly pluralistic.

Last, the original quip has become "If I didn't *love* you, would I be doing this?" It finds its rightful place in *The Nature of Love* when Singer demonstrates how the single expression: "I love you" can be analyzed very differently depending on whether it is spoken (and heard?) from the point of view of falling in love, being in love, or staying in love. (See 3:416–17.)

NOTES

1. Irving Singer, *The Nature of Love* (Chicago: University of Chicago Press, 1987). All references to this text are internalized and refer to volume and page. In *The Nature of Love,* Singer refers to his method as a "synthesis of scientific and humanistic approaches to human affect" (3:345). However, Singer continues to argue that there ". . . is every reason to believe that current work on scientific questions about love and sexuality will eventually alter the humanistic perspectives from which science first arose and later sought to emancipate itself" (3:346). Singer's own movement in this direction is already heralded in *The Goals of Human Sexuality.* In this text, for example, he calls for better questionnaires for understanding human sexuality (see p. 196); better methods of experimentation following those of the Foxes especially vis-à-vis Masters and Johnson; and a host of laboratory studies which include: the effects of the birth control pill on sexual desire in women and coitus-induced ovulation.

2. Irving Singer, *The Goals of Human Sexuality* (New York: W. W. Norton, 1973). All further references to this text are internalized.

3. Singer argues, for example, that, "reproduction is only *one* of the goals of human sexuality, and only occasionally is it the principal one" (p. 19).

4. Compare June M. Reinisch, *The Kinsey Institute New Report on Sex: What You Must Know to Be Sexually Literate* (New York: St. Martin's Press, 1990), p.

202: "We now know that physiologically there is no difference between orgasms, regardless of the type of stimulation used to achieve orgasm." See also pp. 27, 130, and 209.

5. Singer speaks quite vehemently against the claim that human sexuality can be reduced to the physiological alone. For "Once we get to human beings, cultural influences take on such importance that it becomes virtually impossible to separate sexual instinct from sexual learning in any reliable way" (pp. 19–20). Indeed, ". . . human sexuality is pervasively conditioned by social and interpersonal needs as well as physiological processes" (p. 20).

6. Singer argues that the tyranny of the vaginal orgasm which Freud unleashed that rendered the clitoral orgasm imperfect, immature, inferior, and incomplete in comparison to the vaginal orgasm has been replaced in recent times by the tyranny of the clitoral orgasm. However, the vaginal orgasm is not thought to be immature and incomplete in comparison to the vaginal orgasm because, according to Masters and Johnson at least, the vaginal orgasm does not even exist. It is easier to understand why Masters and Johnson want to make the clitoris homologous to the penis and why doing so makes not only all women alike but all men and women as well. Compare Thomas Laqueur, *Making Sex: Body and Gender from the Greeks to Freud* (Cambridge: Harvard University Press, 1990), on the development of the view that the female body is an inferior version of the male body turned outside in. In a nutshell, Singer's question, simply put, is this: ". . . is all orgasmic response a function of stimulation and physiological reaction in the clitoris as Masters and Johnson claim" (p. 28)? His answer, *in nuce,* is this: ". . . to recognize that women are *not* all alike, that in some ways the sexual responsiveness of women does resemble the male's, but that this is not equally true of all women, and that for many women sexuality entails satisfying and health-giving responses which involve a physiological pattern quite different from the kind of sexuality which centers upon the clitoris (p. 29). Singer continues by saying that ". . . we can only conclude that no one female disposition is uniquely indicative of what it is to be a woman, of what she is essentially or by her biological nature" (p. 37). Masters and Johnson, by restricting what is thought to be biologically relevant to orgasm, take only a particular kind of woman as the paradigm or even "*the* epitome" (p. 40) of female sexuality." In claiming that all coital orgasms are physiologically indistinguishable from noncoital ones, they [M/J] take as their norm a preferred sample of the female population . . ." (p. 35). Singer argues that Masters and Johnson's sample must be suspect because the only women whom they assess must meet the criteria of having orgasms after receiving "effective sexual stimulation." This effectiveness includes the ability to orgasm by means of masturbation while being observed. According to Singer, the whole procedure which Masters and Johnson use begs the question because the sample could only contain those women who have the kind of orgasm which Masters and Johnson are looking for and would almost by necessity exclude any other kind of orgasm.

7. There is little doubt that Singer is much more sympathetic to Freud than he is to Masters and Johnson even though "Freudian analysis of female sexuality needs radical revision . . ." (p. 81). "For all its scientific crudity, the Freudian doctrine did at least recognize that orgasm at the superfices of the genital tract need not be fully satisfying. Freud and his followers erred in thinking that women for whom it

was sufficient must be abnormal or pathological. Masters and Johnson err in thinking that other women, those who find libidinal release in blended and uterine orgasms, must be responding to "subjective influences for which there is no biologic correlate" (p. 100). In spite of Freud's basic essentialism, it is very interesting to note that Freud would never have asked the question, "What does a man want?" According to Singer, this is because Freud would never have assumed, in the case of men, that there was simply one thing which all men wanted in virtue of their being male. After all, "Different men want different things on different occasions" (p. 89). What Freud took to be so obvious in the case of men and male sexuality, however, Singer wants to extend to women as well.

8. Singer makes it quite clear that the ". . . pluralistic attitude which I am advocating employs that approach as a correlative to the biases and falsifications that essentialism frequently creates" (p. 125).

9. On the inherent sexism lurking behind the use of the word "penetrate," see Robert Baker, " 'Pricks' and 'Chicks': A Plea for Persons," in *Philosophy and Sex,* edited by Robert Baker and Frederick Elliston (Amherst, N.Y.: Prometheus Books, 1984), pp. 249–67.

10. According to Singer, Masters and Johnson appear either to disregard or to misunderstand their own laboratory evidence for uterine orgasms because of their ideological bias. "It is interesting that Masters and Johnson recognize that a stronger uterine contraction is correlated with a more intense emotional release on the part of the study subject . . ." (p. 162). However (see pp. 94–95, 163), Singer claims that masturbation is generally used for vulval orgasms. But if uterine orgasms are as emotionaly satisfying as Singer suggests, it makes you curious as to why masturbation isn't used more often to induce uterine orgasms. Perhaps Singer has difficulty understanding reports of uterine orgasm which women experience by means of masturbation because he suffers from the reverse ideological bias of Masters and Johnson. In Singer's case, one could argue that if you define uterine orgasm in such a way that it requires the buffeting of the peritoneum by the penis, then masturbation will never result in uterine orgasm by definition. I would add to this two reports which Singer recounts about women who are no longer sexually satisfied, i.e., no longer able to have uterine orgasms, because of a hysterectomy (no uterus to buffet) and because a second husband was not as well endowed as the first.

11. Compare Thomas Nagel, "Sexual Perversion" in *Philosophy and Sex,* p. 271: "It is very important that the object of sexual attraction is a particular individual, who transcends the properties that make him attractive. Singer, on the other hand, asks, "What is the person apart from his qualities? We cannot love another as a person without loving the totality of his attributes. He has no being without them. It is true that we do not love him as a person if we love *only* attributes. For then it would be the particular qualities that we love, and to that degree ours would be a love of things. To love another person is to love him as the unique combination of his properties" (*The Nature of Love,* 3:401).

12. Singer points out that Freud himself never discussed clitoral or vaginal orgasms but only clitoral and vaginal modes of sexual experience (*Goals of Human Sexuality,* p. 85).

13. Singer applies the same pluralistic analysis of human sexuality to variations in the male sexual experience as he does to female sexual experience. After all, "not all male orgasms are alike" (p. 140). Singer claims that the male orgasm ought to involve the same physiological factors and psychological dimensions as those that he uncovered in the case of female orgasm. He wants to see if ". . . the distinction between the sensuous and the passionate can be used for analyzing different kinds of male orgasm" (p. 136). Just as no uniformity could be found for female sexuality, including orgasmic responses, we should expect that there is no simple uniformity to the model of male orgasm either. "By analogy with our description of female orgasms, and employing what we have said about the sensuous and the passionate throughout this book, we may therefore postulate three kinds of male orgasm: the sensuous, corresponding to the vulval in women; the passionate, corresponding to the uterine; and the blended . . ." (p. 139). Although it may seem rather extraordinary to think that a man may experience the equivalent of a uterine orgasm when he lacks a uterus, it must be remembered how important both apnea and peritoneal buffeting are for this particular kind of orgasm to occur. (Compare p. 125.) Since sexology is still very much in its infancy as a science, the question whether or not there are physiological correlates for the three types of male orgasm is unknown.

14. "The issue is whether or not convulsive contractions in the muscles of the outer third of the vagina, or in general those forming the pelvic floor [vulval contractions or contractions of the orgasmic platform], are a necessary element in the female orgasm" (p. 66). According to Singer, ". . . not all orgasms conform to this criterion" (p. 67).

15. Apnea or the involuntary holding of the breath is also characteristic of the emotions of grief, fear, surprise, and joy as well as sobbing, laughing, screaming, and yawning. Recently, I read a newspaper article about dentists who may have been wrongly charged with sexually harassing their patients. It seems that some drug interactions might result in strong sexual hallucinations and the patient's yawning could actually induce orgasm.

16. Compare Singer's use of the terms "jostling" and "beating" on pp. 76, 79, 98, 99, 149, 171, 174, and 191. Singer acknowledges that "uterine" orgasm may be a misnomer for ". . . it is not the uterine *contractions* which prompt the label, but rather the fact that the uterus is repetitively displaced by the penis, thereby causing stimulation of the peritoneum, a highly sensitive organ" (p. 75). Since homosexual anal intercourse can also result in "uterine" orgasm, it might have served Singer's purposes better to have labeled this "peritoneal" orgasm or even "visceral" orgasm.

17. Singer also argues that uterine orgasm is the probable cause of uterine suction, a pressure differential within the uterus which results in the semen being sucked toward the Fallopian tubes.

18. There seems to be considerable similarity between Singer's blended orgasm and the "merged" orgasm described by Sylvia Payne. See Singer, p. 87.

19. Singer points out that in order for a woman to be a test subject for Masters and Johnson, she must be able to "masturbate to orgasm while being observed" (p. 107). Since this is uninhibited behavior, it fits the model of sensuous sex which has vulval orgasm as its goal. (See p. 109). Uterine orgasms require privacy.

20. I have difficulty understanding just how biologically significant this lack of

knowledge may be when Singer confines the significance to "either/or" women. Unless "either/or" women make up a significant percent of the female orgasmic population, then very few women are going to have the same attractiveness, mystery, and charm. According to Malleson, although it is a speculative conjecture on her part, about one-third of the civilized (her word) women experience uterine orgasms, another third vulval, and the remaining third are basically inorgasmic. (See p. 104). However, it is anything but clear from this guideline what percentage of the population fell into the "either/or" camp. Singer, however, makes his own conjecture. "If primatology can reveal anything about innate patterns in *human* sexuality, one may well conclude that either/or tendencies persist in many people" (p. 113). Singer also argues (see p. 108) that for the either/or woman, no simple yes/no will suffice because what she may or may not permit depends entirely on the aim or goal of that particular sexual encounter and will therefore vary.

21. "Though we have described psychological and physiological correlates of harmonization, we have not determined how it may be achieved—or when it ought to be" (p. 154).

22. If harmonization is really a desirable goal in human sexuality, it might be more reasonable to adopt the "either/or" form of sexuality which seems to balance or supplement the sensuous with the passionate albeit on different occasions.

23. "*A priori,* none of these modes of satisfaction . . . is necessarily preferable to any other" (p. 79) because there is and can be ". . . no single correct, definitive, or supremely normal kind of female orgasm" (p. 81).

24. Singer suggests as a reasonable sexual therapy for women that if they feel in themselves a variety of sexual inclinations, they might benefit from learning how to satisfy each in its own way (see p. 123). "Not only is variety worth recommending as a general principle, but also it is in the nature of sexual satisfaction that no one but the participant himself can determine where and how it should or could occur" (p. 135).

25. Heidegger constantly reminds the reader of *Being and Time* that the terms "authentic" and "inauthentic" are not used normatively. Yet would any *Dasein* prefer to exist inauthentically after reading *Being and Time*? Would anyone want to go through life not experiencing passionate, uterine orgasms now that, thanks to Singer, you know they exist?

26. If you are fortunate enough to be able to experience a uterine orgasm, it should never be less than fully satisfying since this seems to be part of its phenomenology. There is no "maybe" or "sometimes" about a uterine orgasm as there is for a vulval orgasm which could leave someone singly shortchanged. A uterine orgasm gives you your money's worth (I hesitate to say "the best bang for the buck") if the two kinds of orgasm are really operating with the same monetary system. The fact that the two orgasms differ in kind rather than degree may help to explain some of this difference in opinion.

27. A further example of a possible restraint on human sexual response may include the following: "Since rapid ejaculation is the norm in all the other primate species, one may plausibly speculate about its being deep-rooted and even instinctive in human beings" (p. 151).

20

Pursuing Love with the Proper Map

Timothy J. Madigan

1. THE PURSUIT OF LOVE

Irving Singer's trilogy, *The Nature of Love*, explores the dichotomy and possible reconciliation between naturalism and idealism. Singer is particularly concerned with mapping out the connection between the biological basis for our love concerns, and the ideals which motivate us and goad us forward. In his latest work, *The Pursuit of Love*, Singer continues this exploration. It is not surprising that one of the philosophers who dominates all these works is George Santayana. For Santayana shared this concern, and postulated what might be called a Platonic naturalism. Can naturalism and idealism be wedded? Is this search for harmony a fruitful one? Where exactly do our ideals of love come from? Is there a biological basis for our love ideals? And how does this influence human development? In this paper, I will be comparing Singer's discussion of the pursuit of love with the recent findings of Dr. John Money and his theory of "lovemaps." In addition, I will be using the figure of George Santayana as an example of someone who might be described as having what Money calls a "vandalized lovemap," and see how this might have influenced his own theory of love. I will be focusing primarily on *The Pursuit of Love*, and in particular Singer's discussion of the pursuit of ideals,
Singer writes:

> Through idealization, the making of ideals, people create a meaningful and even significant life for themselves, The pursuit of ideals is typically human.

It embodies a characteristic search for perfection that is distinctive to our species. Different cultures, and different individuals within each culture, will strive for different ideals; and such divergency can lead to conflicts that cause dissention and sometimes war. But without the plethora of ideals that appear in all civilized existence, there would be neither civilization nor the good life as we recognize it.[1]

This recognition of the importance of ideals (and their potential danger as well as benefit to human well-being) is a constant in Singer's work, as it is in the writings of Santayana. Both philosophers share a naturalistic starting-point. Certainly ideals exist in the imagination, and have a powerful effect on human beings. But how do they arise? What might be the causes of them, and why do different people often have varying—and sometimes competing—ideals? This is a question crucial to the issue of love, since at is the case that the type of love that humans pursue is manifold.

2. LOVEMAPS

Where do our ideals of love come from? John Money, professor of medical psychology and professor of pediatrics at the Johns Hopkins University and Hospital has coined the term "lovemap" to describe a person's idealized lover, love affair, and the activities that cause sexual arousal. In Money's words,

. . . a lovemap is not present at birth. Like a native language, it differentiates within a few years thereafter. It is a developmental representation or template in your mind/brain, and is dependent on input through the special senses. It depicts your idealized lover and what, as a pair, you do together in the idealized, romantic, erotic, and sexualized relationship. A lovemap exists in mental imagery, first in dreams and fantasies, and then may be translated into action with a partner or partners.[2]

Money goes on to discuss what he considers the naturalistic causes of individual lovemaps. In his view, under optimum conditions, both prenatal and postnatal, there is a development toward a heterosexual lovemap without complexities. The prenatal development is susceptible to the influence of sex hormones. Next, sexual rehearsal play between the ages of five and eight is crucial. At around the age of eight, pairbonding rehearsal usually begins. This is a particularly vulnerable age, especially in societies that are antisexual, "Further disruption may take place during the peripubertal years; but after puberty, the lovemap, if it changes, does so chiefly by decoding what has already been encoded into it. Once a lovemap has been formed it is, like a native language, extremely resistant to change."[3]

According to Money, lovemaps may be classified as normophilic (conforming to the statistical norm), hypophilic (characterized by insufficient sexual drive), hyperphilic (excessive), and paraphilic (legally known as "perversion"). Money is quick to point out that normophilic lovemaps are problematic, since there are no exact statistics one can refer to, which means that the term generally applies to a societal or ideological norm. There are no absolute dividing lines between the four categories. Money's research has focused on the growth and development of lovemaps, in particular the possible causes of what he calls "vandalized lovemaps," or those that deviate from the normophilic. He postulates five exigencies for successful lovemap synthesis: (1) pairbondage, first between parent and child, then later between lover and lover; (2) troop bondage, a feeling of belonging to a larger group; (3) a sense of place and sustentation on one's ecological niche; (4) being labeled or classified by one's society and associations in a way that enhances one's sense of self-respect; and (5) an awareness of one's own mortality and the suffering and death of those around one. Normally developed lovemaps allow individuals to deal properly with these five exigencies while unsuccessful lovemaps impede the individual's ability to manage one or more of these exigencies. Money is also relatively nonjudgmental in his exploration, and points out that all four types of lovemaps can meet these exigencies, but in general the normophilic is better adjusted to them.

Money is rather sketchy about what forms the exact images of one's lovemap—those aspects of an idealized lover that one will basically pursue for the rest of one's life. No doubt the images one comes into contact with in one's immediate environment are crucial; also, parents or parental substitutes must play an extraordinarily important role. Indeed, the relationship between the child and the mother or mother surrogate seems to be vital. While Singer does not discuss Money's theories, he is sensitive to this claim:

> Love as an explicit and more or less sophisticated attitude develops out of the realization that one's needed caretaker can be cajoled through agreeableness as well as through demonstrations of annoyance. Seduction of that sort is an important step in love, though not the first or the last.
>
> Before this momentous event occurs, there often exists a sense of mutual enjoyment between mother and infant, hugging and being hugged, feeding and being fed, each delighting in the other's presence. All human love may issue out of this feeling of oneness.[4]

While Singer cautions against making too much of this, the role of mother love is indeed important to consider. In *The Pursuit of Love* and in volume 3 of *The Nature of Love,* Singer discusses the research of biologist Harry F. Harlow on the capacity for love in primates, and the primary and instinctive need for "contact comfort" as the beginning stage of love development. In his famous series of experiments, Harlow reared infant rhesus monkeys with surrogate mother figures. Significantly, he showed that, when offered a choice between a surrogate that provided milk, and a surrogate made of terrycloth that did not provide nourishment, the monkeys time and again chose the latter. The desire for a soft, warm touch superceded their own nutritional needs. Says Harlow:

> We were not surprised to discover that contact comfort was an important basic affectional or love variable, but we did not expect it to overshadow so completely the variable of nursing; indeed, the disparity is so great as to suggest that the primary function of nursing as an affectional variable is that of insuring frequent and intimate body contact of the infant with the mother.[5]

According to Harlow, maternal love, the first stage in his developmental theory of love, has three primary functions: (1) provision of contact comfort; (2) nursing; and (3) security. Through these mechanisms, the infant develops love for the mother or mother surrogate. "Out of these infant-mother inter-actions, augmented by the other variables of warmth and rocking motion, there is built up love for the mother and also basic security and trust."[6] From this initial reciprocity, the next stages of development—peer love, pairbondage of adults, and parental love—can occur. However, if the initial stages are interfered with, the succeeding stages are not likely to properly function. Monkeys brought up without loving mothers, for example, are usually unable to adequately associate with their peers. While neither Singer nor Harlow shy away from drawing implications for human love development from these studies, the former does raise a note of caution. Singer writes that, "Workers in the field may eventually decide that Harlow underestimated the importance of adequate peer-love, and its ability to overcome deprivation at the levels of maternal and infant love. It may also turn out that the analysis into just five systems of love is too impoverished for understanding the intricacies of human nature."[7] Still, he is sympathetic to Harlow's approach, and devotes several pages of *The Pursuit of Love* to a discussion of the importance of maternal love. This leads to an interesting question. To what extent might a person who demonstrably lacked the nurturing of maternal love have anything of importance to say about the nature of love itself?

3. SANTAYANA

George Santayana is a figure who plays a prominent role in all three volumes
of Singer's trilogy, *The Nature of Love*. This is not surprising, for both men
are eager to find a mediation between a Platonic idealistic view of love and
a naturalistic, even materialistic view. Throughout his trilogy, Singer uses
Santayana, sometimes as a guide, sometimes as a foil, but always as a point
of reference. In volume 1, Singer discusses Santayana's writings on the *ideal*
of love.

> For Santayana, as for Plato, all love worthy of the name must have an
> "ideal object." Lovers seek in one another the embodiment of "an ideal form
> essentially eternal and capable of endless embodiments." This "form," or
> "essence" as Santayana was later to call it, is the abstract possibility of some
> perfection, If a man falls in love with a fair-haired woman, he does so because
> his heart has been captured by the ideal of a perfect blonde. It is this ideal
> object, not the woman "in her unvarnished and accidental person," that the
> man truly loves.[8]

This view is similar to Money's theory of lovemaps, if one can equate Santayana's notion of "essences" with Money's idea of "maps." Singer says that
Santayana's essences, which arise from natural causes, act as guides to human
conduct through the medium of the imagination. They cannot be realized
in themselves. "For Santayana, then, love is an imaginative search for un-
attainable ideal objects. No human being—or even the Venus de Milo—can
perfectly exhibit the qualities that have evolved as an ideal of female beauty.
This ideal object does not exist. It belongs to the imagination, where it has
been nurtured by a formal genesis that transmutes the natural into the perfect."[9]
Human beings, according to Santayana, are propelled by their imagination
to seek for lovers who can never meet their ideals. Plato, of course, was
content to postulate an ideal world where such a perfect match could be
attained; but Santayana remains mired in what he calls "my host, the world,"
and does not assume that this can be transcended in any way *other* than
through the imagination. As Singer points out, Santayana ultimately remains
a Platonist at heart, for he cannot see any real satisfaction in earthbound
love relationships. Accordingly, the type of love interest Santayana describes
is not to be found in the world of here and now.

One can speculate as to whether or not Santayana's view of love might
have been influenced by his own situation. For in his autobiography, and
in his other writings, Santayana makes no secret of the fact that he never
received the sort of nurturing from his mother which theorists like Money
and Harlow consider to be crucial for a healthy love development. He presents

a detached but devastating portrait of a woman who seldom showed affection to anyone: "If men did not often make love to her," Santayana writes, "especially not the men who care specifically for women, she amply took her revenge. Her real attachments, apart from her devotion to her father, were to her women friends, not to crowds of them, but to two or three and for life. To men as men, even to her two husbands, she seems to have been cold, critical and sad, as if conscious of yielding to some inevitable but disappointing fatality."[10] Perhaps that revenge was felt most keenly by Santayana himself. The product of her second marriage to a much older man ("my mother always spoke contemptuously of lovemaking and matchmaking: yet she herself was twice married"[11]), Santayana was essentially abandoned by his mother at the age of five, who went to America to live with the family of her deceased first husband, leaving her son behind in Spain with his aged father. At the age of eight, Santayana was brought to Boston by his father, who felt that his education and prospects would be better in the United States. The father then returned to Spain after a year, alone, and Santayana would not see him again until his twentieth year. Santayana apparently was not received with great emotion by the mother who had not seen her son in three years. While his comments about her in his writings are basically matter-of-fact, one can sense his feelings in such statements as, "She could not forgive the shabby side of things for being shabby, or the weak side of people for being weak; while she sternly abdicated all ambition in herself to cultivate the brilliant side, or to hope for it in her children; and this renunciation was bitter, not liberating, because she still craved and needed that which she knew she had missed."[12] Elsewhere, Santayana refers to her as "passionately dispassionate."

It would seem, then, that this lack of maternal affection would color Santayana's later views on love. In *Reason in Society,* for example, he says of mothers in general that their "insight and keenness gradually fade as the children grow older. Seldom is the private and ideal life of a young son or daughter a matter in which the mother shows particular tact or for which she has instinctive respect."[13] He goes on to state that the family unit is in many ways irrational, and responsible for the perpetuation of many false ideas.

Ben-Ami Scharfstein, in his book *The Philosophers: Their Lives and the Nature of Their Thought,* writes that ". . . It is not surprising that Santayana did not want to marry or get very close, biologically or emotionally, to other people."[14] While it is suspected that his basic inclination was homosexual, there is no concrete evidence that he ever engaged in any long-standing affairs with either sex, and he lived most of his life alone. However, Scharfstein goes too far when he writes:

Santayana's philosophy was thus a protective derealization meant to help him to escape the pain and treachery of men and things by depriving them of their biological coerciveness. His shield and his freedom were a peculiarly naturalistic, peculiarly Platonic kind of metaphysics. He believed, as he said, in a desperate but also joyless solipsism which takes metaphysical revenge "on fate, nature, and circumstance." Thereupon he became the withdrawn, vengefully sybaritic spectator.[15]

It is too much to ascribe Santayana's basic philosophy to a protective stance against the world. Indeed, it is wrong to refer to him as withdrawn. While he may have shielded himself against personal relationships, Santayana was deeply interested in the world about him, and maintained affectionate bonds with members of his family and close friends until his death. Also, far from seeking to deprive human motivation of its biological coerciveness, he always stressed the material basis of our emotions and ideals, looking with scorn on Romantic thinkers who were in love with the very concept of love.

    While it would be uncharitable, as well as overly simplistic, to compare Santayana's early life with that of the rhesus monkeys in Harlow's experiments, it does seem that the deprivation of maternal love had a profound impact on him, and probably helped to create what Money would call a "vandalized lovemap." Perhaps Santayana was incapable of either bestowing or receiving the type of love which he himself desired. This may account for his curious mixture of Platonic idealism and hardhearted materialism. Nonetheless, Santayana seems to have dealt with this maternal deprivation in a healthy manner, maintaining an air of detachment to protect himself from further blows. And, as the deep friendships he formed with several individuals throughout his life attest, he was able to advance to the stage of peer love. Santayana may be an example of an individual who pursued love as he saw it, in an idealized form, while recognizing that—for him—there was no possible embodiment, for his lovemap had never developed in a precise fashion (Money would call this a case of hypophilia). His biographer John McCormick observes, "Santayana became his own harshest critic. Of his love sonnets, he remarked: 'They were an evasion of experience.' "[16]

    As Singer, with his pluralistic outlook, recognizes, it is a mistake to assume that all people pursue love in the same manner, or seek the same ideals. Yet each individual has a perspective on love as a whole. And the detached spectator may be able to see aspects of love which those more involved in the battle cannot. Santayana's stoical attitude may have been the best and most advantageous form of life he could forge for himself, given his particular set of circumstances. In writing Santayana's autobiography, McCormick tried to come to grips with the myriad conditions that had helped to shape his subject, including a mother who had always been a distant and cold figure to him. Yet even here, Santayana expressed an affinity. In describing his mother's attitude following the death of her first husband, George Sturgis, Santayana notes a similarity with his own later life:

> . . . I almost think she was relieved, liberated, happy to abandon burdensome superfluities and reduce her life to the essentials . . . the fact was that the most tragic events now could not move her deeply, and the most radical outward changes could disturb her inner life and daily habits very little. She had undergone a veritable conversion, a sweeping surrender of the Old Adam, of all earthly demands or attachments; she retained her judgments and her standards, but without hope. I am confident of this, because at about the same age I underwent the same transformation, less obviously, because in my case there were no outer events to occasion it, except the sheer passage of time, the end of youth and friendship, the sense of being harnassed for life like a beast of burden. It did not upset me, as the revolution in her circumstances did not upset my mother; but it separated the inner life from the outer, and rendered external things comparatively indifferent. I recorded this conversion in my Platonizing sonnets; my mother expressed it silently in the subsequent fifty years of her life.[17]

Santayana thus recognizes a connection between his own views on love and those of his mother, and accepts this common bond between them.

4. HARMONY

One of the themes of Singer's *The Pursuit of Love* is that of harmony, a desire to reconcile seemingly disparate strands. This is, of course, a Platonic theme as well, and like Plato, Singer often describes three elements that need to be integrated to achieve completeness. He speaks, for example, of three objects of love: the love of things, the love of persons, and the love of ideals. These, Singer contends, should not occur in isolation from one another, but rather overlap and interact: "When they do so harmoniously, each love strengthening the other two, are we not assured that the bond that results is better than any alternative? Do we not have good reason to think that the cooperation among the modalities creates an affective unity that may be considered superior to anything proffered by one of them alone?"[18]

I remain unconvinced, however, that this is actually the case. Santayana, for example, seems to have spurned a love of things, and had a rather anemic love of persons, yet his love of ideals was profound. Perhaps it was so deep and abiding *because of* the undeveloped nature of the other two modalities. The type of harmony that Singer seems to be normatively espousing may in fact be impossible—an ideal which cannot be realized, or which may at best be realized only in short durations. Why should the three strands comprise a single experience? The same objection could be made to Singer's discussion of other tripartite modalities: the three concepts of sexual love—the libidinal, the erotic, and the romantic—and the dispositions of sympathy, compassion, and empathy.

I disagree with Singer when he says that the principle of harmonization is a corollary of a satisfactory pluralism. In some cases, harmony may not be a real possibility. He himself discusses the stoical attitude, which holds that humanity must choose between the values of cognition and emotion, and, therefore, if one is to achieve the good life, one must forswear the experience of love. A successful pluralism must make room for such a nonharmonizing attitude, especially if, as seems to be the case for Santayana, this attitude may be the healthiest one a particular person can master.

In addition, it is by no means clear that Singer's own categories are ones that would be generally accepted. He has a predilection for breaking things down into three parts (*The Pursuit of Love* is itself the second volume of a proposed trilogy). This may be a good analytical tool, but one could just as easily break things into five or seven separate aspects. Surely Singer can see the conceptual pitfalls of Trinitarianism. Perhaps he should take a tip from humor writer Douglas Adams, whose latest book is titled *Mostly Harmless: The Fifth Book in the Increasingly Inaccurately Named Hitchhikers Trilogy.*

5. MAPPING OUT THE CONCEPTUAL TERRAIN

In keeping with his pluralistic outlook, Singer closes *The Pursuit of Love* by stating that, while philosophers are unable to formulate rules of love which all people must follow, they can help each individual to determine what is the most likely path of love to pursue. "[The philosophers] can reveal the logical and empirical implications within alternatives that are actually feasible. This is what I call mapping out the conceptual terrain."[19] John Money's theory of lovemaps is a similar, yet more scientifically oriented, mapping of this terrain. Money admits that much work still needs to be done to develop further the scientific aspects of lovemap development. He himself has basically focused primarily on vandalized lovemaps, yet there is still much to learn about the basic process of how lovemaps originate, and how they motivate individuals in their pursuit of love.

Throughout his writings on love, Irving Singer has called for cooperation among scientists, philosophers, poets, and novelists, and has demonstrated a conscious effort to familiarize himself with the literature on love from all three fields. It is fitting that George Santayana should be a major touchstone on all his work. For Santayana, with his level-headed, dispassionate manner, had the eye of a scientist, yet was one of the few people to master the fields of philosophy and literature. While he did not harmonize these disparate activities as successfully as Plato seems to have done, Santayana nonetheless excelled at them both, and from his detached perspective delineated much that is of worth on the topic of love. We can learn from Santayana a great deal about the forms, if not the content of love. Irving Singer, following in his footsteps, guides his readers through the many aspects of love. His works are indeed proper maps for exploring this all-important topic.

NOTES

1. Irving Singer, *The Pursuit of Love* (Baltimore: The Johns Hopkins University Press, 1994), pp. 33–34.
2. John Money, *Lovemaps* (Amherst, N.Y.: Prometheus Books, 1988), p. xvi.
3. Ibid., p. 19.
4. Singer, *The Pursuit of Love,* p. 86.
5. Harry F. Harlow, *From Learning to Love* (New York: Praeger Publishers, 1986), p. 108.
6. Ibid., p. 308.
7. Irving Singer, *The Nature of Love* (Chicago: The University of Chicago Press, 1987), 3:352.
8. Singer, *The Nature of Love,* 1:26.
9. Ibid., p. 28.
10. George Santayana, *Persons and Places: Fragments of an Autobiography* (Cambridge, Mass.: The MIT Press, 1986), p. 9.
11. Ibid., p. 38.
12. Ibid., p. 32.
13. George Santayana, *Reason in Society* (New York: Charles Scribner's Sons, 1936–40), 6:253.
14. Ben-Aml Scharfstein, *The Philosophers: Their Lives and the Nature of Their Thought* (New York: Oxford University Press, 1980), p. 303.
15. Ibid., p. 302.
16. John McCormick, *George Santayana: A Biography* (New York: Alfred A, Knopf, 1987), p. 114.
17. Santayana, *Persons and Places,* pp. 41, 47–48.
18. Singer, *The Pursuit of Love,* p. 176.
19. Ibid.

A Reply to My Critics
and Friendly Commentators

Irving Singer

I am asked occasionally how I became interested in the concept of love. Apart from personal motivation that is relevant to all my work as a philosopher, I recall giving a paper on Plato's *Symposium* sometime in 1954 to the Philosophy Department at Cornell, where I was an instructor. I treated the dialogue as a dramatic vehicle for expressing ideas that Plato was trying to organize into an aesthetic whole, as opposed to making a quasi-scientific investigation that solves problems and reaches some ultimate or definitive solution. I still think that is the most fruitful way to approach Plato's intention. At the time I gave the paper I had discussions about its subject-matter with Gregory Vlastos, who was then a professor at Cornell. Like him I believed that Plato fails to understand the love of persons, and in fact that his philosophy of love seems to rule it out.

This line of reasoning eventually appeared in the first volume of *The Nature of Love* when its first edition was published in 1966, and similar ideas were later developed by Vlastos in an article that has had seminal importance in the field. Whether he originally got these insights from me or I from him, I don't remember. I do know that when the first volume appeared, he wrote me an enthusiastic letter in which he remarked that the chapter on Plato was the best thing on the subject to have been published thus far. Though I was delighted that he should have said this, I also felt he was possibly being too generous, and I am willing to believe that my approach had in fact been conceived under his influence.

My first publication in the philosophy of love was a review article that appeared in *The Hudson Review* in 1958. It is called "Ortega on Love" and contains some ideas that I have since discarded. But it also shows what I had learned from Ortega's emphasis upon love as a confirmation and sustenance of the beloved's being. Soon afterwards I began reading Anders Nygren's *Agapē and Eros.* That book provided my first acquaintance with the Judaeo-Christian concept of *agapē,* which then nourished my initial speculations about love as bestowal.

For some time earlier I had been convinced that philosophers like Nietzsche, Santayana, and Dewey were right when they considered religious thinking of every sort to be imaginative and nonliteral discourse that is basically incapable of yielding factual truth. I took this as encouragement for my desire—which has been with me as long as I can remember—to trace the aesthetic truthfulness in religious or metaphysical writing as well as in great works of literature. It was, therefore, easy and natural for me to reinterpret the notion of agapē, to see it from my own humanistic perspective, to stand it on its head or rather (if I am right) on its feet in order to use it as a tool for understanding processes of imagination that belong to everyday life.

While this fermentation was working in me, I remained what I had been trained to be, an analytic philosopher schooled in the methods and doubtless the prejudices of my Harvard education. I had studied with C. I. Lewis, Henry David Aiken, Donald C. Williams, and, to a lesser extent, W. V. Quine, and like them I believed that only science could give us literal truth about the world, that rigorous analysis was essential for solving all conceptual problems that are capable of being solved, and in general that the unexamined life is hardly worth living. I have not changed much in these beliefs, but from Henry Aiken as well as friends and mentors in literature such as Walter Jackson Bate, I began to glean the possibility of dealing with matters of feeling and human affect as a whole in ways that were then being ignored by almost all reputable professionals writing in English.

I was also influenced by the later Wittgenstein, by ordinary language philosophy centered at Oxford, and by the final efflorescence of existentialist thought on the Continent. These were liberating forces, offering me an escape from the narrowness of American analytic philosophy even though I did not wish to renounce it completely. It spoke with rationality and clarity of thought in the midst of a world that seemed to clothe its confusion in verbiage that was mainly mystical and woolly-headed. Analytic philosophy stood firmly in allegiance with the newest developments in science and technology, to which it promised assistance not only in matters of their methodology but also in their moral and aesthetic implications. It aligned itself with thinkers like David Hume, John Stuart Mill, and Bertrand Russell—each of whom I much admired. From this aspect of my formation, and from the presuppositions of psychiatric writers as well as emotivists in ethical theory such as Charles L. Stevenson and A. J. Ayer, who also belonged to this protoscientific mentality, my thinking about appraisal and bestowal evolved.

At first I was most intrigued by the idea of bestowal. It expressed my intimations about creativity, imagination, and the manner in which love and possibly all of life could be envisaged as an art form. I felt this opened up exciting prospects that suited my temperament as well as my particular talents, which were and are primarily aesthetic rather than deductive or casuistical. My orientation is apparent in the first chapter of the trilogy's first volume, especially in the first edition of that volume. The concept of bestowal, which I introduce in that place, receives a formulation that has misled various readers. It was intended not as a definition that gives necessary and sufficient conditions, but rather as a series of insights into love as related to modes of valuation.

Though I presented bestowal as a necessary condition for love, I did so in a philosophical equivalent of what an impressionist painter does when he portrays a field of poppies or a lady in a parasol as a manifestation of speckled luminosity pervading the visual world, or like Cézanne enabling us to appreciate the phenomenon of spatial depth by revealing it through the contrivance of a two-dimensional representation. I did not wish to suggest that love was *nothing but* bestowal. That kind of approach is alien to me. I see the world through very different spectacles.

A number of years before the first chapter was written, I had concluded that appraisal is both an essential ingredient in human love and a causal agent without which human beings could not love. At MIT in the early sixties, I gave a public lecture in which I explored my thinking about appraisal and bestowal. Some in the audience, particularly my colleague Hubert Dreyfus, complained that I was treating bestowal *almost* as if it were the sole determinant in the definition of love. I remember feeling grateful for my subsequent discussions with Dreyfus. They enabled me to see more clearly that each of the elements needs to be accentuated if one seeks an adequate and comprehensive statement about the human capacity for love: both types of valuation have their varied role within it, and therefore love must be explained in terms of an interaction between them. I was not yet able to depict that interaction in a way that would satisfy me, however, and in the first volume the role of appraisal does receive less attention than it deserves, and certainly less attention than bestowal. By the time I wrote the third volume, I realized how much more I could say about appraisal, and in *The Pursuit of Love* I try to clarify the relation between the two contributing elements by means of several different coordinates as required by a pluralistic analysis.

I do not mean to suggest that I have completed the task. I hope to continue working at it, digesting and possibly learning from new experiences that are constantly arising as life goes on. I have always felt that the doing of philosophy is a thing of the moment, like the eating of our daily bread, and for me, at least, my earlier writings tend to seem dated, and sometimes even stale, after a few years. I often find it hard to think I had a hand in their creation. Yet I know I did, and I recurrently feel that I could, and should, have done a better job. An anecdote about a tenor performing in an opera in Parma may be à propos. Audiences in that Italian city are notoriously censorious about singers who appear on stage before them. On this occasion the tenor was both surprised and gratified when he received an ovation after singing an extremely difficult aria. The audience demanded an encore, and so he repeated the aria. Another ovation ensued, and another demand for an encore. This kept happening, until the tenor felt that his voice could take no more. Flushed with exhilaration and fatigue, he stepped forward and smiled as he addressed the highly receptive audience. "I am very grateful for your applause," he said, "but I have now sung eight encores of the same aria. How much longer must I go on?" To which a voice from the second balcony replied: "Until you get it *right!*"

I don't believe I will ever satisfy a standard as elevated as that. Nevertheless, I am grateful to the participants in the Brock symposium, and to those who did not participate but provided special contributions to this volume, for reminding me of how much more work still needs to be done, in general by everyone struggling with our common subject, and specifically by me. The unfinished cycle of love-operas that I have been writing for so many years may never enable me to get anything right, but encouragement that the different papers offer has helped me keep trying. The effects are already present in my latest book, *The Pursuit of Love.*

❀

In relation to bestowal and appraisal, I am fortunate in having benefited from criticisms that Russell Vannoy leveled against my distinction in his challenging book *Sex Without Love: A Philosophical Exploration.* I assigned that book as required reading in one of my courses and responded to its comments on my philosophy in the third volume of *The Nature of Love.* I had hoped that in the Brock symposium Vannoy would reply to my reply and thus allow us to keep the tennis match going. What he has done, however, may be of greater utility. In making the claim that love reduces to appraisal, rather than depending on bestowal or being a mixture of bestowal and appraisal, he touches on questions that properly force me to reconsider my overall theory.

As I interpret it, Vannoy's argument is the following: romantic, interpersonal love can best be understood in terms of appraisal, not only as a matter of causation but also as the omnipresent determinant in the phenomenology of love itself. At his senior prom everyone sought out as possible objects of amorous relations not the undesirable boys or girls but only the ones who were attractive, the ones amenable to each individual's personal self-interest and/or valued by the group as a whole. At the same time, however, Vannoy recognizes that "passion that is aroused by someone's appealing qualities wants to escalate in intensity" (p. 75). For this to happen, qualities that are only moderately beguiling come to be seen as more desirable than they really are. But "really" poses a problem in this context, and, therefore, Vannoy distinguishes between "reality in the phenomenology of the loveworld" and what we recognize as "ordinary reality." The latter is rational and purposive; the former indulges in those flights of feeling and imagination that would be illusions or even delusions in ordinary reality, but that make a valid contribution to the reality of the loveworld.

If this were the total burden of Vannoy's analysis, there would be no major differences between our two formulations and I could merely admire the inventiveness in his engaging mode of writing. But his distinction between the loveworld and ordinary reality is designed to show that appraisal alone explains the workings of each. Vannoy claims that while aesthetic imagination might bestow upon a baglady value needed for her to serve as a suitable subject for artistic appreciation, she is not likely to be the person anyone falls in love with. At the opposite extreme, it is the beautiful blonde cheerleader whom all the males at Vannoy's prom were in love with, or wanted to love, and, according to Vannoy, she felt the same about the handsome quarterback she finally married. Vannoy recognizes that there may be difficulties in loving a goddess like Marilyn Monroe, since she is *too* desirable and therefore makes one feel worthless. But then, as in the case of his mother's successive choice of seven husbands, Vannoy relies on the concept of what I call individual appraisal to argue that loving someone depends entirely on our finding in him or her just those qualities that may possibly satisfy our own needs and desires.

To me it seems clear that Vannoy's conception is overly reductive, like most attempts to discover a single principle of explanation for anything as complex as interpersonal love. Not only was the real Marilyn Monroe far from being a goddess, but also her image was alluring to many men because it projected a fragility and vulnerability that caused a certain kind of male (Norman Mailer, for instance) to bestow upon it, and therefore upon his idea of her, a value requisite for love to arise in him. This would be even more evident in relation to the blonde cheerleader at the prom. Her fetching qualities in the ordinary reality Vannoy describes might lead every robust boy to hunger for her love, or at least her sexuality, but crossing into the loveworld itself requires responses that are not wholly explicable in terms of appraisive considerations that belong to either reality.

The shy and pimply adolescent with whom the cheerleader deigns to dance will feel the stirrings of love, as opposed to mere desire, only when he perceives that she, too, is insecure in ways that he can appreciate, that for reasons of her own she needs his lowly adoration, that his acceptance of her as the person she is matters to her, and that this makes her more interesting to him than she could ever be as just a curvaceous fleshpot or symbol of the school's athletic standards. The new and greater interest that love induces results from the operation of amorous imagination, which may be present in all of us but is generally hidden or unformed until such time as there occurs a coalescence between individual development, social conditioning, and the good fortune of meeting someone who can help us to cultivate and express this innate potentiality.

For some people the requisite coalescence may never materialize, just as some poetic geniuses may never write a word or sing a song that others can hear in societies that thwart such acts of the imagination. But the loveworld, which interpenetrates our ordinary reality even though it may be studied separately for the purposes of analysis, is of imagination all compact. Love, like the creation of meaningfulness in general, reveals the ability of life—above all, as it appears in human beings—to bestow value upon almost anything that catches our attention and makes itself available for this unique mode of self-realization. Without appraisal there would be no purposive behavior; without bestowal, life would not exist as it does in ordinary reality, for then there would be neither meaning nor love, and purposiveness itself would make no sense at all.

Seen from this perspective, interpersonal love directed toward a baglady becomes more plausible than it could ever be in Vannoy's philosophy. He chooses the baglady as an example of someone who is repellent, unattractive by usual appraisive standards, and therefore unlovable. And, indeed, she is unlovable, if by that word one means difficult to love or lacking in the qualities that normally engender love in most human beings. But all persons, and all objects, are capable of being loved if one has a capacity for love great enough to accommodate them. One need only focus one's attention upon their individual qualities and accept these persons or objects as what they are.

Bestowing value in this fashion, we may find that we can delight in attributes that would ordinarily be distasteful. A person can be loved despite his or her faults and imperfections: they become meaningful to us as the properties of someone who elicits our capacity to bestow. Human beings give great importance to this capacity, for it is deep in our nature and inherently very gratifying. We often treat the bestowing of value—by ourselves or by others—as an ideal condition that matters more to us than anything else in life. Why, then, should Vannoy doubt that some people can feel love for a baglady, or for many other persons he disdains? Out of idealizations such as this arise mighty religions and elevated moralities that civilization cultivates from generation to generation.

In Paul Gooch's paper on friends and lovers in ancient Greek philosophy, I detect a similar confusion about my notion of bestowal. In the course of making interesting statements about the limitations in Aristotle's idea of friendship, Gooch cites the importance of intimacy but then claims that it runs counter to the bestowing of value. "If I thought your love was added from nowhere," he says, "and if I seriously believed that my love for you was entirely a matter of my giving you a gift you didn't deserve, decent relationships [of intimate friendship] would be more fragile than they are" (p. 89). Gooch argues that the intimacy he considers crucial in love can occur only if there is a "commitment to protect, cultivate, and nurture what's grown to be valuable in the other and in the relationship" (p. 89).

Gooch is right in thinking that Aristotle tends to neglect this aspect of friendship and that he overemphasizes mutual admiration of the goodness that already exists in each friend. But Gooch ignores the fact that a commitment to "protect, cultivate, and nurture" what matters to the friends itself involves a bestowal of value that pertains to friendship in love as it does to all other types. For there is nothing in what we judge a friend to be worth appraisively that requires us to commit ourselves to the furtherance of his or her values. That comes from nonappraisive motives in us and issues into an attachment or concern that no mere recognition of deserts can automatically elicit.

In that sense the bestowal of value that occurs in friendship is indeed an undeserved gift. This gift does not belong to the same logical order as gifts that *are* deserved—for instance, a box of chocolates proffered to a secretary who has worked after hours. The gift of love, the value that bestowal creates, is always gratuitous, inherently determined by no prior goodness or valid condition that might require it to exist. There must have been causes for each bestowal to occur, and on analysis we may be able to specify how these involve appraisals related to needs, desires, and hoped-for satisfactions without which we could not survive in the world that we inhabit. The appraisive attitude must also participate in love or friendship as a constituent of the ongoing relationship, and whatever bestowal there is must always interact with this valuational component—either supplementing it, if it is positive, or else compensating for its negativity. But this only proves that bestowal and appraisal both have a role to play.

In friendship, as in all love, we delight in attributes that merit approbation. Yet in itself, by virtue of its own definition, bestowal is not the making or unmaking of positive appraisals on the basis of which it expresses our delight, and therefore Gooch does well to emphasize the danger of its gifts being spontaneously "withdrawn." All that means, however, is that no friendship can be truly indestructible regardless of how meritorious the individuals under consideration remain. Though bestowal is needed for there to be the delight or affirmative concern without which love of any sort could not occur, no experience of delight or affirmative concern can guarantee its own perpetuity. Among human beings at least, bestowal is never the sole factor at work and its continued existence is always precarious.

Perhaps my critics have had difficulty with the concept of bestowal (as I have as well) because it lends itself to so great a variety of explications. Appraisal seems relatively simple: we know that as purposive beings all people have desires and needs, impulses and inclinations in relation to either something or someone whose attributes may provide a relevant consummation; we therefore feel competent to evaluate this thing or person (or ideal), and sometimes even to set a price on it. Our evaluation is an "individual appraisal" if it is based on the object's utility for ourselves alone, as the ones who make the evaluation, or else it is an "objective appraisal" predicting what some community of evaluators would establish as the public worth of this object in relation to individual appraisals that might occur in a hypothetical class of equally purposive human or quasi-human beings.

Bestowal, as I have characterized it over the years, seems much more complex and elusive than either type of appraisal. The truth is that in my pluralistic manner I have wanted to observe it in its variable natural state, to watch it as it flutters through reality rather than to snare it in a net like a butterfly one mounts as a relic next to other forms of life that have been killed and are now also on display. In my description bestowal involves benevolence toward its one or many objects, for value is being created in them, but bestowal equally appears as a means of *enjoying* these objects or some of their attributes. Through bestowal we accept them, not as we accept a trial offer of some household article that arrives in the mail but rather in treating them with respect and in recognizing a dignity in them they have not necessarily earned and that we accord them on our own. Their sheer presence as participants in the universe is highlighted, given special importance. Our bestowal addresses itself to what they are "in themselves," as-is and not in reference to whatever valuational ranking they may also merit from an appraisive point of view.

While imagination operates extensively in appraisal, it is more obvious in the creation of value that is central to the very nature of bestowal. Moreover, bestowal adheres to the individual character of some reality in a way that appraisal does not. Though everything is what it is and not another thing, appraisal cannot bother about such tautological verities. It is geared to the discovery and acquisition of goods needed to flourish as just the organism one is. Many instances of the same type will function and satisfy equally well, and therefore there is little appraisive need to discriminate among them. That fact is built into our concept of a commodity. But bestowal sees *through* the commodityness of anything in order to attend to its uniqueness and autonomy regardless of how it can be used. Bestowal, therefore, aligns itself with a disposition not only to *care about* the object of its attentiveness but also to *take care of* it. Although empathy, sympathy, and compassion are different modes of feeling and behavior, as I argue in *The Pursuit of Love,* each of them reveals one or another of the relations between caring and bestowal.

Since bestowal lends itself to such a wide and intricate network of responses, it appears under varied guises when it operates in falling in love; being in love; staying in love; interdependence; the love of things, persons, or ideals; the libidinal; the erotic; the romantic; the sensuous or the passionate, and so on through all the other phenomena that I try to clarify by using whatever distinctions come to hand, like tools in a workshop that have some utility at the moment. If I am pressed to organize these implements and their possible functions into a comprehensive unity—a total or final resolution of all ambiguities—I find myself embarrassed by a request of that sort. It seems artificial and pointless to me. My life and my experience have never allowed themselves to be regimented in so orderly and precise a manner. I might have been a more accomplished human being if I had acquired at an early age the appropriate habits. But for whatever reason, I did not, and the world as I have known it has always seemed to me somewhat random, highly vivid and creative in itself, but systematically defeating all attempts to package and squeeze it into the limited dimensions of a neatly unified scheme. Perhaps that is why I see reality as novel at every moment and always *re*-creating itself.

❀

In his attempt to explain what I mean by appraisal and bestowal, David Goicoechea says that with the passing years my ideas about appraisal have been "growing." That is equally true of my thinking about bestowal. My conception of both elements keeps changing, just as my lived experience does. In tracing the history of the idea of love, I likewise emphasize its own trajectory of change, from primitive naturalism to transcendental idealism to post-Romantic humanism, as Goicoechea notes. At the same time, I feel that the germs of my later thought are clearly present in the first volume of the trilogy. Even my insistence that bestowal must always be subjected to moral appraisal was already enunciated in my prudential remarks about the dangers of unbridled bestowal and the greed of giving. I do not, however, cite this combination of continuity and development as evidence of growth in the sense of *progress*. My work on successive instances of idealization may help me to understand an important region of mentality that humankind has evolved within a fairly short period of time, and they can tell me much about myself and the parameters of my own developing imagination. For I, too, am a product of the human evolution manifested in the history of these ideas. But unlike Hegel, I do not believe that the Absolute has been marching forward with me or anyone else in mind as its chosen stopping-point in the present. I agree with Nietzsche as well as Santayana in their revulsion against the arrogance of such self-preferment.

My indebtedness to Santayana, despite my repeated criticism of his ideas about idealization, is discussed by Timothy J. Madigan, and Goicoechea elaborates upon my kinship to Nietzsche. At the time I wrote the chapter on Nietzsche in the third volume, I had little sympathy with his conception of *amor fati*. I still have great difficulty with any notion about our loving a universe that is mainly inanimate and apparently meaningless as a totality. I felt, and still do feel, puzzled by the suggestion that one might love the occurrence of gravity, the pervasiveness of thermodynamics, the elements in the periodic table, the forces operating in all molecular structure, or any comparable determinant that is foundational in the universe. I can understand our having love for whatever there is in it that provides gratification to us. But this will not be a love of fated destiny or reality as such.

Nevertheless, what Goicoechea says about the affiliation between Nietzsche's perspective and my own illuminates a line of thought that has become increasingly important for me since the third volume was written. Goicoechea points out that in my later characterization of appraisal's role in the experience of love I see that even the rejecting of the beloved that exists through negative appraisals can engender bestowals that may then interact with disapproval of this sort. And is this not, Goicoechea asks, similar to the cosmic love that the Nietzschean saint attains in loving the world even though he believes it to be nasty, brutish, and hideous? I appreciate the appeal of that suggestion, and in *Meaning in Life: The Creation of Value* I probe the conditions that would make sense of an inclination toward the "love of life," life in its entirety. In that book I suggest that we can love the love in everything, which is to say all animate existence as it strives to achieve a good either for itself or for something else. Although we can extend this love to reality as a whole only through a precarious extrapolation, I recognize that one could treat each individual thing or person or ideal as a *candidate* for love, as not excluded a priori from a love that we might feel even if it is incapable of experiencing love itself. This is less than Nietzschean amor fati, but it marks a step in that direction that I now feel comfortable in taking.

I think Goicoechea is mistaken, however, when he identifies Nietzsche's ideal with the love of God that Piccarda manifests in Dante's *Paradiso*. For her attitude presupposes the dichotomy between appearance and reality that Nietzsche sought to overcome throughout his writings. Piccarda confounds Dante by claiming to be close to the blessedness of God's being, since she accepts his will and finds her ultimate peace in that, even though she inhabits an outer circle of paradise and appears to be removed from the divine presence. It is this distinction between appearance and reality that Nietzsche rejected, more brilliantly than any philosopher who preceded him, and that rejection is fundamental for understanding both his notion of amor fati and the difficulties inherent in it. In my own development, Nietzsche's attack on religious ideas about appearance and reality had an enormous effect that shows itself in almost everything I have written as a philosopher.

My radical repudiation of traditional distinctions between appearance and reality is the underlying cause of John McMurtry's complaints about my outlook. In the afterword to his paper, he responds to three of the criticisms I made to the earlier version that he delivered at the 1991 symposium. The first of them deals with the question of my "subjectivism." Without defining that word too laboriously or even in the detail that I felt McMurtry should provide in order to strengthen his argument, I freely admit to being a subjectivist in the sense that I accept no system of good or bad that claims to have unique authority grounded on some nonempirical structure of Being and apart from the *making* of values that life itself is always enacting. Philosophers, such as Plato, who believe in objective criteria generally do so because they think the world of appearance is too unstable, unreliable, and even illusory to yield a guide to what is truly valuable. In their estimation, only supremely rational insight into "ultimate reality" can do that.

These ideas have always seemed to me bankrupt from the start. They presuppose that the ordinary world is inevitably deficient in ways that force us to renounce it as a homeland to the spirit; they posit a nonverifiable realm of supernature that embodies a meaning of life that precedes rather than issues from the bondage we undergo in our cave-like existence on earth; and they deter us from understanding the infinitely rich and fertile activity of human imagination and idealization as they generate values that burgeon throughout life which we, in our actual condition, consider meaningful.

In emphasizing the unity of appearance and reality, am I guilty of a dubious reliance on bestowals as McMurtry thinks? It is true I believe that we create whatever meaning there is in life and that all value—including the kind that love represents—originates to this extent from bestowal in one or another form. But McMurtry misconstrues the context in which my belief occurs. He asserts that I envisage love as "essentially" bestowal of value; he claims my "introduction of 'appraisive value' in volume 3" is subjectivist in an additional sense, namely "in its confinement of value to what the loved one does for the lover alone"; and he concludes that I have no way of explaining how love can "extend further than the circle of lovers" (p. 280).

But all this imputes to me a kind of subjectivism that is foreign to my thinking, and has been from its beginnings. I have never held that love is *essentially* any one thing. Even in the first volume, I described bestowal only as a necessary condition, and my distinction between objective appraisal and individual appraisal was offered as a means of establishing that love involves social and cultural interests as well as the needs or desires idiosyncratic to each of us as individuals. Appraisal that I call objective recognizes values that we inherit or acquire from the society in which we grow up. This kind of objectivity makes no claims to any ultimate or prior realm of values, and yet it reveals that much more is at stake than goods the lover gets from the loved one in isolation from all social or extrapersonal considerations.

I cannot deny, however, that the trilogy—and, to some degree, *The Pursuit of Love*—ignores many of the questions about the cultural and biological implications of love that McMurtry finds most interesting. I hope that he and others will make up this deficiency. My perspective and my vision are primarily literary and humanistic, in the sense of being concerned with the phenomenology of the good life rather than the resolution of issues related to social science or the logic of decision making. These questions warrant further attention and various approaches may certainly be defended, provided one gives up the search for some transcendental, or otherwise metaphysical, objectivity.

This point is relevant to the last of the three criticisms that McMurtry makes. In effect he finds my pluralistic attitude useless for the assessment of practical issues that love must always involve. I can see the sense in which he may be right. I have no authority as a counselor in matters of the heart. My personal failures and successes, sufferings and joys, have never seemed to me an adequate basis for telling others how to live. My own system of values is present in almost everything I have written in the last thirty-five years, and those who know me well enough can possibly identify the individual reality that lies couched within my judgments and varied points of view. But though I treasure this source of whatever creativity I possess, I have no desire to use it to preach or to proselytize.

Instead I have wanted to make my ideas clear, hence the notion of "mapping" concepts of love that guides me throughout *The Pursuit of Love*. The task of reaching practical and justifiable solutions that all persons need must be carried out by each of those persons separately. Apart from helping others to make their own ideas clear, and beyond any wise saws and modern instances that one can proffer, I do not believe there are universal truths to which any philosopher has special access. As a pluralist, I am content to accept this limitation. It is a rule for playing the game cleanly and with elegance, a formal constraint that turns this mode of cognition into an art form.

In thinking about Marvin Kohl's criticism of my ideas about love in relation to autonomy, I begin to see implications of my pervasive pluralism that I had not noticed before. Kohl's original presentation, as well as his "postscript" to it, were extremely helpful to me in the writing of *The Pursuit of Love*. They led me to distinguish between freedom and autonomy in a chapter of that book, and to reexamine once again my belief that love involves an acceptance of the autonomous condition of the beloved. I am very grateful for the stimulus Kohl provided. My basic position remains unchanged, however, and therefore the differences between us have not been altered.

Kohl argues that a certain kind of love, which he calls "caring love," sometimes requires active intervention by the lover for the sake of assuring benefits to the beloved regardless of the fact that the beloved opposes such intervention. Kohl thinks that this kind of well-intentioned paternalism is indicative of caring love rather than a weakening of it, and he rightly suggests that on my view such behavior would have to be considered a lack of love. Certainly my concept of bestowal implies an acceptance of the other as-is, as he is in himself, his indefeasible autonomy being and remaining paramount in the loving relationship. To say, however, as Kohl does, that I am thereby smuggling covert libertarian doctrine under the abstract guise of a theory of love is unwarranted. Bestowal as I understand it implies no "commitment to . . . unencumbered private property . . . rights" (p. 231). It only means that love ordains boundaries to the lover's benevolent attitude, and that his or her desire to benefit the beloved must be secondary to what this other person wants as a reasonably mature and autonomous being. Love, as I conceive it, inevitably excludes the kind of paternalism Kohl espouses, however moderate it may be.

What can be said definitively on either side? Are we just drawing lines in the sand as an expression of our differing world outlooks? It would seem that we are engaged in formulating what I call idealizations, each of us specifying ideals that matter to us individually and each articulating his own network of philosophic as well as personal bestowals. I am not opposed to that summation of our controversy, but I think there are appeals to disinterested reason that can also be made.

In *The Pursuit of Love* I depict the fragility of love and the fact that as an evolving phenomenon in the lives of two people intimately dependent on one another it is always subject to destructive influences. One of these is the belief that the other person does not understand or appreciate what one "really" wants. I put the loaded word in quotes because there may be no way in which the participants in the relationship can be sure of what the other wants, or even of what they themselves want. They have inclinations, desires, feelings with which they identify themselves, but all this occurs in a fluid and ambiguous flux of vital forces that constitute every moment of life, particularly the life of human beings. The addictive smoker seems to want to kick the habit, but does she *really*? Neither she nor the husband who worries about her health and thinks his love requires him to be paternalistic can ever be certain.

Of course, there are many instances, a great majority perhaps, in which we have a pretty good idea of what the other wants, above all when she consistently tells us about her feelings. But there always lurks the possibility that she is deceiving herself or unaware of her true nature or even acting out the compulsive need created by the harmful addiction. To protect ourselves or others, or this particular person, we may have to intervene. But in the process we always run the risk of eroding the possibility of love. For just as the beloved may be deceiving herself in thinking that she wants what really she does not want, so too may the lover be deceiving himself in thinking that his paternalism is motivated by love rather than a moralistic concern that will eventually undermine the loving relationship.

For love (at least the love of persons) to exist, and to last, each individual must benefit as just the person that he or she happens to be. It is in the name of benevolence that the paternalistic attitude arises in the first place. But if the lover's behavior is indeed paternalistic, it disregards by definition a value that for many people is the greatest benefit of all—namely, the goodness that consists in being allowed to carve out our destiny exactly as we choose and with the assurance that the person we are most attached to respects the autonomy we cherish so much.

Is Kohl prepared to deny the validity of this interest? Is his moral stance so authoritarian and nonpluralistic that he is willing to claim that he or anyone else can ever legislate about the ultimate goodness or badness of a person's freely chosen life, apart from its effect on others? Does he really want to maintain that self-determination is not an indefeasible value to which everyone has a right? Great crimes have been committed in the name of paternalistic love—think only of Cromwell's puritan dictatorship or the Spanish Inquisition, both predicated upon a love of God, or the Soviet dictatorship that justified itself as a means of creating the love of humanity.

I do not know whether these remarks make my position more reasonable than Kohl's. It is possible that I am merely adding new embroidery to my tapestry. But whether or not my argument sways a hypothetical third party trying to reach a decision, I have little interest in scoring polemical points. If I can articulate my vision with clarity and sufficient honesty, I will be happy to let the chips fall where they may. All the same I realize that my view has consequences that many people will find unpalatable. For if one believes that a desire to love requires us to accept anything the other person wants autonomously, this could include her desire to destroy our love, to destroy herself, or even to destroy us. And is not that an even greater contradiction, or paradox, than what I ascribed to Kohl's opinion?

I do not think so. Though love cannot be defined as self-sacrifice, it does involve a willingness to overcome any selfish demands we may have that the beloved serve only as an object of our own desires. If we want her to remain in love with us simply because we cannot bear the idea of living without her, ours is no longer an attitude of love. If we want her to stay alive regardless of her desire for death and despite a terminal medical condition, for instance, that causes her to live in terrible pain, we are not motivated by love. If we loved her, we would yield to the fact that she no longer wants to live.

Kohl's account addresses itself to the fact that love and benevolence are closely interrelated, the lover being concerned about the welfare of the beloved. And surely, death is not a benefit. Death eliminates a life and cannot be considered beneficial to it. But *dying* may be, if that is what a person chooses under specifiable circumstances. The individual who thinks he is acting out of love, although his behavior overrides what the other person is ready to accept, has deluded himself about the nature of love. For authentic benevolence, and therefore love, entails a willingness to forego intervention deemed unwelcome by the object of our solicitude. If we impose our good will despite the other's expressed rejection of it, that may even serve as a paradigmatic example of loveless aggression.

I have greater difficulty dealing with the lover's acquiescence in the beloved's wish that he no longer love her or that he should even cease to exist. There may be a basic contradiction in situations such as those. For they involve not only love as an acceptance of what the other is and wants, but also acceptance of her wanting to destroy one's love for her and possibly for oneself. Can nature endure such inner splitting of the vital roots? To love someone I must control my desire to help her if she does not want me to, but must I also harm myself and my ability to love her if that is what she does want? We may have reached a limiting case, the edge of the world of love beyond which one falls into nothingness. But in fact, I do not think the stated possibilities indicate a condition in which love must terminate. For though we may accept the other as she is and therefore sustain her autonomy, our love does not require us to negate our own autonomy. On the contrary, we could not love her or anyone else unless we remained faithful to what we are ourselves and what we want, which in this case means staying alive and loving her as best we can. If these conditions are unacceptable to the beloved, her love for us may have been destroyed, since she will not be accepting us as we are. But that is another matter.

In making his critique, Kohl raises a number of subsidiary issues that also need to be addressed. First, he asks whether I hold one or another of two different ideas about bestowal: "the negative claim . . . that the bestowal of love does not seek to alter the object in ways that are alien or contrary to its own inclinations and desires" or "the stronger claim . . . that neither in the bestowing of, nor in being in, love is there warrant for intervention unless such an action is consented to" (p. 231). Kohl says that he suspects my view is the latter. His surmise is correct but misleading. I make both of the claims that he refers to, but I do not mean what he implies.

Restating my position as he does, Kohl makes me sound as if I deny that the lover can want to change the beloved. In one place he says I believe that "loving another person we should *only* respect his desires to improve himself" (p. 231). This is something I have never held. To do so would be to ignore the importance of the appraisive element in love. In accepting the beloved as he or she is, the lover affirms the autonomy of this other person. But that does not entail forfeiting standards of good and bad, desirable and undesirable that the lover wants the beloved to live up to. These standards cannot be *imposed* upon the beloved, regardless of how beneficial the lover thinks it would be if the beloved satisfied them. But it would be contrary to human nature for the lover not to want the beloved to have traits that are good rather than bad, desirable rather than undesirable. Playing on the ambiguity in phrases like "seek to alter" and "warrant for intervention," Kohl misrepresents the relationship between bestowal and appraisal as I conceive of them.

Kohl thinks there may be sexist implications in what I believe. He suggests that my " 'autonomy talk' . . . seems to reflect a male story as opposed to a women's story of love" (p. 232). I can't see why he says this. Mine *is* a male story, since I am a male, but it is not one that opposes any woman's story of love. Of greater interest is Kohl's assertion that when it comes to "pluralistic welfare," as he calls it, dignity and autonomy are not always "trumps." But I never claimed they were. I was only giving a theory of love. I was saying that love, which does not constitute all of life or even all of the good life, requires an acceptance of the other's dignity as an autonomous being. Kohl himself recognizes that dignity and autonomy are necessary conditions for the good life and he rightly insists that intervention for the benefit of another person must never be allowed to undermine that person's sense of self-worth. But he fails to realize that acting paternalistically means subordinating respect for dignity and autonomy to the giving of goods that the other person may not value as highly as the benevolent agent does.

To the extent that we force our values upon a person in this way, we are not acting out of love or engaging in an enlightened pursuit of it. Even if we think this person may have what he himself will consider a better life thanks to our paternalistic intervention, our behavior might never issue into a love for *him*. He may only be serving as a means to some well-intentioned goal we have in mind. This could reveal our love of a humanitarian ideal, but it would not be loving another *as a person.*

＊

In Stanley G. Clarke's paper I find an orientation with which I feel very much at home. He characterizes love as a process, as I also wish to do, and like me he recognizes that it is "a process that is historical and not strictly natural" (p. 237). Before considering how one should interpret these beliefs that we have in common, I want to revert to the question about the role of appraisal in love. In a paragraph that alludes to Alan Soble's examination of my philosophy in his book *The Structure of Love,* Clarke says: "Singer claims that appraisals are necessary conditions for love but not constituents or part of the definition" (p. 237). As his reference point, Clarke cites p. 13 in the first volume of my trilogy. If one studies that page, however, one finds a brief discussion that purports to show that love is "primarily bestowal and only secondarily appraisal," and that it "is never elicited by the object in the sense that desire or approbation is." I see my mistake in not explaining my use of the words "primarily" and "secondarily," and in not having inserted "mere" before "desire" and "approbation." I assumed, unwisely as it turns out, that these and similar statements of mine would be understood to mean that even the most favorable appraisals must be accompanied by affirmative bestowals in order for love to exist. Elsewhere in the same chapter I remark that human love includes both appraisals and bestowals, and that appraisals function as constituents within such love as well as being relevant to its causation.

Some of the conclusions that Clarke derives from his belief that love is a process seem to me quite doubtful. For one thing, he maintains that, "The search for necessary conditions tends to encourage one to identify love with only one part of the whole" (p. 238). But this is like saying that writing on a computer makes one's literary style mechanical, or even that an interest in electronics tends to throttle one's aesthetic sensibility. We can find confirmatory examples in each case, but as generalizations neither of these statements is at all plausible. The goals of the different values are not the same. They are easily separable and their competitive effect upon anyone's thinking or experience will vary greatly from person to person. In relation to love, what matters most is how one uses one's definitional analysis as a way of understanding the affective process. When he presents his own ideas, Clarke himself occasionally seems to find the distinction between appraisal and bestowal useful.

The crucial question is what it means to think of love as a process. Clarke argues that science "cannot give us a complete theory of love, and that is because love is not only a process but a historical process" (p. 244). This view is more extreme than mine was, since I held out the hope that someday science might construct a unified and comprehensive theory. I failed to indicate exactly what that would consist of, and I am not suggesting that I can do so now. But Clarke's remarks about the historicity of love, with which I agree, lead me to conclude not that science will never be able to offer an adequate conception of love but rather that it must develop in directions that have hitherto been neglected.

Clarke believes that since the historicity of love creates its "intractability for science" we must turn to literature or other humanistic pursuits for this element of a comprehensive theory. Although he may be right, it is interesting that Clarke draws his example from the work of Turgenev, whose realistic approach to the art of fiction constantly sought to emulate the descriptive methods found in science. Is there anything in Turgenev's account of first love or falling in love as a human phenomenon that cannot be studied scientifically? I think Turgenev would have denied that there is. He wanted to report about imagined human situations much as a naturalist in entomology does in writing about his observations of ants and termites.

In several places in my books I refer to a time when scientists and humanists will join forces and collaborate in an attempt to articulate a persuasive conception of love. Since Clarke seems willing to admit that psychology may someday give a scientific explanation of creativity, an aspect of reality that the humanities have always considered their special province, I do not think he means to exclude the possibility of such cooperation. But if it did exist, with scientists and humanists learning to appreciate each other's expertise and drawing upon each other's methodology whenever that is appropriate, why would the fact that love is a historical process pose a special difficulty for this new science, or prevent it from attaining a comprehensive doctrine of its own? Steps in this direction have already been made in routine investigations by psychiatric theorists, cultural anthropologists, personality psychologists, primatologists, ethologists, and others in behavioral biology. Sometimes in a crude and rudimentary fashion, which needs to be refined through better education at a preliminary level, these investigators already employ fragments of the humanistic imagination. The life sciences regularly deal with historical processes as revealed through case studies, autobiographical statements, anecdotal information, or even works of literature that are taken to include reliable data. As yet the scientific and humanistic communities have not fully combined their resources in the area of love, or human affect in general. But one should not rule out the possibility that they will eventually.

My guarded optimism is developed further in my book on nature and spirit, the still-unfinished sequel to *The Pursuit of Love*. In that book I speculate about the ways in which life is permeated not only by the creation of meaning but also by acts of the imagination that are basic to our acquisition of knowledge about reality. I argue that science depends on imagination (and idealization), just as art or literature does, rather than merely serving the ends of whatever rational faculties we may also have. If this is true, our conception of what is needed for a total and unified scientific theory about affective process will have to be altered considerably. The split between science and the humanities may finally be eliminated, at least in theory and consequently more often in practice than is now the case.

In John Mitterer's paper I find the beginnings of this desirable reconciliation between scientists and humanists. In several places, however, I feel that Mitterer overextends himself. Discussing male domination, for instance, Mitterer—unlike McMurtry—credits my trilogy with having "laid bare the incredible depth of the problem" (p. 249), but then he makes inferences that look to me like non sequiturs. In developing my suggestion that Plato's philosophy of love, like so many others, is an idealization that reveals fundamental values Plato believed in, Mitterer detects a psychology of domination as the basis of Platonic metaphysics. He may be right, and Plato's outlook is clearly interwoven with a male orientation the Greeks took for granted. But Mitterer describes the cognitive structure of their view in a manner that seems rather simplistic.

Mitterer argues that male chauvinism in the modern world derives from Plato's anti-feminine dogma, which he sees as an essential element not only in Plato's theory of forms but also in all subsequent metaphysical and theological thinking in the West. The traditional philosophy is thus shown to be a source of the psychology of inequality: "I believe that Singer's history reveals that the psychology of domination is undergirded by a metaphysic dating back to the Greeks" (p. 255).

I myself do not find sufficient evidence for this statement. If Mitterer had said that previous philosophies of love both presupposed and sustained a sharp distinction between appearance and reality, or feeling and reason, or body and mind, that would have been more credible. But though the psychology of domination does belong to the world of everyday experience out of which traditional Western philosophy and religion arise, it has no unitary role in their content. Even in Plato one finds aspects of egalitarian thinking, in *The Republic* as well as in *The Laws*, together with his more prejudicial assumptions about the sexes. In any event, one cannot derive male chauvinism from the theory of forms itself. The reifications built into that doctrine are such as to deny that males can be the ultimate objects of love any more than females. How, then, can the psychology of domination be undergirded by the resident metaphysics? If anything, the latter weakens the former, since human limitations in this area are thought to apply equally to both sexes. The same is true of Christian ideas about the primacy of God as both an object and a vehicle of love.

All the same, the motive that leads Mitterer into these non sequiturs is one that I applaud. He calls for an alternative to the "grand schemes" we have inherited in the twentieth century. He turns to the "mythopoetic" approach of Jung, Campbell, and Bly, among others, as possibly more relevant to our age than all the metaphysical systems of the past, however splendid they may still seem to some people. I recognize that as a wholesome attitude for someone who wishes to create a world of ideas different from any that has yet occurred. And like Mitterer, I believe in the importance of fashioning what he calls "a naturalistic, humanistic psychology of equality." But I am less sanguine about finding the requisite support in irrationalists like Jung or philosophically naive thinkers such as Campbell, just to mention those two. The permanent merit and continuing utility in the work of great philosophers of the past, and of those in the present who identify themselves with them, consist in their strength of mind, their willingness to follow an argument as far as it will go, their talent for rigorous abstraction, and their love of truth as they understand it. In seeking to clarify concrete experience, and to appreciate insights that only empirical science can provide, we would be boxing with one hand tied behind us if we neglected the great achievements in the history of even metaphysical philosophy.

The writings of Sigmund Freud serve as a case in point in this regard. Pat Duffy Hutcheon's paper stresses, quite cogently, the influence that nineteenth-century philosophers, such as Hegel, Spencer, and Marx, exerted upon non-speculative as well as speculative components in Freud's scientific work. In the chapter from the third volume of my trilogy to which she directs her comments, I tried to systematize Freud's ideas about love and then to examine them critically as if they were the ideas of a philosopher. It is always risky to deal with the thinking of a nonphilosopher in that way. For one can never be sure that an alien discipline is not being imposed upon a creative imagination that is basically very different. I seem to court this danger more than most contemporary philosophers writing in English. I did so with Mozart and Beethoven in my book on their operas, with Kinsey and Masters and Johnson in *The Goals of Human Sexuality,* and with many literary figures in the trilogy and elsewhere. To the extent that this trope of mine is defensible, it would have to be defended anew in each case and with respect to the particular issues involved.

In relation to Freud, the suggestion that he be treated not only as a scientific theorist and investigator but also as a philosopher seems fairly innocuous. He certainly clothed himself in that purple mantle on many occasions. The question is whether I deal adequately with Freud's arguments and criticize him fairly. Throughout my work on love, he serves as a touchstone for the modern mentality into which I was born. Leaving aside my writings on Santayana and my unpublished undergraduate thesis on Dewey's theory of value, I have devoted more pages to Freud than to any other theorist. In the first volume of the trilogy, he served as the main example of what I called "the eros tradition" in its realist mode; in *The Goals* he represented a type of essentialism I pitted against the essentialism of Masters and Johnson in my attempt to reject both alternatives; and in *The Pursuit of Love* Freud is the focus of discussions about civilization, autonomy, and the need for nonmechanistic methods of studying affect.

Possibly because she ignores these other efforts I have made, Hutcheon tends to misread me on several points. First she claims that Freud included in his theory something like my concept of bestowal. Since in the first volume I recurrently cite ideas of Freud that show he has no comparable conception, this strikes me as very strange. Without repeating the detailed arguments in the first volume, I can only say that Freud's notions of idealization and overvaluation of the object, which are central to his ideas about love, derive from his belief that love must be a distortion of some sort, an illusion and a cognitively unwarranted expenditure of surplus energy. Bestowal, as I understand it, is nothing of the sort—at least, not necessarily. It creates value in a manner that Freud does not acknowledge or fully understand. When he mentions "the act of loving" in the passage from *Civilization and Its Discontents* that Hutcheon quotes, he is referring to a circuitous tactic, as in the case of St. Francis, by which we armor ourselves against the fear of not getting the love that everyone wants and that remains constant in human nature. Freud is not modifying his usual claim that giving love must always be reducible to wanting to be loved. He is explaining how a particular act of loving can occur under special circumstances. Whether or not the concept of bestowal provides a better explanation, I see no reason to believe that Freud was using an idea such as mine except (perhaps) at the peripheries of his more characteristic modes of thought.

Similarly, I think Hutcheon misunderstands the nature of my opposition to essentialism, whether in Freud or Plato or anyone else. It is not just a question of reification that blinds one to empirical realities, but also the assumption that the world is well-organized in accordance with unitary categories that yield superior access to ultimate knowledge. It is not even a question of determinism or biological programming that Hutcheon thinks I want to supersede by emphasizing freedom and environmental influences more than Freud did. My pluralism, or anti-essentialism, is based on my belief that no system of analysis, no formula or mold of categorization, can adequately indicate the diversity and equal legitimacy in radically different forms of both sexual response and interpersonal love among human beings.

Ric Brown, who quotes from statements about essentialism and pluralism in *The Goals*, seems to understand what I have in mind.

In part, Hutcheon does too. For in one place she defends Freud's "attempt to seek commonalities or regularities in human nature" (p. 190). That is indeed what I was talking about in criticizing Freud. As against my approach, Hutcheon argues that "digestion and reproduction are similar the world over. Why not certain aspects of sexual development and associated psychic or behavioral complexes?" But her implied assertion is either vague or a non sequitur: the former if "certain aspects" means that some are and some are not similar the world over, though we are not told which is which (or how much similarity is involved in being "similar"); and the latter if she is suggesting that it is reasonable to think that since digestion and reproduction manifest "commonalities and regularities in human nature," then the same must be true of love and sexuality. The complaint I make pervasively against Freud is not only that he fabricated grotesque icons of commonality and regularity, which Hutcheon believes as well, but also that he was mistaken in expecting to find commonality rather than diversity and regularity rather than idiosyncrasy as the basis of human sexuality and our incessant search for love.

Hutcheon wonders whether "social scientific inquiry" can proceed on attitudes such as mine, so greatly different from Freud's in this fashion. I am unable to answer that question, but the mapping of the concept of love that I present in *The Pursuit of Love* offers itself as a theoretical framework for pluralism that social scientists may possibly consider interesting. If they do, they may also want to study a further criticism of me that Hutcheon makes and that I find hard to answer. Defending Freud against my charge of dualism in his main presuppositions, she emphasizes two things that she says I neglect: first, that Freud is monistic in the sense that he firmly assumes all questions about human nature must be settled in terms of nature alone, without any transcendental or religious points of reference; and second, that all his distinctions are constructed with an almost Hegelian intention of showing that opposing realities interact within a process that evolves dynamically in time. In both these comments Hutcheon is correct in what she says about Freud. When she complains that I fail to appreciate that "a passion for dichotomizing is not dualism," I feel the strength of her criticism of me. In stressing the extent to which post-Freudians, and myself, wanted to study human affect as a function of developing processes, I may have minimized the importance of this effort in Freud as well.

This shortcoming on my part, if it exists, is noteworthy in view of my own ways of thinking. Like Dewey, from whom I first learned how to express myself philosophically, I generally formulate my ideas in terms of dichotomies but then become suspicious of attempts by earlier thinkers to turn them into rigid dualisms. As one who still resonates to the genius of Plato, I feel a need to "harmonize" the opposing conceptions, to fit them into a broader and more complex vision of reality. In discussing my interest in harmonization, Madigan suggests that it sometimes turns my pluralism into a kind of trinitarianism. But the number 3 has no special fascination for me even though I find it inherently pleasing, as Hegel must have too, and therefore suitable for establishing a sense of reconciliation. For me, however, there is no possible closure to the dynamic processes of life, and that is what continually propels my thought into further expressions of pluralism. Given his doctrinaire belief in scientific rectitude that must not be sullied by aesthetic excursions such as these, acceptable as they might be in a separate compartment of his being, Freud must have seen his mission somewhat differently.

I am grateful to Ric Brown not only because he realizes how important pluralism is in my thinking but also because he is one of the few philosophers who still pay attention to my book on sexological theory. Not that many of them did when the book first appeared some twenty years ago. Compared to my other publications, it sold very well and was even distributed by two book clubs. But it was largely ignored by my confreres in the profession, who seemed embarrassed by its mere existence. Others were also dismayed. Invitations to polite dinner parties in Cambridge, Massachusetts, and its environs immediately dwindled. On the other hand, my having written *The Goals* helped encourage Alan Soble to proceed with his efforts to create the Society for the Philosophy of Sex and Love, which became a part of the American Philosophical Association, and his inclusion of the chapter on the sensuous and the passionate in his anthology *The Philosophy of Sex* placed that much of the book in the hands of working philosophers. Nevertheless, the main response to *The Goals* occurred among people in sexology and, to a lesser degree, in psychiatric theory.

In the early seventies the sexological world had been given a powerful jolt by the laboratory studies of Masters and Johnson. Radical feminists used them as a massive club to strike back at references to the so-called vaginal orgasm that they charged Freud with having invented for his own sexist purposes. Investigators in the field began to sense the possibility of scientific, experimental work that had never been allowed previously. An exciting new approach to understanding human response in this area seemed to be opening up as never before. At the same time, there arose systematic doubts about Masters and Johnson's methodology, and various sexologists questioned some of their major findings. *The Goals* provided a theoretical, broadly philosophical framework of ideas that opponents of Masters and Johnson could use in order to make sense of their contrasting evidence. Whether it did so well or badly, the book served a function in sexology as well as in philosophy. It was philosophy in action, philosophy having practical implications for people doing scientific work.

For some readers it also had a more personal impact. One letter I received came from a woman whose sexual response had changed dramatically after she had a hysterectomy. She was deeply troubled by an apparent loss of excitation and by the fact that specialists she consulted assured her that Masters and Johnson had proved that sexual potential is unaffected by removal of the uterus. Her medical advisers intimated that her sexual problem was psychological rather than anatomical, which merely compounded her initial worries. After much distress, the woman encountered two doctors who suggested that she look at *The Goals*. They thought it might be relevant to her situation inasmuch as it argues, in its pluralistic manner, that uterine stimulation can have sexual and orgasmic importance for some women on some occasions. She wrote me that my book became a turning point in her life. It convinced her that she was depressed not because of extraneous psychological reasons but because she had lost an organ that was needed for a type of sexual response that she greatly enjoyed. Being a scientist herself, she later went on to write and publish technical articles about the sexological consequences of hysterectomies.

While *The Goals* has had this kind of gratifying reception, entering the lives of at least a few people, it was nevertheless an exploration into a realm that skirts my principal interests. I did not and do not have the aptitude needed for continuous scientific work, and I assume that some of the physiological and biological details on which *The Goals* relied have now been shown to be mistaken. How much of the underlying theory would have to change in order to accommodate later empirical findings I do not know. I am glad, therefore, that Brown's paper concentrates on philosophical problems that transcend the specifically sexological issues. He shrewdly zeros in on two related difficulties that are troublesome in my general perspective.

One of these deals with my distinction between the sensuous and the passionate. This has had a little history of its own that I should mention. The distinction was originally formulated as a conceptual tool for doing the sexological work *The Goals* undertakes. But I also suggested—and in *Mozart and Beethoven: The Concept of Love in Their Operas* I tried to demonstrate— that differences between the sensuous and the passionate can have significant philosophico-aesthetic ramifications. In the latter book I studied them in relation to operatic expressiveness. My venture serves as a backdrop for Marc Widner's paper, which illustrates Mozart's ability, in his piano music as well as in his operas, to express feelings that I characterize as either sensuous or passionate.

This way of approaching works of art is fraught with methodological problems, and possibly the major difficulties Brown adduces in his discussion of *The Goals* may also be applicable to *Mozart and Beethoven.* Brown's most telling point touches on my attempt to be even-handed in distinguishing between the sensuous and the passionate. If I am indeed a pluralist, as I continually insist, I should treat the two elements as, in principle, equal candidates for acceptance by different people on different occasions as they differently prefer. And yet, Brown remarks, my writing seems to reveal that I have "a clear preference for the passionate mode" (p. 302). Nor does he mean that I, as the particular person I happen to be, prefer the passionate, but rather that my philosophical statements presuppose its basic preferability. Brown then goes on, in a very judicious manner, to show how I answer this charge both in *The Goals* and in the last volume of the trilogy. But still there lingers the suggestion that since I say that "something in valuation itself . . . engenders the passionate," I must consider it to be closer than the sensuous to the nature of love. If so, am I not tilting the scales to that extent?

I would be if I were a Romantic extolling passion above all other human interests. That, however, is not my view. Not only do I recognize that there can be equally authentic, albeit calmer, bestowals that constitute sensuous love, but also I am fully aware that although there must be something in valuation that creates passionate response, this response can be a glaring distortion of love and harmful to the individuals involved as well as to others. The sensuous always runs the risk of being overly cool and, therefore, lacking in the interpersonal sensitivity that love requires. But the passionate, in its fevered yearning and mindless ardor, can also render love impossible. As a philosopher, I wish to map out the alternate implications of the sensuous and the passionate. A priori, at least, I see no justification in favoring one over the other. On the contrary, it is because I treat them as equal components in sex or love, or the good life as a whole, that I study their ongoing inter-action and speculate about possible harmonizations between them.

This leads us to the second difficulty in my thinking that Brown explores. It comes down to wondering whether my search for harmonization is really compatible with the pluralism I espouse in *The Goals* and, as Brown points out, develop further in the distinctions sketched in the last chapter of the trilogy. If Brown had seen *The Pursuit of Love,* particularly the chapter on sexual love, he would have found more examples of both my pluralism and my probing into the possibility of harmonization. But do they ultimately conflict with one another? Whether or not my work succeeds in harnessing these different vectors, I do not perceive any necessary incompatibility between them. As a species we are all divided into disparate motives and inclinations that are always clamoring for attention as if nothing else could really matter in life. The essentialist muffles the cacophonous din by choosing one of the voices in the human spirit, anointing it as authoritative, or even god-given, and then sacrificing everything else to the supremacy of this value he has thereby created.

I rebel against such tyranny and raise my pluralist banner as a testament of my desire to love the love in everything. At the same time I recognize the authenticity in our typically human need, which is aesthetic and moral as well as purely cognitive, to quiet the perturbation of the vying forces by harmonizing whatever is compatible within them. For the impulse to experience the peace and unified beauty that comes from harmony is also a need the pluralist can respect. In his paper John R. A. Mayer shows that he understands the role and the importance that this search for harmonization has had throughout my writing.

The outcome of a disposition such as mine must always seem wishy-washy and occasionally vague, as Brown contends. It may also lead to considerable suffering since the world can easily manipulate to its own advantage the ecumenical good will of the guileless and all-embracing pluralist. I have no easy solution and no foolproof recommendation, except that one should remember that some things worth knowing about oneself and others can be learned only by suffering. Let us not fear it unduly.

Reading over Brown's paper, I also found it reminding me of a question that he does not ask but that is very pertinent: Is my philosophy basically realist or idealist? I use that distinction throughout the trilogy, but which of these alternatives applies to my own thinking? I can answer only in a halting fashion. Insofar as I seek the harmonization of interests and admire it when it occurs, I must place myself with the idealists. I sense the grandeur of their quest and feel that life without it would not have much value. But though my writing struggles with problems about the making of ideals and their significance in human nature, I know that the feeling I have just reported is only a feeling. It reflects something deep in me that others may not experience exactly as I do. In fact I think that much of life operates on a level that idealists have usually ignored, and that realists are often right to condemn them as self-deluding, even pompous. Can the idealist and the realist outlooks be truly harmonized? I try to do so in my work, but I am not confident that I am anywhere near that promised land.

Since the future is the past reconstituted by the present, I have always sought to integrate the philosophy I thought I was writing for coming generations with my research into the history of ideas. Here again was a dichotomy that needed to be harmonized, and from the very beginnings I was convinced that a good life for civilized men and women would include the love of previous achievements in literature and the arts, together with a strong desire to create a present culture that constantly renews itself. Like Santayana, who was for me the model in this approach, I wanted to do history as only a working philosopher can and philosophy as only a historian of world outlooks would. Being someone who enjoyed the play of imagination, I relished its magnificence in my forerunners. What could not be acceptable in its literal intention might nevertheless be stimulating and inspirational as metaphorical insight and even truthfulness. I was convinced that abstract forms of speculation can be as beautiful as, I am told, mathematics is. One had only to *humanize* these different disciplines, to see them as expressions of life on earth in its relentless and often pitiful attempt to create meaning in a universe that may otherwise be meaningless.

To scholars who devote themselves to the careful study of texts and their derivations this interest of mine may well appear amateurish. I think that some, possibly a significant portion, of it is. I often began my historical studies in a spirit of general education for myself, which I then hoped to encourage in others by showing how much it meant to me. I never attempted an exhaustive presentation of some author's work. I only looked for nuggets of idealization that would explain and also redeem a philosophic point of view, however flawed it might be in itself or misleading in its conclusions.

For that reason I originally heard and now have read with keen appreciation the papers in this volume that deal with my interpretations of historical figures. In several cases I felt that the commentators neglected, to some extent at least, the perspective from which I approached a particular writer. For instance, in his defense of St. Thomas Aquinas, Walter Principe both understands and does not understand my difficulties with the concept of merging. He perceives that I find no way of making literal sense of religious talk about "mutual indwelling" between God and the human soul, though I recognize the poetic and nonliteral significance of what is being said. But Principe explains my difficulty by suggesting that I have "imposed a material metaphor of physical containment on the highest spiritual intercourse" (p. 136).

I am convinced that I have not done so. I meant to show how chaotic and possibly confused is the language used by St. Thomas and, of course, by Principe himself, when they refer to this "spiritual intercourse." They say it is a "sharing in the divine nature" but they do not reveal how this is possible without a loss of human separateness. It is as if a log consumed by fire can still somehow remain a log. They claim that the persons of divinity do not coerce the human agent in giving it the ability to love, since they just "wisely and lovingly guide" it, thereby allowing it to retain "real, if relative, autonomy" (p. 137). Principe insists that there is no coercion: the Holy Spirit only "modifies" our being.

One might as well suggest that a drug that causes permanent brain damage and recurrent hallucinations has only modified but not coerced the person who imbibes it, having only guided him into another mode of being while leaving intact his real though relative autonomy. In the case of the drug we would be tempted to sneer at such a misuse of language. In the case of divinity allowing a creature to share in its loving nature, we do not sneer because the sentiment is so beautiful and we feel that the inexplicable metaphors reveal a wonderment in life. That is what lures the imagination into this bizarre poetry. We must only recognize it for what it is.

Principe maintains that between "metaphorical language and 'literally' being in one another" there is "the proper (and not metaphorical) ontological or metaphysical reality of union through knowledge and love without destruction of personality" (p. 140). The nature of that "reality" is what he thinks I do not perceive. But my problem is more extensive. I fail to see any justification for this type of utterance beyond the fact that it provides aesthetic values that may possibly help some people go on living. These values are in principle the same as those that are made available to us by great music— not only music like Bach's B-minor Mass or Mozart's Requiem but also music like Beethoven's last quartets or Mahler's Ninth Symphony. In theological language, as in these musical instances, the creative imagination organizes bits of recognizable experience into a crafted totality that enables us to savor the mystery of being alive as sensitive creatures in a cosmos that fills us with awe *because* we cannot understand its enormity and its grandeur. I am willing to leave the matter there and to savor whatever beauty or inspiration I can garner from this characteristically human situation. Those who wish to arrogate for themselves the further dignity of being respectable both as philosophers and as religious adherents must demonstrate that what they say makes sense in ordinary language.

In taking this stand, I have no desire to denigrate attempts to analyze love from a religious point of view. After a public lecture on "Nature and Spirit" that I gave at the University of Madrid in January 1994, the professor of metaphysics there remarked with some amusement that I sounded like a philosopher of religion. The idea amused me, too, although I did not tell him why. In my first academic appointment, at Cornell, I had been hired to teach philosophy of religion but then scandalized some members of the department as it existed at the time by announcing that I had no religious faith myself. When the first volume of the trilogy appeared, I thought that its humanistic approach to religion would elicit the hostility of those who did have religious faith but that it would be greeted by fellow philosophers. I was wrong on both accounts. The philosophers ignored the book and it seemed to survive in those early days only because people who took religion seriously found some merit in it.

I put into the first volume ideas in religious philosophy that had long been forming in me. For many years afterwards, I felt that there was nothing more for me to say in this area of investigation. Only recently, in working on *The Pursuit of Love*, did I find new thoughts welling up as a continuation of what I had previously written. It was therefore very gratifying to see that Graeme Nicholson considered my chapter on *nomos* worthy of his attention as a biblical scholar.

In his paper Nicholson goes far beyond my own remarks about the Bible, but in the issue about the union between man and God, where Principe and I have trouble with each other's formulation, Nicholson expresses my point of view with clarity and insight: "To love and to know God," he says, "is to be desirous of the ever-continuing way into ever-increasing intimacy and concourse" (p. 106). This implies no notion of melting or merging between the human and the divine, and it suggests a sharing of selves that seems to me indigenous to interpersonal love of any sort. Nevertheless, I wish to quibble about the idea of "knowing" God. Since I at least find it very hard to understand what the word "God" means, I cannot imagine what it would be like to *know* him (or her). Surely it is not like knowing the person who lives across the street. God's personhood cannot be knowable in any usual sense, and in its ultimate being presumably not at all. But if the nature of that personhood lies beyond our comprehension, as many religious thinkers would say, I wonder what one gains conceptually by thinking that God is even a person. In order to remain faithful to much of what religion cares about, I can *give* a symbolic meaning to the word "God"—as, for instance, whatever there is in the universe that creates and sustains us at every moment. This does not encompass everything devout believers wish to affirm; but the amorphous residue of theological discourse, which has meant so much to so many others, is not prominent in my own experience and has no immediate reality for me.

❋

In John Nota's paper I detect some of the sources of my alienation from the religious mainstream. Presenting Max Scheler's philosophy of love sympathetically as he does, and rectifying my having neglected it in the trilogy, Nota points out that according to Scheler "love, as the act of the person, is itself spiritual" (p. 197). He contrasts this with my suggestion that we can love inanimate things as ends in themselves, and that loving another person means recognizing the extent to which that person is also a thing. This difference between us is probably insurmountable. To me it seems like presumption (to use the Christian term) for any philosopher to define love in wholly spiritualistic terms. Love exists in nature just as vegetation or locomotion does. It emanates from the realm of matter as an organic process that pervades much of life, possibly all of it, and in human beings it is interwoven with imagination and idealization that constitute our search for meaning. Love in some of its varieties may contribute to, even define, the life of spirit, but in none of its variations can the love that human beings experience be adequately explained in terms of spiritual realities apart from nature.

For this reason, I find philosophers like Scheler and Nota powerless in their attempts to understand love that exists in everyday life. They are like Antaeus, the giant whom Hercules defeats by holding him aloft and thus separated from his mother earth, except that in their puristic thinking Scheler and Nota effect this separation themselves. To me that seems totally unnecessary, and very unfortunate. It leads to a subtle form of impiety toward one's material origins. Nota cannot see why I extol a love of things, or love that is "expressly sensual or sexual." In these ideas he finds a contradiction in terms. For he insists that love is always a love of persons, and he believes that persons ultimately exceed or transcend their materiality. The second of these propositions is true, but the first is not. And neither does the notion of transcendence entail a condition that excludes materiality. Persons are not reducible to things, but in part they are *also* things.

In one place Nota gives an erroneous account of my views which may have been a slip of the typist but is actually quite significant in itself. He says that I, like Kant, think "one should never use a person as a means to an end" (p. 201). Inadvertently, no doubt, Nota has omitted the word "merely" before the concluding phrase. It is indeed central to my conception of the love of persons that another not be used merely as a means to an end. If one does that, one's relationship is something different from a love of persons. But among real human beings, as opposed to hypothetical deities, it is also impossible to love persons as nothing but spiritual entities. For lover and beloved are both products of the physical condition to which they belong. To undergo love as it occurs in nature, which is to say the only kind that we ourselves can actually experience, we must accept one another as inhabitants of the natural order and even as commodities, though not as *mere* commodities. We have no other way of attaining a love of persons.

Holding this view, which I develop further in *Meaning in Life* and in *The Pursuit of Love*, I defend the love of things in a manner that eludes the Christian philosophy of Nota or of Scheler. Nota says that things must be treated as subordinate to persons, just as nature is subordinate to God. He believes that our love of God enables us to love other persons as well as everything that belongs to the subhuman world. But since we can observe and experience only this world and those other persons, can love be anything more than an acceptance of them as they are in themselves, as just the things or persons they happen to be?

Nota does not deny that "sensual or sexual" love may be compatible with a love of persons. But he thinks that happens only when the former becomes "an accompanying aspect of spiritual love." This neglects the fact that men and women are by their nature sensual as well as sexual creatures, and therefore we can love them as persons only by accepting and appropriately responding to those parts of their being. Moreover, at its best, sexual love is itself a form of spiritual love. There is nothing in either to prevent their coalescence.

Spiritual love can also involve interests that are not sexual, as in the love of humanity or of life wherever it occurs. Spirit may possibly try to love all things that exist, as many mystics have wanted to. But even at its highest reach and moment of greatest success in this endeavor, spirit still remains a part of nature. Spirit may rise above the world but can never leave it. Nor would spirit attain its ultimate goal by doing so. Spirituality cannot be love unless it bestows value upon persons, things, or ideals as they appear in nature. If we accept them only insofar as they have a subordinate role within a preordained system of spiritual being, we falsify their inherent individuality and make it impossible for us to love them spiritually, or any other way.

In saying this, I do not doubt that our love for material objects must sometimes be subordinated to a love of persons, and that both may have to be subordinated to a love of ideality or divinity. But a priori at least, these different recipients of love are equal as candidates for bestowal and idealization. Each of us must decide for him- or herself about priorities to be established among them. The justification that can be given for choosing one or another hierarchy of importance will vary in different situations. It is not knowable in advance.

While arguing for pluralism at this level, it is clear to me that my perspective is itself antagonistic to the outlook of a religious theorist like Kierkegaard. Sylvia Walsh's paper makes that point with exquisite precision. She begins by remarking about the superficiality of my treatment of Kierkegaard, to whom I devote only a few pages, although he wrote so many on love and although I give a great deal more space to Nietzsche, who did not write much on it. Walsh is herself a true scholar, compared to a quasi-dilettante like me, and her insight into Kierkegaard's mentality shows what can be learned from someone who is more sympathetic to his views on love than I am. Apart from confessing my own limitations, I can only remind my critics that I was writing philosophical history, a study of past achievements in the history of ideas emanating from interests relevant to my own philosophy in the present. That is why Nietzsche received so much more attention than Kierkegaard. Even when his ideas flounder, as they often do, Nietzsche speaks to my soul in a way that Kierkegaard does not. In giving her superior formulation of Kierkegaard's thinking about religious love, Walsh reveals but does not appreciate why this would have to be the case.

There are two fundamental ideas in Kierkegaard that totally separate his thinking from anything I can find defensible. The first involves his belief that Christian love is not only the highest form of love but also that it is *qualitatively* different from "purely human forms or expressions of love" (p. 168). Walsh relates this idea to Kierkegaard's assertion that Christian love is eternal instead of being transient and determined by action rather than feeling or passion; but these alleged properties seem to me subsidiary to his claim that only Christian love is genuine love since only it enables us to overcome the selfishness in self-love. All views of natural or "pagan" love are condemned on the ground that they cannot eliminate our selfishness. Only Christian love is valid, according to Kierkegaard, because it alone is predicated upon self-renunciation which he considers a necessary condition for love to occur.

This conception of love does not mesh with my sense of reality. Like Luther, I doubt that human beings can truly renounce themselves. Their attempts at self-renunciation usually result in self-deception, self-mutilation, and often the deceiving and mutilating of others. There is an insidious narcissism, to which religious devotees are often prone, in giving so much importance to one's selfishness that one deems it worth destroying totally. Only people dazzled by the bright but blinding light of their own idealism would construct such an ideology. Only they, as in the case of Kierkegaard, would be capable of the self-hatred that must fuel a desire to annihilate this basic element of their natural state.

To me it seems obvious that human beings, like all other animals, are self-oriented in the sense that they cannot survive unless they think and feel and act in pursuit of their own purposive interests. That is why, as Walsh remarks, the concept of appraisal plays so great a role in my outlook on love. If we were gods, or capable of merging with divinity, appraisal would lose all importance except as a stage on the way to perfection. Since we are mortal creatures, however, even at our most spiritual, we cannot hope to break the mold in which we have been cast by nature. The most we can do is to redirect or reshape it in accordance with ideals that transform nature while acquiescing in it. Love is an effort supremely of this sort. In bestowing value upon its object, it enables us to acknowledge the fact that others are also self-oriented and that what matters to them really does matter. In accepting them as they are, in respecting their autonomy and treating it as indefeasible, we compensate for our native selfishness. We cannot, and may not want to, eliminate it entirely, for a love that does not benefit the lover as well as the beloved is not likely to endure. It may even be sick or immoral. And though love controls and sometimes succeeds in curtailing selfishness, love does not undermine or weaken self-love. On the contrary, it strengthens it. For self-love is not the same as selfishness.

Kierkegaard also recognizes the difference between selfishness and self-love. But he interprets self-love not as self-affirmation or acceptance of one's being in nature, which is all that I mean, but rather as personal devotion to a God who is love. This leads to the second major difference between us. Unlike me, Walsh believes Kierkegaard is immune to my claim that Christian idealization of love for God precludes there being an authentic love of persons as they exist in the ordinary world. She insists that Kierkegaard thinks of God as the third person whose presence enables the other two in a love relation to surmount their innate selfishness and thus to treat one another as just the persons that they are.

At the same time, as Walsh also notes, Kierkegaard maintains that God is the ultimate object of all love and that other persons are to be loved not as separate individuals but only as part of a class comprising the humanity God loves. Kierkegaard even states that loving oneself *means* loving God and, in Walsh's words, "the true conception of what it means to love another person is to help that person to love God" (p. 172). These being Kierkegaard's beliefs, however, I do not see how his ideas about the love of persons can even be coherent. For though he insists that a love of God creates a love of persons, as indicated by his claim that God is the intermediary that makes possible all other interpersonal love, his notion is inconsistent or chaotic insofar as he holds that only God can be the *true and essential* object of love. Kierkegaard explicitly asserts that human beings can be loved not as the persons they happen to be but solely because God loves them.

Walsh concludes that for Kierkegaard love of God and love of persons are "integrally connected; one cannot have the one without the other" (p. 177). But she fails to recognize that Kierkegaard's attempt to transform the temporal into the eternal annihilates the preconditions for any human love of persons. Kierkegaard says that loving another as one's friend or spouse means loving him or her primarily as one's neighbor or fellow member of the human race, and, therefore, that all distinctions between individuals are secondary and inessential for love. On my view, Kierkegaard's theocentric religiosity must be taken as a case of throwing out the baby with the bath water, as my teacher Henry Aiken would have put it.

In trying to lead humanity to a spiritual love that makes life worth living, Kierkegaard diminishes, not enriches, the quality of life as it occurs in actual men and women. That consists in our being just the particularities that all of us are, units in the class of general humanity no doubt but also separate from one another and each striving to solve daily problems as they arise throughout our life together. These temporal necessities can eventuate in spiritual achievements that are real and significant, as when love of any sort flourishes in a moral order that sustains it, but this signifies only that the eternal is itself a consummation of our being-in-time. If we treat the temporal and individual condition of everything that exists as merely secondary or inessential, we destroy the possibility of experiencing not only a love of persons but all other kinds of love as well.

❀

It was because Ovid and Friedrich von Schlegel, each in his own way, emphasized the significance of the temporal that I included them among the humanist philosophers. In his paper on Ovid, Kevin McCabe argues that "the attitudes expressed throughout the Ovidian corpus are essentially the same" (p. 116). That was the perspective I also adopted in the first edition of the first volume of my trilogy. But when Winthrop Wetherbee, at the University of Chicago, saw the manuscript for the second edition, he called my attention to the many places in which Ovid appears to speak in a voice that differs from the one I heard. I began to feel that there was more to Ovid than I had realized, and I revised the text considerably. Instead of criticizing his writing as I had done, having assumed it was all an elaboration of sensuous interests that exclude passionate and marital varieties of love, I found a greater diversity in his different statements. My former way of reading Ovid now seemed to me prissy in its condescension toward his love of the sensuous, and unjust in its delineation of his total vision.

McCabe's paper does not commit the first of these faults, but I think he neglects the authenticity of Ovid's admiration for wholesome marital love in the *Metamorphoses* and the *Heroides*. As a result, McCabe also ignores a fringe benefit that I derived from the change in my interpretation. Once I saw that Ovid was capable of understanding and approving at least a fictional version of love between husband and wife, I felt that I better understood his influence on courtly love in the Middle Ages. For not only did medieval courtly love seek to idealize Ovidian relish for the purely sexual or wholly sensuous but sometimes it also professed ideals of married love. In his diversified utterances, Ovid could then be seen as a precursor and sustainer of these alternate directions within courtly love.

In Schlegel I discovered related windows of opportunity. I avoided the mistake of reducing his novel *Lucinde* to the level of tasteless pornography, as so many of his contemporaries—and even Schlegel himself in later years—seem to have done. The book was useful for my purposes because it focusses on the temporal as Ovid had, but then imbues the temporal with spiritual capabilities beyond anything Ovid would have imagined. And above all, it seeks to understand love from the point of view of health or healthy-mindedness.

This importance, this validity of the orientation in *Lucinde*, is greatly understated in Robert L. Perkins's fascinating paper. In one place Perkins does quote Julius, the novel's protagonist, as saying that only health is worthy of being loved. But then Perkins does nothing with this except to remark that "no Nazi eugenicist would disagree" (p. 153). Since I, like Schlegel, was and am searching for an adequate conception of love as a means by which human beings can attain a healthy immersion in nature, I underscored those aspects of Schlegel's novel that contribute to a modern approach as well as to the nineteenth-century movement I called "benign romanticism."

In doing so, I was aware that there are also indications of "Romantic pessimism" in *Lucinde*. Perkins studies them in the context of criticisms by Schleiermacher, Hegel, and Kierkegaard. But the last two were hostile critics whose judgments are not always reputable, and Schleiermacher recognized the affirmative as well as the negative aspects of Schlegel's book. Unlike Kierkegaard, Schleiermacher welcomed its attempt to overcome the split between pagan and spiritualistic types of love; unlike Hegel, he could tolerate many of the utopian implications of Schlegel's thoughts about an ideal relationship between man and woman.

Perkins discusses the points at which Schleiermacher disagreed with Schlegel, and they warrant his scrutiny. But for me *Lucinde* is important in the history of ideas because it points the way to efforts, such as my own, to define spirit in terms of nature, to explain successful love as a fulfillment of organic needs rather than as a supplanting or renouncing of them, to use concepts of health to show how love can be a benign phenomenon that human beings may possibly experience here on earth and in our present dispensation. The differences between this aspect of romanticism and the part I call pessimistic are dramatic, even obvious. Pessimistic romanticism despairs of the likelihood of happiness through love, denies that love can ever resolve the conflict between individuals, between the sexes, between lovers and the society to which they belong. Instead of associating love with a quest for health, Romantic pessimism generally sees it as disease and a pursuit of death, as in the Wagnerian concept of *Liebestod.*

Given the great divergence between these two types of romanticism, *Lucinde* must be classified as an exemplar of the former even though it contains elements of the latter. Nor should there be any ambiguity about my analyses of both or adherence to either. Perkins misconstrues me when he says that my characterization of benign romanticism "suggests that [it] may be just . . . self-indulgence or self-improvement, at best, or a manipulation of the beloved for one's own benefit, at worst" (p. 150). There is no reason to believe that benign Romantics like the early Schlegel thought that love was confined to these alternatives. And neither do I. Perkins complains that my notion of appraisal sounds too "crass" as an insight into love. But life itself is crass, and anyhow bestowal—which Perkins does not mention—is there to make up the deficiencies of appraisal.

In general I do not identify myself with either type of romanticism. Nor is my philosophy particularly Romantic. Although I analyze love as both the pursuit and creation of meaning, I do not consider it an eternal or holy substratum of life. Unlike the Romantics, I feel no need to reverse the Christian slogan that God is love. And unlike most Romantics, both benign and pessimistic, I do not assume that love is always socially or even morally justifiable. I know about the cruelty, deceit, and outright evil that may eventuate from love and that many lovers think their powerful needs or passions condone. I see no reason to commend such behavior, to dignify it in idealistic language, or to deny its underlying heartlessness and lack of decent sentiment. I have no inclination to excuse the hurtful potentiality of love by pretending that it inherently reveals spirit working its way through nature and transforming it into divinity.

All love, including the love of persons, is capable of causing a great deal of misery—not only in those who undergo the experience but also in those who are rejected or abandoned as a result. Artists who glorify love in song and legend have recognized this as well as moralists who systematically condemn it. The Romantic believes that love justifies whatever sacrifice is exacted from oneself or others. Whether the Romantic is optimistic or pessimistic about love's survivability in the world as we know it, he or she is convinced that it is worth any price one must pay for it (and make others pay in different ways). This faith, like all religious belief, is nonverifiable and often pathological. It is not a religion that I share or wish to encourage indiscriminately.

❄

The Puritans and the Rationalists of the seventeenth century, whom John Mayer discusses in his paper, interest me because they too recoiled from romantic love when it is immoral or excessively self-indulgent. This did not prevent the Puritans, at least, from enjoying the pleasures of sexual passion whenever these could be controlled and enclosed within the bounds of marriage. On the contrary, as I argue in The Goals, the Puritans (like the Victorians) learned how to turn restraint imposed by demands for privacy and social decorum into a means of intensifying their passionate sexuality. At the same time the Puritans, the Rationalists, and many of the Victorians rightly understood that this consummation can become a flame that destroys everything else that makes life worth living.

Having learned this from the Puritans and the Rationalists, I respect the horrified realism that pervades the philosophies of love in Schopenhauer, Freud, Proust, and the early Sartre. I have long considered Proust to be the greatest of all philosophical novelists, in view of his unparalled ability to detect problems of philosophy embedded in the concrete phenomena that he portrays throughout his fiction. But Proust has also been a puzzlement to me. For while I admire his analytical and creative powers, I distrust the system of values—many of them unexamined—from which they emanate and which they continually express. I have a similar feeling about Wittgenstein. As much as I relish Proust's perceptive insights, I come away feeling that his project ultimately fails because he remains a *philosophe manqué*. He shows us how close a literary genius can come to being a philosopher, but he is not fully equipped to do the work of philosophy. This is not true of Wittgenstein, of course. In his case I sense an unfortunate throttling of his literary susceptibilities.

Sartre would seem to have had both talents in requisite degrees. His philosophical and literary capacities were ample, and each was sufficiently developed to avoid the limitations in Proust and Wittgenstein. But despite his enormous output, Sartre stopped writing before he could finish his culminating efforts in philosophy and in literature. He never completed the major works of his maturity and he withheld his *Cahiers pour une morale* because he knew it greatly needed revision and rewriting, though he felt he should not prohibit its publication after his death. As a result, Sartre's philosophy of love is thoroughly articulated only in *Being and Nothingness*, which he finally renounced when he recognized the basic inadequacy of its approach to human relations.

In my chapter on Sartre in the third volume of the trilogy, I tried to show the failure of his early philosophy of love as well as the positive promise of his inchoate later thinking. At the time I was writing I was one of the few philosophers to have seen that Sartre's ideas about love belong to three different stages and that the last one contradicts the position in *Being and Nothingness* for which he is most famous. The paper that Thomas Flynn delivered at the Brock symposium acknowledged the nature of my contribution.

In its present version, Flynn's paper makes some criticisms that should be answered. At one point he rejects my claim that Sartre's analysis of love shows no understanding of bestowal by referring to the fact that Sartre talks about the "supreme value" a lover finds in the beloved. But this value, whether or not supreme, must be appraisive, since Sartre presents it as inhering in the lover's attempt to be loved by someone who treats him as an absolute. The passage in which my remark appears is part of my discussion of *Being and Nothingness*. When I reach the ideas in the *Cahiers*, I point out that Sartre's philosophy of love had undergone a sea change by then and that attitudes of acceptance and rejoicing in the particularity of the Other, which do indicate an idea of bestowal, are accentuated as never before. I even quote, in my own translation, the lines from the *Cahiers* that Flynn uses on the last page of his paper.

Flynn also ignores the extent to which my work fleshes out many of the skeletal and loosely written suggestions in the *Cahiers*. One of them that I consider intriguing but finally unacceptable is the notion that love consists in a tension between wanting to attain a merged unity with the beloved and wanting to preserve one's independence. I reject this approach, in Sartre as in the writings of Robert C. Solomon, because it implies an idea of interpersonal merging that makes their overall conception seem inept. In *The Pursuit of Love* I develop my critique of merging further than I had at the time that Flynn was writing, and I also detail tensions in the phenomenology of love that Sartre might have recognized as similar to the ones he possibly had in mind but did not examine thoroughly. In that book I study the ambivalent feelings many people have nowadays, simultaneously wanting to search for love as a source of meaning while also wanting to avoid it. Sartre understood this aspect of our human predicament as well as anyone has.

Some of the other comments that Flynn makes about Sartre's philosophy in relation to mine are very helpful. He points out that for Sartre love is linked with the doing and giving of one's work (*mon oeuvre*) and that "the paradigm of this generous act is artistic creation" (p. 215). That is something I should have discussed in my chapter. It shows what Sartre learned from Proust, and possibly indicates why he had difficulties with the concept of interpersonal love much as Proust did. But also it reveals the role that socioeconomic theory plays in Sartre's general philosophy, including his philosophy of love. Flynn says that if he has "one broad criticism" of my work it is my "tendency to overlook this socioeconomic dimension of love as 'lived' " (p. 218).

I think this criticism is fair. It shows the limits of my talents and imagination. Had I been more *engagé*, like Sartre, or preferably like Dewey, I might have been a better philosopher and possibly a better philosophical critic and historian. On the other hand, if either Dewey or Sartre had been more complete as philosophers of love, perhaps I could have avoided the pitfalls and the potholes that have slowed me down. For all his writing about values and the nature of valuation, Dewey does almost nothing with the concept of love, and his occasional mention of sexual motivation is very primitive. Sartre's involvement with socioeconomic realities as well as those that derive from his devotion to his art did not enable him to solve any of the problems about love that he confronted throughout his intellectual life. I know that one can benefit from Sartre's experience as a philosopher. But as Hutcheon quotes Santayana as having said about the existentialists: "Is all this really necessary?"

That brings us back to my beginnings. In his paper Timothy Madigan discusses the continuities between Santayana's philosophy and mine. Still I have always been a critic of Santayana's neo-Platonism and its effect upon his aesthetics as well as his philosophy of love. As Santayana complained that Dewey was a half-hearted naturalist, so too do I feel that Santayana was a half-hearted materialist. Right as he was in seeing that spirit can occur only as an emanation of psyche, which is itself a province within the realm of matter, Santayana is divided in his appreciation of the love of things. As a novelist and literary critic, and as an observer of human experience (including his own), Santayana has a highly advanced awareness of how the love of things operates in life. Yet as a philosopher of love, he subordinates it to the love of ideals in a way that falsifies our ability to love things, persons, or even ideals. Despite his superlative understanding of the fact that imagination permeates our entire existence, Santayana's neo-Platonism continually prevents him from seeing how creative the imagination can be when it helps bestow value upon things and persons as well as ideals.

What I learned most of all from Santayana was the importance of the humanities as an interdisciplinary resource in all intellectual pursuits. His writings taught me that in the life of the mind there is no absolute chasm between philosophy and literature, the two academic fields that have meant the most to me. In this volume no one has said much about my philosophical literary criticism. By way of conclusion, I feel that I should mention it briefly. At times in the past my work on the myths and legends of love has greatly preoccupied me. Someday I hope to return to it, to revise both published and unpublished chapters on that subject, and possibly to complete the book for which they were originally intended. If I do so, it will be in emulation of what Santayana was able to achieve, at a much higher level, as a humanistic philosopher writing in the tragic and largely loveless twentieth century.

March 1994

List of Contributors

Professor Richard S. G. Brown
Department of Philosophy
Brock University
St. Catharines, Ontario

Professor Stanley Clarke
Department of Philosophy
Carleton University
Ottawa, Ontario

Professor Thomas Flynn
Department of Philosophy
Emory University
Atlanta, Georgia

Professor David Goicoechea
Department of Philosophy
Brock University
St. Catharines, Ontario

Professor Paul Gooch
Department of Philosophy
University of Toronto
Toronto, Ontario

Professor Pat Duffy Hutcheon
Sociologist and former education
professor, and author of
A Sociology of Canadian Education

Professor Marvin Kohl
Department of Philosophy
State University of New York
at Fredonia

Professor John Mayer
Department of Philosophy
Brock University
St. Catharines, Ontario

Mr. Kevin McCabe
Department of Classics
Brock University
St. Catharines, Ontario

Mr. Timothy Madigan
Executive Editor
Free Inquiry
Buffalo, New York

363

Professor John McMurtry
Department of Philosophy
University of Guelph
Guelph, Ontario

Professor John Mitterer
Department of Psychology
Brock University
St. Catharines, Ontario

Professor Graeme Nicholson
Department of Philosophy
University of Toronto
Toronto, Ontario

Professor John Nota
Department of Philosophy
Brock University
St. Catharines, Ontario

Professor Robert L. Perkins
Department of Philosophy
Stetson University
Deland, Florida

Professor Sylvia Walsh-Perkins
Department of Philosophy
Stetson University
Deland, Florida

Professor Walter Principe
Medieval Institute
University of Toronto
Toronto, Ontario

Professor Irving Singer
Department of Linguistics
    and Philosophy
Massachusetts Institute of Technology
Cambridge, Massachusetts

Professor Russell Vannoy
Department of Philosophy
Buffalo State College
Buffalo, New York

Professor Marc Widner
Director of the School of Music
Université de Sherbrooke
Sherbrooke, Québec

www.ingramcontent.com/pod-product-compliance
Lightning Source LLC
Chambersburg PA
CBHW051846090426
42811CB00034B/2232/J